MAPLE LEAF
AGAINST THE AXIS

ALSO BY DAVID J. BERCUSON

The Secret Army
True Patriot: The Life of Brooke Claxton
Battalion of Heroes: The Calgary Highlanders in World War II
War and Peacekeeping (with J.L. Granatstein)
Dictionary of Canadian Military History (with J.L. Granatstein)

MAPLE LEAF
AGAINST THE AXIS

CANADA'S SECOND WORLD WAR

DAVID J. BERCUSON

Stoddart

Published in 1995 by
Stoddart Publishing Co. Ltd.
34 Lesmill Road
Toronto, Ontario
M3B 2T6
Tel.(416) 445-3333
Fax (416) 445-5967

Stoddart Books are available for bulk purchase for sales promotions,
premiums, fundraising, and seminars. For details, contact the **Special Sales
Department** at the above address.

Canadian Cataloguing in Publication Data
Bercuson, David Jay, 1945–
    Maple leaf against the Axis: Canada's Second World War

Includes index.
ISBN 0-7737-2861-9

1. Canada - Armed Forces - History - World War,
1939–1945. 2. World War, 1939–1945 - Canada.
3. World War, 1939–1945 - Campaigns. I. Title.

D766.15.B47 1994   940.54é0971   C95-930059-7

Jacket Design: Bill Douglas / The Bang
Jacket Photographs: National Archives of Canada
Typesetting: Tony Gordon
Printed in Canada

Credits
Map 1   Reproduced from Brereton Greenhous et al.,
*The Crucible of War, 1939–1945: The Official History of
the Royal Canadian Air Force*, volume 3 (Toronto 1994),
with the permission of the Minister of Supply and
Services Canada, 1995.
Map 2   Reproduced from Tony German, *The Sea Is
at Our Gates* (Toronto 1990), with the permission of
Katharine Fletcher.
Maps 3–6   Produced by the Cartography Office,
Department of Geography, University of Toronto.
Illustrations   National Archives of Canada

*Stoddart Publishing gratefully acknowledges the support of the Canada
Council, the Ontario Ministry of Culture, Tourism, and Recreation,
Ontario Arts Council, and Ontario Publishing Centre in the development of
writing and publishing in Canada.*

At 2134 on 16 August 1944, Halifax MZ-899 "O" of the RCAF's No. 433 Squadron lifted off the runway at Skipton-on-Swale, Yorkshire, climbed low over the hills separating the Vale of York from the North Sea, and headed for the coast of Denmark. The Main Force of Bomber Command, including 171 aircraft of No. 6 Group (RCAF), was due to bomb Kiel and Stetin that night, but Halifax MZ-899 "O" and eighteen other RCAF aircraft were assigned to "Gardening," or minelaying missions, instead. Halifax MZ-899 "O" was never seen again; all seven crew members perished.

This book is dedicated to the crew of MZ-899 "O" – Pilot Officer J.G.M. Savard from Montreal, Quebec (pilot); Pilot Officer M.E. Fairall from Toronto, Ontario (air gunner); Pilot Officer B. Bercuson from Regina, Saskatchewan (wireless operator/air gunner); Flying Officer H. Grimble from Sturgeon Creek, Manitoba (navigator); Flying Officer J.L. Baillargeon from Windsor, Ontario (bomb aimer); Pilot Officer A.W.J. Drennan from Windsor, Ontario (bomb aimer); Sergeant R.I. Atkinson of the Royal Air Force (flight engineer) – and to the 42,035 other Canadians and the hundreds of thousands of Allied soldiers, sailors, and airmen who died in the cause of freedom in the greatest war in history.

Contents

✸ List of Maps

The Second World War shaped the modern world, this nation, the people who fought in it or lived through it, and me. I was born two days before the formal Japanese surrender was signed on the USS *Missouri* in Tokyo Bay on 2 September 1945. As a small boy, the recently completed war seemed to have an impact on many important aspects of my life. I vividly remember my mother's European relatives — refugees from the Holocaust — bunking into our small apartment on Maplewood Avenue in Montreal just after they arrived from the Displaced Persons camps of Europe. I thought them strange and somewhat repulsive. They ate herring, had gold teeth, spoke a language I did not understand, and pinched my cheek a lot. My sister was born at the end of 1949 with a congenital hip problem. It was attended to by Dr Breckenridge, who had achieved fame as an army doctor in the war and was still in the army reserves. I remember the photo of him in his office in his army uniform. My uncle, who had been a Halifax pilot with the RCAF's No. 6 Group, Bomber Command, had been badly injured in the crash of his bomber. I remember him telling me about the war and showing me his flying helmet.

The war was all around me as I grew up. At our family table, we talked about Douglas MacArthur, Dwight D. Eisenhower, Harry Truman. My parents took me to Hyde Park, New York, to see where Franklin D. Roosevelt was buried. My father told me about his cousin from Calgary who had been killed in 1944; he had flown away from England one night and had not come back. Most of my friends had dads or uncles who had served in the armed forces. My father had been in the reserves, then worked for RCA Victor designing tank radios. My mother had photos of her two brothers in the living room; both had served in the US armed forces, one just after the war in Occupied Germany. I still have a cigarette case he gave me with a map of the US zone of occupation on it. My mother's uncle had been a US Army doctor in Normandy, her cousin a Boeing B-29 pilot based on Saipan.

At home we avidly watched "Victory at Sea" on television. My father brought home documentary films about the war to show on his new sound projector. Our class collected money for infirm veterans at Christmas. My male high-school teachers were all veterans. One had suffered from battle fatigue (we called it shell-shock) and sometimes grew erratic in front of our class. We feared him when that happened. In class we debated whether it was important to buy poppies on Remembrance Day, whether the war should be remembered year after year. When the Israelis captured Adolf Eichmann, we debated whether they should hang him or let him go, to show the world how truly "Christian" and forgiving they were (I attended a Protestant school). I was glad when he was hanged.

We were "war babies," not "baby boomers." My generation was born during or immediately after the war, when the veterans came home to start families. The streets were filled with mothers wheeling baby carriages. The nursery schools and kindergartens were jammed. War books, war comics, and war movies were the fare of every boy. We refought the war with our toy guns, trying to emulate the scruffy infantrymen we saw shuffling in the newsreels. We were acutely conscious that there had been a war, that it had been very important, and that most of our fathers, uncles, teachers, and friends' fathers had been in it.

Those days are gone. Ask a Canadian high-school graduate today about Dieppe or Juno Beach or the Canadian liberation of Holland, and you will get only a blank stare. To them veterans are old men with blazers, berets, and chests full of medals who march on TV every now and then to mark some occasion no one else seems to remember or care about. Our governments had better things to do after the war than make sure the memory of it stayed alive. In the 1960s, curriculum experts in ministries of education from coast to coast decided that "social studies" were more important than history, and we stopped teaching history — of Canada or anything else — to the next generation. Students learned little about Canada's unique history and heritage, and virtually nothing of its contribution to the defeat of Nazism. That contribution was important both to Canada and to the Allies; Canadian soldiers, sailors, and airmen fought in virtually all the major theatres of war. They were infantrymen, bomber pilots, merchant seamen, corvette captains, tankers, reconnaissance pilots, submarine hunters, and more.

In *Maple Leaf against the Axis*, I have drawn on the latest research in Canadian military history to tell that story, with all its sweep and grandeur, in one volume. I decided to ignore the home front. There is nothing here about the impact of the war on Canadian society, nothing of the rise of trade unionism, the start of the welfare state in Canada, the evacuation of the Japanese, and the role of women on the home front. Two major home-front events — the story of the British Commonwealth Air Training Plan and the two conscription crises of 1942 and 1944 — are mentioned briefly, but only as they had a direct impact on the fighting forces.

This book is about the war itself and about the Canadians who fought it. The library shelves are full of books about those other questions, but there are precious few on the fighting, on the actual killing and dying, that defines war. I make no apology for writing this kind of book. When a widely used university-level textbook can almost totally ignore the fighting effort of the Canadian forces in the Second World War and devote its few pages on that war to a pithy summary of the implications of the war for Canadian society, it is well past time to redress the balance.

But then, I did not write this book to redress a balance. I wrote it to honour those Canadians in the armed forces of Canada and its allies who served their country and the cause of human decency in the years between 1939 and 1945, when the fate of the world hung in the balance. It does not matter to me why each one went — for adventure, out of boredom, for three square meals a day, to save democracy, to stop Hitler. What matters is that they did go and that, when they got to where the shooting was, they gave everything they had to give. What also matters is that many never came back to their wives, sweethearts, parents, children, friends, and siblings. I believe it is essential for the integrity and honour of this country that they be remembered. More importantly, I know it is time that I personally say thank you to all of them. This book is my thanks.

Acknowledgements

I had a great deal of help in the writing and preparation of this book. My agent, Linda McKnight, encouraged me in my belief that it was a good idea and helped me to shape the original concept. Jack Granatstein, Syd Wise, Marc Milner, Norman Hillmer, and Jack English read all or part of the manuscript, and I benefited greatly from their comments, suggestions, and criticisms. Peter Archambault helped with the research, collected the material for the appendices, and drafted parts of the annotated bibliography. Rosemary Shipton did her usual superb editorial job. Sabbatical leave from the University of Calgary gave me the time necessary to complete the manuscript.

As always, Barrie, Sharon, and Alexander put up with my long hours in my "war room" with good humour.

Ultimately, however, I take full responsibility for any errors or omissions.

The approach to the small seaside town of St Aubin-sur-Mer on the northern coast of France is not very different from the approach to any beach resort. Holiday traffic moves slowly on the narrow blacktop road that runs parallel to the beach; cars filled with families pull trailers, young men and women on motorcycles or motor scooters thread their way around the slowly moving vehicles. On warm summer days it is impossible to get a parking spot near the beach; parked cars line both sides of the roads, and the small municipal parking areas are jammed to overflowing. It would be easy to mistake St Aubin-sur-Mer for any other small beach resort on the coast of the English Channel, but it is a resort with a difference, one that has meaning and significance for Canadians. Just a few metres in from the low sea wall that separates the beach from the promenade, a Canadian flag flies from a light standard. Just a few metres from that flag is a low concrete bunker that abuts the sea wall. Inside that bunker is the rusted remains of a German 50-millimetre anti-tank gun.

St Aubin-sur-Mer marks the eastern edge of what is known to history as Juno Beach. At approximately 0745 on the morning of 6 June 1944, Canadian infantrymen of the North Shore Regiment, 8th Canadian Infantry Brigade, 3rd Canadian Infantry Division, backed by the tanks of the 10th Canadian Armoured Regiment (Fort Garry Horse), came ashore there as part of the greatest assault-landing in history. To the left and right flanks of the Canadians, the British landed at Sword and Gold Beaches; away to the west the Americans came ashore at Omaha and Utah Beaches. By the end of the day the Allies were firmly lodged on the Normandy coast, but the British had failed to penetrate inland to the key city of Caen. The long and brutal Battle of Normandy was about to begin.

In St Aubin-sur-Mer and in many other places in Normandy, there are many signs of the passing of the Canadian Army in that hot summer of 1944. In the small beach towns there are markers, memorials, and plaques attesting to the presence of this or that regiment. Near the beach, there is a small museum explaining the D-Day movements of the Canadian troops. There is a Duplex-Drive amphibious tank in a small park near the beach. There are the remains of the formidable German defences that were overcome with bombs, shellfire, and rockets, and, in the end, the sheer determination of mortal men who pitted flesh against steel and concrete, and finally prevailed.

Not far from the beach is the Canadian War Cemetery at Beny-sur-Mer where those Canadians killed in action on D-Day and the fight for Caen lie buried. It is only one of many Canadian war cemeteries that span the globe from Hong Kong to Holland. Each cemetery, each gravestone, is tangible proof that, when called upon to do its part in the struggle to defeat the most powerful evil the world has yet known, Canada did its duty. Each cemetery, each gravestone, marks Canada's final induction into the family of free and independent nations.

In the close to six years that the Second World War ravaged much of the world, some 1.1 million Canadians served in the three armed forces of their country and with Allied (mostly British) forces. In places as far afield as Ceylon, the Aleutian Islands, the North African desert, the ocean run to Murmansk, Hong Kong, Italy, and Northwest Europe, Canadian soldiers, sailors, and airmen played a full role in the Allied war effort. Canadians guarded convoys across the North Atlantic, took part in the bomber offensive against Germany, and contributed close to six full divisions to the Allied armies in the campaign to liberate Europe. That momentous contribution is little remembered in Canada today. A nation without history is no nation, yet at times it seems that the Europeans take more trouble to mark Canada's role in the Second World War than do the Canadians who helped to liberate them.

The Canadian contribution to victory pales beside that of the British, the Americans, or the Soviet Union. The Allies would have prevailed without Canada. But Canada helped immensely and, at certain times and in particular circumstances, Canadians played a decisive role in building the Allied momentum to victory. The Canadian war effort was one that a small nation, barely three-quarters of a century old, could be proud of; one that Canadians today ought to recognize with renewed pride. Amazingly, it started from virtually nothing.

The Canada of 1939 was a very different place from the Canada of today. There were a little over eleven million Canadians, almost half of whom lived on farms or in small towns or villages. Some 5.7 million Canadians considered themselves

British in origin, 3.5 million thought of themselves as French. The other 20 percent were heavily European. Hardly anyone was black. There were few orientals in Canada, except in British Columbia. Most Canadians — about 9.4 million — had been born in Canada.

As a country largely dependent on the extraction and sale of natural resources, Canada and Canadians had suffered greatly in the Great Depression. The products of farm, mine, and forest are usually hardest hit in economic downturns; raw materials are the first thing factories cut back on when orders dry up and the last thing reordered when factories resume full production. There are no accurate figures on the number of unemployed Canadians in the worst years of the Great Depression, but conservative estimates put the number at some 25 percent of the employable workforce. Whole areas of Saskatchewan were virtually depopulated, armies of single unemployed men roamed the country in box cars. Farmers in Ontario, Quebec, and Atlantic Canada were reduced to subsistence level, formerly middle-class families became mired in poverty and were forced to live on handouts or welfare or the meagre money from make-work projects. The social safety net that Canadians take for granted today did not exist.

By the late 1930s a long, slow climb from the depths of the Depression in 1933 had produced a modicum of recovery, but the nation still had far to go before employment and income levels came close to what they had been in 1929. As late as 1938 there were still mobs of unemployed men rioting in the streets of Vancouver. It was little wonder that the great majority of Canadians paid little attention to events taking place in far-off corners of the world as funny-looking little men, strutting about in comical uniforms, made speeches about recovering lost honour, the need for greater cooperation among Asian peoples, or the need to rid the world of Jews, Communists, and other undesirables. There was no instant satellite news then and besides, what did this posturing have to do with putting food on the table? Those who had experienced the war of 1914–18 first hand, or those who listened to isolationists spin yarns about the way the conspiracies of arms' merchants had dragged Canada and other nations to war in 1914, wanted nothing to do with Europe anyway. As one Canadian politician had declared in 1924, Canadians lived in "a fire-proof house, far from inflammable materials."

Many Canadians undoubtedly agreed with that viewpoint, especially after the beginning of the Great Depression in 1929, but other Canadians watched the rise of fascism and Nazism in Europe with growing unease. There was much to be uneasy about. In January 1933 Adolph Hitler's Nazi party took power in Germany, determined to reinvigorate the German military, restore German power, and use that power for a death struggle against communism and the Jews. For the next six years Hitler and his henchmen Benito Mussolini in Italy and Francisco Franco in Spain brought Europe to the brink of war. All Canadians must surely have been aware of the march of events: the Italian attack on Ethiopia in 1935; the German remilitarization of the Rhineland in 1936; the outbreak of the Spanish Civil War in 1936; the German *Anschluss* of Austria in 1938. As the decade of the 1930s dragged on, most Canadians were torn between their desire to avoid participation in another bloody European conflict and their belief that Nazism and fascism were striking at the roots of Western civilization.

No one appeared to be a greater advocate of isolationism than the man who was prime minister for most of the interwar period, William Lyon Mackenzie King. King first came to power in 1921 at a time when Canadians were bitterly divided over issues that had been raised during the war, or because of it. In the months following the end of the war, labour fought capital, the farmers battled the cities, and western Canadians struggled against eastern Canadians. But none of these schisms was as serious as the chasm that had opened between French- and English-speaking Canadians after the introduction of conscription in 1917. King saw himself as a man with a sacred mission to reunite Canadians, to do all in his power to ensure that the fissures that had opened during the First World War never opened again. He refused to allow Canada's young and idealistic diplomats to be active on the world stage. If Canada led a diplomatic crusade against fascism, he reasoned, it might be called upon to participate in a military crusade as well. When that happened, the danger of conscription and national division would rise once again. King made it a policy to say and do as little as possible that might give Quebec, or Canada's isolationists, the notion that the government was preparing for another foreign war.

But King actually played a double game in the late 1930s, as crisis followed crisis in Europe. He studiously avoided any public act, no matter how symbolic, that might be read as preparation for war or support for other nations (especially Britain or France) that were preparing for war. He declared time after time that "Parliament would decide" Canada's course if and when the time came to determine Canadian participation in another conflict. Although there were a few secret meetings with the American military during the late 1930s, there would be no joint planning with Britain for a possible war, no mobilization of Canadian resources for the military, no Canadian resources made available for others to build weapons, no commitments. King played down the importance, or the danger, of Hitler, and was a strong supporter of the British and French policy of appeasing the dictators. No one rejoiced more at the September 1938 Munich agreement that sold Czechoslovakia down the river than he did.

Behind the scenes, however, it was another matter. King was enough of a realist to know that English-speaking Canadians, with the strong emotional ties of loyalty to Britain they then possessed, would never allow their government to remain neutral in a conflict that pitted Britain against Germany. They had fought beside Britain in the last war; most were the sons and daughters of British immigrants; and many had strong family ties to the United Kingdom. Virtually all of them believed that Britain and the British Empire embodied the ideals of Christian civilization, freedom, liberty, and decency that they themselves professed to believe in. As King told Hitler in a private conversation he had with the dictator when he visited him in 1937, Canada would never stand idly by while German bombs rained on London. In fact, at the height of the Munich crisis, the cabinet secretly decided that it had no option but to declare war on Germany if Britain did. In 1914 Canada was only a self-governing colony with virtually no control over its foreign affairs; legally, Canada had gone to war when Britain had. By the late 1930s, Canada was a self-governing nation with the right to total control over its foreign policy, including the decision to declare war. But Canada's strong ties to Britain made it plain to King that the decision to follow Britain into a war with Germany would be virtually automatic, even though Parliament would vote on the declaration of war.

King's double game was thus a game with a purpose: to forestall preparations for war that might divide the nation in peacetime, in order to make sure that if Canada did go to war it would do so as a united country. That plan worked well when the time came. Germany's invasion of Poland on 1 September 1939 set the machinery in motion for Canada's participation in the greatest war of modern times. When Hitler ignored a British and French ultimatum to withdraw from Poland, those two countries declared war on Germany on 3 September. Canada's tiny armed forces had already been put on alert, as had the Royal Canadian Mounted Police. The first stages of the mobilization of the 1st and 2nd Canadian Divisions had already been launched as Parliament gathered in Ottawa on 7 September to debate Canada's declaration of war. That declaration was made on 10 September 1939. For the second time in the twentieth century, tens of thousands of Canadians were called upon to make the ultimate sacrifice.

How ready were Canada's armed forces for war in September 1939? Not ready at all. At the close of the First World War in November 1918, Canada had possessed a tiny navy and no airforce, even though large numbers of Canadians had distinguished themselves in the Royal Flying Corps and the Royal Naval Air Service. Canada's major contribution to the victory of 1918 had come in the form of its four-division Canadian Corps, commanded by Lieutenant-General Sir Arthur Currie, a Canadian who had gained a reputation as one of the best tacticians on the western front. Through trial and error, the Canadian Corps had learned how to fight; a militia-based army officered and manned by weekend warriors had become a tough, battle-hardened force. The Canadians had paid a high price for that transition — some 60,000 Canadians died and 172,000 were wounded out of a total of 720,000 who served — but at least they had learned through their errors. By the end of the war the Canadian Corps had taught itself, or adopted, advanced techniques of assault and defence that rivalled those of any other army on the western front.

When the war ended, neither Canadians nor their government had showed any inclination to maintain the magnificent instrument they had created. As in other Western democracies, Canadians — and most of those who had fought in the Canadian Corps — had had enough of war and soldiering. So the governments of the 1920s and 1930s ignored the entreaties of the military professionals and allowed the Canadian military to wither. They forgot that a modern, well-trained military force, using up-to-date equipment, cannot be plucked off a tree. It takes time to build a capable military, and it takes a sustained effort to inculcate the knowledge and the traditions of military professionalism in an officer corps. That must be done either before a war or during it. When the learning is done during a war, the cost in lost and ruined lives is enormous. At the start of the First World War Canadians had made terrible and costly mistakes at St Julien, St Eloi, Givenchy, and other battles. Eventually, they learned, but at a great cost.

Successive interwar Canadian governments believed that the Canadian military should consist of a small core of professionals whose main job was to train the nonprofessional militia and the air and naval auxiliaries. The professionals of the armed forces were supposed to keep up with improvements in tactics and become familiar with the new military technologies that other nations were developing. It was understood that if Canada ever fought another war, it would do so as part of a greater British Empire war effort, as it had in the First World War. That was fine as far as most of Canada's professional soldiers, sailors, and airmen were concerned. The Royal Canadian Navy slavishly followed the traditions of the Royal Navy, for example, and regularly trained with it. When RCN officers required experience on large ships or in waters far removed from Canada, they sought duty with the RN. The height of a professional Canadian army officer's training came when he passed competitive examinations and earned a place at the British Army Staff College in Camberly, England, or in Quetta, India.

That was the idea; the reality was another matter. A constant round of budget-cutting invariably meant that there were fewer professional soldiers than the military needed to run its training programs, that modern weapons were always scarce, and that the quality of the training that the militia received left much to be desired. When the government's revenues dried up in the Great Depression, the defence budget was slashed to the bone; in 1933–34, only a little more than $13 million was allocated to military spending — just enough to keep the forces alive.

No branch of the service suffered more from the effects of governmental penny-pinching than did the army. The interwar Canadian Army consisted of the Non-Permanent Active Militia and the Permanent Force. The NPAM, or militia, was made up of weekend warriors who gathered at the local armoury once or twice a week to don First World War vintage uniforms and undergo "training." This training consisted largely of drilling and marching and learning essentials such as first aid. Practice with actual arms usually consisted of an hour or two each week on the rifle range (often in the basement) with the handful of .22 target rifles that the regiment possessed. Officers gathered for mess dinners on special occasions, and accompanied their men into the field in late summer or early fall when a militia camp was held. There, rudimentary exercises were conducted with other militia regiments in the region. The pay was virtually nonexistent (officers generally donated their pay to a regimental fund to cover the costs of uniforms and mess dinners), the training was primitive, the weapons scarce. There were no modern weapons to speak of. The militia was supposed to consist of just under 135,000 men in 1931, but it was only about 51,000 strong.

The basic organizational element of the militia was the regiment. Modelled closely after British territorial regiments, Canadian militia regiments gathered men from a particular area or town into one unit. In time of war, the regiment was to be responsible for raising a force of men who would serve in the overseas army and who, it was expected, would maintain their identity and their ties with that particular regiment. Thus, for example, the Calgary Highlanders, a militia regiment that came into existence in 1921, began at the outset of the Second World War to raise men to serve in the 1st Battalion, Calgary Highlanders, which went overseas as part of the 2nd Canadian Infantry Division. A regiment was supposed to be like an extended family, and members of particular regiments were taught the special traditions, history, and culture of that regiment. The theory was that, in combat, men would fight for each other as members of this extended family; that they would stand and die, if need be, for the honour of the regiment.

Modern military historians are of two minds about the regimental tradition. There is no doubt that once in their slit trenches, men do not fight for causes or country; they fight for each other. Thus, there is value in the tradition because it does seem to create a sense of family. On the other hand, the Canadian and British armies tended to seek out officers for regimentally based battalions only from within the regiment, thus cutting down on the pool of potential officer material. The army was reluctant to take a man out of one battalion and make him commanding officer (CO) of another, because of the belief in regimental cohesion. In addition, there is evidence that the regimental tradition strengthened loyalty to the regiment, but blocked the development of loyalties to higher formations such as brigades and divisions. In the German and American armies, a strong sense of divisional loyalty was encouraged, and that seemed to broaden the perspective of battalion COs in planning and executing military operations. Some attempt was made at the start of the Second World War to inculcate divisional loyalties in the Canadian Army, but it did not go very far.

The backbone of the army was the Permanent Force (PF). In 1931 it was supposed to be 6925 men strong, but its actual strength was fewer than 4000. The PF was the professional army, which was intended to train the militia and to train itself for the time when it would be needed. The problem was, what would it be needed for? Until the outbreak of war in 1939, no Canadian government was willing to admit publicly that the Canadian Army's prime mission was to prepare for another overseas war. Thus the interwar years saw a succession of defence plans come and go as the PF tried not only to define a role for itself but to get the politicians to accept — and pay for — that role. The politicians were most reluctant: to admit that a Canadian expeditionary force would once again go overseas was to admit the possibility of conscription and to risk national unity in peacetime.

The Canadian Army had no control over the purse-strings of government, and no real say over its own size or the state of its equipment. It ought, however, to have had a great deal of input into what its young officers-to-be were taught at the Royal Military College in Kingston (or at militia staff courses), and it definitely decided who was to be promoted to what position. The evidence supplied by two leading Canadian military historians — Colonel John English and Dr Stephen Harris — is that it did not do a good job in either training or promotions. The man who dominated the interwar military, Major-General A.G.L. McNaughton, had been a militiaman before the First World War. He was an engineer by trade and, in that conflict, he had learned how to be a very good artillery officer. He had joined the Permanent Force after the war (as many other veterans did not) and had risen to the position of Chief of the General Staff in 1929, a post he occupied until 1935.

McNaughton believed that the proper basis for educating Canadian officers was to teach them how to think scientifically in Canada and then send them to a British staff college. In English's view, McNaughton's army paid "scant attention . . . to developing higher commanders capable of managing a battle."[1] McNaughton seemed to believe that military knowledge or experience was something that a good officer just picked up; he denied that there was something that might be called a profession of arms. Harris echoes English's opinion: "General McNaughton's views on what constituted a sound officer development system were to be proved wrong. It took more than a keen mind, a scientific education, and attendance at British army staff courses."[2] Ironically, McNaughton, who came back to the military in 1939 to command the 1st Canadian Infantry Division and who was later named General Officer Commanding-in-Chief of the First Canadian Army, was the man Canadian soldiers seemed to worship most at the start of the war. Yet his ideas on officer training ensured that when Canadians first went into battle, they would be led, for the most part, by men who had no business on a battlefield. Only a handful of Canadian officers, such as E.L.M. Burns or Guy Simonds, gave any thought to modern tactics in the interwar period, or shared their thinking with their fellows officers in journals like *Canadian Defence Quarterly*. But then, not much more could have been expected from an officer corps of 446 men.

Things changed somewhat for the army after 1935, but not much. Mackenzie King came back to power in October of that year. He was suspicious of the military and no less concerned about national unity than he had ever been. But there was no mistaking that the clouds of war were gathering in Europe and Asia and that Canada was totally incapable of defending itself. The government responded with the first of a number of modest increases in the defence budget and established the Cabinet Defence Committee as the first step towards some coordinated military planning at the cabinet level. King, however, directed that most of the new money would go to the navy and the airforce, because he was as wary as ever of preparing the army for an overseas war. One of the few moves taken in the late 1930s to modernize the army's equipment was the signing of a contract in March 1938 for the manufacture of 7000 Bren light machine guns to replace the army's aging and obsolete Lewis guns. The contract was not tendered, and the press yelled foul. Although a subsequent investigation revealed no wrongdoing, King was stung by this Bren Gun Scandal and became even more reluctant to acquire modern equipment for the army. Still, appropriations for the army were about doubled between 1935 and the outbreak of war, and the size of both the Permanent Force and the militia was expanded; when war was declared, there were 4268 men in the former, 86,308 in the latter. In the spring of 1937 the government reluctantly began to accept the idea that Canada might have to dispatch an expeditionary force overseas in the event of war. Although the army was planning on an overall force of one cavalry and six infantry divisions, no final decision was made on the size or composition of the overseas contingent until after war was actually declared.

The Royal Canadian Navy fared somewhat better than the army in the post-1935 expansion of the defence program, although it almost did not survive until 1935. In the frenzy of defence budget cuts of 1933, McNaughton had decided that Canada really did not need a navy and had recommended that the RCN be disbanded. The navy was saved only when Rear Admiral Walter Hose, Chief of the Naval Staff, argued that Canada had to have a navy in the event of its being dragged into a war between the United States and Japan. Since war was already raging in Manchuria, that possibility was neither wild nor remote and Hose had carried the day.

The backbone of the Canadian fleet in 1935 were the two River Class destroyers — HMCS *Saguenay* and HMCS *Skeena* — which had been built in British shipyards and acquired by the RCN in 1931 (they were so-designated because they were named after Canadian rivers). These were the RCN's first new vessels of any consequence. They were modern warships in every sense of the word, displacing 1360 tonnes, with a top speed of 31 knots, a main armament of four 4.7-inch guns, and a normal complement of 181 officers and men. But there were only two of them, and they were not equipped with asdic, developed at the end of the First World War. Asdic (called sonar in the United States Navy) consisted of a device fitted to the bottom of a warship which transmitted sound pulses through the water and then received them. If a sound pulse struck an underwater object such as a submarine, it was reflected back to the transmitting vessel. The time lapse between the emission of the pulse and its receipt was supposed to tell the asdic operator the distance of the submerged object and also its depth. Successive echoes indicated in what direction the object lay. In theory, these reports would give the captain of the escort vessel all the information he needed to begin a depth-charge attack.

Like the army, the RCN consisted of a professional core and two militia-like auxiliary forces: the Royal Canadian Naval Reserve and the Royal Canadian Naval Volunteer Reserve. The professional core numbered about 1900 at the outbreak of the Second World War. These men were careerists, but the training they received, like that of their counterparts in the army, was well short of what would be required when war broke out. The RCNR had been set up in 1923 with an authorized establishment of 500 men in nine ports. In fact, it was usually only half that size through most of the interwar period. RCNR members were required to have a maritime occupation in civilian life and to possess a professional knowledge of ships and the sea. They received four weeks of training each year aboard RCN vessels. Members of the RCNVR (referred to as the "wavy-navy" because of the wavy gold stripes on the cuffs of its officers' uniforms) came from virtually all walks of life. During the week they were lawyers or accountants or salesmen; they qualified for membership by their interest in the sea — by owning a yacht, for example — and their willingness to devote some time to rudimentary training. They were treated to thirty evenings of training during the winter and two weeks at sea in the summer. There were never more than 1500 members of the wavy-navy between the wars.

It was expected that when the RCN next went to war it would do so as part of a larger Royal Navy war effort and that RCN ships would serve alongside RN vessels under the overall command of RN officers. RCN training, tactics, and equipment in the interwar period therefore followed that of the RN. Most of the RCN's warfare training was carried out in annual summer exercises with the RN's Atlantic and West Indies squadrons. The RN devoted scant attention to anti-submarine warfare in the interwar period, even though it had virtually pioneered it. RN strategists (and, of course, the RCN officers who trained with them) assumed that asdic gave defenders such a powerful tool for the detection of enemy submarines that there would be no repeat of the U-boat scourge that had virtually brought Britain to its knees in the First World War. RN destroyers were not considered primarily as anti-submarine vessels, but as fleet destroyers to protect the main fleet from enemy aircraft and to harass the enemy fleet through daring torpedo and gunnery attacks. Consequently, RCN officers and crew members received virtually no training in modern anti-submarine warfare in the interwar period.

There was one other area in which the prewar RCN was deficient: an appreciation of the need for modern technological advances such as radar and for Canadian sources of supply. As historian David Zimmerman has observed: "Of the three [Canadian] services, the RCN was least committed to a program of scientific research conducted by the National Research Council."[3] The RCN saw no practical need to install radar on its vessels in the late prewar period, for example. It was "content to be totally reliant on the RN for all its technical and scientific needs."[4] When war did break out, the RCN was often a generation behind the RN in using the latest in radar, asdic, and anti-submarine weaponry. The U-boat war turned out to be a highly technical war and the RCN was far from prepared to fight it in 1939, even though convoy escort and anti-submarine warfare eventually constituted the greatest part of the RCN's responsibilities.

In the late 1930s, Ottawa perceived a growing threat from Japan to the Canadian west coast and was anxious not to leave the protection of the coast in the hands of the United States Navy. Four former RN Crescent Class destroyers, similar to the River Class vessels but somewhat larger, were purchased from the United Kingdom as additions to the River Class fleet. These were recommissioned as HMC ships *Fraser*, *St Laurent*, *Restigouche*, and *Ottawa*. HMS *Kempenfelt*, a larger destroyer, was purchased after the outbreak of war as a flotilla leader and recommissioned as HMCS *Assiniboine*. Most of these destroyers were stationed at Esquimalt, on the west coast, in the summer of 1939.

The state of the Royal Canadian Air Force in the interwar years was not much better than that of the RCN or the army. Established as a separate branch of the Canadian armed forces in 1924, the RCAF remained under the overall command of the Chief of the General Staff (the army) until December 1938. Thereafter, it was headed by a Chief of the Air Staff (CAS). The first CAS was George M. Croil, a First World War infantryman who had joined the Royal Flying Corps in 1916. Many of the duties performed by the fledgling RCAF in the 1920s and early 1930s were actually civilian in nature, because the force functioned as the air transport arm of the federal government. That ended in 1936 when the Department of Transport was created to fill the government's civil needs, leaving the RCAF to concentrate on military duties. In the mid-1930s those duties did not include preparation for an overseas war. According to the official history, "Home defence was the principal justification for the RCAF after 1935, overseas commitments were not in favour."[5] RCAF planning concentrated on defending both coasts in the event of war, and, in the meantime, trying to acquire new equipment.

As late as the Munich crisis of September 1938, the RCAF was totally unprepared for war. With fewer than 1000 personnel in its permanent establishment and only obsolete and obsolescent aircraft, it was little more than a flying joke. When No. 1 Fighter Squadron was formed on 1 March 1937, for example, it was equipped with Armstrong-Whitworth Siskin fighters, purchased from the RAF in the late 1920s and early 1930s. The Siskin was a biplane with an open cockpit and a fixed undercarriage. It had a top speed of 190 kilometres per hour. At a time when the Luftwaffe was already flying Messerschmitt Bf 109s (Me 109) in Spain, which had a top speed of 550 kilometres per hour, sending a pilot to war in a Siskin would have been as useful as shooting him in the head.

The government began to get serious about the airforce in early 1939. It acquired twenty Hawker Hurricane I fighters from Britain, one of which was the pattern aircraft for the production of Hurricanes at the Canadian Car and Foundry plant in Fort William; the remaining aircraft went to replace the Siskins of No. 1 Fighter Squadron. The Hurricane was a closed cockpit monoplane with retractable landing gear, a service ceiling of about 11,000 metres, and a top speed of 530 kilometres per hour. It was not a match for the Me 109 in a number of performance areas, but in the hands of a skilled pilot it could emerge victorious in a dog fight. It was more than a match for the Luftwaffe's bombers and the twin-engine Me 110 fighter. The problem was, there were so few of them in Canada.

This, then, was the state of Canada's army, navy, and airforce on the eve of war. Years of neglect and budget cutting had left all three services in a deplorable state. Not only was there a dearth of equipment, but much of the equipment to hand was out of date. There was only a small core of professionals, and the training and skills levels for most of the militia and auxiliaries were patchy and inadequate. Neither the army nor the navy was prepared to fight the type of war that was looming, and the airforce had no overseas mission at all. The government feared a war with Japan much more than a war with Germany, and much of the navy and airforce were assigned to the west coast. The King government, in power since 1935, had moved very cautiously to improve matters, but it was concerned that any outright effort to ready the armed forces for war would produce a political crisis at home. The armed forces of Canada, and the soldiers, sailors, and airmen who served in them, would eventually pay a high price so that Mackenzie King could lead a united nation into war.

The train ride east from Brest in France was slow, halting, and hot. Inside the crowded railway cars, men of the 1st Canadian Infantry Brigade talked, smoked, gawked at the countryside, and drank the cheap wine they bought at every stop. Lieutenant Farley Mowat was one of these men, a platoon commander with the Hastings and Prince Edward Regiment, the Hasty Ps: "The train crawled on and at the first light of dawn it came into the town of Laval, almost 200 miles inland, where it was halted by a frenzied station master. He was beside himself. 'Are you Canadians insane?' he cried. 'Do you not know that Paris has fallen and that all resistance is at an end? Do you not know that *les boches* are only forty miles away?'"[1] It was 15 June 1940 — just thirty-six days after Hitler unleashed his panzer (armoured) forces in the west. France was in chaos, and a handful of green Canadian troops were on the verge of stumbling into the spearheads of Field Marshal Fedor von Bock's Army Group B.

On 10 May 1940 the German army, backed by the Luftwaffe, sliced through Belgium and Holland. Then, in a brilliant execution of tactical surprise, the Germans infiltrated in force through the Ardennes Forest, outflanked France's Maginot Line, split the Allied forces, and caused the virtual collapse of the French armies. The British Expeditionary Force, accompanied by a number of French troops, began to fall back on the English Channel port of Dunkirk. Between 26 May and 4 June, about 340,000 men, mostly British but including about 70,000 French soldiers, were evacuated to the United Kingdom. The remnants of the French army took their stand along the line of the Seine to make a last-ditch effort to halt von Bock and Field Marshal Gerd von Rundstedt's Army Group A. The demoralized French were no match for the Wehrmacht; they were swept aside, and Paris surrendered on 14 June. It was no place for the Canadians to be.

If William Lyon Mackenzie King had had his way, no Canadians would have been there. Just as he had been adamant about delaying a build-up of the Canadian armed forces as late as he could, he also wanted a Canadian war effort with a minimum number of casualties. In effect, he wanted Canada to fight a "limited liability" war by concentrating on providing raw materials, munitions, and war *matériel* to the Allies rather than sheer manpower. He would have been satisfied if the RCAF had restricted itself to the defence of Canada, the navy to guarding the sea lanes on the approach to east-coast ports, and the army to sending as few combat units as possible to European battlefields. This would have kept casualties low and made the possibility of conscription remote.

There were other continuing themes in the government's approach to the Canadian war effort. Ottawa insisted, for the most part, that Canada's contribution be paid for by Canada and that it be as self-contained as possible. That meant that although Canadians would fight under the overall command of British (and later also American) commanders, Canadian units would maintain their integrity and would always be commanded by Canadians. Further, the government wanted to make the Canadian war effort highly visible to both Canadians and others. Sometimes the costs of this Canadianized war effort were high not only in money but in lives lost.

There was a reason for this approach: the government believed that Canadian unity could be guaranteed for the duration only if the war effort was seen by the people of Canada to be Canadian. Fielding an identifiable Canadian army or airforce might do that. It would also make it more difficult for the major Allies to downplay the Canadian contribution to the war. The lesson Ottawa had learned from the First World War was that, when it came to making the peace or playing a role in designing the postwar world, one of the qualifications for inclusion in the process was the importance of a nation's war effort.

Although Canada did not declare war until 10 September 1939, the armed forces began to gear up for the coming conflict in late August. The government's Defence Scheme No. 3 called for the formation of a mobile force to defend Canada and, on 25 August, a number of militia units were activated to assist in the protection of federal property, to guard essential communications, and to man coastal defence installations. On 1 September — the day Germany invaded Poland — an order was issued to establish the Canadian Active Service Force, consisting of two infantry divisions and ancillary troops. Canada's three Permanent Force infantry regiments — the Princess Patricia's Canadian Light Infantry, the Royal 22e Régiment (the Van Doos), and the Royal Canadian Regiment — were mobilized with one battalion in each brigade of the 1st Division to give that division a professional core. The best fourteen militia regiments (infantry, armour, and artillery) from across Canada were also mobilized to form the balance of the two divisions. On 19 September King announced that the 1st Division would be available for overseas service if required (if requested by the British), and that the 2nd Division would be kept under arms in Canada for the time being.

Across Canada, militia regiments opened their doors, set up a rudimentary selection procedure, dug musty uniforms out of storage, and went looking through armoury basements and storage lockers for First World War era Lee-Enfield .303 rifles, Lewis guns, mortars, and any military armaments they could find. There were only twenty-three Bren guns in the entire army. There was virtually nothing else besides rifles. There were no modern uniforms, no combat boots, no field equipment, no overcoats, no prepackaged rations, and almost no up-to-date crew-served weapons such as artillery or tanks. In the militia, new recruits wore crazy combinations of civilian clothes and bits of First World War uniforms. The absence of appropriate army boots posed a particular challenge, because much of the so-called training the men would receive in the coming months was in the form of long route marches. Neither the lack of equipment nor the poor state of readiness seemed to bother the potential volunteers; throughout September and into October they lined up at recruitment centres across Canada. They numbered more than the army needed, and many were turned away.

Why did they join? There is no doubt that many of them sought relief from unemployment or from dreary, low-paying jobs. Others thought that the army and the war would be a chance to get away from home, to see some of the world, and to take part in a great adventure. Still others joined out of genuine patriotism, or from a belief that Hitler was wrong and had to be stopped. There were more than enough volunteers to man two divisions and the expanding navy and airforce, but there was no outpouring of the naive, wide-eyed patriotism that had marked the opening months of the First World War. The prevailing feeling was resignation and grim determination.

Training a man to become a soldier is a long and difficult process, one for which the Canadian Army was not ready in the fall of 1939. Across the country, militia units processed the recruits, rejected those who were unsuitable, and trucked those who were accepted to the nearest training area, where they were housed in temporary shelters (usually tents or wooden shacks) and taught the rudiments of standing at attention, marching, parade drill, marksmanship, first aid, and other military skills. There were lots of physical training and inter-unit sports. No attempt was made to teach small-unit tactics, infantry-artillery cooperation, or advancing with tanks. No one really knew how, and there was no space and too little equipment. The men of the 6th Brigade of the 2nd Division (originally all from western Canada) did not see an artillery piece fired until the late spring of 1940, when a demonstration was mounted for them at Camp Shilo, in southern Manitoba. When the first elements of the 1st Division left Canada on 10 December 1939, most of the men looked like soldiers (they had finally received the new battle-dress uniform, boots, packs, web equipment, and rifles) and had received training in soldierly discipline. But they were totally unprepared for war. They were supposed to receive that preparation in the United Kingdom.

A Canadian infantry division was a large and complex body of men. Commanded by a major-general, its basic war establishment was some 18,376 men. The largest single group of those men were the 8418 infantrymen organized in nine infantry battalions (the eventual infantry battalion establishment was thirty-eight officers and 812 men). Each battalion had a support company, and four rifle companies. Each rifle company was made up of a company headquarters and three platoons of one officer (a lieutenant) and thirty-six men. The support company would eventually comprise a carrier platoon, a mortar platoon, a pioneer platoon, and an anti-tank platoon. Three battalions would be joined in an infantry brigade, commanded by a brigadier; an infantry division had three infantry brigades.

The bulk of the men in a Canadian division were not infantry; they were a combination of field artillery (2122 men), Royal Canadian Army Service Corps (1296), engineers (959), medical personnel (945), Royal Canadian Electrical and Mechanical Engineers (784), signal corps (743), anti-tank artillery (721), and others. A study done after the war by Major-General E.L.M. Burns (who was a corps commander in Italy) concluded that Canadians allocated more men to medical and other ancillary services than they needed to — certainly more than the British did — and that Canadian divisions had far fewer combat troops as a proportion of their total strength than did American infantry divisions (which contained 14,037 men). Yet Max Hastings, who has written extensively on the Second World War, pointed out in his book on the Normandy campaign that only 65.56 percent of an American division consisted of fighting soldiers, against 89.4 percent in a German panzergrenadier (mechanized) division.

In general, therefore, Canadian divisions were far weaker in overall fighting strength than those of their allies and their enemies. That imbalance would later prove a source of great difficulty in combat and would hamper the Canadian Army in its efforts to keep its front-line units up to proper fighting strength. Put bluntly, the Canadian Army contained too many cooks and bottle-washers and too few riflemen, and the blame for this must be laid totally at the door of National Defence Headquarters (NDHQ) in Ottawa, which set the establishment for Canadian divisions.

Lack of equipment, lack of space for training, and a poorly designed divisional structure were not the only difficulties hampering the Canadian Army; leadership was a major problem, especially in the early stages of the war when most of the officers in charge of army units were incapable of leading men into battle. Since most of the army units being prepared for war in the fall of 1940 were militia units, most of the officers were militia officers. Few of them lasted even until their units entered battle; many of those who did succeed them in command proved inadequate. Many were veterans of the First World War and too old or too set in their ways to fight a new kind of war. For one thing, they did not have the physical stamina that younger men possessed.

When British General Bernard L. Montgomery reviewed Canadian units and their commanders in the spring of 1942, he concluded that almost one-quarter of the battalion commanders were totally unsuited to the job of training their men or leading them in combat. As a result, there was a wholesale housecleaning of officers right up to the divisional level. But in an army as wedded to the regimental system as the Canadian Army was, some of the retired battalion commanders were replaced by men who were little better. Still, there were some militia officers who were excellent and, by the time the war moved into its final year, they had come to the fore from the battalion level right up to divisional commands. Two of Canada's best field generals — Bert Hoffmeister, who eventually commanded the 5th Canadian Armoured Division, and A.B. Matthews of the 2nd Canadian Infantry Division — were both militiamen.

It was clear from the start of this war that Permanent Force officers would fill virtually all the staff, planning, and support positions. In the spring of 1939 the PF officer corps numbered just 446 men. In the words of Chris Vokes, who later commanded the 1st Canadian Infantry and the 4th Canadian Armoured Divisions: "Over 50% of the then serving officers in the PF were useless for active service, either from old age, ill health or inefficiency."[2] The vast majority of Canadian Permanent Force army officers were graduates of the Royal Military College, located in Kingston, Ontario, and founded in 1876. RMC taught its students how to command up to platoon level, but no further. In large measure that reflected the approach of A.G.L. McNaughton, whose philosophy of arms and war dominated the army's thinking in this era.

When the government decided it was going to send a Canadian division overseas in the first weeks of the war, there was little doubt that McNaughton was going to be its General Officer Commanding. From that position, McNaughton was eventually elevated to GOC 1st Canadian Corps and then GOC-in-C First Canadian Army. An intelligent and innovative engineer, McNaughton seems not to have thought that a field officer required special knowledge about tactics, uses of weaponry, and leadership techniques. Thus, RMC gave Canadian officers a good education (and was especially effective in technical subjects such as artillery), but did not teach them enough about leading infantry in war.

McNaughton was a strong Canadian nationalist who believed that Canada's army in the Second World War should fight together as the Canadian Corps had done in the First World War. He bitterly resisted any attempt by the British, no matter how trivial, to interfere in the daily administration of the Canadian Army. But the legal and command position McNaughton occupied was full of contradictions. In matters considered operational, Canadian units in the field were under the overall command of the British. In other words, McNaughton always had a British officer above him in the chain of command. Nevertheless, McNaughton was also the ranking Canadian officer in the United Kingdom, charged by the Canadian government with overall responsibility for the Canadian Army there. He could, for example, refuse an assignment that his British superiors wished the Canadian troops to carry out. In administrative matters, he was in *de facto* control of Canadian Military Headquarters (CMHQ), established in London in November 1939, and responsible only to the Chief of the General Staff in Ottawa and, through him, to the Minister of National Defence. Later in the war, when the First Canadian Army was fighting on the continent, a division of function evolved between CMHQ, increasingly seen as the forward echelon of National Defence Headquarters, and Headquarters, First Canadian Army.

On 10 December 1939 convoy TC 1 sailed from Halifax with 7400 men of the 1st Division; it reached the United Kingdom seventeen days later. The rest of the division arrived in subsequent convoys, with the last men arriving on 7 February 1940. The division was settled in Aldershot, near Salisbury Plain, a familiar base to any Canadian who had gone overseas with the army in the First World War. The winter was cold and wet, the housing conditions poor, and the English food unappetizing and difficult to get used to. The Canadians had been sent to

England in the mistaken belief that opportunities for training would be much better there than in the harsh Canadian winter. But it was difficult to train in the cold and wet, and the Canadians were little better trained for war by the early spring of 1940 than they had been when they left Canada. That was not a problem, however, because the German invasion of Poland had long since ended and an eerie quiet had settled over the European battlefields. Over the winter of 1939/ 40, Hitler's generals prepared for an all-out offensive in the west while Hitler held out the hope that Britain and France would now reverse the decision they had made on 3 September, especially since Poland could no longer be saved. It was the time of the "phoney war," or *Sitzkrieg*, and the Canadians could sit as well as the best of them.

Like the army, the Royal Canadian Navy was alerted to prepare for hostilities even before Canada declared war. By the end of August 1939 the RCN consisted of six River Class destroyers (four on the west cost and two on the east coast) and a handful of small minesweepers and other auxiliary vessels, eleven ships in all. On the 26th of that month the Royal Canadian Navy issued orders that no merchant vessel could take to sea from a Canadian port without RCN authority; a similar order had already come from London regarding British merchant ships and the Royal Navy. Then, five days later, *Fraser* and *St Laurent* sailed for the east coast from Esquimalt; they arrived at Halifax on 15 September, and were sent to sea as escort vessels for convoy HX 1 one day later.

The North Atlantic was one of the most important theatres of the Second World War, and the RCN was in the battle from the beginning. If anyone needed proof of how desperate the coming war at sea would be, that proof was provided within hours of the British declaration of war on Germany when the German submarine U-30 sank the British passenger ship *Athenia*, bound for Montreal from the United Kingdom, some 400 kilometres west of Ireland. The attack came without warning, in contravention of rules governing submarine warfare laid down in the 1930 London Naval Treaty and signed by Germany in 1936; 118 lives were lost. Although the sinking of the *Athenia* was clearly the act of one submarine commander and not, at that time, a reflection of a general German policy of embarking on unrestricted submarine warfare, it was only a matter of time before that happened. As an anti-commerce weapon, the submarine was most effective when it struck without warning, wreaked as much damage as it could, and escaped quickly, without stopping to ensure the safety of any survivors.

After the fall of France in June 1940, the outcome of the war in the North Atlantic helped to determine the course of the entire conflict. As Canada's foremost naval historian, Marc Milner, has pointed out, "Without secure use of the sea Anglo-American land and air campaigns could not have been mounted and sustained."[3] The war in the North Atlantic ultimately boiled down to these essentials: to win the war in Europe against Germany, the Allies would eventually have to mount a major land operation supported by airpower. To do so, they needed to have Britain as a base of operations, peopled by a reasonably well-fed and well-provisioned population. And, since British industry could never supply all the tanks, artillery, and aircraft that would be necessary to beat the Germans, much of the war *matériel* — as well as most of the soldiers — would have to come from the United States by sea. None of that was possible unless the sea lanes were secure. The German objective was to stop that transport from happening; the Allied objective was to make sure that the Germans did not succeed.

The best way to ensure that merchant ships got through was to avoid submarines. To have U-boats constantly roaming the sea lanes looking for victims would have been a tremendous waste of submarines. U-boats were assigned particular patrol areas and did not move out of those areas unless told to do so by U-boat headquarters (BdU), the U-boat central command. The challenge to the Allies was to figure out where those patrol areas were. Much of the Battle of the Atlantic involved the undramatic job of finding out where the U-boats were and routing convoys around them. This detection was done through signals intelligence — the breaking of the German naval codes — and radio direction-finding, which pinpointed the location of German submarines from their radio transmissions.

One lesson the British Admiralty learned the hard way during the First World War was that merchant ships travelling in convoys protected by escort vessels were much more likely to reach their destinations than single ships sailing alone. That did not mean that convoys did not create difficulties for the Allies. Convoyed vessels had to waste time gathering in ports of departure, and the arrival of a convoy taxed the unloading facilities at a port of destination, if the port was not well organized. On balance, however, convoys offered significant protection, especially to slower vessels.

The main German weapon in the Battle of the Atlantic, the U-boat, had serious drawbacks as a commerce raider. For one thing, there were never enough of them for the German U-boat commander, Grossadmiral Karl Dönitz, to mount a truly effective blockade of Britain. Even at the height of the war, there were never more than four hundred U-boats available, and, at any one time, part of this fleet was in port for repairs and reprovisioning, part was on its way to patrol areas, and part was on its way back. It was rare that the Germans could put more than a third of their fleet on station at any one time. In contrast, there were literally thousands of Allied and neutral merchant vessels (on charter to the Allies) available to carry cargoes at the start of the war, and thousands more were built during the war. The war at sea was thus a war of attrition in which Dönitz's men attempted to sink Allied merchant vessels (and neutral ships chartered by the Allies) at a much faster rate than they themselves were being sunk.

U-boats were not true submarines. Both main types used by the Germans, the long-range Type IX and the shorter-range Type VIIc, were diesel vessels that ran on battery power when submerged. Their maximum underwater endurance was about one day at a walking speed. Neither type could make more than 7 knots under water; the Type VIIc could do 17 knots on the surface, and the Type IX, 19 knots. Therefore, underwater range and endurance were strictly limited. These boats were really torpedo boats, best used on the surface, but with an ability to submerge to avoid detection. Not until August and September 1940, when the Germans organized "wolfpacks" of U-boats attacking on the surface at night, did they begin to do serious damage to the North Atlantic commerce lifeline.

The Type VIIc was the mainstay of the U-boat fleet in the early stages of the battle of the North Atlantic; it had a limited range of about 10,400 kilometres and, in the early days of the war, had to travel north of Scotland from Germany's Baltic Sea ports to reach the Atlantic. Their limited range led the British Admiralty to believe that they posed a serious threat to commerce only in the eastern Atlantic and on the approaches to UK ports, and that the major threat to transatlantic shipping came from German surface raiders — cruisers, battleships, and pocket battleships. Convoy escort from Halifax to UK waters in the first eighteen months of war therefore consisted of capital ships from the Royal Navy's Atlantic and West Indies squadrons. This left the RCN to escort convoys from Halifax and other east-coast ports to the point in the western ocean where the RN's capital ships took over.

The RCN was not ready to fight an anti-submarine war; two of its six destroyers had still to be fitted with asdic, and neither officers nor ratings (the navy's word for "other ranks") knew how to protect a convoy or kill a U-boat. It was fortunate that there was so little submarine action in the western Atlantic in the first two-and-a-half years of the war. Until October 1941 U-boats rarely ventured into Newfoundland waters. They also generally sailed alone and attacked individual merchantmen one by one; of the 164 ships sunk, only seven were part of an escorted convoy.

The RCN dreamed of putting a small but powerful force of fleet destroyers to sea to help the Royal Navy perform a variety of tasks. That, after all, was what the navy had trained for. The ship the RCN most desired was the new Tribal Class destroyer then being built in British shipyards. Much larger than previous British destroyers, the Tribal had an average displacement of 2000 tonnes, carried six 4.7-inch guns in three double turrets as main armament, and was equipped with a wide array of anti-aircraft and heavy machine guns as well as torpedoes. It also had a top speed of 36 knots. Canadian shipyards were incapable of building these vessels at the outbreak of war; Canadian industry could not even supply suitable steel. If Canada wanted Tribals at that stage of the war, it would have to buy them from Britain, or barter for them.

The ship that Canada proposed to swap for the Tribals was the corvette. A British-designed utility vessel patterned after a whale catcher, the corvette was originally ordered by the RCN as an all-purpose auxiliary ship to operate in Canadian coastal waters. Corvettes would sweep mines, patrol harbour entrances, and do escort duty for coastal convoys. They would definitely not be used in mid-ocean. In February 1940 Ottawa ordered sixty-four Flower Class corvettes to be built by Canadian shipyards. (British Flower Class corvettes were named after flowers; Canadian corvettes were named after Canadian towns and cities.) Ten of these corvettes were earmarked for the Royal Navy, which formally owned them, even though they were to sail under the RCN flag. Of the remaining fifty-four, an additional but undetermined number were to be bartered for four British-built Tribals. The swap fell through, and the RCN kept all the vessels. By the end of the war, 122 had been turned out by Canadian shipbuilders.

The Flower Class corvette displaced 935 tonnes, carried one 4-inch gun as main armament, and had a top speed of only 16 knots. It was a miserable ship to sail on and to fight in. In British and Canadian warships of that day, the men slept and ate in a designated mess deck, the food being brought to them from the galley. The early versions of the corvette had no covered passageway between the galley, which was aft, and the forward mess deck. The corvette was seaworthy, but it pitched and bucked in a heavy sea like a fiend possessed. Sea water sloshed into mess decks, officers' cabins, wardrooms, everywhere. The vessel was not fast enough to catch a U-boat on the surface, and was originally equipped with obsolete asdic and a magnetic compass totally unsuitable for anti-submarine work. When U-boats started to carry 10.5-centimetre deck guns, the corvette did not even have heavy enough armament to fight it out with them on the surface. It often seemed that the best a corvette could do was to ram a submarine, at great risk to itself. When the RCN finally got around to equipping its escort vessels with radar, it first put the obsolete Canadian-built SW1C on board because the better British-built 271 radar was not available. The SW1C was virtually useless in detecting a surfaced U-boat. The only thing a corvette could do better than any other escort vessel was turn on a dime.

Few regular RCN personnel ever served aboard the corvettes; the "corvette navy," as James B. Lamb has called it, was manned almost exclusively by the men of the Royal Canadian Naval Reserve or the Royal Canadian Naval Volunteer Reserve. The RCN began to mobilize both the RCNR and the RCNVR at the outset of the war and, as with the army, it was not long before volunteers began to pour into RCN recruitment centres. The men of the "real" or "pusser" navy served aboard the River Class destroyers, the Tribals that Canada finally put to sea in 1943, and on the other major ships that joined the Canadian fleet before the end of the war. The Canadian side of the Battle of the Atlantic was fought mostly by men who, until 1940 or so, had rarely seen the ocean.

The man who commanded the burgeoning Canadian fleet was Percy W. Nelles, Chief of the Naval Staff (CNS) since 1934. Nelles had had a career typical of RCN officers; he had served aboard British destroyers in the First World War and had risen to command of a British cruiser in the America and West Indies Squadrons in 1929. He was the first captain of the destroyer HMCS *Saguenay*, and spent a year at the Imperial Defence College in the United Kingdom before returning to Ottawa to become CNS. A strong supporter of the Royal Navy, he was a traditionalist. He also failed to grasp the importance of the RCN's having the most advanced anti-submarine warfare (ASW) technology. But then, almost no one else in the upper echelons of the RCN did either. In the words of Marc Milner, Nelles was "a quiet, competent, but uninspired man, one promoted well beyond his limits."[4]

Even if Nelles had been more attuned to the need for the latest in asdic, radar, and other equipment, the RCN would still have suffered tremendous teething problems. As the U-boat war widened after May 1940, there was no time either to train men at specific tasks or to get them used to working with each other and under their assigned officers. The unreliability of the corvette and other RCN ships initially made it almost impossible for the RCN to set up permanent escort groups (a specific group of corvettes working with a destroyer) to work and train together. These problems stemmed from the navy's unpreparedness for war, an unpreparedness based on the government's prewar defence policy.

❧

Like the army and the navy, the Royal Canadian Air Force also hurried to ready itself for war. Before Parliament declared war, the RCAF's eight permanent and eleven auxiliary squadrons were placed on active service, even though none was properly equipped or manned. Official historian W.A.B. Douglas has summed up the state of the RCAF at the outbreak of war: "Of the fifty-three aircraft 'able to take their place on active service,' including eight on the west coast and thirty-six in the east, many were civil types converted with floats for patrol work and most of the others were obsolescent."[5] Of the fifteen squadrons that the RCAF was capable of putting into the air, twelve were allocated to home defence and three were selected to be sent overseas.

On 17 December 1939 Canada, Britain, Australia, and New Zealand reached agreement on the establishment of the British Commonwealth Air Training Plan, with costs to be borne by all four countries. Canada was to pay the largest portion, as part of its contribution to the war effort. The BCATP would use Canadian bases and training facilities to train Commonwealth aircrew who would then enter overseas service with the Royal Air Force. The RCAF was to operate the BCATP, which began to graduate aircrew in late 1940. By 1942 the BCATP operated 107 schools across Canada; by the end of the war more than 131,000 flight crew had been turned out, 73,000 of them Canadians.

Two provisions of the BCATP directly affected the development of the RCAF. Article 14 of the agreement guaranteed Canada a supply of aircrew for what the RCAF termed its Home War Establishment — the squadrons to be used for the defence of Canada, including anti-submarine defence — while Article 15 provided that a number of RCAF squadrons would be formed overseas using Canadian BCATP graduates. This last provision became the legislative framework for the eventual formation of No. 6 Group (RCAF), Bomber Command.

A number of RCAF personnel were already in the United Kingdom serving with the RAF when war began, but the first all-RCAF squadron to go overseas, No. 110 "City of Toronto" Squadron, left Canada for Britain in February 1940. An "army cooperation" (reconnaissance) squadron, it was equipped with single-engine Westland Lysander aircraft. Since there was little for the squadron to do in the United Kingdom, it continued to train for its army cooperation role after it arrived. It was redesignated No. 400 Squadron on 1 March 1941. No. 110 Squadron was followed in June 1940 by No. 112 Squadron, also an army cooperation squadron, and by No. 1 Fighter Squadron equipped with Hurricane I fighters.

On 9 April 1940 Germany invaded Norway and occupied Denmark; within days the British began to mount a counter invasion aimed at Narvik and other sites. They planned a second strike on Trondheim, and approached CMHQ with a request that infantrymen from the 1st Canadian Division be made available for this attack. They initially asked for eight parties of about one hundred men each to help seize a number of German-held forts at the head of Trondheim fjord in a frontal assault. McNaughton agreed, allocated the men from the 2nd Brigade, and appointed acting-brigade commander Lieutenant-Colonel E.W. Sansom to command the operation. On 18 April 1300 men of the Loyal Edmonton Regiment and the Princess Patricia's Canadian Light Infantry left Aldershot by rail for the Scottish port of Dunfermline; they never left for Norway. The British Chiefs of Staff changed their minds about the operation, always considered risky, primarily because of the danger that the Luftwaffe posed to the invasion fleet. Since British troops to the north and south of Trondheim seemed to be doing well, there was no need for the operation. The Canadians remained in Scotland for several days as CMHQ and the British tried to decide how they were to be used, if at all. By 26 April they were back in their barracks at Aldershot. The British and French troops in Norway fought on against growing odds, but finally began to pull out early in May. The last Allied soldier departed on 8 June, and Norway was occupied by the Germans until the end of the war.

Although strategically important, Norway was a sideshow; the main feature began on 10 May, with the German invasion of the Low Countries and France. Much has been written about the brilliance and daring of the German attack, on the failures of Allied strategy and tactics, on the collapse of morale of the French army, and on the Dunkirk evacuation. It was only after most of the damage had been done and the Dunkirk evacuations had been completed (3 June) that the British decided to try for a second time to save France — or, at least, a piece of it — by scraping together enough units to form a second British Expeditionary Force. The 1st Canadian Division was to be part of that new BEF.

McNaughton thought that his troops would land at Brest and then concentrate in an assembly area to the northeast of that port, but he was wrong. When the lead elements of the 1st Brigade, the artillery, and the Royal Canadian Army Service Corps (RCASC) supply column landed on 12 and 13 June, the British put them aboard trucks and railcars bound for an assembly area near Laval and Le Mans, more than 100 kilometres from the line they thought they were going to help hold across the base of the Brittany peninsula in the vicinity of Rennes. There is strong evidence that the British and French had planned to try to hold Brittany as a redoubt, but the situation had deteriorated to such an extent that this was impossible. Churchill changed his mind and ordered all British and Canadian troops not already under command of the French army to be evacuated.

With the German spearheads drawing dangerously close to the Canadian concentration area, the lead troops of the 1st Brigade, the artillery, and the RCASC began to move back the way they had come. Farley Mowat recorded the retreat in his history of the Hasty Ps: "The holiday mood was certainly at an end. As the train retreated coastward, the face of the country underwent a terrifying change. Every little station was jammed with refugees fleeing westward."[6] It seemed impossible that the train would reach Brest without suffering German air attack, but reach Brest they did without incident.

There, all was confusion. Refugees crowded the port to escape the German juggernaut; everyone who could beg, borrow, or steal a ferry ticket to Britain jammed the quays. Those Canadians who had not left their ships simply sailed back to the United Kingdom, but those who crowded in by rail and by road seemed at first to have no means of escape — there were no ships to take them to England. It was not until a whole day had been lost that three ships arrived and the men began to embark. Their vehicles were left outside town and destroyed, while guns and ammunition trailers were taken to the east quay. They, too, were supposed to be destroyed, but the local British garrison commander, an RMC graduate, was persuaded to let the Canadians try to load them. He told them to get as much as they could aboard ship by 1600; that was less than two hours away. Working at a feverish pace, all twenty-four field guns and much other equipment was put aboard; the remainder was rendered inoperable. The ships sailed at 1715 on 17 June and arrived back in England the next day; six men had gone missing, but the formation had survived, something that most certainly would not have happened if it had pressed on to meet the Germans. The Royal Canadian Horse Artillery war diary called it "a rout."

The fall of France put a different complexion on the war; Britain now had no major partners, and Canada was its largest ally. Mackenzie King's limited liability war effort was dead. Henceforth Canada would have to do all it could on land, sea, and air to aid the cause. Back home, Parliament passed the National Resources Mobilization Act on 21 June, providing for universal conscription for the defence of Canada. NRMA conscripts would not be sent overseas, but could volunteer to "go active" (switch to the Canadian Active Service Force) if they desired. Then, on 18 August 1940, King and US President Franklin D. Roosevelt concluded the Ogdensburg Agreement to establish the Permanent Joint Board on Defence to be in charge of joint Canada–US defence planning. To shore up British defences and to strengthen the Canadian overseas contingent, Ottawa announced on 20 May that the 2nd Canadian Infantry Division would be sent to the United Kingdom as soon as possible, that the two divisions would form a Canadian Corps, and that a third infantry division would also be raised for overseas service. Eventually, a fourth and a fifth division were formed and sent to the United Kingdom, a 2nd Canadian Corps was set up, and First Canadian Army was authorized.

The brigades of the 2nd Division had been concentrating at training areas in Canada since the spring; in June, seventy-six officers and 2577 of these men were sent from Canada to Iceland as "Z" Force, to help the British guard the vital island from a possible German takeover. The Royal Regiment of Canada and the Fusiliers Mont-Royal stayed in Iceland until October, and then rejoined their division in the United Kingdom. The Cameron Highlanders stayed the winter and arrived in Britain in the spring of 1941. The rest of the 2nd Division landed in Britain between 1 August and 25 December 1940.

The fall of France drastically changed the nature of the U-boat war. Suddenly Dönitz had French ports available from which his submarines could be sent to the mid and western Atlantic. No more was a long and hazardous voyage north of Scotland required; once through the Bay of Biscay, the U-boats could reach their patrol areas within days. The reduced transit time meant that more boats could be sent to sea at one time than before. That fact, and the lengthening nights of late summer and early fall, made it an ideal time to introduce the *Rudeltaktik*.

The *Rudeltaktik* involved numbers of U-boats setting up patrol lines across the main transatlantic shipping lanes. If a submarine spotted a convoy, it shadowed it and radioed news of its find to BdU, which ordered the rest of the pack to rendezvous with the shadower. The wolfpack waited for dark, slipped through the escort screen, and attacked on the surface. The almost total lack of air cover allowed the submarines to stay on the surface as they shadowed their prey by day; the longer nights of the fall and winter of 1940/41 gave them plenty of darkness to cover their approach. The result was a slaughter on the high seas as the submarines sunk hundreds of thousands of tonnes of Allied shipping with few losses to themselves. U-boat commanders called it the "happy time."[7]

The Royal Navy was virtually alone in trying to cope with the U-boat packs in the mid-Atlantic in the last half of 1940. The RCN still awaited its first corvettes, while the bulk of its River Class destroyers had been dispatched to UK waters to help the RN cope with the Dunkirk evacuations and to guard the English coast. It was while performing this duty that *Fraser* was sliced in two by the British cruiser HMS *Calcutta* in the Gironde Estuary on 25 June 1940. She sank with the loss of forty-seven of her crew, the first Canadian naval vessel to be sunk in the Second World War. *Fraser* was replaced by *Margaree*, another River Class destroyer acquired from the Royal Navy. On 22 October 1940, while sailing on her first escort mission some 500 kilometres west of Ireland, *Margaree* was also sliced in two, this time by a merchant vessel in the convoy. She went down with 142 officers and men. After the fall of France, *St Laurent*, *Restigouche*, *Ottawa*, *Skeena*, and *Margaree* were sent to join the Clyde Escort Force, taking convoys from UK ports to about 15 degrees west and then meeting inbound convoys. On one of these escort missions, *Ottawa* joined with HMS *Harvester* on 6 November to sink the Italian submarine *Faa Di Bruno*, Canada's first submarine kill. On 1 December *Saguenay* was torpedoed by another Italian submarine while it was escorting a convoy from Gibraltar. It did not sink, but twenty-one crew members were killed.

The RCN's escort force was augmented in the third week of September 1940 when six US-built, First World War vintage destroyers arrived in Halifax to be commissioned into the RCN. These vessels were the RCN's allotment of fifty old destroyers obtained by Britain from the United States in exchange for ninety-nine-year leases on a number of bases in Newfoundland and the Caribbean. Known as Town Class destroyers (because the RN named them after British and American towns with the same name), the RCN named most of them for rivers that flowed along the Canada–US boundary. The Towns were flush-deck, four-stack destroyers with a top speed of 36 knots, but they had serious drawbacks; they were top heavy, they were narrow of beam, and their steering gear was obsolete and prone to breakdown in winter conditions. The RCN cut several metres off the top of the three aft stacks, removed the four outboard multiple torpedo launchers and replaced them with a single multiple launcher amidship, and removed as much extraneous equipment as possible to reduce top weight. Still, the ships rolled badly and were almost impossible to handle in a beam or a heavy following sea.

One of these Town Class destroyers was HMCS *St Croix*, originally commissioned into the United States Navy on 30 April 1919. *St Croix* arrived in Halifax on 20 September and sailed for the United Kingdom on 30 November with *Niagara* and *St Clair*. The latter two arrived safely, but *St Croix* was pounded mercilessly by a North Atlantic storm and suffered extensive superstructure damage. Unable to steer easterly, and suffering from frequent failure of its steering equipment, it was forced to "heave to" to ride out the storm and was roughly handled by a following sea. For two days the ship struggled against the storm until, on 10 December, it turned south in search of calmer seas. It then limped back to Halifax via St John's, Newfoundland. It arrived on the 13th and, four days later, went out again to escort the battleship HMS *Revenge*. Given its long range and basic reliability, *St Croix* was destined to become a mainstay of the RCN's anti-submarine war.

As the U-boat war intensified, the Germans completed their occupation of northern France (the Vichy regime controlled southern France) and prepared for the next stage of the war. Plans were laid for an invasion of the United Kingdom — Operation Sea Lion — but before the assault could be launched the RAF had to be vanquished. The Battle of Britain, the epic struggle for control of the skies over the United Kingdom, began in mid-July. Luftwaffe attacks on British coastal shipping intensified as the date of the projected landing drew near. In mid-August the Luftwaffe began to concentrate on British ports, airfields, aircraft factories, and radar sites. At the end of August the first deliberate bombings of British cities began; on 7 September the Luftwaffe turned its attention to London, first in daylight raids, then in night attacks that lasted into the spring of 1941.

Much has been written about the Battle of Britain, and the full story of that battle will not be repeated here. It is important to point out, however, that the Luftwaffe suffered from the disadvantage that its best fighter — the Me 109 — had too short a range to give the German bombers all the protection they needed. The other German fighter mainstay — the Me 110 — was no match for the single-seat fighters of the RAF. The RAF also fought over its home territory, which meant that pilots who survived dog fights in badly damaged aircraft could bail out to fly and fight again; the German pilots could not. Damaged German aircraft had to struggle home over hundreds of kilometres of enemy country and the English Channel. Nevertheless, the Germans had a significant numerical advantage, and, had they concentrated from start to finish on destroying RAF fighters and bombers, airfields, and radar installations, they might well have won the battle through sheer attrition. Throughout the war, Hitler was the greatest asset the Allies had. It was he who insisted that his airforce turn from its task of attacking the RAF to punishing London, after a small British air attack on Berlin. That insistence saved the RAF, and probably Britain as well.

The RCAF's No. 1 Fighter Squadron had arrived at RAF station Middle Wallop on 21 June. It brought its Hurricane Is with it, but they were outdated and were replaced with newer models by the end of the month. On 17 August the squadron became operational at Northolt; on 24 August it went into action for the first time and promptly shot down two RAF Blenheim patrol bombers that its pilots mistook for German JU 88 bombers. That disastrous introduction to battle was kept secret for years; RCAF headquarters in London did not inform Ottawa about it until 1947. The squadron's next engagement two days later was very different. Taking off in the mid-afternoon, the Canadians were vectored to a formation of about 30 Dornier 215s flying at about 4600 metres. The German Me 109s were drawn off by RAF Spitfires, and the RCAF Hurricanes dove into the formation. German gunners poured fire into the attacking fighters, which shot three bombers down and severely damaged three others. But the Canadians paid a heavy price — three fighters were lost and one pilot was killed.

The Battle of Britain dragged on, day by day, and the lone RCAF squadron did its part. So did other Canadians flying with the RAF, including the well-known group that formed part of No. 242 Fighter Squadron. Canadian Johnny Kent helped No. 303 Polish Squadron to become operational, and was then given command of the RAF's No. 92 Squadron. Recent estimates indicate that some ninety Canadian pilots flew with the RAF during the Battle of Britain and that twenty of them were killed in action. But the largest concentration of Canadians was in the RCAF's No. 1 Fighter Squadron, which flew out day after day to do battle and which suffered heavy casualties in dead and wounded and in destroyed aircraft, as did the rest of Britain's aerial defenders. Possibly the best day the squadron had was on 27 September, when it is estimated to have shot down seven German aircraft even though it could put up barely half-a-dozen fighters. On that day the unit war diary, usually sparse and laconic, recorded: "By the end of the day the Squadron was a very tired, unshaven group of warriors. They are so tired that they immediately drop asleep, not hearing or caring about the funny noises that go on in the neighbourhood."[7]

No. 1 Squadron would continue to lose planes and men at a rapid pace until the German daylight raids petered out and the night blitz of London intensified towards the end of September. Hitler postponed Operation Sea Lion indefinitely on 17 September; his Luftwaffe had badly hurt the RAF, but it had not won air superiority over the United Kingdom. As the winter nights grew long, the Luftwaffe pounded London night after night, but had little impact on the overall British war effort. The RAF recovered much of its strength and the RCAF began to build up its presence on British soil.

In those same months, Hitler turned away from the west, gave up his dream of conquering Britain, and began to plan the invasion of the USSR. The war was just a little more than a year old, but already Canadians were in it up to their necks. For much of the next year, the little escort ships of the RCN would bear the brunt of the nation's war.

Four hours before midnight on 11 July 1941, convoy HX 138 slowed as it entered foggy waters west of the Strait of Belle Isle. HMCS *St Croix* moved to the flank of this motley collection of plodding merchantmen to give the ships as wide a berth as possible. More than ten hours earlier, *St Croix* had slipped its moorings at HMC Dockyard, Halifax, and, in company with *Annapolis*, another Town Class destroyer, had headed for a rendezvous with HX 138, already escorted by HMS *Aurania*. *St Croix*, *Annapolis*, and the other escorts were slated to accompany HX 138 eastward until they met Royal Navy escorts that would take the convoy the rest of the way to the United Kingdom. As *St Croix* had steamed to the rendezvous point, her crew had completed calibration of the recently installed medium-frequency direction-finding (D/F) gear, a navigational aid.

St Croix's career as an RCN destroyer had had an inauspicious start; severely damaged in its first attempt at passage to the United Kingdom in December 1940, the ship had been laid up for repairs until mid-March. On 14 March 1941 *St Croix* had taken to sea again, but had been relegated to escort duties in Canadian coastal waters and to checking on fishing boats from St Pierre and Miquelon. Since those two islands now came under the jurisdiction of Vichy France, the RCN feared that their fishing boats might radio reports of convoy movements to the Germans.

St Croix and the other ships of HX 138 cleared the fog bank in the predawn hours of 12 July, but slowed again just after noon when the fog closed in once more. At 2035, still enshrouded in fog, the convoy began a preplanned change of course. Suddenly, from out of the gloom came the unmistakable sound of steel grinding against steel; in two separate collisions four ships, including that of the commodore, were badly damaged.

The damaged ships left the convoy and, unescorted, proceeded slowly back to Halifax. The rest of the convoy sailed on to meet another section of HX 138 out of Halifax. The two groups of ships joined up on the morning of 14 July and moved to the narrow strait that separates Newfoundland from Labrador. About 355 kilometres west of the entrance to the strait, the convoy ran into a large field of icebergs, and reduced speed to 6 knots. After dark, fog rolled in again, increasing the danger from the ice field. *St Croix* lost much of its power the next morning when a main steam pipe collapsed on its starboard engine; it returned slowly to Halifax, arriving three days later.

There was little that was dramatic about the passage of HX 138 through Canadian waters: there was no deadly encounter with German surface raiders, neither were there running battles over many nights with U-boat wolfpacks. But the story of this convoy's departure does reveal the constant frustration of doing convoy escort with outmoded equipment, the dangers of inclement weather, and the problems posed by the almost constant presence of ice in northern waters. It was routine in one way, but not routine in another; a head-on collision with one of the 60-metre-high icebergs that drifted near the entrance to the strait would have been the end of *St Croix*, and, in these northern latitudes, men in the water would quickly die from hypothermia.

At the outbreak of the war the Admiralty had feared that German surface raiders would pose the major threat to transatlantic shipping. There had been some dramatic encounters between German ships and Allied merchantmen and naval vessels in both the North and the South Atlantic. The epic fight of the British armed merchant cruiser *Rawalpindi* against the cruiser *Scharnhorst* in November 1939 and the Battle of the River Plate off the coast of Uruguay one month later seemed to bear out British fears. For the most part, however, the small German surface fleet was successfully bottled up by the Royal Navy in Germany's Baltic Sea ports. When the powerful battleship *Bismarck* tried to break out into the North Atlantic in May 1941, it managed to sink HMS *Hood*, but was then destroyed by a large British fleet. In the end, the surface-raider threat turned out to be mostly illusory.

That was not true of the U-boats. After the fall of France in June 1941 the U-boat fleet, based at French ports, pushed farther west, beyond the range of the RN's escort vessels based in Britain. The Royal Navy still did not have enough escorts to accompany convoys all the way across the Atlantic, but Dönitz now had close to one hundred submarines under his command, enough to put at least thirty boats to sea at any one time and three times more than he had had a year earlier. Sinkings increased dramatically. In March, Winston Churchill declared that Britain was now fully engaged in the Battle of the Atlantic, and he charged the RN with closing the escort gap between Canadian waters and Ireland. The Royal Navy set up a supply base in Hvalfjordhur, Iceland, in April to replenish and resupply RN escorts in the mid-ocean, but Dönitz countered by deploying his wolfpacks even farther to the west, in the waters between Newfoundland and Iceland. In May one unprotected convoy lost five merchantmen before it dispersed in panic; U-boats then picked off some of the lone ships as they scurried away.

In recent years a persuasive argument has been put forward by some historians that Britain had so much merchant carrying capacity at its disposal in 1941, and so much food and productive capacity of its own, that it would have been well-nigh impossible for the German submarine campaign to strangle the United Kingdom at that point in the war. According to Marc Milner: "The German campaign against trade in the winter of 1940–41 could only have been successful had a total blockade of Britain been established, and that was an extremely difficult thing to do."[1] Thus, even though U-boats were sinking about 250,000 tonnes a month over the winter of 1940/41, it would not have been enough to knock Britain out of the war. That is a moot point, however. Britain's ultimate war aim was not simply to survive, but to win. To succeed, it needed to expand its military capability with raw materials and weaponry from North America. It had to preserve and even increase its carrying capacity. At this point, however, Britain was facing the need to stretch its own naval resources to new theatres of war ranging from Southeast Asia to the coast of North Africa. Meanwhile, Dönitz's deadly fleet continued to expand. The balance sheet was unmistakable: three merchant ships were going down for every new one built, and eight new U-boats were being launched for every one destroyed.

On 20 May 1941 the RN requested the RCN to close the escort gap by sending its growing corvette fleet (along with its small destroyer force) to St John's, Newfoundland, where it could begin to assume mid-ocean escort duties. The new arrangement would work this way: convoys would sail from Sydney or Halifax escorted by the RCN's smaller and more outmoded ships to a point off Newfoundland. Those escorts would then put into St John's, replenish supplies and fuel, and return to Nova Scotia. The escorts based at St John's — the Newfoundland Escort Force (NEF) — would pick up the convoy and accompany it to a point near Iceland, where they would hand it over to Royal Navy escorts. The NEF ships would then proceed north to Hvalfjordhur, replenish and refuel, and sail south to pick up westbound convoys.

St John's, or "Newfyjohn" as the sailors called it, was at first in no shape to function as the western terminus of this transatlantic lifeline. The harbour itself is not large, and the entrance is a mere cleft in the ancient rock of Newfoundland. Built on the hillsides around the harbour, St John's consisted largely of clapboard houses on steep and narrow streets. Often shrouded by fog and lashed by gales, it was difficult to approach in inclement weather. As James B. Lamb was later to remember: "In Newfyjohn . . . you are either in the harbour or out of it; there is no long estuary leading to the sea. The transition is brief and dramatic; one moment you are trundling along in the comparative serenity of harbour, and the next you are in the midst of open ocean, amid all the fury of the North Atlantic."[2] Eventually radar and radio approach beacons were constructed to help ships find the harbour entrance, but the approach was never ideal.

Ashore there were few amenities for officers and ratings, and virtually none of the support facilities — quays, fuel dumps, repair shops, storage warehouses — that the navy would need to maintain the NEF at sea. For much of 1941 and into 1942, the RCN devoted considerable manpower and resources to expanding and improving its base facilities in St John's while communications and command facilities were also constructed. In charge of it all was Commodore Leonard W. Murray, then Commodore Commanding Newfoundland Force, and a small staff.

If Newfyjohn was primitive, the facilities at Hvalfjordhur were stone age by comparison. The base consisted of support and supply vessels anchored in a shallow harbour whose barren surrounding hills offered little protection from the weather. Ships in harbour were as exposed to the winds and seas of a heavy gale as they were on the open sea. When one storm hit in early 1942, the Canadian destroyer *Assiniboine* was almost lost inside the harbour. Milner describes the base as "a dreary and unforgiving haven, by far the worst of those used by escort forces in the Battle of the Atlantic."[3]

In assuming its new responsibilities, the RCN added mid-ocean escort to the coastal escort it had been doing since the outbreak of the war. Those duties had been both boring and routine, since few U-boats ventured near the coastal shipping lanes. Now the Canadian corvettes and destroyers of the NEF would sail directly into the dangerous waters of "torpedo alley." There they would find U-boats; there they would have their time of testing.

The business of mid-ocean convoy escort had been pioneered by the RN during the First World War; it was something that the RCN would now have to learn.

The basic function of ocean escort was carried out by an escort group. For most of the war the Royal Navy had enough men, ships, and training time to forge permanent escort groups that almost always worked together. In the first years of the war, however, the Royal Canadian Navy was so shorthanded in men and so lacking in seaworthy escort vessels that it could barely keep up with the demand. It did not have the luxury of removing four or five ships at a time from escort duty so they could spend several weeks training together. Frequent breakdowns in equipment also meant that Canadian escort groups usually had to be scrabbled together from whatever vessels were available.

At the beginning of the war an escort group usually consisted of at least one destroyer and three corvettes. With its slow speed, the corvette was not well suited as an anti-submarine vessel; only a destroyer could move quickly from one flank of the convoy to another, from ahead to behind to close a gap in the escort screen, or to come to the aid of an attacking corvette. Generally the destroyer, with the escort group commander aboard (Senior Officer of the Escort or SOE), sailed at the head of the convoy, the corvettes on the flanks and astern. The convoy was organized in columns, with the commodore's ship in the centre of the front rank. The escort vessels zigzagged to cover more ocean with their detection gear.

In the early stages of the war at sea there were at least two schools of thought about the role convoy escorts should play. Some officers advocated an offensive strategy: escorts should seek out and attempt to destroy enemy submarines. Churchill subscribed to this school and believed that the Royal Navy should be doing more to patrol the sea lanes and sweep them clean for the following merchant ships. Others believed that escorts should stay close to their charges and do everything they could to ensure that the merchantmen got through. There was a real conflict between these two approaches until 1941. In April of that year the Royal Navy's Western Approaches Command, in overall charge of convoy escort, decided that the prime duty of escort ships was the "safe and timely arrival of the convoy." There were to be no wild-goose chases after submarines; the escorts were to stay with the convoy no matter what. The professional RCN, with its interwar offensive training, had trouble accepting this doctrine, and it became a frequent cause of British complaint about the way the RCN was carrying out its duties.

The RCN also gave the RN other cause for complaint. In 1941 Canadian escort ships had either no radar or radar that was ineffective. They also had obsolete asdic. They still used wireless for ship-to-ship communication rather than radio-telephone (R/T). Their machine-gun armament (Lewis guns) was obsolete or too light to be effective against U-boats. At a time when the U-boat war was becoming highly technical, the RCN failed to measure up. With the lack of ships and the dearth of trained manpower, the RCN was clearly at a severe disadvantage in doing escort work. The case of the corvette HMCS *Amherst* was all too typical. The keel for *Amherst* was laid at Saint John, New Brunswick, on 25 May 1940. Launched on 4 December, *Amherst* was completed in the early summer of 1941, underwent sea trials in July, and was commissioned on 5 August. The ship left Saint John on 21 August and arrived in Halifax the next day. Then, between 27 August and 6 September, *Amherst* engaged in a grand total of five days of training alongside a number of other corvettes and destroyers before putting to sea on 18 September for her first escort assignment. British training was far more extensive, and used RN submarines to teach asdic and radar operators what U-boats sounded like and looked like on their radar screens.

The RCN had one other serious disadvantage: the greatest part of its escort fleet was made up of Flower Class corvettes which had not been designed for mid-ocean escort duty and which were, for all intents and purposes, unfit for the job. The RN began to make major modifications to its corvettes early in the conflict, changes designed to make them more seaworthy, more stable, and more comfortable for the crews. Although the RCN eventually moved in that direction, such improvements were out of the question in 1941 because the navy needed all the ships it could get for convoy escort. RCN crews lived for weeks at a time in cold, wet, cramped quarters in ships that tossed and twisted at the first sign of a heavy sea. James Lamb chronicled what life aboard a corvette was sometimes like: "A wall of water, tons of it, sweeps across our fo'c'sle to hurl itself against our bridge structure with a resounding thump. Water sweeps everywhere; even in the shelter of the dodger we are drenched, and from below comes a series of bangs and crashes, from mess decks and galley and upper deck, where a hundred items, big and small, have bumped and smashed and clanged and rattled under the impact of the heavy sea."[4] With galley fires constantly doused, a hot meal was a rarity. If it left the galley hot, food was usually cold and wet when it arrived at the mess deck. This life was debilitating, draining men of their energy and grinding them into a numbing tiredness. Even when ships blew up around them on a dark night, the adrenalin rush was barely able to outstrip their fatigue.

In the last half of 1941, two breakthroughs, one technological, the other in the realm of intelligence, held promise for effective defence against U-boats. The first was Ultra, the code name given to Allied intelligence gained from cracking the most secret German ciphers. Using a mechanical encoding device known as

Enigma, top-secret German diplomatic, governmental, and military information was broadcast hourly to and from German land, air, and naval forces and diplomatic posts around the world. Tipped off to Enigma even before the war began, the British were able to build a decryption machine; they were eventually able to crack the German codes, and the naval code was first deciphered in the summer of 1941. This allowed the RN to read some of Dönitz's radio traffic to his submarines and to determine his plans. At this stage of the war, however, deciphering was slow and could be done only on a selective basis.

The other development was the perfection of ship-carried high-frequency direction-finding (HF/DF) equipment capable of detecting U-boat radio messages. Shore-based HF/DF had been in use since the First World War, but shore stations could not give a convoy escort immediate information on nearby U-boats. Thus the Royal Navy and the United States Navy developed HF/DF that could go to sea on the escort vesels. Henceforth, whenever a U-boat transmitted, the emissions could be picked up on these ships, the direction determined, and the position fixed by cross-referencing. This information allowed the SOE to organize his defences to best protect the convoy from enemy submarines. By the end of 1941, many British escort vessels had that equipment installed, and at least one ship in every escort group was able to pick up U-boat transmissions. Canadian ships did not fit HF/DF widely until 1943.

There was one bright spot in the RCN's escort picture in mid-1941; Commander J.D. "Chummy" Prentice, one of Canada's little-known war heroes, was beginning to leave his mark on the state of preparedness of RCN escorts. Born in Victoria, British Columbia, in 1899, Prentice had served twenty-two years in the Royal Navy before retiring to the business world in his home province in 1937. When war broke out, he volunteered for RN service, but was offered a commission in the RCN. Eventually, he was posted to Murray's staff in Halifax, prior to the formation of the NEF. With a rimless monocle ever present in his right eye, a British accent, and a cigarette almost always in his right hand, Prentice quickly became a legend throughout the fleet. His real contribution to the RCN was not as some flamboyant imitation of a Royal Navy gentleman; he strongly believed that thorough training was necessary not only to familiarize men with their vessel and teach them the demanding skills of anti-submarine warfare, but also to work with other ships to provide effective escort. The hallmark of Prentice's service in the RCN, aside from his command of an escort group at sea, was his constant push to train escorts in groups and to do it as soon as newly commissioned vessels arrived in St John's. In the last half of 1941, that goal was to prove well-nigh impossible; later in the war, Prentice's efforts would pay large dividends.

The NEF was scarcely a month old when it fought its first full-scale convoy battle. On 21 June convoy HX 133, with fifty-eight ships, sailed from Halifax; near St John's the local escort handed HX 133 to a group of four corvettes (three Canadian and one British) led by *Ottawa*, a River Class destroyer. The convoy was spotted by U-203 south of Greenland on 23 June; the submarine then radioed its position and sought permission to attack. Interception and decryption of the traffic between BdU and U-203 indicated that Dönitz was trying to organize a wolfpack of at least ten submarines to attack the convoy. To counter the threat, the Commander-in-Chief (C-in-C) Western Approaches directed two escorts from a second escort group, led by *Wetaskiwin*, then sailing south from Iceland to meet westbound convoy OB 336, to go to the aid of HX 133.

U-203 waited for nightfall, then moved in on the surface, penetrated the escort screen, and torpedoed one ship. On board the *Ottawa*, Commander E.R. Mainguy tried to coordinate the defence, but the Canadian corvettes did not have R/T and their wireless sets were not working properly. The submarine escaped unscathed. At about 2300 the following night another ship was torpedoed and a U-boat surfaced astern of the convoy. *Ottawa* and another corvette chased it briefly, but turned back at the sound of still another torpedo explosion. Mainguy again tried to mount a coordinated hunt, but inadequate equipment and poor seamanship foiled the effort. When C-in-C Western Approaches received Mainguy's report of these latest sinkings, he ordered *Wetaskiwin* and its two consorts to go to the aid of HX 133. *Wetaskiwin* had, at that point, been unable to locate OB 336. As it prepared to comply, it intercepted an urgent radio message that the unescorted OB 336 was now also under attack. The escort commander decided to take matters into his own hands, ignore the order to join HX 133, and proceed as fast as possible to the more vulnerable convoy. *Ottawa*'s escort group handed HX 133 over to a powerful RN force shortly after; eventually, the British ships went on to sink two U-boats. The convoy itself lost a total of six ships and OB 336 lost another two. Although not a heavy loss, the performance of *Ottawa*'s escort group was cause for serious concern and an indicator of the many obstacles the RCN still had to overcome.

For the remainder of the summer the Admiralty maintained an edge over the U-boats by using Ultra information to route convoys past danger. But that edge seemed to have disappeared entirely after nightfall on 9 September when torpedoes slammed home against SS *Muneric*, a ship in convoy SC 42 in the waters south of Greenland. With its bottom blasted out, *Muneric* sank quickly and the epic battle of SC 42 was on. It would demonstrate all too clearly just how poorly equipped the RCN was to guard convoys even two years after the outbreak of the war.

Sailing from Sydney, Nova Scotia, on 30 August, SC 42 was a slow convoy consisting of sixty-four merchant ships. It was guarded by a Canadian escort group from the NEF, which initially consisted of the destroyer *Skeena* and three corvettes. The convoy was making for the Strait of Belle Isle when, on 1 September, Ultra intercepts carried warnings of a major U-boat concentration in the northwestern Atlantic. In St John's, Prentice obtained permission to sail to the area of danger in *Chambly*, accompanied by *Moose Jaw*; both of these ships were supposed to be part of a training group of five vessels that he was trying to put together. As Prentice proceeded eastward, he received garbled instructions to go to the aid of convoy SC 43, but he chose instead to sail to a position about 500 kilometres east of Cape Farewell, the southern tip of Greenland, and bide his time until it became clear whether SC 42 or SC 43 was in greater danger.

In the meantime, convoy SC 42, then to the south-southeast of Cape Farewell, altered course and sailed due north, towards the Greenland coast, in an attempt to pass around the concentration of U-boats. The sea was rough and the convoy could make only 5 knots. Darkness began to envelop the ships, spread out over the seascape, as they turned northeastward towards Iceland. Inside the ships the men prepared for the long night with a sense of foreboding; if nothing else, the course change told them that somewhere, far to the east, their fate was being decided on the chartboards of the Admiralty and the U-boat headquarters. Those not on watch turned in fully dressed, the better to abandon ship if a torpedo struck home. As the darkness deepened, the moon rose, silhouetting the ships to any submarine stalking them. That was when the first torpedoes struck; SC 42 had run into a wolfpack of eight to twelve U-boats.

In the chaos of the next few hours, *Skeena* and her consorts raced about, asdic pinging, lookouts straining in the explosion-lit dark to spot the surfaced U-boats. They were easy enough to see; every few minutes it seemed as if another surfaced submarine was reported by another merchantman. Tracer whipped across the sky as the gunners aboard the freighters tried to hit back at their attackers. Explosion after explosion gave notice of yet another German triumph, as the tell-tale sounds of submarines were lost to asdic operators in the swirling waters stirred up by the screws of advancing merchantmen. The escorts sometimes gave chase, sometimes turned back to protect their charges, and sometimes stopped to rescue men still in the water.

Just after midnight, as the beleaguered convoy made ready for a change in course, a U-boat was spotted on the surface inside the convoy, running up between two columns of freighters. *Skeena* turned into the convoy and raced after it. The U-boat cut across a column of ships, reversed course, then speeded back in the opposite direction. The destroyer and the U-boat ran past each other, each in a separate lane; the two vessels closed too quickly for *Skeena* to bring its guns to bear, especially since a line of merchantmen lay between them. The U-boat began a crash dive as the convoy began to execute its turn. For one panic-stricken moment, the slender *Skeena* lay directly in the path of a lumbering freighter; *Skeena's* captain, Commander J.C. Hibbard, ordered all astern, and *Skeena* backed away just in time to avoid being cut in two.

As the submarines attacked again and again, Prentice was ordered to come to SC 42's aid. He was not certain of the exact position of the convoy, and his 15-knot maximum speed put him the better part of a day's sailing away. In the meantime, the U-boat attacks continued through the night and into the early dawn of 10 September. With the exception of Hibbard aboard *Skeena*, the escort captains seemed confused about what was happening and what their responsibility was. They wasted valuable time pulling men from the water when they ought to have been keeping to their stations and deterring further attacks.

Daylight brought no immediate respite; the U-boats dove and continued their onslaught against the slow convoy, which tried to twist and turn out of danger as it proceeded inexorably up the east coast of Greenland. Each turn seemed to bring it into torpedo range of yet another submarine. As darkness fell once again, the U-boats came to the surface and the attacks were stepped up. Once again the night was illuminated by starshells, tracers, and exploding ships; but this time they helped guide Prentice and his small flotilla of reinforcements to the stricken convoy. *Chambly* and *Moose Jaw* had actually sailed past the convoy, but spotted the pyrotechnics and turned back. Prentice reasoned that the enemy submarines would be on the surface on the dark side of the convoy and that he might catch them illuminated to the south, as they had caught their victims. His asdic operator obtained a firm contact close inboard some twenty-six minutes after midnight, and *Chambly* moved in quickly to drop a pattern of depth charges. Prentice then brought *Chambly* around in a tight turn to try to regain contact. As he did, U-501 popped to the surface about 350 metres from *Moose Jaw*. Hal Lawrence was aboard the second corvette: "Water streaming from her sides, U-501 set off in the general direction of Germany. We gave chase, the captain manoeuvring to ram. With our primitive weapons, this was the surest way for a kill; a corvette in exchange for a U-boat was a bargain."[5] *Moose Jaw* rammed the U-boat and raked its deck with gunfire to keep the Germans from their deck guns. Then Prentice pulled along-side and put a boarding party onto the German submarine to see what might be salvaged. But it was obvious that the Germans had opened the seacocks and that the vessel was going down; the Canadians retreated from their victim, and U-501 sank with one Canadian seaman still inside. *Chambly* and *Moose Jaw* then joined the convoy escort screen.

The following day nine RN escorts, including five destroyers, came to the aid of *Skeena* and her consorts, and the Battle of SC 42 effectively ended. One submarine had been sunk, but sixteen merchantmen had been lost. It was more than obvious that the Canadian escorts had been unable to mount an effective and coordinated defence of their charges. The four escorts not only had been outnumbered but, with the exception of Hibbard, had been outmanoeuvred too. This pattern would happen time and time again until the RCN could bring better-equipped vessels, more trained men, and more advanced weapons and detection gear into the fight. In mid-September SC 44 lost four ships and the corvette *Levis* in one night. One month later, SC 48 suffered a terrible mauling despite a much heavier escort. At the beginning of November, SC 52 was actually driven back to port by U-boats, the only North Atlantic convoy to take such action in the war.

There was no let-up as the winter gales began to lash the North Atlantic. In fact, the load on the RCN increased as the RN pulled escort groups out of the North Atlantic and redeployed them to the South Atlantic. RCN ships and men were pushed to the limit. Ships like *Chambly* spent virtually every day at sea. The strain on the men and the equipment took its toll. What was worse, there was no time for men to learn better ways, for crews to jell, for ships to be refitted with better equipment. Each time a new corvette was commissioned, existing crews were stripped of their most experienced men, who were then ordered aboard the new vessels. The Admiralty asked the RCN to strengthen its escort groups by adding one corvette and one destroyer to each, but there were nowhere near enough destroyers to go around.

The slaughter at sea that occurred with SC 42 might have been avoided had the British and the Canadians been able to mount effective air cover over the convoys. For the wolfpack tactic to work, the U-boat that initially spotted a convoy had to stay on the surface, shadowing its prey, until the other submarines arrived and a night attack could be coordinated. Aircraft circling over the sea on the fringes or in the path of a convoy forced shadowing submarines down. Once under, U-boats were usually too slow to track the convoy. Constant air patrol over SC 42 and the other convoys might have helped the escort overcome the long odds against it. But this solution was simply not possible in the fall of 1941.

The RAF's Coastal Command had consisted of nineteen squadrons at the start of the war, but most of the aircraft available to it were both obsolete and short range. The RCAF's Eastern Air Command suffered from the same disadvantage, but it was in worse shape because it was even smaller. It counted only a single bomber reconnaissance squadron (No. 10) in its order of battle when war broke out, although a second squadron (No. 11) was formed shortly after. The BCATP added to the problem of building up these and other anti-submarine reconnaissance squadrons because it limited the number of aircrew that the RCAF could divert to Eastern Air Command from overseas operations.

The two mainstays of the anti-submarine squadrons of Eastern Air Command in the first months of the war were the short-range twin-engined Douglas Digby and Lockheed Hudson; not long after, Consolidated PBY/Catalina flying-boats were added (the Canadian-built version was called the Canso). They had a much longer range, but were very slow and carried a modest bombload. Eventually, the aircraft of choice was the four-engine Liberator, a US-built bomber which was capable of great endurance when fitted with extra fuel tanks (the Very Long Range or VLR version), and which carried a large load of bombs or aerial depth charges. But the RCAF did not begin to acquire these aircraft until 1943. Although the RAF's Coastal Command was flying Liberators in anti-submarine roles from Northern Ireland and Iceland in 1941, it always had to compete for these aircraft, mostly unsuccessfully, with Bomber and Transport Command, the United States Army Air Force, and the United States Navy.

The greatest part of the North Atlantic crossing was beyond the range of shore-based aircraft for all of 1941 and 1942. Even when British or Canadian aircraft caught a U-boat on the surface, however, poor training or inadequate weapons and equipment generally stymied a successful attack. Like the RCN, the RCAF lagged behind its British counterpart in acquiring the latest radar and anti-submarine weapons. Its ability to cooperate with the surface forces was also handicapped by poor organization and communications. Whereas Coastal Command

and the RN had been cooperating since the late 1930s (and Coastal Command came under the operational control of the RN in April 1941), the RCAF jealously guarded its independence until much later in the war.

For the crews of Eastern Air Command, the battle of the North Atlantic was a contest of endurance more than anything else. Each day they took off from east-coast bases, sometimes in appalling weather, to fly long, boring hours over the open ocean. Hour after hour they scanned the seascape for the tell-tale signs of a submarine in hull-down position, when U-boat captains held the decks of their vessels just at or under the surface so that only the conning tower was above the waves. It took only a minute for a submarine in this position to crash dive. If anything went wrong in the attack, the vessel would escape. At the end of each patrol, the crews had to battle the prevailing westerly winds to return to their sometimes fog-shrouded bases and attempt a safe landing.

One reason why the build-up of Eastern Air Command units was so slow in 1941 was that it was generally assumed by the Canadians, the British, and the Americans that the United States, not Canada, would be primarily responsible for hemispheric defence, even though the United States was not then a participant in the war. According to war plans drawn up by the British and the Americans in early 1941, Canada would take responsibility only for its own airspace and coastal waters; the Newfoundland Escort Force was to be only a stopgap measure until the United States Navy could deploy its strength more fully in the North Atlantic theatre of operations.

As long as the United States was not officially at war, President Franklin D. Roosevelt had to be careful about the use of US naval vessels in convoy escort, lest the neutralists at home accuse him of provoking Germany. Nonetheless, US naval units began to involve themselves more fully in the Atlantic battle as the U-boat offensive intensified; even though it was a neutral, Roosevelt declared, the United States had a right to protect its own shipping. US air units from Argentia, Newfoundland, and US destroyers began to patrol the sea lanes in the late summer of 1941. On 4 September the US destroyer *Greer* came under torpedo attack in the waters south of Iceland. It sustained no damage, but the incident gave Roosevelt the excuse he needed to involve the USN more fully in the campaign. On 11 September Roosevelt ordered US ships to "shoot on sight" any

U-boat that appeared to endanger them or their merchant charges; for all intents and purposes, this response committed the United States to the battle. Roosevelt's command had a double impact on the RCN. The defence of the sea lanes in North American waters now fell under the command of Rear Admiral A. LeRoy Briston, USN, in Argentia, and it was agreed that the United States Navy, operating primarily with fast destroyers, would escort the fast convoys to the United Kingdom, while the RCN would guard the slow ones. Those convoys, like SC 42, were the most vulnerable; ships in slow convoys had a 30 percent greater chance of being torpedoed.

The United States Navy was just getting its sealegs in the battle of the North Atlantic when Japan attacked Pearl Harbor on 7 December 1941. The United States now officially joined the United Kingdom and the USSR (which Germany had attacked the previous June) in a full global war against the Axis. Eventually, the industrial might of the United States would tip the scale against the Axis, but the immediate result for the RCN was that the USN virtually pulled out of the battle of the North Atlantic as it redeployed its destroyers to the Pacific. For most of the next year, the RCN would fight the western Atlantic battle virtually alone.

That battle was merciless; it was a fight not only against the German enemy but against the sea itself. On 12 December 1941 a Canadian escort group of seven ships, led by *Restigouche*, sailed from Hvalfjordhur to pick up a west-bound convoy and bring it to the Canadian coast. Early that afternoon, radio messages from the convoy revealed that it had run into heavy weather and was considerably behind schedule. *Restigouche* raced ahead, tried to locate the merchantmen, failed, then returned to the corvettes. All seven ships proceeded in line abreast lest they miss their charges. The next morning, the glass began to fall precipitously; in the afternoon, the storm broke in all its fury. *Restigouche*, the corvettes, and the convoy were in the middle of a hurricane. The official report is graphic:

> It was still daylight but the wind-driven spray had reduced the visibility to practically zero. The seas were mountainous, the wind was a thing of indescribable power. The stubby corvettes bobbed up and over the sea. The thin-plated destroyer, with her long, narrow hull, knifed into them and was slugged unmercifully. Worse still was her tendency to fall off into the trough . . . Within half an hour . . . all the destroyer's canvas covers, splinter mats and carley floats had been ripped off or torn to shreds and her boats reduced to matchwood. At 1700 the foremast split, with a tremendous

47

crack, below the crowsnest. The upper section broke off and the steel lower
section bent back . . . To the eerie shrieking of the wind was added the wail
of the ship's siren; aerials and halliards from the mast had been borne down
on the siren wires.

The ship was badly damaged and had to make port, but heading back to Halifax
(where the repairs could be done) was out of the question. Instead, *Restigouche*
headed for the Clyde. On the afternoon of 16 December, *Restigouche* steamed into
the harbour at Greenock. With a marked list to port and heavy structural damage
topside, she was bent but not broken. As the destroyer slipped alongside the quay,
the "dockyard mateys" gave it a rousing cheer. It was a fitting end of the year for
this hard-working destroyer and symbolic of the state of her sister ships still plying
the North Atlantic run. After more than two years of war, they, too, were bent but
not broken.

There is a happy ending to the story of *Restigouche*'s battering. During the
ship's refit her captain, Lieutenant-Commander D.W. Piers, "purchased" a HF/DF
set for the destroyer for a bottle of liquor. Thus *Restigouche* became the only RCN
vessel to mount a HF/DF set in 1942.

As 1941 slipped into history, the RCN turned with fresh determination to
face the remains of another North Atlantic winter. It was obvious that the long
nights in cold northern waters and the murderous torpedo fire of the wolfpacks
would further test this raw young navy in the year ahead. But few could anticipate
that the next stage of the RCN's battle would be fought, not in the mid-ocean,
but at the navy's very doorstep — in the home waters of the Gulf of St Lawrence
itself.

III Canada against Japan

On 19 December 1941, as dawn began to lighten the fog-shrouded peaks that dominated the eastern portion of Hong Kong Island, small parties of Japanese infantry advanced towards the strategic Wong Nei Chong Gap. The gap, or pass, was the key to the centre of Hong Kong Island; the main north–south road from Victoria Harbour to Repulse Bay and Stanley passed through it and intersected with an east–west road from Aberdeen to the Ty Tam Tuk Reservoir. The gap was where Canadian Brigadier J.K. Lawson had established the headquarters of West Brigade, a mixed force of Canadian, British, and Indian troops along with Hong Kong volunteers, charged with the defence of the western part of the island. The rest of the island was defended by East Brigade, another mixed force commanded by British Brigadier C. Wallis. The defenders were under the overall command of British Major-General C.M. Maltby.

From Stanley in the south and Victoria in the north, artillery fire poured down on the advancing Japanese. They took heavy casualties, but pushed ahead and around Lawson's headquarters. A First World War veteran, Lawson had remained with the Permanent Force after the war. He was Director of Military Training at National Defence Headquarters in Ottawa in the fall of 1941, when the government decided to accede to a British request to send a small force of Canadians to help garrison Hong Kong. Now he and that force were in mortal danger in a far-away place where Canada seemed to have no real interests at all.

As the Japanese advanced, the circle around Lawson's headquarters grew tighter. A small group of reinforcements managed to reach Lawson before the ring closed completely, but there were not nearly enough to make any real difference. The Japanese infiltrated around the high ground overlooking the gap and poured rifle and machine-gun fire at the headquarters. Snipers were spotted on the roof of the aid station, only 30 metres away. Lawson telephoned Maltby to report that "his headquarters was virtually over-run and that the Japanese were firing into his position at point blank range."[1] He and his men were going to go outside to fight it out "rather than be killed like rats."[2]

Lawson and several others destroyed the telephone exchange and then charged out and ran for cover. He did not make it; he crumbled and fell as Japanese machine-gun fire decimated the remainder of his headquarters group. Despite Lawson's death, the Japanese had no easy time of it; they suffered heavy casualties, and the fighting for the gap raged for three more days before they secured the position. Lawson was the first senior Canadian commander to be killed in action in the Second World War.

Lawson's death at the hands of the Japanese, and the entrapment of two Canadian infantry battalions on Hong Kong, were the latest events in a larger drama rooted in great power rivalry stretching back at least four decades. The modernization of Japan in the late nineteenth century had been accompanied by militarization and a strong desire to take part in the worldwide competition for colonies. By the outbreak of the First World War, Japan had seized Korea, defeated Russia in a war for the domination of Manchuria, and forged a powerful army and navy. Japan sided with Britain in the First World War and benefited by gaining possession of important former German colonies in the southwest and central Pacific. In 1931 Japan seized Manchuria, and in 1937 launched a war against China. In September 1940 Japan joined the Axis. Japan's march to domination of Southeast Asia seemed inexorable, and its challenge to the United States and the European colonial powers in Asia, inevitable.

But Japan lacked natural resources. The oil to fuel her fleet and the tin, rubber, and other materials to equip her army lay to the south, primarily in the Dutch East Indies and Malaya. To gain those territories, Japan would need to take them by force. It would first have to neutralize the Americans, who then ruled the Philippines. Japan's rulers eventually decided that the Imperial Japanese Navy would have to strike at the very heart of the United States Pacific Fleet stationed at Pearl Harbor, Territory of Hawaii. They began to lay plans for that attack in March 1941. In July, Japan invaded Indochina. Two months later the United States froze Japanese assets and cut off oil exports to Japan. During the five months of fruitless diplomatic sparring between the United States and Japan that followed, the Japanese military completed its preparations for war. On 26 November 1941 a powerful Japanese task force of six aircraft carriers and escorting ships sailed for Hawaiian waters. At 0755 on 7 December they struck.

The attack against Pearl Harbor was the opening blow in a whirlwind Japanese offensive also aimed at the Philippines, the Malay Peninsula, and Hong Kong. Since Canada was not a Pacific power and had nothing to do with the long train of events that led to the Japanese assault, many Canadians then and since have wondered why 1973 Canadian soldiers organized in two battalions — the Royal Rifles of Canada and the Winnipeg Grenadiers — and a brigade headquarters lay in the path of the Japanese juggernaut. That puzzlement increased after the war, when Canadians discovered that the British military had considered Hong Kong indefensible, and that Winston Churchill himself had declared early in 1941 that it would be the height of foolishness to reinforce the men already stationed there.

Hong Kong had first come into British possession in the nineteenth century. The colony consisted of the island, a settlement on the Kowloon peninsula to the north, and what became known as the New Territories on the mainland. The area is small — some 35 kilometres from the southern tip of the island's Stanley peninsula to the border with China to the north. The island itself is only 16 kilometres across at its widest point, and is separated from the mainland by Victoria Harbour and Lye Mun passage, which is less than 500 metres in width. The island and the Kowloon peninsula are mountainous; the island's western end is dominated by Victoria Peak, and its eastern section by a small mountain chain consisting of Mount Parker, Mount Butler, Jardine's Lookout, and Violet Hill. The New Territories were mostly flat, with part of the landscape heavily treed and part covered by scrub.

A defensive line consisting of linked fortified positions had been built across the mainland, north of the Kowloon peninsula, from Gin Drinkers Bay on the west to Port Shelter on the east. Around the circumference of the island were pillboxes designed to house machine guns. The island's garrison before the Canadians arrived consisted of four battalions of regular troops: the 1st Battalion, the Middlesex Regiment, a machine-gun formation; the 2nd Battalion, the Royal Scots, infantry; and the 5th/7th Rajputs and the 2nd/14th Punjabis, both infantry units of the Indian Army. In addition, there were about 2000 militia — the Hong Kong Volunteers. Given the distance between Hong Kong and the major British naval and air base at Singapore, the lack of air cover at Hong Kong, the colony's proximity to major bodies of Japanese troops in China, and the terrain, there was almost no chance that Hong Kong could hold out for any significant length of time against a determined Japanese assault. That was why the British refused to reinforce it.

In mid-1941 the British changed their policy. As tensions mounted in Southeast Asia and the Japanese launched their offensive in Indochina, the British shifted ground. Some British strategists came to the conclusion that Hong Kong might serve them well as a forward base for operations against the Japanese in southern China; others, including Maltby and his predecessor, Edward Grasett, a Canadian serving in the British Army, believed that reinforcing Hong Kong might even help deter war. In August 1941 Grasett visited Canada on his way back to the United Kingdom from Hong Kong and shared his views with H.D.G. "Harry" Crerar, an old classmate from RMC who was then Canada's Chief of the General Staff. There is controversy to this day about what was said and what assurances were given at that meeting, but Grasett certainly arrived in the United Kingdom believing that Canada would, if asked, send troops to help garrison Hong Kong. That request was made in mid-September 1941, and Canada agreed. It is important to point out here that Britain believed those troops would not have to fight, at least not any time soon, and that their presence in Hong Kong might deter war completely. Although conspiracy buffs have declared ever since that Britain knowingly sent young Canadian soldiers to be sacrificed in a place that the British themselves had no intention of defending, there is not a shred of evidence for this view. In September 1941 war in the Pacific was not inevitable; the Japanese were planning for the possibility of an attack against Pearl Harbor, but they did not actually decide to launch that attack until 5 November, when it finally appeared that the negotiations with the United States would fail.

There is no doubt that the two battalions Canada sent to Hong Kong were not ready for war. The Winnipeg Grenadiers had recently returned from Jamaica, where they had been engaged in garrison duty; the Royal Rifles had performed similar tasks in Newfoundland. The only other formations that might have been sent were units earmarked to join the 3rd Canadian Infantry Division in the United Kingdom, but National Defence Headquarters had no wish to disrupt the build-up of that formation. The fact that the two battalions sent to Hong Kong had nothing like the intense training that units destined for battle ought to have received is beside the point, since no one thought they were going to war. Both units had been mobilized for some time and were considered "of proven efficiency" — good enough for what they were intended to do. The truth is that none of Maltby's units were adequately prepared for battle and, even if they had been, Japan's overwhelming air and sea strength in the area would have prevailed anyway.

The Canadian Hong Kong force, consisting of a brigade headquarters, the two battalions, reinforcements, a detachment from the Signals Corps, and two nursing sisters, gathered in British Columbia in late October and sailed for Hong Kong aboard the cargo ship *Awatea* on 27 October, escorted by the armed merchant cruiser HMCS *Prince Robert*. Before departure, Lawson, who had helped select them, was promoted to Brigadier and placed in command of the force. Most of the vehicles assigned to the units were put aboard the US cargo ship *Don José*, due to take a more circuitous route to the Far East, even though there was still space on the *Awatea*. The Canadians arrived in Hong Kong on 16 November and disembarked the next day, but the *Don José* never reached them. It was still at sea when war broke out, and US military authorities refused to allow it to leave Manila. The Hong Kong vehicles ended up, with Canadian permission, in the hands of the United States Army.

Maltby's plan for the possible defence of the colony was to divide his 13,000-man force into two brigades. One, under Wallis, would defend the mainland and particularly the Gin Drinkers Line; the other, under Lawson, would be stationed on the island to guard against an invasion from the sea and to reinforce the mainland garrison if necessary. The former brigade was made up of the Royal Scots, the two Indian battalions, and the Canadian signallers. The latter formation consisted of the two Canadian units and the Middlesex battalion. Although destined for the island, the Canadians were barracked at the Sham Shui Po camp on Kowloon, where they began active training as soon as they settled in.

At 0800 on 8 December (7 December in Canada), some six hours after the Pearl Harbor attack, Japanese aircraft struck Kai Tak airport, wiping out the tiny contingent of obsolete British aircraft stationed there, and also bombed Sham Shui Po. Three regiments of the Japanese 38th Division then began to infiltrate across the Hong Kong–China border, forcing the Punjabis to blow a bridge over the Sham Chung River and withdraw to the Gin Drinkers Line. The Japanese plan of attack was simple: force the defenders back to the Gin Drinkers Line, break through it, clear the mainland area, then assault the island itself. Although they did not greatly outnumber the defenders, they enjoyed the advantages of air and artillery superiority; moreover, their troops were tough, well-trained, highly motivated, and had seen combat in China. They knew how to fight as a cohesive force. The defenders were a motley group by comparison, and help was a long way off.

At first the Japanese thought they would encounter serious difficulty with the Gin Drinkers Line defences; they originally gave themselves up to a week to organize a proper assault. But on the night of 9/10 December a Japanese battalion assaulted the Shing Mun redoubt, the highpoint on the defence line and the key to the line's western sector. The redoubt overlooked the Jubilee Reservoir to the north and commanded a key ridge just to the south. The British defenders were taken by surprise; after a few hours of fierce fighting, the Japanese took the position. A counter-attack was out of the question; the nearest defenders were too far away, and the ground between them and the redoubt was too broken and rocky. The mainland defence line had been compromised.

On 11 December the Japanese began to roll up the left flank of the defence line. Maltby gave some thought to reinforcing the rest of the line and ordered the Winnipegs brought forward from the island. It was soon obvious, however, that the mainland defences were no longer tenable and, at midday, he ordered virtually all his troops to pull back to the island. The Rajputs were to stay at Devil's Peak peninsula, on the north side of the Lye Mun passage, to cover the withdrawal. On the morning of 13 December they, too, pulled back, taking a number of artillery pieces with them.

With the mainland lost to the Japanese, Maltby set about reorganizing his defending force. Again he created two brigades — west under Lawson and east under Wallis. Lawson had under his command the Royal Scots, the Punjabis, and the Winnipeg Grenadiers, along with a number of Hong Kong Volunteers. Wallis commanded the rest of the defending forces. Although it was obvious that the main Japanese thrust was coming from landward, Maltby was still concerned about a possible landing to seaward, and he positioned the Royal Rifles in the southeast part of the island to counter-attack a Japanese landing.

On the morning of 13 December, the Japanese sent a small delegation across Victoria Harbour in a motor launch to demand the surrender of the garrison. The Hong Kong governor, Sir Mark Young, refused. A party of Japanese infantry then tried to gain a foothold across from Lye Mun passage on the night of 15/16 December, but were beaten back. On the 17th came another demand for surrender and another refusal. The defenders were in a hopeless position, but they were determined to delay the Japanese as much as possible.

The Japanese came across the water after dark on 18 December. Under cover of heavy shellfire, three regiments in line abreast crossed the harbour and Lye Mun passage in small boats pulled by ferries, and poured ashore. The Rajputs held the pillboxes that dominated the landing ground and cut down hundreds of attackers with their machine guns, but the Japanese pushed past them and made for the gullies and valleys that led into the centre of the island. The Rajputs were virtually wiped out. On the left flank the 229th Regiment sent one battalion to take the walled redoubt on Sai Wan Hill, while the rest of the regiment rapidly climbed Mount Parker and seized its summit. The Royal Rifles of Canada attempted to counter-attack the advancing Japanese and succeeded in inflicting heavy casualties with automatic weapons, but they could not take Sai Wan Fort back and were forced to withdraw. Less than 2 kilometres to the southwest another contingent of the Royal Rifles attacked the Japanese on Mount Butler; they, too, were beaten back, with many killed and wounded.

Throughout the night of 18/19 December, the Japanese pushed to the centre of the island and across. Their intention was to seize the main passes, and especially the Wong Nei Chong Gap, take control of the centre of the island, and split the defenders. By dawn on the 19th, Japanese infantry had reached Repulse Bay and were closing in on Lawson's brigade headquarters. Among the defenders, all was confusion. Through the night they had received no solid information as to how many Japanese had landed, exactly where they had come ashore, or what direction the main body of their troops was heading in. The darkness was made darker by smoke from oil fires burning in Victoria. Japanese sympathizers and fifth columnists cut telephone wires to disrupt the defenders' communications. When Lawson learned that two Japanese regiments were closing in on the summits of Jardine's Lookout and Mount Butler, he first ordered three platoons, each acting as a "flying column," to stop the attackers. Outnumbered by about six to one, the results were predictable; the Canadians were pushed back and two platoon commanders were killed. Lawson then ordered A Company of the Winnipeg Grenadiers to attack the advancing Japanese.

The men of A Company were last seen climbing up through the dark and fog to meet the enemy; most were never seen alive again. Survivors later described how part of A Company, under Company Sergeant Major J.R. Osborne, took the peak of Mount Butler with a bayonet charge and held it for three hours. They were then forced to pull back towards Lawson's position, but ran into a Japanese ambush and were virtually wiped out. Osborne himself was killed when he threw himself on a Japanese grenade to save his men; he was posthumously awarded the Victoria Cross when the story became known after Japan's surrender. As the Japanese closed in around Lawson's position, Maltby ordered a group of naval ratings to go to his aid. They rushed forward on trucks, but ran into a Japanese roadblock; a small number managed to get through, and the rest were forced back. It was then that Lawson decided to try to break out and was killed.

In the east, Wallis decided he could not mount any sort of effective defence with his troops scattered among the hills, so he sought Maltby's consent to withdraw southward towards Stanley. He intended to defend a line across the peninsula, then counter-attack. Permission was given and, by nightfall on 19 December, Wallis's troops had pulled back south of the Ty Tam Tuk Reservoir. This left the bulk of the island's fresh-water reserves in Japanese hands and also resulted in a break in communications between the west and the east brigades. On the morning of 20 December, Wallis tried to re-establish contact with West Brigade by sending the Royal Rifles northwest between Violet Hill and Repulse Bay towards Wong Nei Chong Gap. But the Japanese had already taken up positions in the path of the Canadian advance; a company of the Royal Rifles managed to dig in around the Repulse Bay Hotel, but could make no further headway. Wallis tried again the next day, sending another company of the Royal Rifles to the south edge of the Ty Tam Tuk Reservoir. Although the Canadians were able to reach the south edge of the reservoir, they could not hold. Towards evening, the company that was entrenched at the Repulse Bay Hotel moved north and made contact with a British unit just south of the Wong Nei Chong Gap. The Japanese counter-attacked and inflicted heavy casualties, but the Canadians held on until the night of the 22nd, when they were forced to pull back.

In the western sector, the Royal Scots and the Winnipeg Grenadiers made the Japanese pay dearly for every square centimetre of the Wong Nei Chong Gap. The Japanese held the police station in the gap for most of this time, but D Company of the Grenadiers occupied a position dominating the north–south road and killed and wounded large numbers of Japanese who tried to dislodge them. The fight for the gap finally ended on the morning of 22 December after the last defenders had withdrawn into a shelter behind steel doors, taking their wounded with them. The Japanese brought up a mountain gun and blasted the doors in; further resistance was useless, and the officer in charge of the remains of D Company surrendered.

Throughout the 23rd and the 24th, the Japanese consolidated their hold on the centre of Hong Kong Island. They pushed the remainder of the West Brigade back to a line between Victoria in the north and Aberdeen in the south, and forced Wallis's men to withdraw to the vicinity of Stanley Prison. On Christmas

Day the Japanese tried once again to secure a surrender, but were refused, even though the position was clearly hopeless. In the early afternoon, Japanese attacks resumed on both fronts, and casualties among the defenders mounted as ammunition and other stores dwindled. In mid-afternoon, Maltby finally decided that further fighting was useless; the white flag was hoisted and a small party was sent to Wallis to confirm the order to lay down arms.

Although all fighting ended in the early hours of 26 December, the killing did not stop. In various parts of the island, Japanese soldiers embarked on a killing frenzy, bayoneting and machine-gunning prisoners, medical staff, and wounded men lying helpless in hospitals and aid posts. That was not the end of the ordeal for the Canadians or for the other survivors of Maltby's force. Kept in appalling conditions in prison camps and forced to work as slave labourers for almost four years, many more died in captivity. Of the 1973 officers and men who left Canada in October 1941, 555 never returned, and many of those who did were so broken in body and spirit that they died premature deaths in the years that followed.

❈

Although the Battle of Hong Kong marked Canada's most significant role in the war against Japan, it was not Canada's only contribution to Allied victory in the Pacific. Three squadrons of the Royal Canadian Air Force served in Southeast Asia. No. 435 and No. 436 were both transport squadrons that flew Dakotas (C-47s) in support of the British Fourteenth Army in Burma. Formed in the Punjab in the second half of 1944, the squadrons flew air supply missions until the end of the war. Together they flew more than 56,000 tonnes of freight and about 29,000 passengers — civilians, troops, and casualties. Seven aircraft were lost on operations and a number of aircrew were killed.

The third RCAF squadron to take part in the Pacific war was No. 413, a general reconnaissance squadron attached to the RAF's Coastal Command which flew Consolidated Catalinas. The squadron moved to Ceylon (Sri Lanka) from the United Kingdom in March 1942. As aircraft and crews arrived they were pressed into service flying reconnaissance missions over the Indian Ocean, on the lookout for a possible Japanese carrier strike. At 1600 on 4 April 1942, Squadron Leader L.J. Birchall sighted Japanese Admiral Nagumo's fleet, including aircraft carriers, some 560 kilometres south of Ceylon. As the radio operator tapped out news of the discovery, Birchall ducked into cloud cover to try to avoid the inevitable combat air patrol that the carriers most certainly had aloft. His signals were picked up at home and by the Japanese, who directed their fighters towards his aircraft. The warning was heard in Ceylon, but the Japanese also found Birchall and shot him down. Birchall and his crew were retrieved and beaten, then sent to prison camp, where they survived the war. The feat earned Birchall the nickname "saviour of Ceylon." No. 413 was involved again in searching for Nagumo's force in the next few days as the Japanese carriers roamed the southern reaches of the Indian Ocean mounting raids on Columbo and Trincomalee, on the north side of the island. For the rest of the war No. 413 flew anti-submarine reconnaissance, but saw no further action.

Canadians were also involved in the campaign to expel Japan from the Aleutian Islands. On 3 and 4 June 1942 Japanese carrier aircraft attacked the US base at Dutch Harbor, on Unalaska Island, about 1400 kilometres from Anchorage. The air attacks were followed on 7 June with landings on Attu and Kiska, at the western end of the Aleutian chain. These attacks were diversionary; they were designed to draw US naval and air forces towards the Aleutians and away from Midway Island at the end of the Hawaiian chain, the target of a powerful Japanese task force intent on seizing Midway and forcing a showdown battle with the United States Pacific Fleet. The Japanese had no plans to work their way up the chain towards the Alaska mainland. Nevertheless, neither US nor Canadian military leaders knew this at the time; the Japanese presence on "North American" soil was considered serious enough that it had to be expunged as early as possible.

By the spring of 1943 Japan had been put on the defensive throughout the Pacific theatre. The destruction of four Japanese carriers at Midway in early June 1942 was a blow from which the Imperial Japanese Fleet never recovered. The United States began to lay plans to retake Attu and Kiska, and sought Canadian help. Ottawa agreed, and authorized a brigade group under Brigadier Harry W. Foster to take part in the attack on Kiska. A Permanent Force officer, Foster was brought back to Canada from the United Kingdom to oversee the organization and training of the force. The fighting edge of the Kiska contingent was to be provided by the Winnipeg Grenadiers (re-formed after Hong Kong), the Rocky Mountain Rangers, the Régiment de Hull, and the 24th Field Regiment, RCA. Since the Aleutians were considered part of North America, NRMA conscripts were used. The force was virtually re-equipped with US weapons and other *matériel* to keep supply problems to a minimum.

The estimated strength of the Japanese on the two islands by May 1943 was

2500 on Attu and 5400 on Kiska. On 12 May US troops landed on Attu, beginning a bloody fight for the island that ended two weeks later with a Japanese *banzai* charge; only eleven Japanese survived from the entire garrison. Plans were then laid to assault Kiska. A force of 34,000 men was assembled for the operation, 4800 of whom were Canadian. On the morning of 15 August the assault began, led by the First Special Service Force, an elite Canadian-American commando unit which was later labelled the "Devil's Brigade" and saw extensive action in Italy. To the surprise of the invaders, the Japanese were gone. A small Japanese task group had slipped past US surveillance aircraft and vessels — something easily done in those fog-shrouded waters — and evacuated the garrison. The Canadians remained on the island for three months, then withdrew to British Columbia. Foster returned to the United Kingdom, where he was given command of a brigade in the 3rd Canadian Infantry Division prior to the Normandy landings.

The Canadian contribution to the naval war in the Pacific was minimal. That should not have been surprising, given the state of the RCN at the beginning of the war. Nevertheless, as the Battle of the Atlantic wound down in late 1944 and the need for the RCN's Atlantic fleet diminished, plans were laid for a Pacific fleet of some sixty ships, including two light fleet carriers, two cruisers, and a large number of escort vessels. The first of this contingent to sail for Pacific waters was the *Uganda*, a light cruiser built for the RN and transferred to the RCN in October 1944. Crewed by 700 officers and men, the cruiser's main armament consisted of nine 6-inch guns. Commanded by Captain Rollo Mainguy, *Uganda* joined a Royal Navy task force in the western Pacific in April 1945 and served as an anti-aircraft screening vessel during carrier strikes at the Japanese home islands and the Japanese naval base at Truk, in the Caroline Islands. The main danger to the task force came from kamikaze pilots determined to smash their bomb- and fuel-laden planes into Allied ships, killing themselves in the process. The two British carriers, *Victorious* and *Formidable*, were main targets for the kamikazes, so *Uganda* was not hit. *Uganda* left the Pacific theatre, and the war, in July. As it had announced in April 1945, the King government was determined that all Canadians serving in the Pacific theatre would be volunteers. The crew of the *Uganda* was therefore given the unique opportunity to vote on whether to continue to serve in an active theatre of war, and chose not to. That was surely the strangest vote ever held aboard a Canadian warship.

The war in Europe officially ended on 8 May 1945, and Canada began to turn its attention to the Pacific theatre. Plans were laid to contribute a small fleet, a bomber force, and an infantry division for the final assault against Japan. The division — designated the 6th Canadian Infantry Division — was to be commanded by Major-General Bert Hoffmeister, who had commanded the 5th Canadian Armoured Division in Italy and Northwest Europe since March 1944. Close to 80,000 officers and men from existing units volunteered for the Pacific Force, but only about 39,000 were found to be suitable. The force was to be organized along US lines and to use US equipment. It never saw action. In early August 1945 the United States dropped two atomic bombs on Japan, ending the struggle in the Pacific.

Canada played only a small role in the war against Japan, but the sacrifices of those who gave their lives in that struggle are not lessened by the size of the overall contribution. On 9 August 1945 Pilot Robert Hampton Gray, of Nelson, British Columbia, sunk the Japanese destroyer *Amakusa* in Onagawa Bay, Japan, before his Corsair crashed into the sea; he was posthumously awarded the VC. The Canadian headstones in the Sai Wan military cemetery overlooking Sai Wan Bay on Hong Kong Island are also evidence of Canada's contribution. They are evidence, too, of the soft-headed British thinking that the presence of two thousand Canadians might help deter Japan from its aggressive intentions in Southeast Asia.

✤ IV The Agony of Dieppe

At 0550 on 19 August 1942, Captain Denis Whitaker of the Royal Hamilton Light Infantry was pinned down with his men in front of the sea wall that separated the stony Dieppe beach from the broad grassy promenade that lay in front of the town. Although the Canadian landing was barely twenty minutes old, German bullets and shells had transformed the beach into a maelstrom of fire. Whitaker knew that he and his men had no chance where they were: "As I lay there, one tank a few yards to my right had its six-pounder gun shattered by an enemy solid-shot shell. I was determined to get my men off [the beach] before the enemy artillery, mortars and M[achine] G[uns] annihilated us."[1]

Whitaker spotted the partially demolished casino about 500 metres to his right and led his men there in a desperate charge to get under cover. The casino was filled with German defenders, but Whitaker and his men fought with an intensity born of desperation and, within minutes, cleared the position and some slit trenches on the building's east side. They then jumped through a window, headed through the slit trenches, and ran towards a low wooden building. As they arrived, a German mortar barrage began to explode around them. They dove to the concrete floor of the shelter and discovered it was a German latrine: "It was impossible to move, as the mortaring continued without interruption; we lay in this crap for twenty or thirty minutes, feeling great revulsion for every German alive."[2]

Whitaker survived the hell of the Dieppe beach; he was the only Canadian officer to return to the United Kingdom untouched after one of the most tragic days in the history of the Canadian military; he was awarded the Distinguished Service Order (DSO) for his leadership. Most of the Canadians were not nearly as fortunate: of the 4963 officers and men who had embarked for the landing the night before, only 2210 returned. There were heavy casualties: 807 were killed in action, 100 died of their wounds, 586 were wounded, and 1874 were taken prisoner. Of the Canadians who were killed at Dieppe, 770 are buried in the Dieppe Canadian War Cemetery in the little town of Hautot-sur-Mer, 5 kilometres south of Dieppe itself.

❧

As the fall of 1940 gave way to the winter, and the German bombers returned night after night to pound London and other British cities, the Canadian presence in the United Kingdon continued to grow. France had fallen, the United States and the USSR were not yet in the war, and Canada, with its 11.5 million people, was Britain's largest ally. Prime Minister William Lyon Mackenzie King's dream of a limited liability war effort had evaporated with the collapse of the French armies, and Canada was now determined to give all it could to help Britain survive. During June, July, and August 1940, close to 78,000 Canadian men joined the Canadian Active Service Force. As the Battle of Britain raged, the main body of the 2nd Canadian Infantry Division arrived in the United Kingdom, and the 3rd Division concentrated in the Maritime provinces. It, too, was transported to Britain, arriving for the most part in late July and early August 1941. The 1st Canadian Army Tank Brigade, Canada's first armoured formation, arrived just ahead of it. Later renamed the 1st Canadian Armoured Brigade (it would eventually fight as an independent brigade), it was the first unit of the Canadian Armoured Corps, which was formed in August 1940. The 1st Canadian Army Tank Brigade was followed in November 1941 by the 5th Canadian Armoured Division and, in the late summer and early fall of 1942, by the 4th Canadian Armoured Division. The 2nd Canadian Armoured Brigade, also an independent brigade, was organized in the United Kingdom in the first half of 1943. To command this field army of five divisions and two independent armoured brigades, Canada established the Canadian Corps in July 1940 (later renamed 1st Canadian Corps), the 2nd Canadian Corps in January 1943, and the First Canadian Army, commanded by Lieutenant-General A.G.L. McNaughton, in April 1942.

Over the winter of 1940/41 and for the rest of the year, the Canadians were engaged almost exclusively in training and mounting a defence against a possible German invasion of the United Kingdom. For this defence role, the 1st Division was stationed in Surrey, and the 2nd in barracks at Aldershot. Units from both divisions rotated in and out of defensive positions on Britain's south coast throughout this period. It was not until Hitler attacked the Soviet Union in June 1941 that it became obvious that Germany was no longer interested in or capable of invading the United Kingdom.

As the Canadian Army built up its numerical strength, it also completed the task of equipping itself for a modern war. By February 1941 the line infantry companies received their final allotment of the Bren light machine gun. The field artillery regiments, whose task it would be to provide close artillery support for the infantry battalions, were fully equipped with the new 25-pound gun/howitzers by September 1941. The tank selected as the main armament of the armoured regiments was the British Churchill, a heavily armoured (for then) but slow and cumbersome vehicle mounting a 6-pound gun. Anti-tank guns were to remain a problem throughout the war. The initial anti-tank weapon was the Boys anti-tank rifle, which was useless. In the spring of 1941 Canadian and British infantry formations began to receive 2-pounder anti-tank guns as a replacement, but these, too, lacked stopping power. Eventually, the anti-tank platoons of Canadian and British infantry battalions were given the 6-pounder anti-tank gun.

The war widened dramatically in 1941; the struggle for North Africa, which had begun in September 1940 with an Italian attack from Libya against the British in Egypt, took a dramatic turn in March when the newly arrived Afrika Korps under General Erwin Rommel opened its first offensive, sweeping all before it. In the Balkans, German troops came to the aid of the floundering Italians, who had sought an easy conquest of Greece; the Germans defeated the Greek army and their British allies, and followed through with a costly but victorious parachute invasion of Crete. In the desert, the British Eighth Army counted among its troops Australians and New Zealanders, but no Canadian formations (though individual Canadian officers served there). The only action the Canadian Army in Europe saw in 1941 took place in August and September; a small Canadian force took part in a joint Canadian-British-Norwegian expedition to destroy mining and communications facilities on Spitzbergen, less than 1000 kilometres from the North Pole, and to evacuate its population. For the most part, the Canadian Army, growing stronger by the day, sat in Britain and trained.

When Canadian divisions left Canada or arrived in the United Kingdom, there was invariably much crowing in the press of both countries that these formations were fine bodies of fighting men ready to take on anything the Germans could throw at them. But they were not. Although the men had usually been taught the rudiments of marching, drilling, and other basics of military life, along with how to handle and fire the standard infantry weapons, they knew little else. They did not know how to coordinate an attack or a defence. They did not know how to work with artillery, mortars, or armour in advancing against an enemy position. They did not even know how to move a battalion by truck from one place to another. They had to be taught virtually everything that an infantryman ought to know before setting foot in a battle zone. That was what training was for.

In general, training proceeded from the individual fighting man to the highest formations. Men had to be taught how to fight in sections, platoons, and companies. Then companies had to be taught how to fight in battalions, battalions in brigades, brigades in divisions, and so on. While individual soldiers learned elementary infantry skills, the formations they were part of engaged in ever-larger exercises that covered more of the English countryside. Month after month the men left their barracks, climbed aboard trucks, and took part in exercises such as Waterloo, Bumper, Beaver, Maple, or Tiger, as officers and men tried to learn the ways of modern war. They acquired much technical know how, but was it enough?

In the late fall of 1941 the idea of battle drill — pioneered by the British but adopted by the Canadians — seemed to seize the imagination of Canadian formation commanders in the United Kingdom. Battle drill was based on three simple but interrelated ideas: training should be as physically tough as possible; it should take place in terrain and under conditions as near to actual combat as possible; and it should teach small units (sections and companies) a series of basic battlefield moves that they would do almost automatically when under fire. The proponents of battle drill believed, for example, that the best way to react to an enemy ambush could be taught in advance, even on a parade ground, though it was better done in the field. Thus, when the time came, the men would know instinctively what to do. Battle drill was an unabashed British and Canadian effort to train their infantry to fight as they thought German infantry fought.

There is controversy to this day about the effectiveness of battle-drill training in preparing Canadians for combat. Field Marshal Bernard Montgomery, for one, was not opposed to it, but believed that it did not teach what men truly needed to know: how to maintain contact with the enemy and to fight him at the same time. And it most assuredly did not teach Canadians how to fight as effectively as the German infantry did. The Germans trained their men to fight in small units. They encouraged the leaders of those units to be imaginative and innovative under fire, and they gave them considerable freedom to manoeuvre. The German infantry relied on their own battalion weapons to fight themselves forward, pin the enemy down, manoeuvre around him while he was pinned down, and then destroy him piecemeal.

In early 1942 Montgomery began to visit every Canadian formation training in the United Kingdom, examining the state of their training and commenting on the effectiveness of their leaders. Whatever may be said of "Monty" as a tactician — and there is still controversy about the way he organized his battles — he was a superb trainer of men. His comments were as incisive as they were cutting. He found much of the training inadequate and many of the leaders lacking — from divisional commanders on down. In May he observed the Canadians on Exercise Beaver IV and concluded: "The weak point in the Canadian Corps at present is the knowledge of commanders in the stage-management of battle operations, and in the technique of battle fighting generally, on their own level." Although he found J. Hamilton Roberts, GOC 2nd Division, acceptable as a division commander, he concluded that George Pearkes, GOC 1st Division, and C. Basil Price, GOC 3rd Division, were "no good . . . Pearkes would fight his Division bravely till the last man was killed; but he has no brains and the last man would be killed all too soon. Price not only has no military ability, but he is not a fighter by nature and has no 'drive.'" Both men were replaced soon after.

Although training was clearly necessary in an army that was militia-based and manned almost entirely by volunteers with no military background, the men grew bored and angry as the war raged elsewhere; morale plummeted with each passing week and each new exercise. As Strome Galloway, serving with 1st Division, put it: "Barrack square routine and large scale manoeuvres . . . had started to turn us into a fed-up, browned-off, disillusioned band of volunteer warriors."[3] A strange paralysis of will regarding the use of the Canadian Army seems to have gripped Canadian military and political leaders in the wake of the fall of France. Here was a relatively large force, well equipped, consisting of men who had volunteered to fight, sitting in Britain, training and training, and training some more. Part of the problem undoubtedly lay in McNaughton's insistence that the Canadians stay together. That meant that if the British wanted to use Canadian units in, say, North Africa, they would have had to use all of them at once. That was not possible, because the British did not want to leave themselves with virtually no defence and because transporting the entire Canadian Army to North Africa would have caused massive transportation difficulties. Thus Canada's military leaders were reduced to grasping at straws; one of those straws was a cross-channel raid on the French resort town of Dieppe which the new head of Combined Operations, Vice-Admiral Louis Mountbatten, was beginning to consider in March 1942.

Combined Operations was essentially a planning organization responsible for mounting military operations, such as cross-channel raids, which combined land, naval, and air forces. In October 1941 the head of Combined Operations, Admiral Lord Keyes, was replaced by Captain Louis Mountbatten of the Royal Navy, a well-connected member of the royal family whose military experience to date had consisted in having three ships sunk under him. Mountbatten had been urged by Churchill to put some life into Combined Operations. Mountbatten responded by increasing the tempo of cross-channel raiding, with escapades such as the British commando raid on the German submarine facilities at St Nazaire, France, in late March 1942.

The raid on Dieppe clearly had its genesis in pressure from the Soviet Union to do something on the western front. The Americans also wanted action on the western front and were, in fact, hoping to mount a full-scale cross-channel invasion of France by the end of the year — an unrealistic notion if ever there was one. It was apparent to most Allied political and military leaders that an invasion of France would come at some point, however, and a Dieppe raid might just provide experience in how to take a French port intact. To this day the source of the idea and the planning for the raid have been subjects of contention. Montgomery's official biographer, Nigel Hamilton, summed up Dieppe this way: "The Dieppe operation bears the traces of hasty planning, of obtuse enthusiasm on the part of those units desperate to see 'action,' and of amateur, even tragic, overambitiousness." His view of Mountbatten is even more harsh: "As Chief of Combined Operations [Mountbatten] was a master of intrigue, jealousy, and ineptitude. Like a spoilt child he toyed with men's lives with an indifference to casualties that can only be explained by his insatiable, even psychopathic ambition."[4] But if Mountbatten was ultimately responsible for the fiasco of Dieppe, it was the Canadian commanders Andy McNaughton and Harry Crerar who were directly responsible for selecting this mission to be the baptism of fire of the Canadian Army in the United Kingdom.

Dieppe is a small resort town on the channel coast some 100 kilometres from the English coast at Sussex. It was close enough to be in fighter range of the United Kingdom, but not so close as to be an obvious target for a raid. Besides, there was really not much there of strategic value to the Germans. The port was small and incapable of being a major supply base. The town was an attacker's nightmare. To the east and west rise high, dominating cliffs. Between the front of the town and the sea wall is a wide, flat promenade offering no cover to advancing troops. The beach itself is narrow, steep, and covered with a type of shingle that is hard on the feet and even harder on wheeled and tracked vehicles.

Dieppe was strongly held by well-equipped German troops of the 302nd Infantry division. German strongpoints on the cliffs on either side of the town dominated the beach. The Germans were lavishly equipped with automatic weapons, large- and small-calibre artillery, anti-aircraft guns, anti-tank guns (not particularly effective against the Churchill tanks), and mortars. They had large reserves to hand, including the 10th Panzer division at Amiens. Most importantly, British intelligence badly underestimated their numbers and weapons strength.

The plan for the Dieppe operation evolved through a number of stages, until the Combined Operations staff decided that a strong frontal assault of close to division strength, aided by tanks, would constitute the main thrust. It would be supported by landings on each flank. The frontal assault would be proceeded first by air bombing, then by a low-level attack by Hurricanes against the front of the town. The troops were to seize the port, penetrate through the town to take and destroy the radar station and other important facilities, and, if possible, secure the German divisional headquarters, take prisoners, and capture any important documents that might be located there. At the same time, parachute troops were to attack and destroy the airfield at St Aubin, just south of Dieppe.

The Canadians were first introduced to the operation by Montgomery. He was to be in overall command, since the raid would be launched from his operational area. He mooted the idea to Crerar, whose corps was under Monty's command. Monty preferred to use an all-Canadian force for the main invasion rather than a composite British-Canadian force. Crerar was eager to accommodate him, because it was a chance to get his troops into action; he suggested the 2nd Division. Since McNaughton was still in overall charge of the Canadian Army in the United Kingdom, his approval was sought and given on 30 April. Roberts, the divisional commander, then selected the 4th and 6th Brigades for the landings; they were to be accompanied by the 14th Canadian Army Tank Regiment (the Calgary Tanks) and a small force of engineers. The raid was eventually scheduled for 4 July, and the units destined to take part embarked on intensive training in landing and assault operations. The Canadian staff played almost no part in drawing up the overall plans for the raid, but accepted them as sound despite some reservations about the use of tanks on the Dieppe beaches.

On 2 and 3 July the troops embarked and were fully briefed; the weather deteriorated on the night of 3 July and the sailing was postponed repeatedly, until it was decided to launch the attack on 8 July. But on the morning of 7 July, the Luftwaffe attacked the small fleet lying just west of the Solent. It was obvious that the Germans knew something was up owing to the concentration of shipping. That, and the failure of the weather to improve, prompted the naval force commander to cancel the operation. The disappointed troops were disembarked and, since the plan was no longer a secret, everyone assumed that the attack would be permanently shelved.

It was not. Mountbatten was determined to go ahead and, apparently at his own initiative and without the approval of the British Chiefs of Staff, he revived the operation about one week later.[5] Most of the original plan was to be kept, but some important differences were introduced. Instead of concentrating the landing force on transports, part of the infantry would cross the channel on the same LCIs (infantry landing craft) that would take them up to the Dieppe beach. This was done to preserve the element of surprise. The parachute landing was discarded as too complicated, and landings by British commandos to silence German batteries flanking the beaches were laid on instead. Thus the assault would be spread out over some 16 kilometres of coastline, with the flanking attacks scheduled to begin thirty minutes before the main landing. The air bombardment, the only heavy support that the landing was to have, was cancelled when the Bomber Command chief, Air Marshal Arthur Harris, refused to allow his heavy bombers to attack after dawn. A precision night attack was virtually impossible, and, since the accuracy of the bombing was in question, Mountbatten's staff concluded that little would be gained from it other than to alert the Germans. Thus, in essence, the plan for Operation Jubilee (the code-name for the Dieppe raid) was that the attackers would emerge from the sea in the early dawn, rush ashore before the Germans could react, and seize their objectives by surprise; there was absolutely no room for error. The landing force embarked again late on 18 August and slipped into the English Channel as the dusk melted into a beautiful, clear night. The little fleet, accompanied by British destroyers, formed up and made for the French coast.

Things began to go wrong just before 0400. A small German convoy proceeding from Boulogne to Dieppe came across several British vessels on the left flank of the attacking fleet, and a short, sharp, sea battle ensued. On the French coast the sound of guns rolled in from the sea; in some of the German defensive positions the defenders rushed to their posts. A part of the invading force — that carrying the British commandos destined for the landing on the far left flank — was scattered. The landings were not called off. The commander of the group that had run into the Germans was unable to report the extent of the battle because of damage to his radio equipment. Even if he had, it was probably too late: the transports carrying the troops due to make the flank attacks had already lowered their landing craft. That had been done in the hope that the smaller craft could slip into shore undetected by German radar.

The scattered contingent of British commandos was due to assault the coastal battery at Berneval, about 8 kilometres east of Dieppe; only seven of the twenty-three landing craft put their troops ashore. The Germans had been fully alerted by the noise of the sea battle, and most of the commandos who did land were quickly killed or captured. One small group managed to infiltrate close to the battery; they kept the German gun crews away from it for some two-and-a-half hours, until they escaped to the beach and were evacuated.

The Royal Regiment of Canada came ashore at Puys, about 2.5 kilometres east of Dieppe. The plan was to have the battalion land in three waves, with a contingent from the Black Watch (Royal Highland Regiment) of Canada, from the 5th Brigade, in the last wave. The beach here was narrow, dominated by high cliffs, and with only one exit up a brick path commanded by a German pillbox. The Royals' attack depended on surprise; they didn't get it. They came in late, as dawn was breaking; the Germans were on the alert and the Royals ran into heavy fire even before they hit the beach. Private Steve Michell's experience was all too typical; he had to push his way through a pile of bodies just to get out of his boat. As he waded through the chest-deep water he found one of the younger men trying to stuff his intestines back inside his body. Michell reached shore, but found only about a dozen men of his company still standing out of 120.

A handful of men managed to get over the sea wall, but they could accomplish nothing. The second and third waves should not have come ashore, but, owing to faulty communications, they did. The Germans had less than a single company guarding the exit from the beach, but it was all they needed. Those Canadians not killed were pinned down all morning and part of the afternoon, until they were forced to surrender; there was no way to get them off. Of 554 Royals who had embarked, 225 were killed in action, died of their wounds, or died in captivity, and thirty-three of those who did return were wounded. The remaining 264 were taken prisoner. Only sixty-five returned to the United Kingdom. The Black Watch suffered only four fatalities, but only forty-four men of the 111 who had embarked returned to Britain.

The disaster at Puys had a direct impact on events at Dieppe, because the Royals had been given the task of clearing the headlands that dominated Dieppe from the east. Their failure to do so allowed the defenders to pour fire down on the Canadians as they came in to the beach. The landing took place at about 0520 under cover fire from the guns of four destroyers, and was preceded by a low-level strafing attack by five squadrons of cannon-firing Hurricanes. Then the Essex Scottish on the left and the Royal Hamilton Light Infantry (RHLI) on the right hit the beach. The tanks should have landed at the same time, but the LCTs (tank landing craft) carrying them were delayed by navigational errors.

On the right flank of the main beach, German fire from the cliffs near the radar site, the casino, and the large stone castle that nestled against the cliff engulfed the beach and the RHLI men on it. Despite the storm of shot and shell, Whitaker's men managed to clear the casino; another group, led by Captain A.C. Hill, actually got across the sea wall and the promenade, and penetrated about two blocks into the town before they withdrew to a position near the casino. On the left, however, the Essex Scottish got nowhere at all; German gunners on the east headland and in the buildings that fronted on the promenade kept them pinned down and exacted a heavy toll. One small group of about twelve men got across the promenade, but were forced back.

About ten minutes after the main landing, the tanks came ashore. One by one the LCTs approached the beach to land their tanks. Most were hit before they could do so, some immediately after. Some of the tanks never made it out of the water, some were hit by shellfire as they churned over the sea wall. About half seem to have got on to the promenade itself, but none made it into the town. Many were disabled by shells exploding in their tracks (some writers contend that their tracks broke on the stony beach), but were not destroyed because the bulk of the 37-millimetre German anti-tank guns at Dieppe could not penetrate the Churchill tanks' frontal armour. Most of those tanks that were immobilized but not destroyed continued to give covering fire to the infantry to the last.

The right flanking attacks were the only part of the operation that seemed to go at least partially according to plan. The British troops of No. 4 Commando got ashore as scheduled; one party landed at Vasterival and moved overland to attack a coastal battery about 750 metres inland; the other landed about a kilometre further west and swung behind the battery. The South Saskatchewan Regiment and the Cameron Highlanders of Canada ought to have come ashore astride the mouth of the River Scie at Pourville. This would have allowed the South Saskatchewans to climb the high ground between Pourville and Dieppe, position themselves to dominate the battleground, and attack the radar station. Instead, the two battalions were landed on the beach to the west of Pourville, about 2 kilometres from the main Dieppe beaches. The beach there was also dominated by high cliffs, but somewhat wider and longer than those at Puys.

To gain their objective, the South Saskatchewans had to cross the Scie on a bridge in the centre of Pourville and move up the main road towards Dieppe. But the Germans were fully alerted by the time they started their push, and they could make no headway; the bridge was soon covered with dead and wounded. At that point Lieutenant-Colonel Cecil Merritt walked towards the bridge, waving his helmet and shouting to his men to follow him across. They did (and Merritt won the Victoria Cross for his feat), but they still could not gain the heights. Off to their right, the Camerons landed late but managed to push inland despite the death of their Commanding Officer. They reached the hamlet of Petit Appeville, where they were stopped short of the airfield, their ultimate objective. Then they, too, fell back to the beach.

As the battle ran its course on the ground, German aircraft rushed to the sky over the blazing beaches and were met by the fighters of the RAF's No. 11 Group. Charged with command of the raid's air operations, Air Vice-Marshal Trafford Leigh-Mallory ensured that from three to six squadrons of fighters were kept over Dieppe at all times. The air battle between the RAF and the Luftwaffe was more intensive than anything else since the Battle of Britain. At the end of the day, the RAF had been bested, losing 106 fighters to the Germans' forty-eight destroyed and twenty-four damaged.

One of the squadrons taking part was Canada's No. 1 Fighter Squadron, now renumbered No. 401. After escorting a group of American B-17s on a raid against the Luftwaffe fighter base at Abbeville, the squadron swung south towards Dieppe. When Squadron Leader K.L.B. Hodson saw four twin-engine German bombers, he came in behind one and shot it up. He claimed it as damaged. Flight Sergeant Zobell fired at another and damaged it too, before he was attacked by a German fighter. Despite damage to his fighter and an eye injury, Zobell managed to reach home safely. The pilots returned from their first sortie over Dieppe (they made three that day) to report, "the town . . . covered by smoke."[6] The Canadian squadron shot a number of German aircraft down, but also lost several fighters of its own.

Aboard command ship HMS *Calpe*, J. Hamilton Roberts was unaware of the full extent of the unfolding disaster. Radios were malfunctioning, radio men were being hit, officers were lying low trying to avoid being hit. At about 0610 a message was received reporting that the Essex Scottish were "across the beaches and into the houses," a gross exaggeration. Roberts decided to send in his reserves. He ordered the rest of the Royal Regiment (there *was* no "rest"; the entire contingent had gone ashore at Puys) and the Fusiliers Mont-Royal (FMR) to land on the left beach behind the Essex Scottish.

The craft carrying the FMR approached the maelstrom at about 0700 and were met by heavy, accurate, and deadly fire. The current pushed their vessels to the right and they put ashore virtually under the high cliffs on the west side of the main beach. When the boats were about 75 metres out, the Germans opened up: "Every gun and mortar in Dieppe seemed to open fire on the ill-fated Fusiliers de Mont-Royal. Two boats were immediately blown out of the water. The remainder were badly holed and many of the men killed and wounded while still at sea."[7] Most of those who did get ashore were unable to move past the headland into the area of the main beach. Because Roberts still had no clear idea of how events were shaping up, he sent a contingent of Royal Marines to land in front of the casino. Their CO, Lieutenant-Colonel Joseph Phillips, came ashore with a group of about seventy men; he saw what was happening and stood up to wave off the craft following him. He was killed, but some two hundred of his men were saved as a result of his quick thinking.

The Royal Regiment survivors at Puys had already surrendered when Roberts received a message from the FMR at about 0900 declaring that they were in severe difficulty and would be wiped out if they were not immediately evacuated. Five minutes later they radioed that they were totally surrounded. Most surrendered shortly after, just as Roberts issued an order to evacuate the beaches by 1100. Across the beach, now littered with burned-out or crippled tanks, damaged landing craft drifting on the swells, and dead and wounded men, those still alive tried to scramble to the water's edge. Some huddled in the shelter of immobile tanks. Those who were too severely wounded to move lay where they were, comforted by comrades or by Padre J.W. Foote of the RHLI, who chose to stay behind and accompany his men into captivity. The RN destroyers, *Calpe* included, came dangerously close to shore to cover the withdrawal with their guns; overhead the fighters of No. 11 Group tried to keep German bombers and fighters from attacking the evacuating men. Immobilized tanks kept up their fire with 6-pounders and machine guns as long as they could, so the infantry could get away. By 1400 the last Canadians were either off the beaches or had surrendered; the survivors limped back to the United Kingdom.

Dieppe was Canada's greatest disaster in the Second World War. More Canadians were taken prisoner there than in all the rest of the campaign in Northwest Europe. Canada suffered more killed in action in the one-half day of fighting at Dieppe than in any other day of fighting in the war. The casualties were horrendous, but were they worth it in terms of lessons learned? It is hard to escape the conclusion that whatever was learned at Dieppe ought to have been known anyway, or could have been figured out in a tactical exercise: that it would be hard to take a port in a direct assault and that a landing must be preceded by careful planning and heavy fire. It ought not to have taken any stroke of military genius to figure out that men coming ashore in boats in daylight are extremely vulnerable to heavily armed, well-protected, and well-supported men on shore who want to do them great harm. Of course, the men were not supposed to land in daylight. But a successful landing in total darkness on a distant shore, near enough the intended objectives to allow the infantry to seize them without resistance, and with boats subject to the vagaries of current, would have been almost impossible anyway. The planners ought to have known that up front.

In his otherwise authoritative history of the Canadian Army in the Second World War, Canada's official historian, Colonel C.P. Stacey, observed that although the Canadian military could have sidestepped the operation, they were loath to do so because of "how violently resentful the ordinary Canadian soldier would have been had an enterprise like the Dieppe raid been carried out at this time without the participation of the Canadian force which had waited so long for battle."[8] That is an explanation of why McNaughton and Crerar accepted the mission, but it is not an excuse. At bottom, the success of Dieppe depended on two factors: first, absolutely everything had to go right so that the men could rush ashore, on schedule, out of the dark, and seize their objectives before the Germans could react; second, once the Germans did react, they would forget how to function as trained soldiers. The whole history of warfare made both assumptions extremely unlikely.

In the weeks and months after the disaster at Dieppe, the job of trying to prepare the Canadian Army for war continued. It was made harder by the simple reality that the bulk of the 2nd Division had been left on the beach at Dieppe; most of the division would have to be rebuilt virtually from scratch. A case can be made that that task was never properly carried out; 2nd Canadian Infantry Division suffered a disproportionate number of casualties — the highest casualty ratio in the Canadian Army — from the time it returned to combat in early July 1944 until the end of the war.

One of the most important exercises in the process of preparing the Canadian Army for war was Spartan, mounted in the first two weeks of March 1943. For the first and only time in the war, the entire Canadian field force took part in a single exercise; it was the first real test for McNaughton as army commander and for his First Canadian Army Headquarters. Spartan revealed McNaughton's real weakness as a field force commander. General Sir Bernard Paget, Commander-in-Chief of the British Home Forces, was especially critical of McNaughton. In his words, the Canadian was guilty of "a lack of confidence [which] resulted in missed opportunities, delayed decisions, changes of orders and frequent and conflicting short moves of units and formations."[9] Paget was right; much of the Canadian "battle" suffered from confused and contradictory orders, poor movement planning, and a lack of direction from McNaughton's headquarters. As usual, he seemed more interested in tinkering with minor problems than in tackling the major difficulties that plagued his forces.

Major-General J. Hamilton Roberts lost his job after Spartan. Although he was awarded the DSO for his leadership of the Dieppe raid, Crerar engineered his removal after Spartan, ostensibly for his performance in that exercise. In a letter to McNaughton written in early April 1943, Crerar claimed that he had not had time to assess Roberts's performance in the field "until recent months," but now that he had, he had found him wanting: "I have examined the actions of 2 Cdn Div [in Spartan] . . . My conclusion is that there was, in fact, very considerable confusion, loss of time and inadequate co-ordination of effort . . . It is also to be remarked that 2 Cdn Div suffered very heavy losses by umpire decision." No one should have expected otherwise less than eight months after Dieppe.

Roberts was placed in charge of Canadian reinforcement units in the United Kingdom and was never again given operational command. Before the raid, he had told his men that Dieppe would be a piece of cake; each year on the anniversary of the debacle a small parcel would arrive in his mail bearing a stale piece of cake to remind him of his words.[10] Roberts might have refused the Dieppe assignment, but the real responsibility for the massacre belonged to Mountbatten, McNaughton and Crerar, two of whom went on to bigger and better things before the end of the war.

❦ V The Deadly Skies

By 30 May 1942, Sir Arthur "Bomber" Harris, known as "Butcher" or "Butch" to the aircrews of Bomber Command, had conceived a bold stroke to bring the RAF bombing campaign against Germany to new heights of power and destructiveness. He would marshall a force of one thousand planes, drawing on operational squadrons, operational training units (OTUs), and virtually anything else he could get his hands on, and send the entire force to bomb a single German city on a single night. His superior, Sir Charles Portal, Chief of the Air Staff, strongly supported the scheme and helped Harris win over Prime Minister Winston Churchill. Now, on the afternoon of 30 May, Harris stood in front of a large wall map of Europe and contemplated his target. He lit an American cigarette and moved his finger slowly across the map; it stopped at Cologne. That city was to have the distinction of being the first in history to be bombed by a thousand planes at one time.[1]

Within a few hours, 1046 bombers took off in the gathering gloom and headed for Cologne; sixty-eight aircraft of the Royal Canadian Air Force's bomber squadrons were among them. The bombers proceeded to Cologne on a single track; each aircraft's time of arrival over the target had been carefully calculated to produce the utmost devastation in the shortest possible time. The first bombs fell at forty-seven minutes past midnight; the last at 0225. In the intervening ninety-eight minutes, some 898 aircraft dumped their loads — a rate of one bombload every 6.5 seconds. (As in every raid, some aircraft failed to reach the target for a variety of reasons.) The fires from the heart of the ancient city were visible to approaching crews from as far as 240 kilometres out. One Canadian pilot later described the scene: "There are other aircraft around us as Ole [the bomb aimer] gives me directions until the moment when he shouts, 'Bombs gone!' . . . As I drop a wing to turn away, I get a full view of the target area. Immense fires are raging now, and bomb flashes are practically incessant."[2]

When aerial reconnaissance photos were taken early the next morning, the damage to Cologne seemed extensive. More than 5000 houses were destroyed or badly damaged, 7000 were partly damaged, and 45,000 people were made homeless. Thirty-six factories were permanently put out of action, and seventy more were forced to curtail production. There were fewer than 500 deaths, but more than 5000 people were injured. The RAF official history later concluded that Cologne's total war production loss from this one raid amounted to about one month: it was much harder to destroy a factory than Harris and his experts yet realized. But then, destroying factories was only a part of what Bomber Command was trying to do in its "area" offensive against Germany.

In the early months of the war, it had been anticipated that the RCAF would keep the bulk of its strength in Canada for home defence and send only three squadrons overseas. One of those squadrons — No. 1 (Fighter) Squadron (later No. 401) — had participated in the Battle of Britain. Other Canadians had taken part in the battle, flying for the RAF. As late as March 1941 there were still only three RCAF squadrons in the United Kingdom — Nos. 401 and 402 (Day-Fighter) Squadrons, and No. 400 (Army Cooperation) Squadron. Then, over the next twenty months, the RCAF's presence in the United Kingdom increased tenfold to thirty-two squadrons, including eleven bomber, eight day-fighter, and three night-fighter units. RCAF squadrons could be found in Bomber, Fighter, and Coastal Commands of the RAF, and RCAF pilots performed duties as varied as torpedo bomber attacks on enemy shipping and night intruder missions against German airfields. It was not only the size of the mid-war RCAF that was stunning compared with its immediate prewar establishment, but also the range and the complexity of its operations.

The RCAF's wartime role and size were largely determined by the British Commonwealth Air Training Plan. When the original BCATP agreement was signed in December 1939, it contained provision that an indeterminate number of RCAF squadrons would be formed overseas (primarily in the United Kingdom) manned by Canadian graduates of the plan. Further negotiations ensued and, in January 1941, Canada and the United Kingdom reached an initial agreement that twenty-five RCAF squadrons might be formed, in addition to the three already in Britain, to be paid for by the United Kingdom to balance the fact that Canada paid for the bulk of the BCATP. In addition, Canadians serving with the RCAF would wear their own uniform and, most important to the men, they would be paid according to the RCAF rank scale, which was considerably higher than that of the RAF. These "Article 15" squadrons formed the backbone of the fighting RCAF, which, by war's end, would expand its overseas strength to forty-eight squadrons. That expansion began soon after the Canadian-British agreement, with the formation of No. 403 Squadron on 1 March 1941 (initially as an army cooperation, then as a day-fighter squadron), No. 405 — Canada's first bomber squadron — in April 1941, and Nos. 404 and 407 with Coastal Command in May 1941. On 1 March 1941 Canadian squadrons in the United Kingdom and other theatres of war were assigned numbers in the 400 block, beginning with No. 400, to distinguish them from RAF squadrons. Thus No. 110 became No. 400, No. 1 became No. 401, and No. 2 (formerly 112) became No. 402.

From the beginning of the war to the end, a majority of Canadians served either directly in the Royal Air Force or as members of the RCAF in RAF squadrons. One of the most famous was George Frederick Beurling of Verdun, Quebec, a fighter pilot who earned the nicknames "Screwball" from his fellow pilots and "Buzz" from an admiring public when he became Canada's highest-scoring fighter ace of the war with 31 1/3 kills. Beurling had tried to join the RCAF on the outbreak of war, but even though he had more than one hundred hours of solo flying time in his log book he was rejected, apparently because he was not considered to have had enough formal education. He made his way to the United Kingdom and joined the RAF. After a stint with the RCAF's No. 403 Squadron (though still with the RAF), he was assigned to the RAF's No. 41 Squadron. There he shot down his first two German fighters, but earned a reputation as a troublesome lone-wolf incapable of bending to the discipline of squadron flying. In truth, Beurling was a brilliant pilot and fighter tactician with very good eyesight. He trained himself in the art of deflection shooting — shooting at an enemy aircraft from the side by aiming ahead of it. But he was also moody, temperamental, and difficult to get along with. Not long after he joined No. 41 Squadron, he transferred out and found himself aboard an aircraft carrier sailing to the besieged island of Malta.

In the late spring of 1942 the British were locked in mortal combat with the Germans and the Italians in the Battle for North Africa. The British used Malta as a base to attack enemy shipping bringing supplies and reinforcements to North Africa; the Germans and the Italians relentlessly attacked Malta in an attempt to stop the British attacks on their shipping. The only way the British could reinforce Malta was by sea from Gibraltar, but the resupply convoys invariably took a terrible beating from Axis aircraft and submarines. If new fighters were going to be sent to the besieged island, they would have to be flown there, but Spitfires did not have the range to reach Malta from Gibraltar. Thus, the fighters were brought as close to Malta as possible on board Royal Navy aircraft carriers, then flown on one-way missions to the island. Beurling made the hop from HMS *Eagle* on 9 June 1942 and landed at Takali, a small fighter strip not far from Valletta, the capital.

At first Beurling had trouble here, too; he insisted on breaking formation and hunting on his own. Under the stern discipline of P.B. Lucas, his squadron commander, however, he settled down and soon began to shoot German and Italian aircraft out of the sky at a furious pace. Beurling knew that the pilot who survived air-to-air combat was not the better flier, able to do aerobatics in a whirling dog fight, but the one who spotted the enemy first, positioned himself above and behind, then pounced, closed the range as quickly as possible, and fired only when too close to miss. After barely two months on Malta, Beurling's confirmed kills had climbed from two to sixteen.

Even in the Second World War, the press tended to depict air-to-air combat as somehow gallant and chivalrous. Men like Beurling knew better, as he later recounted in a description of one of his victories over an Italian pilot:

> I closed up to about thirty yards . . . I was on his portside coming in at about a fifteen-degree angle . . . it look[ed] pretty close. I could see all the details in his face because he turned and looked at me just as I had a bead on him . . . One of my can[non] shells caught him right in the face and blew his head right off . . . The body slumped and the slipstream caught the neck, the stub of the neck, and the blood streamed down the side of the cockpit."[3]

Beurling stayed on Malta and his tally continued to mount, but the strain of constant flying against invariably larger numbers of enemy aircraft took its toll. He began to exhibit unmistakable signs of combat fatigue. In Canada, his exploits had made him a legend — the Knight of Malta — and an asset too valuable for the government to allow to be destroyed. At the end of October 1942, with twenty-nine enemy aircraft to his credit and a chestful of decorations, Beurling was pulled out of action and sent back to Canada to help with recruiting and the sale of war bonds. He was not to meet his end until 20 May 1948, when he was killed at Rome's Urbe airfield. He and another man were in the process of flying a single-engined Canadian-built Norseman to the fledgling State of Israel, to volunteer for the Israeli airforce, when they crashed and were killed. "Buzz" Beurling now lies buried in the Holy Land.

🍁

In late November 1940 Air Marshal Sholto Douglas assumed leadership of the RAF's Fighter Command, and a new phase in British air operations began. Douglas believed that Fighter Command should adopt a more offensive strategy against the Luftwaffe; instead of sitting back and waiting to defend its home ground, the RAF should mount fighter operations over Occupied Europe. The objective was to attack enemy airfields and other important targets and to entice the German fighters into combat. Massive fighter sweeps — dubbed Rhubarbs — over France and Belgium began soon after; when bombers, escorted by fighters, were sent to hit targets in daylight, the operations were called Circuses. The strategy was less than a success. The Germans avoided combat unless they found conditions favourable; when they did choose to meet the RAF, they generally took a heavy toll owing to their greater experience, better fighters (the improved Me 109F and the new Focke-Wulf FW 190), and the advantage of fighting with full gas tanks near their own bases. In fact, Fighter Command now found itself in combat under the same disadvantageous conditions that had plagued the Luftwaffe during the Battle of Britain: they were forced to fly long distances, much of the time over water, in short-range fighters, and were fighting over enemy-occupied country. The RAF also discovered that German radar and German anti-aircraft fire were superior to those the British had used only a few months before to defend the United Kingdom. In January and February 1941, 190 bomber and 2700 fighter sorties resulted in the destruction of only twenty German fighters for the loss of fifty-one Fighter Command pilots; over the course of the year, Fighter Command seems to have lost about four aircraft for every German plane downed. The operations should have been discontinued, but were not. In fact, when Germany attacked the USSR in June 1941, these RAF operations were stepped up in the belief that Rhubarbs and Circuses would force the Luftwaffe into siphoning aircraft from the eastern front. That did not happen. Still, these operations remained a mainstay of Fighter Command until 1944, a waste of precious resources.

The RCAF squadrons attached to Fighter Command took part in these Rhubarbs and Circuses with results not much different from those of the RAF squadrons. May 1942, for example, was a typical month for No. 401 Squadron. On 1 May a section of four fighters was circling below cloud some 24 kilometres west of Le Havre when it was jumped by twelve or thirteen ME 109s. Two Canadian fighters were destroyed, although one pilot was pulled from the sea by a rescue boat. On 9 May the squadron was again in the air over France, this time patrolling inland from Calais. The crew heard reports of three German fighters, but saw only the splash of an RAF Spitfire hitting the sea. It was two weeks before the squadron took part in another sweep; on 24 May Flight Sergeant Morrison closed to within 100 metres of an FW 190 and poured a burst of cannon fire into the enemy fighter. He saw his shells hit the starboard wing, causing a small explosion. He followed the German down towards the water, but pulled up again when he spotted more enemy aircraft above him. He was in mid-channel at 6000 metres when he spotted an FW 190 on the tail of a Spitfire heading for home, about 1500 metres below him. He pulled sharply to the right and fired a long burst at the German. He later reported that the FW 190 "did a slight left-hand turn and dense white smoke poured from both wing roots when at approximately 8000 feet he (Morrison) broke away and left the [enemy aircraft] still going down in a steep dive with the white smoke still pouring out."[4] Since he had seen neither pilot bail out or the fighter actually crash, he could claim only two enemy fighters as damaged. Five days later, on 29 May, No. 401 Squadron aircraft again came under attack off the coast, but suffered no losses.

The worst single day suffered by RCAF fighters in the war came on 2 June 1942. On that day No. 403 Squadron, the first RCAF fighter squadron activated in the United Kingdom, took off in its Spitfire Vs and headed for France as part of a Rhubarb with several RAF squadrons. The unit was led by a New Zealand veteran of the Battle of Britain, Squadron Leader A.C. "Al" Deere. The gaggle of RAF and RCAF fighters was picked up early by German radar, and the Luftwaffe decided to set an ambush. Several squadrons took off, clawed for height, and then bounced the Canadians and British. In virtually a single pass, seven Canadian fighters were destroyed, only one pilot bailing out, and another fighter was so badly damaged that it crashed on landing. Just four aircraft from No. 403 Squadron returned safely to base.

By late 1942 the RCAF was fully engaged in operations against the enemy on several fronts. No. 417 (Fighter) Squadron was transferred from the United Kingdom to Egypt in the spring of 1942, leaving its Spitfires behind. The unit was stationed in the Nile Delta, but, since there were no aircraft available, the groundcrew worked on maintaining other aircraft while the pilots flew ferry missions. In

September 1942, newer model Hurricanes arrived, modified for desert flying, and, later, Spitfire Mark VBs. The squadron stayed in the Nile Delta until the spring of 1943, when it was attached to the famed Desert Air Force. It flew escort and fighter bomber missions for the British Eighth Army in the last stages of the fighting in Tunis and again in the Sicily campaign.

No. 418 Squadron, formed in November 1941, was the RCAF's only intruder squadron with the task of flying day and night strikes deep into enemy-held territory. Equipped initially with American-built twin-engine Boston bombers, the squadron flew its first night mission in late March 1942, attacking enemy airfields in the Abbeville area of France and in the Netherlands. The main purpose of night intruder missions was to disrupt enemy bomber and fighter operations by attacking their airfields. If the squadron's timing was especially good, it might even find itself approaching Luftwaffe bases while German bombers or night-fighters were taking off or landing. One of the most effective tactics for a night intruder, German and Allied alike, was to join the enemy's landing pattern and approach the field as if it was a bomber returning home. Then, at the last minute, the intruder might shoot down a landing bomber and shoot up or bomb just-landed aircraft before they reached their dispersal areas. At other times intruders were used as low-level strike aircraft against a variety of enemy targets. No. 418 gave up its Bostons in mid-1943 and acquired the fast, light Mosquito, which it flew to the end of the war.

As many as six RCAF squadrons flew with the RAF's Coastal Command during the war. The first, No. 404, was a coastal fighter unit formed in the United Kingdom in April 1941. Flying twin-engine Blenheim, Beaufighter, and Mosquito aircraft, it flew anti-shipping missions and escort for heavier Coastal Command aircraft operating in the Bay of Biscay. No. 423 Squadron, formed in May 1942, flew the heavy four-engine Short Sunderland flying-boat on convoy escort and anti-submarine patrols until the end of the war. Its crews destroyed two U-boats and shared in the sinking of one other, beginning with U-753 on 13 May 1943.

After the bulk of German U-boat strength was shifted to French Atlantic ports such as La Rochelle and St Nazaire, the German submarines had to transit the Bay of Biscay before heading for their patrol areas. To save time and fuel, they usually attempted this crossing at night and on the surface. Improvements in Coastal Command tactics, weapons, and equipment increased the RAF's chances of finding and destroying these raiders. Better radar allowed the aircraft to detect the submarines from further away, while the Leigh Light — a blindingly powerful searchlight mounted under the wing of an aircraft — fixed the U-boat in the final moments of attack. Hunting surfaced U-boats was not like shooting at sitting ducks. As the war progressed, the U-boats carried better aircraft detection radar and more and heavier anti-aircraft weapons. One No. 423 Squadron Sunderland discovered these advances to its cost on 4 August 1943, when it was shot down by a mortally stricken U-489, which it had just attacked. Five of the Sunderland's crew were killed, and the rest — all wounded — were picked up by a British destroyer along with the U-boat's survivors.

Although the RCAF made an important contribution to Fighter and Coastal Commands, its most significant contribution to the war effort up to the end of 1942 was in the form of its eleven bomber squadrons. The first of these, No. 405, flew its first operational mission as part of the RAF's No. 4 Group of Bomber Command on the night of 12/13 June 1941, when its Vickers Wellington twin-engine medium bombers attacked Schwerte, southeast of Dortmund. No. 405 was to have an illustrious career with Coastal Command, with No. 6 Group (RCAF), and with No. 8 Group (Pathfinders) of Bomber Command before the war ended.

No part of the Allied war effort was as technically complex, as destructive to Germany's cities, and as controversial as the night area bombing campaign waged by the RAF's Bomber Command from late 1940 to virtually the end of the war. German statistics gathered after the war indicate that more than half a million German civilians were killed in this campaign and more than three million dwellings were destroyed, but the verdict is still open about how effective the area bombing campaign was in shortening the war. To this day there is considerable controversy about the aims, methods, and results of the Bomber Command offensive against Germany.

The night area bombing campaign was rooted in the experience of the First World War. In that war both sides initiated long-range bombing operations ostensibly designed to destroy "strategic" targets such as key rail junctions, aircraft factories, and munitions plants. The Germans used both lighter-than-air Zeppelins and bombers; they usually came at night. They bombed not only factories but also neighbourhoods. Given the extreme difficulty of hitting anything with a bomb from a high altitude, especially in the dark, that was not surprising. Nor was it unwelcome to the attackers, because of the impact it might have on civilian morale.

The British and the French, using bombers only, followed suit. For all intents and purposes, air defence against this sort of bombing was nonexistent. Anti-aircraft guns were crude and inaccurate, and fighters did not have sufficient warning time to reach an altitude high enough to intercept the raiders. Although there was no wholesale panic in the streets of London, many civilians were demoralized by the helplessness they felt as the Zeppelins droned above them in the dark. The Royal Flying Corps and the Royal Navy transferred a large number of fighter squadrons to the United Kingdom from the fighting front in France to bolster the air defences of the capital.

In the interwar years, a number of air-power theorists speculated that long-range strikes at so-called strategic targets would not only impair the enemy's ability to fight but create mass panic among civilians, shorten wars, and eliminate the need for large armies. One of the most important of these men was Hugh Trenchard, the first Chief of the Air Staff of the RAF, who was responsible for what became known as the Trenchard Doctrine. That doctrine held that an independent airforce, mounting a strategic bombing offensive, would do incalculable damage to an enemy and might even win a war by itself. The bombing of civilians by the Japanese in China and the Nationalists in Spain in the late 1930s seemed to bear these theories out. The RAF was closely wedded to these notions in any case, since the independent war-fighting role envisioned for it by Trenchard and others rationalized the RAF as a force independent of the army and the navy, with its own command structure, and drawing separately on the resources of the nation. Thus, as war clouds gathered in Europe in the 1930s, the RAF embarked on an ambitious program of bomber development and construction, even diverting important resources from the production of modern fighters for air defence.

But what was strategic bombing anyway? To some theorists, especially in the United States Army Air Force, strategic bombing involved pinpoint attacks at important industrial targets whose destruction would hurt the enemy war effort. Such targets would include factories building weapons, or factories supplying parts such as ball bearings that were vital to modern weapons systems. Civilians would most certainly be killed, but they were civilians whose labour directly aided the enemy war machine. Besides, it was not the civilians who were the targets, but the factories they worked in. The problem with this theory was that it assumed great accuracy on the part of the bombers. As the experience of war bore out, that was a large assumption, even for daylight bombing. It would prove well-nigh impossible at night.

The early months of the war produced mixed evidence about the effectiveness or the importance of strategic bombing. The Luftwaffe, unlike the RAF, had been built primarily with a tactical mission in mind; its prime purpose was to aid, supplement, and even complement the striking power of the ground forces. German bombers were used not so much to bomb cities but to hit enemy strongpoints, blast enemy forces, help clear the way for the mobile forces on the ground, and harass the enemy as he fled. The Germans certainly bombed cities and civilians — Warsaw and Rotterdam stand out — but these were not primary targets. This difference had nothing to do with morality, and everything to do with German military doctrine. Although German bombing of cities and civilians produced spectacular damage and many casualties, it was not clear that it contributed anything significant to German victories.

As for the RAF, its early bombing campaign was a disaster. RAF bombers, such as the single-engine Defiant light bomber and the twin-engine Hampden, Whitley, and Blenheim, were too slow and lightly armed to fend off fighter attacks successfully during daylight raids. The twin-engine Wellington was the best of the RAF's medium bombers and was kept on operations long after the others had been removed from service, but it, too, was extremely vulnerable to fighters. These bombers suffered frightful losses when they were used to attack enemy installations or troop concentrations during daylight. After the Battle of France, the RAF began to switch almost exclusively to night bombing, which brought a whole new set of problems.

Just as the darkness hid a bomber from defenders, it also hid the target and the route to the target from the bomber crew. The Germans had partially solved this problem by using radio beams to guide their bombers during the London Blitz and the other night attacks on British cities in the late fall of 1940 and the winter of 1940/41. Although the Germans could locate large cities using such devices, they could not pick out individual targets within those cities. Thus, German night bombing had amounted to area bombing — the bombing not of specific targets but of whole areas of cities with their houses, apartment blocks, hospitals, and schools, as well as factories, dockyards, and government buildings.

The RAF's night-bombing campaign began in earnest in May 1940 with attacks on the industrial Ruhr. From then until early 1942, the campaign essentially consisted of RAF crews trying to pick their way over the blacked-out European countryside, find their targets in the dark and often in bad weather, hit something, and get home before dawn. The bomber force was small, and too many targets were usually attacked in one night to allow any real concentration of effort. The crews were often unable to locate, let alone bomb, their targets. When they did, little damage was done because accuracy was virtually impossible. The RAF bombed fields and forests, lakes and rivers, peaceful farming villages and city neighbourhoods; it even, occasionally, bombed something important, but not very often. On many occasions the Germans had a hard time trying to figure out just what the RAF had been trying to hit. RAF bomber losses were lower than in the previous daylight raids, but there were still losses from enemy night-fighters, anti-aircraft fire, mechanical failure, collisions, and crash landings in the United Kingdom, especially when morning fog hid runways from the tired eyes of fatigued pilots. In August 1941 D.M. Butt of the British Cabinet Secretariat issued a report on the effectiveness of the RAF's bombing, and concluded that of the two-thirds of RAF bombers that had claimed to have attacked their assigned target on any given night (the other third had returned early or gotten lost), only one-third came within even 8 kilometres of their targets. When the Ruhr was attacked, only one crew in ten came close. On dark moonless nights, the average was one crew out of fifteen. The search for more effective bombing techniques intensified.

The Germans were not idle either. Under General der Nachtjagd Josef Kammhuber they developed a system of night-bomber interception that used early warning Freya radar and Würzburg interception radars working in conjunction with night-fighters. The German coastal defence belt was divided into territorially defined boxes. In each box, ground radar guided a single night-fighter to its target. Searchlights were supposed to illuminate the enemy bombers to allow the night-fighters to home in on them. German anti-aircraft fire within these boxes was also radar controlled. In early 1942 the night-fighters began to be equipped with airborne Lichtenstein radar. Thus, a bomber was tracked from the ground, the night-fighter pilot was guided to the bomber by a ground controller, the radar operator aboard the night-fighter then detected the bomber on his own set, and the fighter bore in from below and to the rear and opened fire, aiming at the bomber's wingroots where the gas tanks were located.

Across the English Channel, a number of developments from early 1941 to early 1942 marked an intensification of the RAF's bombing campaign and a dramatic escalation in Bomber Command's ability to find and attack targets. In February 1941 the four-engine Short Stirling entered RAF service. It was the first of what would eventually prove to be a massive fleet of heavy bombers. The Stirling suffered from too low an operational ceiling and was largely removed from front-line service by the beginning of 1943, but was replaced by two other mainstays of the heavy bomber force, the Handley Page Halifax and the Avro Lancaster, both of which began to enter service with Bomber Command in early 1942. The Lancaster was by far the better of these two aircraft; the Halifax suffered from a large number of serious design flaws that afflicted most of its marks until late in the war.

In late February 1942 Arthur Harris took over Bomber Command. A dedicated follower of the Trenchard Doctrine, he wanted to knock Germany out of the war by air bombardment alone. He was a strong supporter of area bombing and scorned what he called "panacea" targets — factories that produced strategic materials or weapons systems. He believed that intensive bombing of German cities would not only kill and wound the civilians who worked in the war plants, but would also destroy their homes and their morale. This view was strongly supported by Sir Charles Portal who, along with Churchill, thought of the bombing campaign as the only "second front" Britain might mount against Germany at that stage of the war. That belief had intensified after Germany invaded the USSR in June 1941; bombing seemed to be one of the few ways the United Kingdom might aid its new ally, both by attacking Germany's war-making capacity and by forcing it to divert resources to air defence purposes.

The introduction of the Gee navigational device and the bomber stream seemed to provide Harris with the means of achieving his objective. Gee consisted of ground stations in the United Kingdom sending out intersecting radio beams that were picked up by a receiving set in each bomber. When the beams intersected over the intended target, the bomber dropped its load. But there were two major problems with Gee: it could not be used for targets deep inside Germany, owing to the curvature of the Earth, and it was easy to jam. Later in the war, Gee would be replaced by Oboe — another radio navigation device — and H2S airborne targeting radar. The bomber stream was a method of concentrating the main bomber effort on a single target, and hitting that target with all available aircraft in the shortest possible time. It was also a way of overwhelming the German night defences by putting many more bombers through the defensive boxes than the Würzburg radars and night-fighters could possibly handle. By the end of 1942, elite pathfinder crews dropped a series of target marking and illumination flares to guide the bombers that followed. The bombloads also changed; the bombers started to carry a mix of high-explosive bombs designed to blow the roofs off buildings, and incendiaries to start fires inside the building shells. The first time these techniques were used together in a raid was in March 1942, when 234 bombers were sent to attack the German port city of Lubeck; 191 aircraft pressed home the attack and dropped about 270 tonnes of bombs, including 129 tonnes of incendiaries. Only 312 people were killed, but more than 15,000 were made homeless.

The first of the RCAF's bomber squadrons, No. 405, took part in these attacks, as did the other RCAF bomber squadrons as they became operational. No. 405 began flying the four-engine Halifax in April 1942, while the rest of the RCAF bomber squadrons stayed on twin-engine aircraft for some time after; No. 419 converted to Halifaxes in November 1942 and No. 408 did the same one month later, but the other RCAF bomber squadrons continued to fly Hampdens or Wellingtons until well into 1943. The Canadian squadrons were placed with existing Bomber Command groups — No. 419 Squadron with No. 3 Group, No. 405 with No. 4 Group, and Nos. 408 and 420 with No. 5 Group, generally considered the best all-round group in Bomber Command. A French-Canadian unit — No. 425 "Alouette" Squadron — went operational in June 1942 with No. 4 Group.

A typical night mission was a harrowing experience for the young men of Bomber Command. After the crews were briefed in late afternoon, they were taken out to their aircraft in the gathering dusk to wait for the final word on whether the mission would go ahead. This decision usually depended on last-minute weather updates received from high-flying reconnaissance aircraft that had been sent out over Germany earlier in the day. Lolling under the wings, they would smoke or talk or daydream as they tried to keep their minds focused on anything but the dangers they were about to face. Then, when word came that they would go ahead, they each urinated on the tail wheel for good luck before they squeezed into their respective crew positions. Equipment was checked, lucky charms and talismans were stowed away, and engines were started and run for instrument checks; then the wheel chocks were pulled away and the aircraft began to roll towards the perimeter track. As each bomber reached the takeoff point, the pilot stood on the brakes and ran up the throttle; then brakes were released, the heavily loaded bomber gathered speed, and, if all went well, it pulled away from the runway and into the darkening sky over southern or eastern England. Sometimes all did not go well and several tonnes of metal, bombs, gasoline, and human flesh hurtled off the runway and crashed into power poles, trees, or low hills, creating a massive explosion and leaving a funeral pyre to mark the way for the aircraft that followed.

And follow they did, climbing out in silence over the burning wreckage that had once borne friends and comrades.

Once airborne, the bomber began the long climb to its assigned altitude as the navigator guided the pilot into the bomber stream. At their crew stations, the men tried vainly to keep warm in the freezing night air and to perform their various tasks — the wireless air gunner monitoring the airwaves and peering out into the dark, the navigator watching his Gee set or taking star shots, the pilot sweating to keep the aircraft flying straight and true in the night air made turbulent by the passage of hundreds of other bombers. If there was moonlight, the crew could sometimes see other bombers and there was less chance of collision, but there was also a better chance of being spotted by night-fighters. If there was no moon, or if the bomber was flying in cloud, the men felt as though they were trying to move about a room blindfolded, never knowing when they were going to crash into some dangerous obstacle. In an instant, the tailwheel or the propellers of another bomber could come smashing through a windscreen or into the top of the fuselage. Worse, a night-fighter could sidle up underneath and blast away with cannon fire at the wingroots, setting gas tanks ablaze or exploding bombloads in one terrifying flash.

Throughout the bomber war the crews of American bombers, flying in daylight, could easily see incoming fighters and had time to bail out if their aircraft were stricken. The majority of them escaped their crippled bombers and survived. Flying in the dark, most of the crews of Bomber Command had little or no warning before they were attacked, and not enough time to make their escape; the great majority of those attacked died in their aircraft. Crew members, especially rear gunners, strained to catch a glimpse of an approaching night-fighter in time to warn the pilot to go into the stomach-wrenching corkscrew dive that offered the one reasonable chance of survival.

If they made it across the North Sea, across Occupied Holland or Belgium, across Germany, they approached the target, a confusing maze of searchlights, tracer, flares, and coloured target-markers cascading down from the pathfinders. As one pilot later remembered: "Gun flashes, photoflashes, bomb bursts, streams of tracer of all colours, and everywhere searchlights. Our target runs were like the weavings of a demented bird. With bombs away, we would turn breathlessly into the waiting darkness; sometimes we left fires behind us that could be seen for a great distance."[5] Always they left comrades behind, too. Often the passage of the bomber stream was marked by the flaming wreckage of shot-down bombers, some destroyed by night-fighters, others by flak. Loss rates climbed steadily, as more and more German targets were attacked and the crews' chances of completing their allotted thirty missions shrunk. The night-fighters did not let up as the bombers left the target area, but if the crew survived its run up to the target, it had a better than even chance of coming home. Occasionally they arrived to clear skies in a breaking dawn; often they came back to fog-shrouded runways. Thousands of crew members made it back to England only to die near their own airfields. The ones who did return, body and soul intact, were debriefed, ate a hearty breakfast, tried to sleep, and prepared to do it all over again.

Although Harris mounted two more thousand-plane raids after Cologne, on Essen and on Bremen, the results were not nearly as spectacular. In both cities, the bombers failed to achieve sufficient concentration to do extensive damage. It was clearly not possible to scrape enough aircraft together to continue these operations. There were too many losses in the Operational Training Units, both of crews and instructors, and Harris was in danger of mortgaging the future in exchange for a dubious advantage in the present. For the remainder of the year, Bomber Command sent smaller forces to attack targets at night and even during the day, when there was sufficient cloud cover to hamper day-fighter defences. The search for a means of improving accuracy also continued, even though official RAF bombing policy was changed in October 1942 to stress area attacks aimed at undermining German morale rather than the hitting of individual strategic targets. This change was little more than recognition that hitting specific targets at night was virtually impossible at that stage of the war.

This aspect of the bombing campaign has drawn the most controversy: attacking the morale of German civilians was clearly tantamount to attacking the civilians themselves and killing as many as possible. If, as some historians have alleged, this was done as the deliberate and sole objective of a campaign that actually contributed little or nothing to the war, and Harris, Churchill, Portal, and others knew this to be the case, then the campaign was at best immoral and at worst plain murder. The popular version of this argument was most spectacularly advanced in "Death by Moonlight," a television program first broadcast by the Canadian Broadcasting Corporation in *The Valour and the Horror* series in 1992. The conclusion reached by the authors of *The Crucible of War*, volume 3 of the official history of the RCAF, also reflects this view to some extent, though in a more scholarly fashion.[6]

There is no doubt that area bombing targeted civilians. In doing so, however, did it help to bring the war to a victorious conclusion as speedily as possible? Did it seriously damage the German war effort, and did it undermine German morale and contribute to the victory? If area bombing did contribute significantly to the Allied victory, then the killing of German civilians was an unfortunate but necessary component of the Allied war effort, a war effort intended to defend against Nazi aggression and to bring about the collapse of one of the most immoral and murderous regimes in modern history. It is important to this discussion to point out that Hitler started the war, that the Nazis waged a "total" war from start to finish, and that the Nazis aimed not only at the domination of Europe but at the wanton murder of millions of civilians.

Harris forecast many times that the RAF bomber offensive would win the war; the Allied ground forces would need only to occupy surrendered Germany after heavy bombing from the air. That was fantasy. The RAF did not have the capacity to defeat Germany from the air; it could have done so easily with a fleet of American-built B-29 Superfortresses and a score of atomic bombs, but such a bomber force was still some years in the future. On a small number of occasions, bombing attacks were mounted under conditions that allowed Bomber Command to achieve both accuracy and concentration and to wreak havoc on a German city, greatly damaging its capacity to produce war materiel, at least for a time. For the most part, however, the results of the bombing campaign were mixed, if the attacks are to be judged solely by their impact on war production; Cologne suffered great damage, but industrial production was back to normal a short time afterwards. That was primarily because there were few factories in the centres of German cities; most were located in the suburbs, which usually suffered only marginal damage from Bomber Command attacks.

In recent years there have been many claims that German industrial capacity did not suffer unduly from the bombing campaign: there was great slack in the German economy and the Germans showed a remarkable capacity to recover and rebuild; moreover, German morale was not undermined by the bombing. If true, these claims call the morality of Harris's bomber offensive into question because they imply that Bomber Command killed civilians simply to pile up bodies. This, however, is not the conclusion of American historian Williamson Murray, who has written extensively on the air war. While not discounting the damage Bomber Command did to industrial targets in its area bombing campaign, Murray points to another important Bomber Command contribution to victory:

The night bombing campaign's greatest contribution to the winning of the war was precisely what Harris claimed and what the conventional wisdom has so often discounted: The "area" bombing attacks did have a direct and palpable effect on the morale of the German population, and the German leadership, in response to that impact, seriously skewed Germany's strategy.

Murray points out that recent German scholarship shows that, as early as 1942, night bombing was having a serious impact on German morale and that, in 1943, it caused "a dramatic fall off in popular morale." Reports of the *Sicherheitdienst* (SD), the secret police, showed that the German people were increasingly restive, bitter, and angry with their leaders and that they blamed them for the tribulations of the bombing campaign. In Murray's view, this growing feeling of despair and anger forced German leaders to continue to waste resources on offensive weaponry in order to placate the demand for revenge:

> The SD reports, reflecting the popular mood, explain the leadership's demand for retaliation weapons (the V-1 and V-2), its willingness to waste the Luftwaffe's bomber fleet over the winter of 1944 even though faced with the threat of an Allied invasion, and its refusal to provide the necessary support to the fighter forces until military defeat was obvious and inescapable.[7]

In May and June 1942 the representatives of fourteen nations met in Ottawa to review and revise the British Commonwealth Air Training Plan. The Canadian government had already decided to push for the establishment of an all-Canadian bomber group to operate under the overall direction of Bomber Command. The British were less than ecstatic about this decision, fearing it might set a precedent for other Commonwealth countries in breaking up the operational unity of Bomber Command. The UK government knew, however, that it had little choice, given the Canadian government's contributions to the war, Canada's independent status, and the precedent already set for an independent Canadian army and navy. The RAF was also not happy, and the decision was particularly opposed by Harris. The RAF dragged its heels on this "Canadianization" until the Canadian government decided it would pay for the full cost of what was to become No. 6 Group (RCAF) Bomber Command, as well as the other RCAF squadrons in the United Kingdom. After that, there was no excuse for delay. No. 6

Group was to consist of the Canadian bomber squadrons then in England and whatever new ones would be formed; it was eventually supposed to be composed of Canadian groundcrew and aircrew commanded by Canadian officers, and flying Canadian-built aircraft (the Lancaster X). As we shall see in chapter 7, that goal was a long way away and, in fact, was never fully achieved.

On 1 January 1943 No. 6 Group went operational, with its headquarters at Linton-on-Ouse. Its order of battle consisted of eight bomber squadrons located at six bases in Counties Durham and York; two other squadrons were still attached to No. 4 Group, and one was on loan to Coastal Command. At its peak, it would include thirteen squadrons (with No. 405 being attached to No. 8 Group [Pathfinders]). It was a proud day for Canada, but it was also a day that ushered in a year of grave difficulties for No. 6 Group, high casualties, and the near defeat of the overall night-bombing offensive.

On 14 October 1942 the passenger ferry SS *Caribou* was on the last leg of its usual run between North Sydney, Nova Scotia, and Port aux Basques, Newfoundland. It had departed the Canadian coast at 1900 the previous evening and, escorted by the Bangor Class minesweeper *Grandmère*, headed across the Cabot Strait with its 237 passengers and crew. The ship was the sole link between the Canadian National Railways railhead in North Sydney and the Newfoundland Railway railhead in Port aux Basques. For seventeen years the *Caribou* had carried passengers and freight across the Gulf of St Lawrence and, on this night, as on most others, many of the passengers and crew were part of a closely knit gulf community that had sent its men to the sea in ships for generations.

The night was clear and cold, with a brisk breeze, no moon, and a faint glow from the aurora borealis. The *Caribou* and the *Grandmère*, keeping station to the rear as current regulations for night escort of a single vessel dictated, zigzagged through a slight swell. Most of the passengers aboard the darkened ferry were asleep. It was approaching 0221 Atlantic Standard Time; less than one kilometre away, Oberleutnant Ulrich Graf and the crew of U-69 waited for the two-ship convoy to pull into torpedo range. With the *Caribou* silhouetted against the faint northern glow, Graf could not miss. Lookouts on the *Caribou* and the *Grandmère* saw no hint of the low-lying submarine. The minesweeper carried no radar, and its position astern of the ferry gave it no chance of detecting the German on asdic. As the *Caribou* pulled into range, Graf gave the order to fire; moments later a single torpedo exploded amidship and the *Caribou* began to list. Then came a second explosion as the ferry's boilers blew up. The ferry settled quickly then, its guardrails almost to the water within a few minutes. From below, the engine and boiler-room gangs tried to scramble to the open deck. Passengers and crew made for the lifeboats amid the sounds and sights of their vessel breaking up. Some of the lifeboats had been shattered by the exploding torpedo; the rest were quickly jammed with fleeing people. Rafts and carley-floats drifted in the wake of the still moving ferry, carried forward now by its own momentum. Then, in less than five minutes, *Caribou* was sucked under; 136 of her passengers and crew perished in the cold waters of the strait.

The communities that ring the shores of the Gulf of St Lawrence were shocked by the heavy loss of life in the sinking of the *Caribou*, but by the fall of 1942 they were not surprised by the attack. They were all too aware that U-boats had been hunting in Canada's coastal waters since May of that year and that they had already accounted for many sinkings and much loss of life. It is ironic that while the RCN was struggling to meet its commitments for mid-ocean escort, it did not have sufficient strength to guarantee the safety of passenger or cargo vessels operating between Quebec City and the Cabot Strait. And although news of these sinkings could not be totally suppressed from a country at war (the matter was even debated in the House of Commons), the fact that U-boats operated not only in the Gulf of St Lawrence but also in the St Lawrence River itself remained unknown to most Canadians for many years after.

❋

What Canadians would eventually call the Battle of the St Lawrence had its roots in the Japanese attack against the United States Pacific Fleet at Pearl Harbor on the morning of 7 December 1941. That attack prompted the United States not only to declare war on Japan but to pull virtually all its destroyers out of the Atlantic battle and send them to support the now dangerously weakened Pacific Fleet. It also brought the United States into the war against Germany, when Hitler declared war on the formerly neutral power on 11 December 1941.

In the long run, the US entry into the war was the crucial difference between a Nazi victory (or a Nazi-dictated stalemate in Europe) and Allied victory. In the short run, it added to the already tremendous burden on the Royal Canadian Navy. The US doctrine of anti-submarine warfare held that only fast, well-equipped destroyers should be used to escort merchant convoys, and the United States refused to use smaller, more make-shift anti-submarine vessels similar to Canada's corvettes, minesweepers, or Fairmile motor launches. Thus, with the exception of a handful of US destroyers and Treasury Class Coast Guard cutters (roughly equivalent to corvettes in speed, but larger and better armed), few US anti-submarine ships remained in the Atlantic by early 1942. That meant that the Royal Canadian Navy had to fill the gap left by the Americans and throw its largely corvette navy more fully into mid-ocean escort work. Henceforth the RCN would not

hand over convoys to the RN at the mid-ocean meeting point and head for Iceland; from February 1942 on, RCN vessels shepherded their charges all the way
across the North Atlantic. This change was marked by the termination of the
Newfoundland Escort Force and its replacement by the Mid-Ocean Escort Force
(MOEF), which consisted primarily of British and Canadian escort groups and a
handful of US warships.

In the new convoy scheme, fast merchant convoys would depart from Halifax
(or New York after September 1942), and slow ones from Sydney (later Halifax),
Nova Scotia. They would be escorted to the Western Ocean Meeting Point
(WESTOMP), southeast of Newfoundland, by the largely Canadian ships of the
Western Local Escort Force (WLEF). At WESTOMP, the WLEF would hand its
charges to the MOEF and proceed to St John's for refuelling and provisioning,
before heading back to sea to pick up a westbound convoy for Halifax or New
York. The route travelled by the WLEF was dubbed the "triangle run." The MOEF
would take charge of eastbound convoys at WESTOMP and accompany them to
a point just off Ireland — the Eastern Ocean Meeting Point — where they would
hand their charges to the RN and then head for Londonderry, Northern Ireland.
From there, they would return to sea and meet a westbound convoy, which they
would take to WESTOMP, before heading back to St John's. As this system was
inaugurated, the main convoy routes were also shifted south, away from Iceland,
to shorten the convoy track. This rerouting somewhat alleviated the requirement
for additional escort vessels, but it also put the main convoy track more squarely
into the wider part of the air gap — that area of the mid-ocean which could not be
reached by shore-based anti-submarine patrol aircraft and which was known as
the black hole.

SC 47, sailing in early February, was the first convoy to follow the new routing; it was accompanied by six RCN corvettes, including *Spikenard* as the escort
commander's vessel. On the night of 10 February the U-boats attacked, sinking
Spikenard and a tanker; the corvette went down so quickly that no distress call was
possible. It was only after she could not be raised by radio that her consorts noticed her absence; a search for survivors turned up eight men clinging to a carley-
float in the bitterly cold water.

Londonderry, or Derry, as it became known, was a great improvement over
Hvalfjordhur, Iceland. The westernmost port in the United Kingdom, it had
been chosen by the Admiralty in the summer of 1940 as a major base for anti-
submarine operations in the North Atlantic. By September 1940 the sights and

Troops arrive in Hong Kong aboard HMCS *Prince Robert,* 16 November 1941. PA 114820

Disaster on the Dieppe beach, 19 August 1942. C 17291

The corvette HMCS *Agassiz*. PA 115875

Admiral L.W. Murray presents an award to a *St Croix* crew member after the sinking of submarine U-90 by the *St Croix* on 24 July 1942. PHOTOGRAPHER H.A. IRISH. PA 37456

HMCS *St Croix* off Halifax, March 1941. The ship in the distance is HMS *King George V*. PA 105306

The captured German submarine U-190 is escorted from the Bay of Bulls to St John's, Newfoundland, 3 June 1945. PA 112877

The frigate HMCS *St Stephen* near Esquimalt, British Columbia, 14 August 1944. PHOTOGRAPHER KEN MACLEAN. PA 150156

The River Class destroyer HMCS *Restigouche* in Halifax, 1940. PA 104199

Commander J.P. Prentice on the bridge of HMCS *Chambly*, 1941. PA 151743

Pilot Officer George G. Beurling on his return from Malta in November 1942. PA 176977

Vice-Admiral P.W. Nelles (RIGHT), Air Chief Marshal L.S. Breadner (SECOND FROM RIGHT), and other officers at the Quebec Conference in 1943. C 8853

Canadian troops land in the Aleutian Islands, Kiska, Alaska, August 1943. PA 163415

Canadian troops in an assault landing craft during an invasion training exercise in southern England, July 1942. PA 116273

A Sherman tank of the Three Rivers Regiment amid the ruins of Ortona,
Italy, 23 December 1943. PHOTOGRAPHER T.F. ROWE. PA 114029

Bomb damage at Pontecorvo, Italy, as Canadians advance through the Hitler Line,
24 May 1944. PHOTOGRAPHER R. NYE. PA 144723

Burnt-out German Tiger tank on the
Agira–Regalbuto road, Sicily.
PHOTOGRAPHER J.E. DE GUIRE. PA 130337

A captured German 88-millimetre
anti-aircraft gun, without the carriage,
at the Royal Canadian School of
Artillery, Petawawa, Ontario. C 4796

Canadian stretcher-bearers carry a wounded soldier, Italy, October 1943. PHOTOGRAPHER TERRY ROWE. PA 141622

Major-General E.L.M. Burns at Larino, Italy, 18 March 1944. PHOTOGRAPHER C.E. NYE. PA 134177

sounds of construction dominated harbour vistas as refuelling facilities, repair shops, drydocks, and warehouses were built, rebuilt, or expanded. In June 1941 the Americans arrived and built a destroyer base, complete with a new repair yard and a fuelling facility, next to the RN base. The Royal Navy could use the US facility as long as the United States Navy had first call on it.

Entering Londonderry after a storm-tossed crossing of the North Atlantic was balm to a weary sailor's soul. In the words of James Lamb: "To arrive at Derry after a hard east-bound crossing was a little like approaching the pearly gates."[1] As the rust-streaked corvettes entered the mouth of the River Foyle, the deep green of the Irish countryside engulfed them; each kilometre they sailed up river was one step closer to respite and one farther from the brutal war at sea they never became inured to, no matter how many merchantmen they saw blown up or how many human remains they spotted drifting in oily waters. The quaint old town welcomed them and offered them succour. Too often they had little time for anything more than a quick turn around, and then they were out again to face the grey Atlantic; for most of 1942 there were still too few escort vessels to afford the luxury of a week in port to heal minds and bodies and to make minor repairs on ships. There was always another westbound convoy to shepherd, another escort group that needed the addition of one more corvette.

The entry of the United States into the war as a full participant removed the last restraints on Dönitz's U-boats in the Atlantic; now American shipping was fair game wherever it could be found. It did not take long for the U-boat captains to discover that it could be found in great abundance right off the coast of the United States itself. Despite all that the history of submarine warfare from 1917 on should have told them, the Americans were unprepared for the onslaught against their shipping. They did not convoy, preferring to send their ships out alone; and they insisted on sweeping the empty sea lanes for U-boats, rather than letting the U-boats come to them. What is even more puzzling is their failure to recognize the importance of air cover to keep U-boats down and to impede their surface access to the shipping lanes. By far the majority of the ships sunk off the US coast in this period were lost within range of shore-based aircraft. Why, then, should the German submarine headquarters, BdU, risk losses attacking convoys in mid-ocean, when fat cargoes were there for the sinking up and down the eastern seaboard of North America, often within sight of land? Thus Dönitz launched Operation Paukenschlag (Drumbeat), pulling boats out of the mid-Atlantic and the Mediterranean and sending them to US coastal waters. There they experienced their second "happy time" of the war and sunk close to two million tonnes of shipping in the first six months of the year. In May and June alone the German submarines accounted for more than a million tonnes of sinkings in US coastal waters. Some of this shipping was local, but much of it was destined for the eastbound North Atlantic convoys. If these ships continued to sink even before they reached the western convoy terminuses at Halifax or St John's, there would be precious little for the transatlantic convoy escorts to guard on the sea lanes to Britain. The point was not lost on the British Admiralty, which constantly urged the United States to institute a convoy system of its own. Slowly, as the coastal losses increased, so did the wisdom of the USN; with help from the RN and the RCN, the rudiments of a coastal convoy system were constructed by the summer of 1942.

The withdrawal of most of the USN's destroyers from the North Atlantic and the enlarging of the sea-war theatre increased the strain on the RCN. By mid-1942 half the escort vessels and a quarter of the aircraft patrolling the Atlantic sea lanes north of New York were Canadian. From December 1941 to July 1942 Ottawa effectively administered the shipping system in the western Atlantic north of the equator. The initial failure of the Americans to protect shipping in US coastal waters meant that the tanker routes from eastern Canada to the Caribbean were vulnerable. Any serious diminution of the fuel-oil supply to east-coast ports would have had a serious impact on the Canadian war effort. In May, seven precious corvettes were diverted from North Atlantic duties and placed on the Trinidad–Halifax tanker run; seven more were added to the southern convoy routes in August. The warm sun of the semi-tropics, the blue of the Caribbean, and the lure of exotic islands were welcome relief to those sailors lucky enough to be assigned to the southern tanker routes, but the loss of these escorts to the WLEF and the MOEF was serious.

On 8 May 1942, U-553, commanded by Korvettenkapitan Karl Thurmann, slipped through the Cabot Strait into the Gulf of St Lawrence and took up station about 80 kilometres north of the Gaspé coast; in the early hours of 12 May Thurmann torpedoed and sank the steamers *Leto* and *Nicoya*. The sinkings were not unexpected; the RCN had believed for some time that U-boats might penetrate the gulf and even the river itself, and had prepared a defensive plan based on the scarce air and surface resources then available. There was not much. The RCN's gulf strength consisted of five Bangor Class minesweepers, three Fairmile motor launches, and an armed yacht, while Eastern Air Command was already pressed to the limit supplying air cover for the Atlantic convoys.

Although the RCN and the government believed it was important to keep the gulf open to ocean-going ships, there were only so many anti-submarine resources to go around. Virtually all the important war cargoes that crossed the gulf in ships could have been sent to Halifax or Sydney or any number of US ports by rail for shipment to the United Kingdom. True, the rail network in eastern Canada and the northeastern United States was already heavily burdened, but at least cargoes sent by rail would not end up at the bottom of the gulf. Even before the battle of the gulf broke out, it was decided to resist stripping escorts from Canadian ocean escort groups so as to protect gulf or river shipping. Such diversion would only have weakened those escort groups doing the most important job, and would have given the Germans an advantage.

Though gulf waters were shallower than those of the North Atlantic, anti-submarine operations there were more difficult than they were at sea. The mixing of the fresh water from the St Lawrence River with the salt water of the gulf, compounded by the tricky tides and currents, layered the water into different zones of temperature and salinity that bent asdic beams. Submarine captains learned to take advantage of these conditions to hide both before and after attacks.

The two sinkings on 12 May sparked off intensive air patrol activity and led the RCN to inaugurate cross-gulf convoys for ships carrying strategic goods. These measures, in addition to heavy fog, effectively prevented Thurmann from scoring any more kills and, on 22 May, he left the gulf to hunt elsewhere. A little over a month later, U-132 took his place with orders to attack gulf shipping and scout the eastern end of the Belle Isle Strait. Commanded by Korvettenkapitan Ernst Vogelsang, U-132 proceeded up the gulf virtually to the mouth of the St Lawrence. Late on 5 July Vogelsang attacked a Quebec–Sydney convoy, sinking three ships before dawn. Depth-charged by the minesweeper *Drummondville*, U-132 sustained minor damage but escaped to resume its war patrol in the gulf. This latest attack shook Naval Service Headquarters from its previous policy of holding the line in the gulf, and six corvettes were taken off North Atlantic duty and assigned to the Gulf Escort Force until the close of the gulf shipping season. This move did not prevent Vogelsang from scoring one final sinking off Cape Magdalen on 20 May in a daylight periscope attack. Then he, too, escaped.

The third incursion of German submarines into the gulf in 1942 was by far the most serious. Towards the end of August, U-517 and U-165 entered through the Strait of Belle Isle; on 27 August U-517 torpedoed and sank the United States Army transport *Chatham* in a daylight periscope attack at the western end of the strait. Later, towards evening, it and U-165 sank the freighter *Arlyn* and badly damaged the *Laramie*, another merchantman. Less than a week later U-517 struck again, slipping past two escorting corvettes to attack a small convoy and sink the freighter *Donald Stewart*. Eastern Air Command now concluded that two submarines were operating in the gulf, and it increased its air patrols over the gulf convoy routes. On the night of 6/7 September, however, the two U-boats sank the armed yacht *Raccoon* and four freighters. Four days later U-517 torpedoed the corvette *Charlottetown*, which sank in four minutes. Most of the crew escaped into the water, but many were maimed and killed when the corvette's depth charges exploded as the hulk went down: there had been no time to disarm them before the crew abandoned ship.

The choices now facing the navy and the government were stark: reinforce the Gulf Escort Force significantly or close the gulf to all but local shipping. The former course was out of the question; in August the Admiralty had requested Canadian help for the forthcoming assault on North Africa (Operation Torch), and the RCN had agreed to scrape seventeen vessels together for the task (see chapter 8). That could only be done by closing the gulf and releasing the Gulf Escort Force corvettes for duty in the Mediterranean or to relieve other corvettes going there. The fate of gulf shipping was sealed; on 9 September the order was given to close down the convoy and escort system for ocean-going cargoes. The railways would have to carry the extra burden.

The closing of the gulf did not stop local sailings carrying freight and passenger traffic between gulf ports. There were still targets for U-boats to shoot at, and shoot they did. U-517 and U-165 sank four more ships and damaged another on the night of 15/16 September, before making for the Atlantic. Not long after their departure, U-69 passed through the Cabot Strait to spearhead the last German war patrols inside the gulf in the 1942 shipping season. It was joined several days later by U-106 and U-43, which set up station in the Cabot Strait. U-69 torpedoed and sank the freighter *Carolus* early on 9 October, and U-106 torpedoed and sank the *Waterton* at midday on 11 October. The *Waterton* and its cargo of paper sank in eight minutes, and U-69 moved off in search of other targets. It found what it was looking for in the early morning hours of 15 October, when the

Caribou hove into view. The sinking of the *Caribou* was the climax of the 1942 Battle of the St Lawrence. U-69, U-106, and U-43 departed soon after. In mid-November U-518 entered the gulf to land a German spy on the Gaspé shore, then left the area to begin a patrol off Halifax. The spy was quickly discovered and arrested; U-518 sank no ships in the gulf.

The gulf incursions were as successful as they were daring. In five months the U-boats had sunk one corvette, one armed yacht, and nineteen freight or passenger vessels and had heavily damaged two other merchantmen. The government had been forced to divert escorts to the gulf, even though escorts were in short supply elsewhere; then it had closed the gulf altogether, causing additional problems for the already overburdened rail network. The Germans paid virtually nothing for the havoc they had wreaked. In the entire five-month period, not a single German submarine was sunk in gulf waters; not one was even severely damaged.

🍁

In the larger scheme of things, the Gulf of St Lawrence was not an important theatre of war; the North Atlantic was. Shortly after the Americans became full-blown allies of the British and the USSR, Churchill and his staff travelled to the United States to lay joint plans for the future conduct of the war. He and Roosevelt agreed that their first priority was to knock out Germany, then to turn to Japan; they also agreed that an invasion of Occupied Europe was the only way that Germany could eventually be defeated. Before they could begin to think seriously of launching that invasion, the United States would have to build up its land and air forces in the United Kingdom to the point where a combined Allied assault would stand a reasonable chance of success. That build-up was dubbed Operation Bolero; it would not succeed if the slaughter at sea continued. The RCN, responsible for the protection of the convoys in the western Atlantic, would play a vital role in the success or failure of Bolero. This was an important challenge that the RCN had great difficulty in meeting in 1942.

The biggest problem, as always, was that the RCN had too little of everything. True, corvettes were now being launched in large numbers, but not large enough to allow the RCN to cover the Caribbean oil routes, escort convoys through the Gulf of St Lawrence, and still build permanent escort groups for the MOEF and the WLEF. Ideally there should have been enough corvettes to give escort groups sufficient time in port for rest, recuperation, and replenishment, but there were not. There were not enough to allow the RCN to set up permanent support groups, such as the RN was doing in 1942, dedicated and trained only to hunt submarines and positioned at sea to come to the aid of the escort groups of hard-pressed convoys. Canadian escort groups were chronically overworked, were usually short at least one vessel, and often contained a new vessel or two that were not used to working with the other ships. Although an escort group was supposed to have at least two destroyers by mid-1942, Canadian groups usually had only one. Even when they did have two, Canadian destroyers often ran low on fuel and were forced to make for the nearest port, leaving the escort group shorthanded. Refuelling at sea would eventually overcome this problem, but it was not standard operating procedure for convoy escorts in early 1942.

For most of 1942, the corvettes of the RCN remained at least a generation behind those of the RN in both design and equipment. As RN corvettes began to receive the excellent 271 radar, capable of detecting a surfaced U-boat, the Canadians were installing the SW1C, a Canadian variant of the British 286 which was good for little more than convoy station-keeping; it could almost never detect a surfaced U-boat. Canadian corvettes began receiving the 271 radar during refits at Derry, but not until late 1942. Even then, they could expect no more than ten sets installed each month. Nor did the Canadians have the latest in gyro-compasses, asdic equipment, or shipborne anti-aircraft weapons. Since the British were in short supply for this newer equipment, it was natural that they would put it on their own vessels first. On British corvettes the lengthening of the forecastle also meant that men would no longer have to cross the open deck to reach the forward mess decks. In addition, "hedgehog," a new anti-submarine weapon, was being installed. A multiple mortar that threw bombs ahead of an attacking vessel, hedgehog enabled the attacker to keep asdic contact as it approached its target during an attack. It also had the advantage of exploding only on contact, providing almost certain evidence of a hit. But the Canadians did not have enough corvettes for most of 1942 to pull more than a handful out of service for any length of time, in order to make these modifications and improvements.

Well into 1943 most Canadian captains continued to command their vessels from bridges that were almost totally exposed to wind and sea, protected only by a canvas "dodger" hung from the bridge railing. When mounting an attack against a submarine, they had to jam themselves inside the asdic hut at the rear of the bridge platform because it housed the only compass on the bridge. Aboard the corvette *Sackville*, Alan Easton found the task exceedingly difficult.

It was a bit of a squash inside the asdic house . . . Once wedged in alongside the compass it was a job to get yourself out. And to be able to make an exit was important. It was almost better to crane your neck in from outside through an open window. But that would have given you a distorted view of the compass card, and you would have needed the sight of a seagull to read the degrees.[2]

By early 1942, U-boat wolfpack tactics were familiar and even predictable. A line of U-boats would take up station across the usual convoy routes and would try to make visual contact with a convoy (unless they had prior intelligence about a convoy's position and direction). When one submarine made contact it would shadow the convoy, usually on the surface, from as far astern as possible, and would radio its position to BdU. BdU would then direct the rest of the pack to the appropriate place to make an attack. The U-boats preferred to attack at night, when they could fight on the surface and use their diesel engines to work their way in between the escorts and the merchantmen.

The RCN's lack of adequate radar during this period of the war meant that Canadian escort groups were, for all intents and purposes, fighting blind when they tried to counter these night attacks. By day they would sweep the flanks of the convoy to the limits of visual range. As night began to fall, the destroyer would leave its position at the head of the convoy and sweep far astern, trying to force any shadowing U-boats to dive. That would usually be combined with a convoy course change to throw any shadowers off. As darkness enveloped the ships, the escorts would move in close and sweep with asdic. In late 1942 some escort groups began to use the "major hoople." When the SOE (Senior Officer of the Escort) suspected that surfaced U-boats were lying in wait on the fringes of a convoy at night, he would order his escorts to carry out a major hoople to port or starboard. Then all the escorts on either the right or the left flank of the convoy would quickly do a 45-degree turn and begin firing starshells 90 degrees to the course of the convoy. The hope was that lurking U-boats would be illuminated and driven under. It was innovative, but no substitute for radar.

The RN, by contrast, was relatively well-equipped to fight this kind of war. By late 1942 virtually all its escort vessels carried high-frequency direction-finding devices (HF/DF), as did the convoy rescue ships. Thus U-boat transmissions could be intercepted, and the positions of shadowers or wolfpacks plotted by the convoy while at sea. Ultra intercepts were always helpful, but a

German code change in early 1942 deprived the Allies of U-boat Ultra for almost a year. Still, even if the U-boat signals could not be understood, their intentions could usually be discerned from their positions, giving the RN escorts a chance to spot them at night with their 271 radar.

The RCN's shortcomings trapped it in a vicious cycle. Prior to the US entry into the war it had been decided that the United States' destroyer-heavy anti-submarine force would shepherd the fast convoys (the HX series) across the mid-ocean, while the RCN, with its largely corvette fleet, would escort the slow convoys. This division was made partly because a corvette's top speed was 15 knots, and partly because of the overall state of training and equipment in the RCN. In practice, this meant that the RCN was given responsibility for convoys which, because of their slow speed, were more likely to be attacked, which would remain in danger longer, and which would spend more time in the black hole of the mid-ocean air gap. It also meant that the loss rates of RCN-escorted convoys would invariably be higher than those of the RN convoys, apparently "proving" to the British that the Canadians were incapable of doing the job properly.

Although these problems eventually put RCN escorts at a serious disadvantage once at sea, they had not become obvious even by mid-1942; in fact, the RCN performed well in a number of convoy battles in the summer of that year. While shepherding eastbound convoy ON 113 towards the end of July, *St Croix*, leading Escort Group C 2, sunk U-90; the convoy lost three freighters, two sunk and one damaged. Within days ON 115, escorted by Escort Group C 3, produced similar results. Though the convoy was constantly shadowed by as many as six U-boats, it lost only two merchantmen but accounted for U-588 sunk (by *Skeena* and *Wetaskiwin*) and one or two other submarines badly damaged. One of the latter was attacked by *Sackville*, whose captain, Alan Easton, later described the moment of sighting.

> The gun went off and I opened [my eyes] again. After what seemed like a long wait the star shell burst. There she was. A U-boat silhouetted against the falling ball of light. I had no need of my binoculars now. The U-boat lay broadside on, about fifteen degrees on the starboard bow, less than four hundred yards away. Her bow was pointing directly across our course and I saw a short boiling wake at her stern.[3]

Easton tried to ram, but the submarine crash-dived just in time to avoid the onrushing bow of the Canadian escort. As he passed over the turbulent water left by the diving boat, Easton called for depth charges. The submarine was blown to the surface, its bow pointing to the stars, before it disappeared once again, but it was not sunk.

For a time in the late summer of 1942 it might have appeared that a combination of better tactics, improved battle management, and more skilled crews and commanders was finally pulling the RCN even with the RN in anti-submarine warfare performance. Although merchant ships were still going down at a rapid rate, U-boat kills were climbing also. In late 1942, RCN escort vessels sank four U-boats in the North Atlantic and the Caribbean (U-94 sunk by *Oakville*). In the battle for SC 94, for example, the Germans sank eleven freighters but lost two U-boats, a rate of exchange they could not afford. Still, the real key to victory in the North Atlantic lay in closing the air gap in mid-ocean, something that was still far beyond the capabilities of the RCAF's Eastern Air Command. That failure would become jarringly apparent as the summer of 1942 slipped into fall.

❦

Eastern Air Command had come a long way since 1939. The armament carried by its aircraft improved greatly in the first two years of the war; by mid-1942 they were using more powerful depth charges, specifically designed for air dropping, which used detonators that could set off the explosives at much shallower depths. That was important, because the nature of airborne anti-submarine warfare was that attacks on U-boats invariably took place while the boats were either diving or just under the surface. Through trial and error, and with the new equipment, EAC crews began to patrol at higher altitudes, where they were more likely to catch a U-boat without being spotted and still have time for a well-planned attack.

Two major problems remained. The first was tactical. As historian Roger Sarty has written:

> Eastern Air Command responded to the German offensive with a wasteful and largely futile effort to fly close cover over as many convoys and independently sailed ships as possible. U-boats, easily evading these rigidly organized and widely dispersed defences, were able to press into and sink scores of ships in the heavily travelled coastal shipping routes and near approaches to harbours.[4]

The RAF's Coastal Command had learned the hard way that positioning aircraft to orbit over convoys might well keep shadowing U-boats down, but it accomplished little else. Coastal Command kept the coastal waters near the United Kingdom relatively U-boat free with offensive tactics: its aircraft swept far ahead of convoys, catching any waiting U-boats on the surface; and it sent aircraft to patrol only over those convoys that were definitely known, through Ultra or through HF/DF, to be threatened.

EAC Squadron leader N.E. Small, Commanding Officer of No. 113 Squadron based at Yarmouth, Nova Scotia, was a great believer in these Coastal Command tactics. He ordered white camouflage paint applied to the bottoms of his aircraft to make them harder to spot from a surfaced U-boat, and he urged his crews to use intelligence reports to pinpoint likely spots where submarines might be lurking on the surface. On 31 July he himself caught U-754 on the surface southeast of Cape Sable and sent it to the bottom. Despite Small's success (the first U-boat sunk in the war by EAC), it was not until late 1942 that EAC began to follow Coastal Command's approach to convoy protection. It was then that improved tactics and a good dose of luck produced one of EAC's best days of the war. On 30 October 1942 a Digby of No. 10 Squadron, based at Gander, Newfoundland, spotted U-520 on the surface while it was returning home from patrol duty with convoy ON 140; it sank the submarine in a quick attack with four depth charges. That same day a Hudson of No. 145 Squadron, based at Torbay, attacked and sank U-658 while it was on a routine air patrol about 510 kilometres east of Newfoundland.

EAC's second major problem was with the aircraft it was forced to use. Its fleet was composed primarily of twin-engine, medium-range Douglas Digbys, Lockheed Hudsons, and Consolidated Catalinas (PBYs). The PBY was probably the best of these aircraft, but it was agonizingly slow; when German submariners spotted the lumbering Catalinas from the bridge of a surfaced U-boat, they usually had ample time for a crash dive before they were attacked. None of these aircraft was in the same league as the major types coming into service with the RAF's Coastal Command — the long-range four-engine Short Sunderland (a flying-boat) and the American-built Consolidated B-24 Liberator.

The Liberator was the aircraft of choice. Designed as a strategic bomber, it was meant to carry a crew of ten and was heavily armed with machine guns. It had a range of approximately 3500 kilometres when it carried its normal 2268-kilogram load of bombs. When field-modified as the VLR (Very Long Range), it was stripped of most of its machine-gun armament and other equipment not needed for anti-submarine warfare and had extra fuel tanks installed in the bomb-bay. In this configuration, the aircraft range was virtually doubled. Had sufficient numbers of VLR Liberators been stationed on both sides of the ocean and in Iceland in early 1942, the mid-ocean air gap would have been eliminated.

The RAF began to fly VLR Liberators out of Iceland in late 1941, but the RCAF was denied these aircraft even though it tried desperately to get them. Everybody else seemed to want them, too, and Canada was low on the priority list. The B-24 was one of two heavy bombers (the other being the B-17) that equipped the heavy-bomber squadrons of the United States Army Air Force. Thus the USAAF had first call on all the B-24s it needed to build its heavy-bomber strength in the United Kingdom, the Pacific, and other theatres of war. The RAF also wanted B-24s, both as bombers (although few RAF B-24s were ever used in this way) and as anti-submarine aircraft. It was Coastal Command's firm belief that the best time and place to attack U-boats was when they were crossing the Bay of Biscay on the surface. Coastal Command demanded and received B-24s to be converted into radar-carrying, Leigh Light aircraft, even though the statistics proved conclusively that, on average, it took more than 300 hours of air patrolling to sight one U-boat in the Bay of Biscay, but only thirty hours of air patrolling to sight a U-boat when escorting ahead of convoys. The simple fact was that heavy bombers were a rare and valuable war-fighting commodity through most of 1942, and none were to be spared for Canada. Thus EAC would continue to push its twin-engine aircraft as far out to sea as it dared, knowing that the black hole beyond would continue to swallow up large numbers of merchantmen and their crews until it was eliminated by long-range aircraft.

On 5 September 1942 the RCN's Escort Group C 4, consisting of the destroyers *St Croix* and *Ottawa*, the RN corvette *Celandine* (equipped with a 271 radar that worked only intermittently), and the RCN corvettes *Amherst*, *Arvida*, and *Sherbrooke*, slipped their berths at Londonderry, sailed down the Foyle, and joined the westbound, thirty-two merchant-ship convoy ON 127 just before noon. Acting Lieutenant-Commander A.H. "Dobby" Dobson aboard the *St Croix* was SOE. C 4 was as experienced a coterie of RCN escort vessels as could be found in the late summer of 1942.

Unknown to Dobson or anyone else in ON 127, the convoy was spotted by a U-boat one day out of Londonderry; at BdU, Dönitz mobilized his charges for an attack. Although ON 127 sailed peacefully towards mid-ocean for the next five days, thirteen U-boats from two packs, *Vorwarts* and *Stier*, began to form a patrol line across the convoy lanes out of range of shore-based aircraft. ON 127 was spotted by the Germans on the night of 9 September, lost, then spotted again on the morning of the 10th. Then the U-boats moved in. The submarines worked in pairs as they approached the convoy; they came in from ahead during daylight, then dove under the lead escorts to deliver their first attacks from periscope depth.

The first sign the escorts had that ON 127 had run into a wolfpack came at 1430z (zulu or Greenwich Mean Time) on the 10th, when torpedoes fired by U-96 slammed into the sides of the *Elizabeth van Belgie*, the *F.J. Wolfe*, and the *Svene*. The *F.J. Wolfe* survived the attack, but the other two sank. Three more vessels were torpedoed later that day, one was sunk and two damaged. Dobson had neither the time nor the resources to press home attacks against his tormentors, but he also seems to have conducted a disorganized defence. With his small number of escorts, he should have realized the seriousness of his predicament and kept his ships together and in close proximity to the convoy, but he did not. At about midday on the 11th he took *St Croix* on a sweep far ahead of the convoy, sighted a surfaced U-boat, but was unable to press home his attack. He sent *Sherbrooke* on a long sweep astern that separated that corvette from the convoy for many hours. And he inexplicably ordered *Amherst* to stand by a stricken Norwegian ship to pick up survivors and then to sink the hulk. This left only four escorts to guard the convoy most of the day, clearly not enough. Three more ships were lost. The escorts fought back, but the attacks continued. In the early morning hours of 12 September another tanker was damaged (but not sunk), while a Panamanian steamship went down at noon on the 13th. So far the U-boats had damaged three merchantmen and sunk nine. At dusk on the 13th the RCN Town Class destroyer *Annapolis* and the RN destroyer *Witch* from the WLEF rushed to join *St Croix* and its consorts. The night was very dark and the seas were rough, but ON 127 was rapidly approaching EAC's eastern patrol limit. With two destroyers coming to reinforce the escort screen, it might have seemed that the battle of ON 127 was soon to conclude.

Ottawa was steaming ahead of the convoy, to port, and proceeding at about 15 knots as *Witch* hove into view, aldis lamp flashing signals. *Ottawa* turned slightly to the RN destroyer to return the signals, then turned back on course. Just then an explosion blew a large hole in its hull abeam the No. 1 gun turret. Its captain, Acting Lieutenant-Commander C.A. Rutherford, ordered all engines stopped as *St Croix* raced to her aid. *Ottawa* was settling evenly, but did not appear in danger of imminent sinking; the crew began to shore up bulkheads to contain the seawater in the open compartments. Then, as *St Croix* pulled alongside, a second torpedo tore into the starboard side of the stricken destroyer. The ship began to sink rapidly; the gunnery/torpedo officer raced to remove the depth-charge pistols lest they explode as the ship went down. As the water level rose, two men trapped in the asdic room could be heard in the voice tubes yelling for help. They could not be reached. About twenty stokers, some wounded in the first explosion, were also trapped in their mess deck. They, too, went down with the destroyer. Rutherford appears to have made it into the water, but was last seen handing his life belt to a rating. Within moments, *Ottawa* slipped beneath the cold North Atlantic; five officers and 109 ratings died with her.

ON 127 was a tragedy. A seasoned escort group had lost one of the RCN's precious River Class destroyers and nine merchantmen without taking any toll from Dönitz's submarines. The RCN thought that Dobson had done a competent job, but the British and the Americans had serious doubts. One British officer severely criticized Dobson's decision to waste escort resources by ordering his corvettes to stand by to destroy damaged freighters. The Americans thought his defence too tame. They believed that if he was going to strip escorts from the close screen to sweep his front and rear, he ought to have been far more aggressive in those sweeps. They and the RN began to doubt the ability of the RCN to carry out its assigned tasks in the mid-ocean; the RCN's reaction to the defeat was to mount an immediate effort to replace its lost destroyer and to accelerate the installation of the 271 radars on its vessels.

The RCN's fortunes did not improve in the weeks that followed. On 30 October C 4 sailed from St John's to escort convoy SC 107 to the United Kingdom. *St Croix* had been detached for a refit and *Ottawa's* place was taken by *Restigouche*, another River Class destroyer, but one fitted with HF/DF equipment. U-522 sighted the thirty-six ship convoy near Cape Race, and BdU placed a seventeen-boat wolfpack across its path. The attacks began with the torpedoing of *Empire Sunrise* after nightfall on 1 November. The escorts did what they could, chasing asdic and radar contacts, but the screen was far too weak for the number of attackers. In the early morning hours of 2 November, seven ships were torpedoed within a four-hour period. Two Canadian corvettes joined C 4 after daylight, but *Restigouche* remained the lone ship with the speed and endurance for long-range sweeps; one destroyer was not enough. In the next two days, seven more ships were torpedoed. The total count of merchantmen sunk before the convoy was further reinforced by three USN vessels at dawn on 5 November was fifteen; not a single U-boat had been sunk.

ON 127 and SC 107 were major convoy defeats for C 4 and reflected on the overall ability of RCN escorts to perform at this point in the war. But the final blow to the prestige of the RCN was yet to be struck. That came with the voyage of ONS 154, another westbound convoy. It was escorted out of Londonderry by C 1, which consisted of the HF/DF-equipped (but not yet calibrated) River Class destroyer *St Laurent* and five RCN corvettes. All were newly equipped with the 271 radar, but their radar operators had had no time to train. The fate of the convoy might have been different if C 1 had had time for sea trials with its radar sets, or if it had not been routed on a southern track, across the widest part of the air gap.

ONS 154 was spotted just after leaving the reach of shore-based aircraft by the twelve-boat wolfpack *Spitz* on 26 December. The battle began in heavy weather soon after, when U-356 passed through the convoy, sinking three ships and badly damaging a fourth. Spotted by *St Laurent* and attacked with gunfire and depth charges, U-356 went down with all hands. The Germans lost contact with the convoy for most of the next thirty-six hours and only one ship was lost, but firm contact was re-established on the morning of 28 December. From that point on the convoy was under constant attack. The special service ship HMS *Fidelity* was sunk, as were nine more merchantmen. Despite the sinking of U-356 (not confirmed until after the war), ONS 154 was the last straw for the Admiralty.

As early as mid-December, the Admiralty had started pressuring Churchill to request that Ottawa pull the RCN out of the mid-Atlantic battle and take over the UK–Gibralter run under decent air cover. They were becoming convinced that the important North Atlantic convoys could not be left in the hands of the C groups any longer — or not until the C groups had been properly trained and their equipment brought up to par with that aboard RN ships. They were all too aware that the vast majority of ships being lost at that point of the war were being escorted by Canadian groups. Vice-Admiral Percy Nelles and the senior RCN staff bitterly resented the suggestion that the RCN was not adequate, and they were not entirely wrong. The Canadians, after all, had the short end of the stick with the slow convoys; no one will ever know if RN escort groups might have done any better.

After ONS 154, the RCN could no longer deny that its contribution to the battle left much to be desired. Nelles gave in and, on 9 January 1943, Ottawa acceded to the British request. For the hard-pressed RCN, the withdrawal from the mid-Atlantic battle was the lowest point of the war.

O n 21/22 January 1944, somewhere in the darkened skies of northern Europe, a Halifax of the RCAF's No. 419 Squadron, based at Middleton St George in County Durham, struggled to reach its assigned bomber-stream altitude en route to Magdeburg, a key German rail centre. Staying in the bomber stream was no guarantee of survival, but it certainly increased the odds of returning. Bombers that drifted off track or flew too low were choice prey for the German night-fighters; they were easily spotted and just as easily picked off. The pilot of the Halifax was Warrant Officer I.V. Hopkins. He and his crew had heard a loud bang just fifty minutes after takeoff and had discovered that the landing gear would not retract all the way. Something was wrong with the aircraft's hydraulic system. As the fully loaded bomber crossed the Dutch coast, Hopkins could manage no better than 3900 metres, well below its assigned 6100-metres altitude. Hopkins ordered his bomb aimer to jettison some incendiaries, then managed to nurse the Halifax into the bomber stream.

Hopkins's bomber was one of 645 dispatched by Bomber Command to attack Magdeburg that night. The target offered some respite from Air Chief Marshal Arthur Harris's campaign against Berlin, which had started the previous August with three preliminary raids. The main Battle of Berlin had been launched in earnest in mid-November 1943; No. 6 Group and the other Bomber Command groups had hit Berlin with the ninth attack only the night before Hopkins took off for Magdeburg. There would be many more attacks on Berlin before Harris would call the battle off in late March. Casualties had risen as German night defences had improved. On the previous night's raid, the Luftwaffe had introduced a new tactic known as "tame boar": radar-equipped night-fighters directed to the bomber stream by ground controllers entered the stream and sought targets of opportunity as they flew along with the bombers. Many of the night-fighters were armed with a new weapon — Schräge Musik (jazz music) — 20-millimetre cannon mounted to the rear of the night-fighter cockpit, usually at a 60-degree angle, to fire upward into the vital spots of the bombers. Using this device, a night-fighter could sidle underneath an unsuspecting bomber, open fire at wing-tanks or bomb-bays, and blow bomber and crew to eternity with no warning at all.

Bomber Command was also using different tactics from those it had employed earlier in the war. Spoof raids were now routinely mounted to other cities in Germany to fool the ground controllers (usually by Mosquitoes spreading aluminum chaff), while the main force headed to its target. A new Pathfinder Force had been set up in late 1942 and had then been consolidated in a new No. 8 Group, established in January 1943, to lead the way to the target and to mark it with coloured pyrotechnics. A variety of newly developed technical wiles that both sides had been developing throughout the war — radar, radar jamming, spoof raids, radio-telephone transmission interception, IFF (Identification Friend or Foe) — were in use to achieve one of two basic aims. For Bomber Command, it was to bomb Germany long enough and heavily enough to win the war; for the Germans, it was to make the British bombers pay so high a price that they would stop their campaign before they achieved their objective.

Although much high strategy was being played out in the skies over Germany, little of that was in the minds of Hopkins and his crew as they approached Magdeburg. All they could see was a rolling plain of cloud; the target was totally covered. As usual in conditions like this, they aimed for the skymarkers that had been dropped by the Pathfinder Force — coloured flares descending beneath parachutes — and hoped they had done some good. Then they turned for Leipzig, with nose down, trying to pick up more speed for the run back to the coast. A German fighter flashed by in front of them from left to right. Hopkins pulled sharply right and dove. He did not hear the fighter's shells strike, but he saw his outer starboard engine burst into flame. He managed to get the fire out, feathered the engine, then resumed course, this time just under 3000 metres. Then the Halifax was attacked again, raked from below at least three times, probably by Schräge Musik. As Hopkins would later remember: "Upon starting evasive action the [starboard] inner [engine] burst into flame, cannon-shell hit the selection box and shrapnel hit me in [the] leg and shoulder, also wiping out some instruments." The bomb-bay was on fire, the gas tanks were leaking, the port engines were overheating, wind screamed through a hundred bullet holes, and Hopkins's controls were not responding. The Halifax was losing altitude fast; Hopkins ordered his crew to bail out, held the bomber steady as they did so, then jumped himself and watched his plane flip over and dive into the ground.[1] He and his crew were captured and spent the rest of the war in prisoner-of-war camps (one was later killed by Allied fighter bombers). They were lucky; the vast majority of Bomber Command crews whose aircraft were hit by German fighters did not survive.

No. 6 Group sent out 114 aircraft that night: thirteen returned early or aborted the mission because of some mechanical failure; eighty-six managed to locate and attack the primary target; and fifteen bombers with ninety-eight crewmen aboard did not return. That was a disastrous loss rate of 12.3 percent. In total, Bomber Command sent more than six hundred bombers to Magdeburg and lost fifty-seven — a loss rate of almost 9 percent. The attack was also a disaster; most of the bombs fell outside the city and little damage was done. No military force can survive when its losses are as high as those suffered by Bomber Command, and especially No. 6 Group, that night. And yet, five nights later, Hopkins's comrades took to the skies once more to continue the Battle of Berlin. There would be many more losses before the bomber offensive against Germany ended.

No. 6 Group (RCAF) was intended by the Canadian government to be one of the most important and highly visible symbols of Canada's independence and of its war effort against the Axis. Ideally it would be composed of Canadian pilots, aircrew, and groundcrew, commanded by Canadians, flying a Canadian-built aircraft — the Lancaster X. It would not act as an independent airforce, deciding its own strategy or choosing its own targets. It would have virtually complete administrative leeway, but operationally it would fall under the aegis of Bomber Command in the same way that the other Bomber Command groups did.

The man appointed Air Officer Commanding (AOC) No. 6 Group, Air Vice-Marshal G.E. Brookes, was forty-seven years of age at that time. British-born, he had come to Canada in 1910 and served in the Royal Flying Corps in the First World War. He had joined the fledgling RCAF and had filled a number of posts in the interwar years. Although he had no operational experience on bombers (but then, neither did Harris), he was considered a good trainer of aircrew, something that the neophyte No. 6 Group would definitely need.

Brookes had been one of three men considered eligible for the job of AOC; there were much fewer qualified Canadians, especially Canadians in the RCAF, available in Bomber Command for virtually all other levels of command in the new group. RCAF Canadians were appointed where possible; RAF Canadians were brought in where necessary and when available to be taken out of their own units without too much difficulty. But invariably many posts, including squadron leaders, went to British or other Commonwealth officers serving in the RAF. There was simply no choice.

There was also difficulty Canadianizing the aircrews themselves. In the United States Army Air Force it was standard practice to organize a heavy-bomber crew at home and then have that crew fly an aircraft to the assigned theatre of operations. That was not the case in Bomber Command. Canadian aircrew and others who had graduated from the BCATP's schools in Canada were brought to the United Kingdom and assigned to an Advanced Training Unit (ATU) to learn the basic craft of bombing, and then to an Operational Training Unit (OTU) where crews were assembled and training on actual bombers (usually obsolete or wornout aircraft) began. The assembly of crews was done in a large room (usually a hangar) in a haphazard way that resembled a high-school dance — most men stood about eyeing the others, while a few bolder ones went from cluster to cluster, often selecting crew members on the basis of a quick first impression. Until the RCAF established its own purely Canadian OTUs, there was no way to guarantee that the crews assigned to it would be all Canadian or even predominantly Canadian. Even then, there was a shortage of Canadian flight engineers; consequently, there was usually at least one Australian, South African, or Briton in most RCAF aircrews. For most of No. 6 Group's first year of operations, many of its flying personnel and most of its groundcrews were not Canadian. Indeed, in the whole course of the war, more Canadians served in the RAF, wearing either RCAF or RAF uniforms, than in the RCAF.

The group's problems with Canadianization of personnel did not impede its operational efficiency; other difficulties were far more serious, and there were a goodly number of them. It was important that all the bases of a particular group be located in the same general area of the United Kingdom. Such proximity made communications, personal travel, and shipment of everything from mail to equipment much easier. It also made it easier to service aircraft, since different squadrons usually flew dissimilar aircraft types, especially in the mid-years of the war. It was standard practice to station squadrons flying Hampdens, for example, near other squadrons flying the same aircraft.

Base location became a problem for No. 6 Group because it was the last bomber group formed in Bomber Command and because it began operations just as the US Eighth Air Force initiated a rapid expansion of its aircraft and bases. The Americans were apportioned the best base locations in the flat country of East

Anglia; No. 6 Group was assigned to the Vale of York farther to the north. Most of the bases were in Yorkshire, though Nos. 419 and 420 Squadrons were based at Middleton St George, in Durham, to the north of the other bases. Between the Canadian bases, which were almost at sea level, and the North Sea was a range of hills with a few peaks as high as 450 metres. Fully loaded bombers taking off for a night's mission had to clear these obstructions, sometimes in fog or low cloud; damaged bombers returning from long flights had to avoid them while they searched for their home fields. Because these bases were much farther away from the continent than the other Bomber Command bases, No. 6 Group aircraft sometimes had to land at airfields closer to the south coast so as to top up with fuel on either an outgoing flight or a return. Statistically, the chances of a bomber being damaged or destroyed climbed with each takeoff and landing cycle it made. Finally, the location of No. 6 Group's bases meant that the RCAF bomber squadrons often had to join the bomber stream near the Dutch coast, well within German night-fighter range. This gave them less protection as they neared the coast than bombers joining the stream closer to the United Kingdom.

For much of its history, No. 6 Group squadrons were also plagued with poorly performing aircraft. Although the Canadian-built Lancaster X with its Rolls Royce Merlin engines was a virtual copy of the Avro Lancaster I or III, it could not be built quickly enough or in sufficient numbers to equip an entire group. In fact, the first of these Lancaster Xs, named "The Ruhr Express," was not delivered until September 1943 and did not see action for some time after. Fewer than 500 were built in the entire war. The first RCAF bomber squadron to go operational on Lancaster Xs, No. 419, did not begin to receive the aircraft until March 1944; at war's end, only six of the group's fourteen squadrons were flying the Canadian-built bomber.

When No. 6 Group was born on 1 January 1943, only two of its squadrons — No. 408 and No. 419 — were flying heavy bombers, the Handley Page Halifax Mark II and Mark V. (No. 405 was also flying Halifaxes, but was under command of Coastal Command on 1 January 1943.) The remaining squadrons were flying twin-engine Wellingtons. Ottawa insisted that No. 6 Group be an all-heavy-bomber group (in fact, an all-Lancaster group), but there were not enough "heavies" available to convert quickly. When the Canadian squadrons did begin to make the changeover, it was usually to the Halifax, not the Lancaster.

The two versions of the Halifax most used in the first years of the bomber offensive — the Mark II and the Mark V — were killer aircraft. Poorly assembled, with lower operational ceilings than the Lancaster, they were cold and uncomfortable to fly. Worse, they were dangerous. Their exhaust flames were easily seen at night, they offered poor downward vision, their tail assemblies were badly designed, and their controls were too sensitive for the sort of violent manoeuvres required to evade night-fighters. When a pilot of a fully loaded Halifax II or V put his aircraft into the corkscrew turn and dive called for when a night-fighter was spotted, the bomber tended to go into a flat, upsidedown spin. Recovery was all but impossible. Loss rates of Halifax aircraft were consistently higher than the Merlin-equipped Lancasters. Harris hated them and had no use for Handley Page, their manufacturer.

Why was it that No. 6 Group squadrons tended to receive Halifaxes at the same time that RAF units such as No. 5 Group were being equipped with the much superior Lancaster? Some observers then and since have chalked it up to Harris's biases against dominion crews and his particular opposition to the forming of No. 6 Group. He had not been alone in that opposition. In general, the RAF and the British government would have much preferred to have had Canadians streamed into the RAF in the same way that other Commonwealth flight crew were. They believed it made for a stronger and more effective RAF, and they were not wrong from the point of view of war-fighting capability; it would have been less disruptive to Bomber Command if all its crews and groups had been mixed in with each other. But there is no evidence that Canadians were denied better aircraft simply because of their nationality. In fact, No. 426 Squadron began to receive the radial-engined Lancaster II as early as July 1943, while No. 408 Squadron, based with No. 426 at Linton-on-Ouse, was equipped with the same aircraft in October of that year. This was a stop-gap aircraft, made necessary because of the shortage of the better Merlin engines. When the US-built Packard variant of the Merlin engine was wedded to the Lancaster airframe to produce the Lancaster III, the Lancaster II was withdrawn from service. But most Canadian squadrons flying the Lancaster II received the supposedly improved Halifax III, rather that the Lancaster III; four RCAF bomber squadrons were still flying Halifax bombers at V-E Day.

The Lancaster II was not as good an aircraft as the Lancaster I or III; moreover, new aircraft of the better variants tended to go first to No. 5 Group squadrons. Harris believed, and not unreasonably, that his best aircraft should first equip his best and most experienced crews. The seven new Canadian bomber squadrons formed in the last half of 1942 (Nos. 424, 425, 426, 427, 428, 429, and 431) would have to wait in line for their Lancasters behind more established squadrons. The bulk of No. 6 Group's aircraft were bound to be inadequate for the task for some time to come.

The most serious problem afflicting the group in its first seven to eight months of operations was the inexperience of many, if not most, of its crews. The night-bomber war was a highly technical and a physically and emotionally demanding business. It grew even more complex in 1943 as it began to rely more heavily on electronic measures and countermeasures. In January 1943 the British first introduced H2S — airborne target-finding radar. Over the next six months a myriad of electronic devices was added to the bombers in an effort to evade German defenders and to increase the ability of crews to hit their targets at night. Although prewar theory had held that a large enough force of fast bombers would always get through the enemy defences in sufficient numbers, even in daylight, to inflict heavy damage on the enemy, both sides had learned that this was not so. Day-bombers needed fighter escort to survive. They needed to have air superiority to and from and over their target in order to carry out their mission in relative safety.

Night-bombing was supposed to solve the air superiority problem by hiding the bombers in the dark. But radar was rapidly stripping the dark away, and night-fighter defences were beginning to inflict heavy damage on unescorted night-bombers, though not as heavy as that wreaked by German day-fighters on unescorted American bombers. They lost seventy-four aircraft shot down, damaged beyond repair, or crashed on landing out of 291 sorties, or 25.4 percent, in a raid on 14 October 1943 against the German ball-bearing manufacturing centre of Schweinfurt. Harris might have called for the creation of a large force of radar-equipped night-fighters and intruders to aid his bombers (the excellent Mosquito fighter/fighter-bomber nicely filled the bill), but he resorted to evasion rather than air superiority to gain the upper hand. In other words, he would not try to defend his night-bombers with night-fighters, but would instead try to hide his night-bombers by attempting to blind or deceive the enemy in a variety of ways. At the same time, he would try to increase the chances that his bombers would do the job assigned to them in finding and hitting their targets in the dark. This task would have been hard enough in ideal conditions, but it was made even more difficult by the poor weather that usually prevails over northern Europe during the long nights of winter. Summer weather was better, but the nights were not long enough for deep penetration raids.

The Germans were well aware of these efforts and were determined to neutralize every new device and technique that the British came up with to hide their bombers or hit their targets effectively. The night-bomber war became a highly technical war of measure and countermeasure. Among these contrivances were Naxos, a night-fighter device that homed in on H2S; Monica, bomber-borne radar to detect night-fighters; and Boozer, another type of bomber-borne radar device to detect fighters. The Germans also improved their main airborne radar, the Lichtenstein, and their ground radars and control systems.

After the Battle of Hamburg in late July and early August 1943, the war of jamming, radar detection, electronic counter-measures, spoof raids, and ghost raiders became even more complex. In fact, Bomber Command established a special electronic warfare unit — No. 100 (Bomber Support) Group — in November 1943 to jam German radio and radar, broadcast fake ground-controller instructions, and carry out other highly technical tasks in aid of the bombers. It should not be surprising, then, that "sprog" (or green) crews who had not even honed basic skills, such as how to stay in the bomber stream or how to search for night-fighters, were disadvantaged. Statistics showed clearly that inexperienced crews were far more likely to be lost on operations than those that had served at least half of their normal thirty-mission tour of duty. The large number of sprog crews was the primary reason why No. 6 Group's performance was so poor, through much of 1943, compared with that of the rest of Bomber Command.

No. 6 Group's inferior performance showed in almost every category: fewer sorties per aircraft, owing to poor maintenance; a higher rate of aircraft returning before reaching the target; a lower percentage of aircraft placing bombs within 5 kilometres of the aiming point; and higher loss rates. The high rate of early returns was partly due to poor maintenance, but it was also partly due to fatigue, low morale, and unwillingness to press on. Too many times a crew would return complaining of some malfunction in the aircraft, only to have the bomber check out in perfect working order. All these difficulties were linked, of course, and all were symptomatic of the group's teething problems. Put simply, No. 6 Group was learning the art of night aerial bombardment by doing it; such an induction guaranteed a host of serious problems and a higher casualty rate than those among the other groups. This was the ultimate price for Canadianization. If Canadians had been mixed in with other crews in squadrons and groups, they would probably have learned the skills necessary for survival from other more skilled crews and commanders, and would probably have had a better chance to complete their thirty-mission tours of duty.

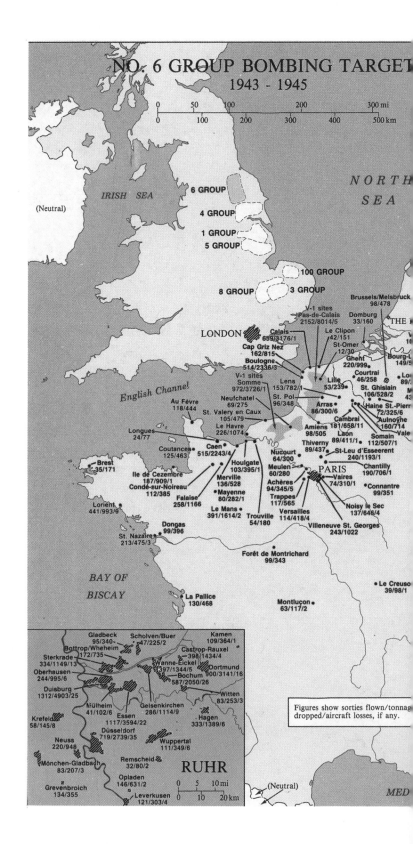

NO. 6 GROUP BOMBING TARGET
1943 - 1945

| 0 | 50 | 100 | | 200 | | 300 mi |
| 0 | | 100 | 200 | 300 | 400 | 500 km |

IRISH SEA

(Neutral)

NORTH

SEA

6 GROUP

4 GROUP

1 GROUP
5 GROUP

100 GROUP

8 GROUP   3 GROUP

Brussels/Melsbruck
98/478

V-1 sites
Pas-de-Calais   Domburg
2152/8014/5   33/160   THE

LONDON   Calais   Le Clipon   V
659/3176/1   42/151   10
Cap Griz Nez   St-Omer
162/815   12/30   Bourg-L
Boulogne   Gheht   149/5
514/2336/3   220/999
V-1 sites   Lens   Lille   Courtrai   Lo
Somme   153/782/1   53/239   46/258   89/
972/3726/1   St. Ghislain   M
Neufchatel   St. Pol   106/528/2   43
Au Fèvre   69/275   96/348   Haine St-Pierr
118/444   St. Valery en Caux   Arras   72/325/6
105/479   86/300/6   Aulnoye
Longues   Le Havre   Cambrai   160/714
24/77   226/1074   Amiens   181/658/11   Vale
Coutances   98/505   Laôn   Somain
Caen   125/463   Thiverny   89/411/1   112/507/1
Brest   515/2243/4   Nucourt   89/437   St-Leu d'Esseerent
35/171   64/300   240/1193/1
Ile de Cezembre   Houlgate   Meulen   PARIS   Chantilly
187/909/1   103/395/1   60/280   190/706/1
Condé-sur-Noireau   Merville   Achères   Vaires   Connantre
112/385   136/528   94/345/5   74/310/1   99/351
Falaise   Mayenne   Trappes
Lorient   258/1166   80/282/1   117/565   Noisy le Sec
441/993/9   Le Mans   Versailles   137/646/4
391/1614/2   Trouville   114/418/4
Dongas   54/180   Villeneuve St. Georges
99/396   243/1022
St. Nazaire
213/475/3

Forêt de Montrichard
99/343

BAY OF
BISCAY   La Pallice   Le Creuso
130/468   39/98/1

Montluçon
63/117/2

RUHR

Gladbeck   Scholven/Buer   Kamen
95/340   47/225/2   109/364/1
Bottrop/Wheheim   Castrop-Rauxel
172/735   398/1434/4
Sterkrade   Wanne-Eickel   Dortmund
334/1149/13   397/1344/5   900/3141/16
Oberhausen   Bochum
244/995/6   587/2050/26
Duisburg   Witten
1312/4903/25   83/253/3
Mülheim   Gelsenkirchen   Hagen
41/102/6   286/1114/9   333/1389/6
Krefeld   Essen
58/145/8   1117/3594/22
Düsseldorf
Neuss   719/2739/35
220/948   Wuppertal
111/349/6
Mönchen-Gladbach   Remscheid
83/207/3   32/80/2   0   5   10mi
Opladen
Grevenbroich   146/631/2   0   10   20km
134/355   Leverkusen
121/303/4

Figures show sorties flown/tonnag
dropped/aircraft losses, if any.

(Neutral)

MED

English Channel

(Neutral)

Bergen
123/571/1

COPENHAGEN

BALTIC SEA

Heide/Hemmingstedt
299/1078/3
Heligoland
110/328/2
Wangerooge
190/902/4
orden
1/2
Emden
139/380
Oldenburg
6/14/3

Kiel
688/2335/9

Peenemünde
63/155/12

Hamburg
1298/4666/43
Wilhelmshaven
304/924/5
Bremen
95/323/1

Stettin
116/349/4

Hannover
575/1764/29

Berlin
1070/2573/84

BERLIN

Osnabrück
284/1033/4
Wesel
2/5
Münster
293/1090/3
Dorsten
96/3141/16
Soest
186/726/2

Brunswick
111/442/9
Hildesheim
87/382/2

Magdeburg
228/675/29

Dessau
81/260/3
Kassel
155/402/17
Merseburg
156/567/3
Leipzig
406/1137/27
Böhlen
110/253
Dresden
66/20

RUHR

Cologne
1138/4248/14
Wesseling
150/598/1
Bonn
96/460
achen
703/10
Troisdorf
146/510
iesbaden
60/277/2
Mainz
299/1044/1
Ludwigshafen
264/1021

Frankfurt
545/1292/36
Hanau
193/570/2
Worms
111/349/6
Mannheim
586/1621/23
Karlsruhe
196/670
Zweibrücken
192/755
Pforzheim
50/189

Zeitz
242/711/14
Chemitz
286/748/9

Schweinfurt
87/172/5
Rüsselsheim
33/119/1

PRAGUE

Pilsen
26/65/4

Nuremberg
290/689/17
Schwandorf
118/492

Stuttgart
782/2120/33
Augsburg
58/113/6
Gablingen
17/45
Munich
69/174/5
Friedrichshafen
19/55

(Neutral)

Milan
48/120/1

Turin
14/42

ADRIATIC SEA

EAN SEA

On the night of 3 January 1943 six Wellington bombers of No. 427 Squadron took off from their base at Croft, in Yorkshire, and headed out over the North Sea for the Frisian Islands off the coast of Holland. They were to take part in an aerial minelaying operation. These Gardening missions, as they were called by Bomber Command, were an important but little-known duty carried out by Coastal and Bomber Command aircraft throughout the war. They were intended to sow mines in strategic locations, such as harbour entrances or river estuaries, in order to disrupt commercial traffic or to hinder the movements of German naval vessels, especially U-boats. Over the course of its operational life, No. 6 Group aircraft would mount 2407 additional Gardening sorties, lay more than 5000 tonnes of mines, and lose forty-four aircraft doing it. Gardening was a good way of giving sprog crews experience flying over, or close to, enemy waters and coasts. Since it was far less demanding than bombing, it was also something that could be done with obsolete aircraft such as the four-engine Stirling, the older marks of the Wellington, or the Halifax IIs and Vs. Gardening raids could also be used to draw the German night-fighter force out and direct it away from the main-force attack, which was usually scheduled for later in the same night.

On this particular night, half the contingent from No. 427 Squadron completed the mission, but the other three aircraft returned early. No. 427 had been operational for only a little more than two weeks, and the mission was the first mounted by No. 6. Group; it was not an auspicious beginning. Less than two weeks later, group aircraft took part in their first bombing mission, sending nine Wellingtons and six Halifaxes to bomb German U-boat facilities at Lorient, on the French coast. One Wellington from No. 426 Squadron was lost.

Bomber Command's assault on Germany's industrial cities was intensified on the night of 4/5 March 1943 with the opening attack of the Battle of the Ruhr. Located in western Germany, the Ruhr was one massive industrial basin, home to steel works, manufacturing facilities, munitions factories, and synthetic oil and rubber plants, all fed by a large rail and canal network. The cities of the Ruhr were jammed with industrial installations and with the workers who laboured in them. The Ruhr lay at the heart of the German war effort.

The Ruhr was easy enough to find in the dark, but bombing a particular target or even a particular city was not easy to do. In Essen the sprawling Krupp works so dominated the city that it was almost impossible to miss them even from a good bombing altitude, but Essen was the exception. The cities of the Ruhr were jammed together, were hard to distinguish from one another at night, even with H2S, and were often obscured with industrial smoke and haze. They were defended by a formidable array of radar-guided searchlights and flak guns, and the route from the coast was dominated by night-fighter fields and beacons.

No. 6 Group took part in the opening Battle of the Ruhr and in most of the raids against the Ruhr that followed throughout the war. On this night, the target was Essen. The Canadians put up seventy-seven aircraft, of which sixty-five attacked the primary target and eight returned early. Only three aircraft were lost, which equated to a loss rate of almost 4 percent. Canadian pilot Walter Thompson, who flew a Lancaster with No. 105 Squadron of the RAF's No. 5 Group, wrote of an attack against Essen that took place later that same month:

> There was a great deal of illumination from three or four cones of searchlights . . . Bombs were now going off below — one could see the rippling shock waves from the explosion of 4000 pounders (these bombs were dubbed "cookies") across a smoky surface, like ripples from rocks on a pond. Small fires were blazing in the middle, getting larger as one approached. Flak was twinkling . . . ahead . . . We flew through the smoke puffs left by the exploding shells in the sky . . . red target indicators, dropped . . . by Oboe-equipped Mosquitoes were clearly visible far below.[2]

Thompson's aircraft was coned by searchlights, and he was half-blinded. But he managed to slip into the darkness, bomb, and return safely to base.

On the night of 24 July 1943 Bomber Command launched 791 aircraft at the German port city of Hamburg in the opening attack of what Harris had labelled Operation Gomorrah. No. 6 Group dispatched seventy-eight aircraft. The bombers were carrying a new weapon in the night air war against Germany, millions of strips of aluminum foil cut to precise lengths and designed to jam the German radar with a fog of blips. Fed down the flare shoots of the bombers at timed intervals, the aluminum strips, called Window, registered on German radar screens as if they were aircraft. Both ground and airborne radar were rendered useless. German night-fighter pilots and ground controllers filled the dark with radioed cries of frustrated anger. German flak guns and searchlights went blind. Flight Leader G.F. Pentony, flying a Wellington from No. 429 Squadron, later remembered: "The master searchlights and all the others were waving aimlessly about in the sky . . . My crew were delighted. My bomb aimer said that his bloody hands were frozen with dropping Window but that it was well worth it . . . he asked if we could do as many trips as soon as possible . . . before the enemy found a solution."[3]

Hamburg began to die that night; in three subsequent raids on the 27/28 and 29/30 of July and on the 2/3 of August, Bomber Command mounted 3095 sorties against the city, with about 2500 aircraft actually bombing the target. On 25 and 26 July, the Americans bombed by day. Close to 50,000 people were killed, another 40,000 were injured, and some 61 percent of the city's residential accommodation was destroyed. The worst damage was inflicted on the second night, when a combination of concentrated bombing, hot weather, and an almost complete lack of fire-fighting equipment (water mains had been destroyed) resulted in an immense firestorm. To the aircrews it seemed as if the heart of the city was in flames; smoke billowed up more than 7000 metres into the night sky. One member of No. 427 Squadron recalled: "It was incredible. The place was a great mass of flame. Halfway home we could still see the smoke rising from Hamburg."[4] In all, Bomber Command lost eighty-six aircraft (2.8 percent of the attacking force), with another 174 damaged (5.6 percent). It was not a high price for the result. Hitler's minister of war production, Albert Speer, warned the Führer that six more such attacks would "bring Germany's armaments production to a halt."[5] But Bomber Command could not easily replicate the results of the Battle of Hamburg; the combination of conditions that had caused the firestorm were rarely duplicated. More to the point, the Germans quickly devised means to counter Window.

Hamburg epitomized the type of war that Harris meant to wage against Germany. He strongly believed that his crews were incapable of precision strikes against specific targets. He also believed that such strikes were useless. He scorned suggestions that attacking industrial "chokepoints" — synthetic oil plants, ball-bearing factories, and the like — would shorten the war. He called these targets "panacea targets," and those who advocated attacking them, "panacea merchants." He believed that burning the heart out of Germany's major industrial cities, killing as many Germans as possible, and destroying their houses and places of work would win the war. Thus he stubbornly resisted attempts to harness Bomber Command to specific campaigns against strategic objectives. "Pointblank," a plan for a combined US–British bombing assault on the factories that produced German fighter aircraft, was such a campaign; Harris all but ignored it.

Harris had wide popular support for his position. By all measures, the civilian populations of the United Kingdom and Canada supported this endeavour of making the German people reap what they had sown in Warsaw, Rotterdam, Coventry, and London. Many political leaders also backed Harris's area offensive. One British MP put it best in 1942 when he wrote: "I am all for the bombing of working class areas of German cities. I am Cromwellian — I believe in 'slaying in the name of the Lord' because I do not believe you will ever bring home to the civil population of Germany the horrors of war until they have been tested in this way."[6]

The Canadian government had no say in the making of RAF bombing policy; it was interested strictly in the administrative control of the RCAF overseas, not operational control. But the Prime Minister, for one, had no regrets about Harris's way of waging war against Germany's civilians. This was, after all, total war, one forced on the world by the German nation. Although there were some voices raised in moral outrage at these attacks against German civilians, it was inconceivable to most people in Britain and in Canada that the population of Germany should be spared from the horrors of a war they had brutally inflicted on everyone else.

Harris was the commander of Bomber Command. In the RAF's peculiar administrative set-up, he was virtual master of all he surveyed. His immediate superior, Chief of the Air Staff Sir Charles Portal, had no authority to tell Harris what targets to bomb or not bomb. But Harris, like all commanders, was capable of being swayed, persuaded, and brought on side when necessary. Thus Bomber Command, and No. 6 Group, attacked much more than the built-up centres of German cities. They also assaulted industrial, transportation, and military targets, sometimes with great effectiveness. One such attack was on the German experimental rocket installations at Peenemünde, on the Baltic Sea coast, on 17/18 August 1943, when Bomber Command sent 541 aircraft (fifty-seven from No. 6 Group) to destroy or delay the German V-2 effort. The attack was a reasonable success, forcing the Germans to disperse V-2 production and delaying that production by several months, but No. 6 Group suffered grievous losses: twelve aircraft, representing 19.7 percent of the number dispatched compared with 6.7 percent for the total attacking force. Part of the reason was that the group's aircraft bombed towards the end of the raid, when German night-fighters had been fully alerted and had congregated near the target. But part was also due to poor discipline among the crews. As Martin Middlebrook wrote: "Canadian Main Force crews were not notoriously rigid followers of flight plans and timetables, and a study of the records of the 6 Group squadrons reveals a characteristic spirit of independence."[7] It was clear that the problems that had plagued the RCAF bomber group from the start were troubling it still.

As the summer gave way to fall and longer nights, Harris launched the preliminary phase of what would later prove to be a prolonged assault on Berlin.

Between the 23/24 of August and the 3/4 of September, Bomber Command attacked Berlin three times. No. 6 Group sent 129 aircraft to the target (only three on the last raid); ninety-six actually bombed Berlin, nineteen returned early, and twelve were shot down, for an overall loss rate of 9.3 percent over the three missions.

Bomber Command did not return to Berlin until the night of 18/19 November; in the meantime, it and No. 6 Group attacked a variety of other targets, concentrating on the Ruhr. From 3/4 September to 18/19 November, the RCAF mounted twenty bombing attacks and eight minelaying operations. Hanover was the most frequent target — attacked four times — and the object of No. 6 Group's first sortie of one hundred aircraft or more on the night of 8/9 October. Its losses that evening were six aircraft (6 percent), still too much for sustained operations.

But however much Bomber Command attacked other targets and engaged in other missions that fall of 1943, Harris's real objective was the destruction of Berlin. He appears to have believed that such an accomplishment would pave the way for an Allied victory. In early November he penned a memo to Churchill which has since become famous as an example of his gross overestimation of the abilities of Bomber Command or of his enormous ego: "We can wreck Berlin from end to end if the USAAF will come in on it. It will cost between 400 and 500 aircraft. It will cost Germany the war."[8] The USAAF did not come in because its emphasis was on bombing strategic industrial chokepoints, not on area campaigns, and Bomber Command never had the capability of winning the war by itself.

The first raid of the main phase of the Battle of Berlin took place the night of 18/19 November, when Bomber Command dispatched a mixed force of Stirling, Halifax, and Lancaster aircraft to the German capital; 444 bombers took off from the United Kingdom and only nine were lost. No. 6 Group sent twenty-nine aircraft to the target and suffered no losses at all. It was a good start as far as losses were concerned, but a failure in that Berlin was covered by thick cloud and the skymarking was ineffective. The city suffered little damage. The next attack, five nights later, was much more successful, with more than 3000 buildings destroyed and about 2000 people killed. But as the bombers returned to Berlin in the weeks that followed, Bomber Command's losses began to mount precipitously. German controllers could guess the target and direct the radar-equipped "tame boar" fighters and the single-seat "wild boar" fighters (without radar) to the bomber stream and the target. After the first three raids, Harris ordered the Stirling squadrons to stand down from the attack; their losses were much too high.

One of the Canadian pilots in the thick of the action was J. Douglas Harvey, from No. 408 Squadron. One night he had just settled into his bomb run over Berlin when something made him look up through his Lancaster's perspex canopy: "A Junkers 88 was crossing directly over my cockpit, going from left to right. The huge iron cross on its side looked larger than a billboard. I literally could have reached out and touched it. Three feet lower and it would have smashed directly into us. It was obvious it hadn't seen us."[9] Harvey was one of the lucky ones. The growing effectiveness of the German ground controllers, the increasing skills of the night-fighter force, and the appearance of better radar and radar-detection devices allowed the Luftwaffe to take a heavy toll of the attackers. Over the course of the main phase of the Battle of Berlin (from the nights of 18/19 November 1943 to 24/25 March 1944), Bomber Command launched 10,813 sorties at the city and lost 625 bombers, or 5.8 percent of the total. No. 6 Group dispatched 1086 sorties and lost sixty-five bombers, or close to 6 percent of the total. The heavy losses, the long flights, and the lack of any respite in the campaign sapped crew morale. In the early winter of 1944, many Bomber Command crews came closer to cracking than at any other time in the war. And yet they did not crack. Somehow, they dragged themselves to their aircraft night after night, took off into the gathering gloom, and did their best to fulfil their missions. It was their greatest time of testing.

Despite the persistence and the courage of the crews, the Battle of Berlin was an unmitigated defeat for Bomber Command. The heavy losses of bombers were not nearly balanced out by the destruction visited upon the city. There were many reasons for this result. Berlin was far from the United Kingdom and it was difficult for the crews to keep to the main path on so long a trip. The winter weather over northern Europe was usually poor; high winds, cloud, and icing of aircraft control surfaces made navigation a nightmare. Once over Berlin, the size of the city and the almost perpetual cloud cover, not to mention the heavy concentration of searchlights and flak, made accurate marking all but impossible. The primitive H2S sets carried by most of the Pathfinder Force could not pick out any distinguishing features of the city; Berlin was one great splotch of white light on their radar screens. And the main-force crews often failed to bomb the markers properly. The intense flak and heavy concentration of night-fighters exacerbated the problem of "creep-back" — bombing short of the markers to get away from the target area more quickly. As a result, many tonnes of bombs fell in forests and fields.

Harris's preoccupation with Berlin did not stop him from ordering attacks on a host of other targets in the early months of 1944. He even sent his bombers to participate in the so-called Big Week, a combined bomber offensive between

Bomber Command and the USAAF Eighth Air Force designed to destroy German aircraft factories. But Berlin was his main target. He knew that the long-expected cross-channel invasion of France was looming, and he feared that his bomber force would be pressed into pre-invasion preparatory attacks on defence installations and communications facilities. He was desperate to complete his self-appointed task of destroying Berlin before that happened.

Although No. 6 Group's performance had been improving by the end of 1943 as Brookes tightened up on training and as the survivors of the early disasters became more experienced, it was still not up to that of the other groups. Thus, on 12 February 1944 Brookes left his post as Air Officer Commanding No. 6 Group and was replaced by Air Vice-Marshal Clifford "Black Mike" Mackay McEwen. A First World War ace with twenty-seven enemy aircraft to his credit, McEwen had become an RCAF career officer in the interwar years, AOC of the RCAF's No. 1 Group based in Newfoundland, and a base commander in the United Kingdom before assuming command of No. 6 Group. He was determined to make his new command one of the best in Bomber Command. A hard taskmaster and a stickler for discipline on the ground and in the air, he made sure his crews lived up to his high standards of performance. He stressed good navigation and the maintenance of as high an altitude as possible both to and from the target. Under his leadership, No. 6 Group would become one of the best groups in Bomber Command in almost all areas of performance, from early returns to accurate bombing of the target.

In early March, Bomber Command began to shift its attention to the French rail network. As a preliminary to D-Day, a "transportation plan" had been worked out to deny the Germans the use of the French railways as a way of reinforcing their troops in the landing zones once Operation Overlord began. British and American medium and heavy bombers and fighter-bombers attacked rail centres, marshalling yards, railway bridges, and rolling stock. Harris and the Commander of the US heavy-bomber forces, Ira Eaker, had resisted using their aircraft in this way, but they had little choice after they were brought under the overall command of General Dwight D. Eisenhower, who had been selected as Supreme Commander of the Allied Expeditionary Forces for the Normandy landings.

Harris had one more chance for a massive area attack on a German city before going under Eisenhower's command on 1 April 1944 and he chose Nuremberg as his target. On the night of 30/31 March, 795 bombers took off for Nuremberg, flying most of the way in a clear, moonlit sky. Gordon W. Webb was one of the No. 6 Group pilots flying that night. "The moon . . . was the brightest moon any enemy night fighter could have asked for. Visibility was virtually unlimited for a night sky. At our altitude cloud cover simply did not exist. What cloud there was hung low to the ground providing a perfect back drop, silhouetting the bombers."[10]

Webb saw that the bombers flying at his assigned altitude were leaving vapour trails, ghostly white in the night air, which no German pilot could possibly miss. He decided to climb as high as he could in the hope that the colder air would dissipate his bomber's trail.

Given the moonlight and the visibility of the bomber stream, Bomber Command's usual deception tactics did not work. German air controllers determined the direction of the bomber stream early in the night, and the German nightfighters had little difficulty spotting the bombers; ninety-five were shot down — almost 12 percent of the attacking force. No. 6 Group put up 118 aircraft and lost thirteen or 11 percent of the total. Webb saw one destroyed: "We were at 21,000 feet and our air speed just over 200 MPH . . . Suddenly, a Lancaster dived across from right to left directly ahead and just below us . . . Right on the Lanc's tail was a ME 110. The fighter closed quickly and fired both his cannon and machineguns. The shells hit across the fuselage of the Lanc and entered the starboard outer engine. The coolant released from the engine burst into flames." The fighter turned, fired again, and a wing tore off the bomber. It went into a "twisting, spiraling dive" and crashed. Webb saw no parachutes.[11]

In April the bomber offensive was harnessed to the needs of Overlord. Although there would be attacks on German cities in the months that followed, the main effort was over France and the Low Countries, both in aid of the D-Day landing and the ground battles that followed 6 June. In March 1944, 70 percent of the bombs dropped by Bomber Command had been against German targets; that number fell to less than 25 percent in May and almost none in June. The switch of targets was reflected by dramatic falls in loss rates both for Bomber Command and for No. 6 Group. The respite would prove to be temporary for Germany's cities; when Eisenhower relinquished control of the British and American heavy-bomber forces on 25 September, the bomber offensive against Germany resumed. In fact, the last seven months of the war would see some of the heaviest raids of any phase of the RAF/RCAF bomber campaign.

By the beginning of the fourth year of war in the North Atlantic, HMCS *St Croix* had become one of the stalwarts of the RCN and the Mid-Ocean Escort Force. Despite repeated problems with minor equipment failures, the old four-stacker had put to sea time and time again to help guard the vital convoys that made up the Allied lifeline to the United Kingdom and the supply line for the eventual invasion of the continent. After several refits, *St Croix* was about as well equipped as could be expected of a quarter-century-old ship; she and her crew had themselves destroyed U-90 in late July 1942 and had assisted the Canadian corvette *Shediac* in the destruction of U-87 in early March 1943.

In August 1943 *St Croix* was transferred from the Mid-Ocean Escort Force (MOEF) to the Royal Navy's Western Approaches Command, along with the RCN Town Class destroyer *St Francis* and the RCN corvettes *Chambly, Morden,* and *Sackville,* to become part of Escort Group 9, a support group for North Atlantic convoys. These support groups were designed to reinforce the close escort of endangered convoys or to hunt submarines in mid-ocean and kill them. Unlike regular escort groups, support groups could stay in one locality long enough to sink a trapped U-boat while the convoy sailed on. The work of escort groups was invariably defensive — protecting convoys. But the role of support groups was inherently offensive — finding U-boats and destroying them.

Escort Group 9 was only one of several new Allied support groups that had been patrolling the waters of the mid-ocean since the late spring of 1943; the presence of those groups reflected a new strategy towards the U-boats. That strategy can be summed up in simple terms; henceforth the chief task of the Allied navies in the Atlantic would be to hunt U-boats and sink them. In other words, the Admiralty now believed (as the USN had since the entry of the United States into the war) that the safe and timely arrival of convoys ultimately depended on the destruction of the U-boat fleet. Since there was still a need for convoy escorts — and for those escorts to stay close to the convoys — the U-boat killing would be done by support groups. Thus the RN put increased emphasis on channelling the bulk of its resources, and its newest and best equipment, into support groups with the specific task of sinking German submarines. By the end of 1943 both the RN and the RCN were actually stripping ships away from convoy escort work and turning them to submarine hunting instead.

On 15 September 1943 Escort Group 9 sailed from Plymouth to carry out an anti-submarine patrol in the Bay of Biscay, but it was diverted to rendezvous with convoy HX 256. When it was clear that HX 256 was in no danger, Escort Group 9 was ordered to reinforce Escort Groups B 3 and C 2, which were guarding the westbound convoys ONS 18 and ON 202, respectively. The slow convoy — ONS 18 — had sailed from the United Kingdom on 13 September; the faster ON 202 had departed several days later on a similar track and was now coming up behind the first convoy. At sea, a patrol line of U-boats awaited. On 20 September, after the Admiralty picked up increasing signs of a German submarine concentration, it ordered the two convoys to merge. An official report later described the rendezvous:

> As darkness fell on the evening of the 20th the junction of the convoys ONS-18 and ON-202 was still not complete and 63 merchant vessels (nb: other reports say 88 merchantmen) were spread out in comparative disorder over miles of sea. Earlier in the day, two American merchantmen had been sunk and there was strong evidence that a large pack of submarines was gathering. In the words of the Senior Officer, Commander M.J. Evans, OBE, RN, 'the two convoys gyrated majestically round the ocean, never appearing to get much closer and watched appreciatively by a growing swarm of U-Boats.'

Escort Group 9 had arrived in the vicinity of the convoys the previous afternoon and had taken up outer screening positions ahead and astern of the gaggle of merchantmen, on the port side. The weather was deteriorating, with fog and rain, as the collection of escorts and their charges headed west into a weather front. All around them, the U-boats of Group *Leuthen* gathered for the attack. RAF patrol aircraft and the convoy's escort had no shortage of contacts to attack. One such contact was U-305, shadowing the convoys to their rear. In the late afternoon of 20 September, *St Croix* was on station behind the convoys when the Senior Officer of the Escort (SOE) ordered it to proceed astern to check out a possible U-boat sighting reported by an orbiting Coastal Command aircraft. At that point, the combined convoys were about 640 kilometres southeast of Greenland.

In the gathering gloom, *St Croix* turned eastward and headed back along the convoy track, zigzagging at about 20 knots. As it approached the spot where the sighting was reported to have taken place, her captain, Lieutenant-Commander A.H. Dobson, ordered the *St Croix* to turn and to begin an asdic sweep. The ship was just settling back, bow wave subsiding, when a massive explosion detonated just near her port propeller. She had been hit by a single acoustic torpedo fired by U-305. *St Croix* glided to a stop and almost immediately took on a heavy list; as the crew took to the sides, a second torpedo tore into the stern of the warship. Within three minutes of this torpedo hit, *St Croix* was gone; eighty-one members of her crew remained in life rafts and on carley-floats, clinging to whatever they could. When the SOS reached the escort commander, he dispatched the RN frigate *Itchen* to pick up the *St Croix* survivors, but *Itchen* found *St Croix* belching smoke from two stacks and settling by the stern; it drew close just as the second torpedo hit the already stricken destroyer. *Itchen* radioed news of the sinking and was close to the destroyer when an acoustic torpedo exploded prematurely in its wake. *Itchen*'s captain decided that his ship was in mortal danger and withdrew from the scene to await reinforcement from the RN corvette *Polyanthus*. But as *Polyanthus* steamed towards *Itchen* and *St Croix*, it too was hit. It sank quickly with the loss of all hands, save one.

The next day, *Itchen* returned, searching back over the convoy track and finding the lone survivor of the *Polyanthus* and the eighty-one crew members from the *St Croix*. All were hauled from the cold sea some thirteen hours after the two sinkings. The next night *Itchen* was pursuing a surfaced U-boat when an "ear-shocking explosion" tore across the water. *Itchen* blew up in a spectacular display of pyrotechnics, another victim of an acoustic torpedo. Only three men were rescued, two from *Itchen* and one from the *St Croix*.

The *St Croix* was the thirteenth RCN ship lost in the Second World War and the one that produced the heaviest loss of life — only one man survived out of a crew of 147. It was the first Allied warship sunk by the deadly new German device, the acoustic homing torpedo (Gnat), which homed in on the propeller noises of a target vessel and was especially designed to sink escort ships. One of the dead from the *St Croix* was Surgeon-Lieutenant William Lyon Mackenzie King, nephew of the Prime Minister.

By the beginning of 1943, Allied, especially American, shipyards were building merchant vessel tonnage faster than the U-boats could sink it, but the loss in

Allied cargoes, crews, and cargo-carrying capacity was still very high. The U-boats continued to pose a serious risk to Operation Bolero — the build-up of troops, planes, tanks, and other material in the United Kingdom preparatory to an invasion of the continent. In December 1942 alone the Allies lost more than 300,000 tonnes of shipping to U-boats; total losses for 1942 amounted to more than 8 million tonnes and more than 1100 ships. In the United Kingdom there were barely more than 300,000 tonnes of non-military oil reserves, enough for only three months of rationed usage, though the Royal Navy still possessed a reserve of about 1 million tonnes. By January 1943 Dönitz's fleet consisted of some 390 submarines, and his operational strength hovered over the 200 U-boat mark. Allowing for the usual allotment of one-third at sea, one-third in port, and one-third proceeding to or coming from station, that still meant a formidable force to place in the mid-Atlantic, beyond the reach of shore-based aircraft.

In late December 1942 and January 1943, shipping losses plummeted, owing to unusually bad weather at sea. Convoys were often forced to heave to so as to ride out storms with monstrous waves, high winds, driving snow, and sleet. Escorts iced up, making them dangerously top heavy. Radars could not distinguish between giant waves and ships, let alone low-hulled submarines. The pounding of the sea made the asdic useless. But then, the bad weather also hampered U-boat operations. Alan Easton's corvette HMCS *Sackville* was caught by one of these storms:

> Where the other ships were we had no idea. The radar could not tell us because it was useless now . . . At times the fo'c'sle was buried down under water, the foredeck submerged, the green seas battering the bridge. Spray thrown up by the pounding of the bow flew high over the funnel. I knew the agony of the men below, the sickening torment as the bow plunged down incline after precipitous incline like a runaway roller-coaster.[1]

When the weather abated, the slaughter of merchantmen picked up anew. Trinidad–Gibralter convoy TM 1 lost seven of nine tankers; more than 100,000 tonnes of fuel went to the bottom. A convoy bound for the United Kingdom out of Sydney lost ten ships in a three-day battle. In late February another Atlantic convoy lost fourteen ships in a four-day fight. Losses in February rose to more than 290,000 tonnes, and although twelve U-boats went down, Dönitz's mid-Atlantic fleet continued to grow.

On 14 January 1943, just as the two surviving tankers of the much mauled convoy TM 1 dropped anchor at Gibraltar, Churchill and Roosevelt met at Casablanca to decide key questions on the future course of the war. One of the topics covered was the war at sea; the conclusion they reached was that the defeat of the U-boat menace must have top priority, otherwise an invasion of the continent could not be mounted. In fact, the high Allied losses at sea meant that no invasion would be possible that year. There were simply not enough merchantmen to feed Britain and to bring sufficient men and weapons to the United Kingdom to mount a successful cross-channel attack. The Americans would have to return to the Atlantic battle in sufficient numbers to allow them and the British to form support groups, with escort carriers wherever possible, which could hunt and kill U-boats at sea. Escort carriers, or CVEs, had first been used by the Americans in the Pacific theatre in the fall of 1942; these "baby" flat-tops were built by welding a flight and hangar deck as well as a control island to a hull originally designed for a merchant ship. At the same time, enough VLR Liberators were to be diverted to the combined navies to close the air gap. As naval historian Dan van der Vat has put it: "The absolute necessity of providing end-to-end air-cover was thus clearly identified, together with the measures necessary for supplying it."[2]

That was all well and good. The politicians and their staffs made their pronouncements, then departed the sunny clime of North Africa for their cold capitals and let their naval commanders fill in the details. But Admiral Ernest J. King, Commander-in-Chief of the United States Navy, was in no hurry to implement the decisions made at Casablanca. He dragged his feet on the build-up of USN escorts in the Atlantic; the first US escort carrier, USS *Bogue*, did not begin operations until March. In addition, the RCAF was still denied VLR Liberators for Eastern Air Command, although the British intended to station RAF Coastal Command Liberators in Newfoundland, while the command structure in the western Atlantic was chaotic. By the late winter of 1943, for example, the RCN was supplying just under 50 percent of all the escort vessels available in the theatre and the United States just 2 percent, yet a US admiral based in Newfoundland (Commander, Task Force 24) was in overall charge of naval forces in the area. The Canadians insisted that this inequality would have to change, but Admiral King would have none of it. Until these very real problems were resolved, the U-boats would continue to reap a full harvest at sea.

In January 1943 the RCN Escort Group C 1 accompanied a fast HX convoy to the United Kingdom, then remained for rest, refitting, the installation of newer anti-submarine equipment, and the beginning of a long training regimen. First the crews were trained ashore in basics such as gunnery, signalling, asdic tracking, depth charging, and damage control. Officers were sent to the Western Approaches tactical unit in Liverpool for table-top exercises and other tactical training. Then the entire group sailed for Tobermory, Scotland, where the RN had its extensive work-up and training facilities for its own escorts — HMS *Western Isles* — and where the Canadians would receive hands-on training at sea, aided by British submarines.

According to former RCN Commander Tony German, the RN commander of *Western Isles*, Commodore G. Stephenson, was known as the "Terror of Tobermory." He made sure that the Canadians got no rest and that they were constantly kept on the move with battle problems, special manoeuvres, and un-pleasant surprises, such as having their vessels attacked by frogmen and boarded by saboteurs. On one occasion he stepped aboard a Canadian corvette, flung his hat to the deck, and proclaimed to a startled bosun's mate: "That's an incendiary bomb. Get on with it." The young sailor promptly kicked the hat overboard. In German's words: "It is said to be the only time Commodore Stephenson was seen to be non-plussed."[3] As C 1 finished its training, it was joined by an RN destroyer and SOE and was assigned to the UK–Gibraltar convoy run. The other three Canadian groups then followed suit.

The Gibraltar run, and the convoy route from there to North Africa in sup-port of the Torch landings that had taken place the previous November, was thought to be a good training ground for the refurbished RCN crews and ships. There were fewer convoys, allowing more time for rest and repair between sailings, and virtu-ally the entire route to Gibraltar was under land-based air cover. In addition, the Canadian escort groups could continue their training whenever they were back in the United Kingdom, and they could reinforce the seventeen RCN corvettes that had been sent to the Mediterranean in the fall of 1942. Those vessels were doing yeoman work accompanying merchant ships to and from North Africa, particu-larly in the face of German and Italian air attacks. Between 13 January and 8 February 1943, for example, *Ville de Québec*, *Port Arthur*, and *Regina* sank one German U-boat and two Italian submarines. But these victories did not come without loss. On 6 February, convoy KMS 8, sailing from Gibraltar to Bone, Alge-ria, and escorted by six British and nine Canadian corvettes, was hit by a large force of Italian dive and torpedo bombers; *Louisbourg* was hit by a torpedo and sank within four minutes, taking half her company with her. Another RCN corvette, *Weyburn*, was lost after hitting a mine as it left Gibraltar for the United Kingdom. In both cases the death toll was higher than it might have been owing to the explosions of the ships' depth charges as they sank below the surface, an ever-present threat when escort vessels went down.

By the end of March the Canadian escort groups started to return to the mid-Atlantic, though for a time they remained under RN control and commanded by RN SOEs. Before that, however, C 1 got in its licks in the Mediterranean theatre when it was escorting KMS 10 to North Africa. While still in the North Atlantic, the convoy was attacked by three U-boats; two merchantmen were sunk before *Shediac* and *St Croix* destroyed U-87.

Although most of the Canadian MOEF escorts went to Tobermory, not all did; the corvettes *Rosthern* and *Trillium*, both equipped with the 271 radar, stayed at sea with the US-commanded Escort Group A 3, which included the US Coast Guard cutters *Spencer* and *Campbell*. On 12 February 1943, A 3, augmented by the Canadian corvettes *Dauphin* and *Chilliwack*, and the RN corvette *Dianthus*, joined the westbound convoy ONS 166, with forty-nine merchant vessels, to assume close escort duties.

A 3 assumed its task at a most inopportune time. The severe weather of late December and January had abated; the U-boat wolfpacks were back in force in the mid-Atlantic air gap, and this time they were armed with a significant advantage over the Allies — the Germans had broken a key Royal Navy convoy code. From February to July 1943 the German submarine headquarters, BdU, had available Admiralty U-boat position reports to convoys and escorts at sea; from these reports the Germans were able to determine convoy routings. Although the Allies had themselves rebroken the German naval codes in December 1942, they temporarily lost their ability to decipher them in early February 1943 as the Germans made one of a number of periodic adjustments to their encoding machines.

On 18 February, as ONS 166 pounded westward, high-frequency direction-finding devices picked up U-boat transmissions indicating that submarines were concentrating on the convoy track. Shortly after midnight on 21 February, *Spencer* chased a radar contact that turned out to be U-225, which was then sunk in a depth-charge attack. It was the opening round in a running battle that lasted for six days. Before it was over, ONS 166 lost fourteen ships, although one more U-boat was sunk by *Campbell*. The four Canadian corvettes scored no kills, but they did a good job of keeping U-boats at bay and working in coordination with the American and British vessels (and the Polish destroyer *Burza*, which arrived on

22 February) to avoid even more horrific losses. Considering that the wolfpack strength was eighteen submarines, two U-boat sinkings for fourteen merchant vessels was thought by the RN to have been a qualified success.

Qualified success was better than the unmitigated disaster that had marked the war at sea in 1940 or 1941, but it was still not good enough by far to sustain Operation Bolero. What was needed were more convoys, more frequent sailings, and reduced losses. That meant more escorts, among other things. C 3 was scheduled to return to the MOEF by 11 March, with the three other Canadian groups following in short order. For the time being, however, they would return to their old role of close escort, while the job of seeking out and attacking the wolfpacks would devolve on British and American support groups.

One of the most important but little-known gatherings of the Second World War opened in Washington, DC, on 1 March 1943. The Atlantic Convoy Conference brought together representatives of the USN, the RN, and the RCN to discuss the command organization, tactics, and equipment needs of the three navies in the Battle of the Atlantic. The meeting was held just as the great struggle for control of the North Atlantic was beginning to climax; the Germans were putting more U-boats to sea in larger packs than ever and were determined to reprise the "happy times" of earlier days of the war. The Allies were equally determined to pour more and newer ships, aircraft, and anti-submarine technology into the Atlantic campaign to break the U-boat packs and to increase the convoy tonnage moving to the United Kingdom. If they could not do so, the war in the west might degenerate into stalemate.

The conference opened on a sour note. US Admiral E.J. King, never happy about US escorts sailing in mixed groups (such as A 3) but still unable to commit large numbers of destroyers to the North Atlantic battle, threatened to pull the USN out of the fight altogether. The Canadian delegates renewed their demands to take over full command responsibility for naval and convoy operations in the northwest Atlantic. In the end, the conferees decided that the position of Commander, Task Force 24, would be abolished, that the USN would take general responsibility for southern convoy routes (from the Caribbean to the Mediterranean), but that it would leave one support group in the North Atlantic. The United Kingdom's Western Approaches took charge of the anti-U-boat war in the mid-Atlantic, while Canadian Rear-Admiral Leonard W. Murray would become Commander-in-Chief, Canadian Northwest Atlantic Command. He assumed this new post on 30 April, taking responsibility for all Allied convoy and naval operations north of latitude 40 and west of longitude 47. He became the only Canadian to command a theatre of war in the Second World War, though it was, in fact, not a large one.

Then forty-seven years of age, Murray had been born in Nova Scotia and had entered the Royal Naval College of Canada in 1912, when he was just sixteen. Like all interwar career officers, Murray put in his time aboard Royal Navy vessels, making important connections and learning the ropes of a big-ship navy. He never affected the British accent that so many other Canadian officers did after serving with the RN. He loved sports, particularly hockey, and did not hold himself aloof from his men or his roots in rural Nova Scotia. Soon after the outbreak of the war he was appointed to command the Newfoundland Escort Force, and was promoted to Commanding Officer, Atlantic Coast, in 1942. By all accounts, he was a popular leader with a good grasp of the essence of the anti-U-boat campaign. He was backed by an increasingly skilled and knowledgeable RCN staff, a far cry from the earlier days of the war.

The Atlantic Convoy Conference marked a significant change in the Allied approach to the war against the U-boats. There were to be more escorts, more escort groups, more support groups, and more escort carriers; eventually, the United States would have four such groups in the Atlantic. This would allow for larger convoys and more frequent sailings. Moreover, the RCAF was promised its long-sought VLR Liberators, to fly air cover over the western Atlantic from Newfoundland.

As if to underscore the importance and necessity of the decisions made in Washington, convoys SC 122 and HX 229 departed New York on 5 March and 8 March, respectively, just as the conference broke up. The two convoys were escorted to the Eastern Ocean Meeting Point (EASTOMP), mainly by Canadian ships, then handed over to two RN groups, B 4 and B 5. Alerted by deciphered British radio transmissions, Dönitz was able to concentrate four wolfpacks, with a total of forty-four U-boats, in the path of the convoys (for a few days he thought there was only one). On the night of 16/17 March the battle began; when it ended on the 19th, twenty-one merchant ships had been sunk and not one U-boat had been destroyed.

The slaughter of SC 122 and HX 229 was the last of its kind. The US support group built around the escort carrier USS *Bogue* and the four British support groups (one with the escort carrier HMS *Biter*), along with the VLR Liberators of Eastern Air Command and the RAF's Coastal Command, began to take their toll. These ships and planes augmented the close escorts in two ways: they came to the aid of convoys believed to be threatened or they swept far ahead of the convoy track, searching for gathering U-boat packs. The US-built Grumman Avenger torpedo bombers and Grumman Wildcat fighters, flying off the baby flat-tops, were especially effective in this role. They could cover thousands of square kilometres of ocean in a single day. Flying low, the fighters and bombers surprised the U-boats on the surface, sweeping in with machine guns and bombs. If they did not sink or badly damage their prey, they pinpointed it for the fast escorts that accompanied the escort carriers.

Operating with the aid of Ultra intelligence, the support groups were especially effective in destroying the U-boat supply system that Dönitz had built up since the beginning of the war. That system depended on the 1700-tonne Type IX "milch cows" that rendezvoused with U-boats on war patrol and provided them with fuel, food, mail, and spare parts. The meetings were arranged through coded radio transmissions. Once the Allies were able to decipher the German naval codes again, it was easy to arrange ambushes. Of ten such milch cows operating in the spring of 1943, only two were still afloat by the end of the summer. The impact on U-boat operations was immediate and dramatic; war patrols had to be shortened, and it became necessary to arrange meetings of several U-boats at the same time — a dangerous move. Former U-boat captain Peter Cremer later recalled one such resupply operation in August 1943: "We were five boats dawdling away the time without fuel or food. The situation was not only grotesque, it was desperate . . . here we were, five of us confined in the narrowest space, a prey to anything that might happen."[4]

At first the support groups were formed by stripping existing escort groups of warships, but the Americans were soon pouring hundreds of new escort vessels and three additional escort carriers into the Atlantic battle. One of the most important types of the new escort ships was the purpose-built destroyer escort (DE), which was considerably smaller than a fleet destroyer. Most DEs were armed with two 5-inch guns (earlier models were less well armed), depth charges, hedgehog, and the newest in radar and sonar (as the Americans referred to asdic). Though the DEs had a top speed of only 20 to 25 knots — well below that of most contemporary destroyers — they were considerably faster than a surfaced U-boat (unlike a corvette) and had a tight turning circle, essential for anti-submarine work.

The Canadians also acquired new escort vessels in mid-1943. First came a second generation of River Class destroyers, ex-RN vessels, which were more heavily armed than the original prewar types. The first into commission in March 1943 was the *Ottawa II*, which became the nucleus for a new Canadian escort group, C 5.

Eventually six of these destroyers were acquired, and all were assigned to the MOEF to give the Canadian groups more punch. In June the RCN also took delivery of the first of what would prove to be a fleet of more than seventy River Class frigates, virtually all of which were built in Canada. The RCN knew that its corvettes, still the bulk of its fleet, though barely adequate in the first two years of war, were not suitable for sustained ocean operations, even when they were modified with extended forecastles, better electronics, and other advances. The frigates were designed to fill the bill. They had been chosen by the RCN over the American DEs and were similar in size and armament, though several knots slower.

The RCN played almost no role at all in the Allied offensive against Dönitz's wolfpacks which peaked in May 1943, when forty-seven U-boats were destroyed in one month. The climax of that campaign came with the voyage of convoy ONS 5, which sailed from Liverpool on 21 April escorted by the RN group B 7. The first shots in the battle of ONS 5 were fired on 26 April, when a Coastal Command aircraft sank U-710 ahead of the convoy. Then the struggle was joined, as two RN support groups rushed to the aid of B 7. The U-boats managed to sink twelve merchant ships despite rain, cloud, and heavy seas. An RCAF Canso accounted for one U-boat during a brief break in the weather, but it began to look as though another slaughter was in the offing. On the night of 6/7 May, however, when fifteen submarines tried to drive home their attacks in calm but foggy seas, the escorts, using their radar effectively, drove off some twenty-five attacks. The U-boats failed to launch a single torpedo. More disastrous still for Dönitz, six submarines were lost that night. In the end, ONS 5 lost twelve merchant ships, but the Germans lost eight submarines sunk by escorts, two more submarines lost through collision, and seventeen submarines damaged, some severely. It was the clearest sign yet that the tide of battle was turning.

Although the RCN did not share in the May mass killing of U-boats, it carried out its close escort missions with as much determination as ever, but with a great deal more skill, as the story of convoy HX 237 shows. Sailing to the United Kingdom in early May, that convoy was escorted by C 2, consisting of three RCN corvettes, two RN corvettes, and one RN destroyer. HMS *Biter* and her support-group consorts swept well ahead of HX 237 and enabled it to break through a well-guarded U-boat patrol line. The RCN corvette *Drumheller* combined with an RCAF Sunderland of No. 423 Squadron of Coastal Command and the RN destroyer *Lagan* to sink U-753 on 13 May. No ships were lost.

Dönitz lost his own son that month, a watch officer serving aboard U-954.

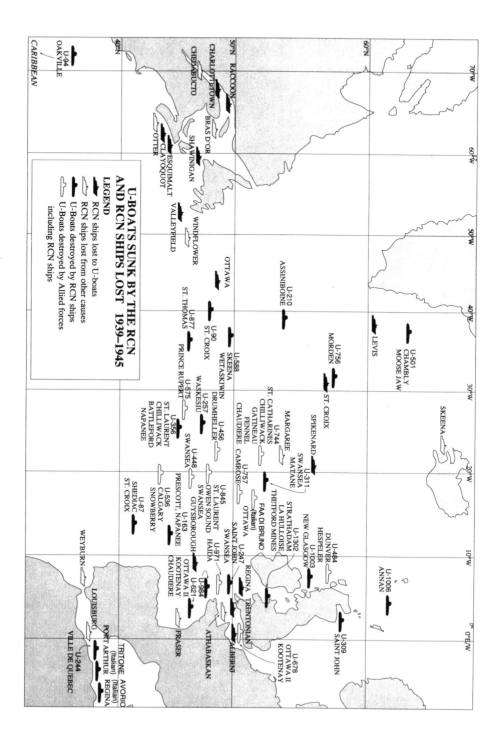

U-BOATS SUNK BY THE RCN
AND RCN SHIPS LOST 1939–1945

LEGEND

RCN ships lost to U-boats
RCN ships lost from other causes
U-Boats destroyed by RCN ships
U-Boats destroyed by Allied forces
including RCN ships

CARIBBEAN

U-94
OAKVILLE

40°N

50°N

60°N

70°W

60°W

50°W

40°W

30°W

10°W

0°E/W

CHARLOTTETOWN RACCOON
CHEDABUCTO
BRAS D'OR
SHAWINIGAN
ESQUIMALT
CLAYOQUOT
OTTER
VALLEYFIELD
WINDFLOWER

OTTAWA
ASSINIBOINE
U-210

U-756
MORDEN
ST. CROIX

LEVIS

U-501
CHAMBLY
MOOSE JAW

SKEENA

U-588
SKEENA
WETASKIWIN
U-877
ST. THOMAS
U-90
ST. CROIX
PRINCE RUPERT

DRUMHELLER
WASKESIU
U-257
U-575
ST. LAURENT
CHILLIWACK
BATTLEFORD
NAPANEE
U-356

CHILLIWACK
ST. CATHARINES
MARGAREE
MATANE
GATINEAU
FENNEL
CHAUDIERE CAMROSE

SPIKENARD
SWANSEA
MATANE
U-311

SWANSEA
U-448
U-757
OTTAWA
FAA DI BRUNO
(Italian)

STRATHADAM
LA HULLOISE
THETFORD MINES
U-1302
NEW GLASGOW
U-1003

DUNVER
HESPELER
U-484

U-1006
ANNAN

U-845
ST. LAURENT
SWANSEA
OWEN SOUND
GUYSBOROUGH
PRESCOTT, NAPANEE
SWANSEA
U-163
U-536
CALGARY
SNOWBERRY
U-87
SHEDIAC
ST. CROIX

SAINT JOHN
REGINA
OTTAWA
U-247
SWANSEA
HAIDA
U-971
ST. ALBERNI
OTTAWA II
KOOTENAY
CHAUDIERE
FRASER
U-984
U-621
TRENTONIAN

U-678
OTTAWA II
KOOTENAY

U-309
SAINT JOHN

ATHABASKAN

WEYBURN

LOUISBURG
PORT ARTHUR
TRITONE AVORIO
(Italian) (Italian)
VILLE DE QUEBEC
U-244
REGINA

141

The tide had clearly turned to the point where heavy U-boat concentrations now invariably meant heavy losses. The mid-Atlantic air gap had finally been closed, and the Allies now had enough high-quality escort vessels, escort carriers, and aircraft to shepherd large convoys safely to their destinations with small loss. On 14 May Dönitz told Hitler: "We are facing the greatest crisis of the U-boat war. The enemy are making it impossible to fight."[5] It was time to rethink tactics, and to re-equip his submarines with advanced new weapons and detection gear to give them a fighting chance. At the end of May he pulled his U-boats out of the North Atlantic for the first time since the beginning of the war and assigned them to the area west of the Azores.

Although it was the British and the American navies that bore the brunt of the offensive against the U-boats in the spring of 1943, they could not have been successful without the RAF and the RCAF. Most historians who have written about the Battle of the Atlantic are agreed, first, that the Allies could have closed the mid-Atlantic air gap much sooner than they did and, second, that their failure to do so until mid-1943 remains one of the great enigmas of the war. By all measures they surely realized that the greatest U-boat victories always occurred beyond the reach of aircraft, and that aircraft were of inestimable value not only to sink U-boats but to keep them down and to render them virtually blind while the convoys manoeuvred around them. They ought to have recognized these points, but they did not, even though the aircraft and the technology had been available at least since the beginning of 1942.

The RCAF's contribution to turning the tide against the U-boats was made at both ends of the Atlantic. No. 10 Squadron of Eastern Air Command, based at Gander, began to receive VLR Liberators on 22 April 1943; by the end of May the entire squadron had converted to the new aircraft. No. 11 Squadron, located at Torbay, Newfoundland, began to convert to the Liberators in July. No. 10 Squadron had already sunk one submarine (U-520) the previous October, when a Douglas Digby had spotted it on the surface while it was returning from patrol over convoy ON 140. Its new Liberators would account for two more U-boats before the end of 1943. Its first victim was U-341, spotted and sunk on 19 September as the aircraft was returning to Gander from Iceland after escorting HMS *Renown*, which was carrying Winston Churchill back to the United Kingdom after the first

Quebec Conference. The second victim, U-420, was destroyed on 26 October. No. 11 Squadron made ten sightings and mounted eight attacks, but did not sink any U-boats.

At the other end of the transatlantic lifeline, five RCAF squadrons served with the anti-submarine squadrons of the RAF's Coastal Command in the United Kingdom at various times during the war. Nos. 405 and 415 Squadrons later reverted to Bomber Command. Nos. 422 and 423 Squadrons, which flew Sunderland IIIs out of Castle Archdale, Northern Ireland, together (and in combination with other Allied units) accounted for four U-boats during the war. The most successful anti-submarine squadron in the RCAF was No. 162, which flew Canso patrol bombers. Originally based at Yarmouth, Nova Scotia, the squadron was loaned to the RAF's Coastal Command in January 1944 and transferred to Iceland. Its first victory came on 17 April 1944 and, by the end of the war, it had accounted for five submarines sunk, one shared sinking, and one U-boat damaged. On 24 June 1944 a No. 162 Squadron Canso flown by Flight Lieutenant D.E. Hornell attacked U-1225 and sank it, but it was hit by return anti-aircraft fire in the course of the engagement and crashed. The crew spent nine hours in the water before being rescued (seven were rescued, one had drowned). Hornell died shortly after rescue and was posthumously awarded the Victoria Cross.

From the beginning of 1943 to the end of the war, RCAF squadrons sank or shared in the sinking of seventeen U-boats. It was a solid performance, aided by the fact that from early 1943 on the RCAF was no longer the step-child of the Allied anti-submarine airforces, but began to receive the newest in an ever lengthening list of high-tech anti-submarine devices. For example, EAC's Liberators were equipped with the newest US-designed anti-submarine radar, a 10-centimetre radar that could detect a surfaced U-boat from about 20 kilometres away but which could not be picked up by the U-boats' Metox radar-detection receivers. EAC also received the newest US-built homing torpedoes, designed to be used in conjunction with air-dropped sono-buoys. The system was intended to detect prowling U-boats and to radio their location to patrolling aircraft, which would then drop the homing torpedoes to hunt the submarines down. A highly technical and temperamental system, it never worked properly during the war, but became the mainstay of anti-submarine weaponry in the years afterwards. The same was true of the new magnetic anomaly detector (MAD) gear, designed to pick up a submerged submarine from the changes in the Earth's magnetic field which were caused by the passage of a large metallic object.

If there was one man who, compared with his Allied peers, was least in tune with the ever more complex and technical nature of the anti-submarine war, it was Vice-Admiral Percy W. Nelles, Chief of the Naval Staff in Ottawa since 1934. Nelles was not at fault for the many shortages of vessels and trained men that had plagued the RCN since the outbreak of war, though he had been over-eager to take on more than his fledgling navy could handle, such as the dispatch of corvettes to the Mediterranean in late 1942. But there is no question that he had great difficulty in coming to grips with the fact that anti-submarine warfare had changed dramatically since the First World War. A navy that was not prepared to give its men the very latest in equipment and training could not hope to pull its weight in the Atlantic battle. Nelles had constantly failed to ensure that the RCN kept up with its Allies in that regard, and the RCN's anti-U-boat score had suffered as a result.

In early August 1943 Angus MacDonald, Minister of National Defence for Naval Services, received a private memorandum from William Strange, Director of Naval Information at NSHQ, which made a singular point: the RCN was not equipped to fight an anti-U-boat offensive in the North Atlantic because most of its vessels, particularly the corvettes, still lacked basic modern equipment such as gyro-compasses and hedgehog. MacDonald, who as minister in charge of the navy surely ought to have been aware of this problem, conducted a behind-the-scenes investigation while he tried to get answers from Nelles to the questions posed in the memorandum. By the end of the year he concluded that Nelles must go, since RCN vessels had been "putting to sea inadequately equipped as compared to British ships . . . over an unduly long period of time."[6] Nelles was moved out of the chief's post in January 1944 and replaced by Vice-Admiral G.C. Jones. Though at least as culpable as Nelles for the RCN's problems, MacDonald kept his cabinet post to the end of the war.

No one was more aware of the impact of the battle of new technologies on the war at sea than Dönitz. He was determined to re-equip his submarines before he sent them back into the mid-Atlantic; between the end of May and the beginning of September 1943, he did just that. The long-run answer to the Allies' new ships and equipment was to be the Walter boat which, equipped with an advanced turbine motor operating on hydrogen-peroxide fuel and the new snorkel device, would be able to remain under water indefinitely. Its smooth hull design would allow it to reach speeds of up to 25 knots under water, compared with the 7 knots top speed of the submerged Type VII and Type IX U-boats. The Walter boat was only a dream: the concept never reached a practical stage of development during the war. But Dönitz had another variant up his sleeve, the Type XXI boat. Conventionally powered, but with a larger battery capacity, it had a streamlined hull to achieve much higher speeds while underwater than the Type VII and Type IX. The Type XXIII, a smaller version of the Type XXI and intended for inshore operations, was also under development. Until the Type XXI and XXIII boats were available, however, Dönitz would have to rely on improving his conventional submarines. This was done by adding additional anti-aircraft guns, new radar-detection equipment, and the snorkel device that allowed U-boats to use their diesel engines while they travelled just below the surface. This device enabled U-boats to attain higher speeds, and gave them the ability to recirculate stale air, recharge batteries, and stay under water for much longer periods than previously. Each submarine was also allotted four *Zaunkonig* homing torpedoes (Gnats) intended to destroy escort vessels by homing in on propeller noise.

In early September the re-equipped U-boats returned to the mid-Atlantic. As we have seen, Group *Leuthen* with twenty submarines intercepted ONS 18 and ON 202 about 640 kilometres southeast of Iceland and inflicted heavy damage; six merchantmen were destroyed, under cover of night and bad weather, and three escorts — *St Croix*, *Polyanthus*, and *Itchen* — went to the bottom with heavy loss of life. When the skies cleared on the afternoon of 22 September, RAF and RCAF VLR Liberators were there, orbiting the convoy, ready to provide cover; the RAF's No. 120 Squadron then accounted for one U-boat sunk.

The battle of ONS 18 and ON 202 was, without a doubt, a German tactical victory. But it was also one of the last Dönitz was to have and it was a clear exception to the general trend of events in the North Atlantic in the last months of 1943. Within days the RN and the RCN began to equip their escorts with towed decoy devices to counter the homing torpedoes — the British used Foxer and the Canadians used the simpler and lighter CAT gear — thus effectively neutralizing one of Dönitz's most important innovations. In one convoy fight lasting from 18 to 21 November, for example, the Germans threw twenty-three U-boats and twenty-five long-distance Focke Wulf 200 Condor bombers at a convoy of twenty-eight escorts and sixty-six merchant ships, but sank only one merchantman while losing three U-boats. One of the submarines destroyed was U-536, which fell victim to the RCN corvettes *Snowberry* and *Calgary* and the RN corvette *Nene*. In the first six months of 1943 the U-boat fleet had sunk 1.7 million tonnes of Allied shipping; in the last six months its total dropped to 500,000 tonnes, while it lost 142 submarines. Many more merchant vessels and escorts would be sunk and several thousand more merchant seamen and naval personnel would lose their lives before the end of the war, but the tide of the war at sea had clearly turned.

✹

On 30 November 1942 the Tribal Class destroyer *Iroquois*, built in the United Kingdom, was commissioned into the Royal Canadian Navy. It was the first of four Tribals built for the RCN in Britain during the war; the other three were *Athabaskan* (commissioned in February 1943), *Huron* (commissioned in July 1943), and *Haida* (commissioned in August 1943). The Tribals were by far the most advanced and most powerful of the destroyers acquired by Canada during the war. Designed for RN fleet service in the late 1930s, these ships displaced close to 1800 tonnes, had a top speed of 36 knots, were manned by fourteen officers and 245 ratings, were armed with six 4.7-inch guns and four torpedo tubes as main armament, and carried a large complement of medium and light anti-aircraft weapons. In every sense, the Tribals were designed for fleet action and not for escort duty. In 1941 the Canadian government, at the urging of the RCN, decided to build four modified Tribals in Canada, even though the RCN's Chief of Naval Engineering and Construction, Rear-Admiral George Stephens, opposed the move as extravagant and unnecessary. The Canadian Tribals were not commissioned until after the war, and it is clear from the historical record that the RCN saw them as the backbone of a modern and moderate-sized postwar fleet, not as ships to help win the current war.

Based in Scapa Flow for much of 1943, the Canadian Tribals performed a variety of duties, from anti-submarine patrols in the Bay of Biscay to anti-aircraft escort on the convoy routes from the United Kingdom to Murmansk, USSR. There were trials aplenty for these destroyers, ranging from equipment failures and a short-lived mutiny on the *Iroquois* to the damaging of *Athabaskan* by a German glider-bomb off the coast of Spain in late August. *Athabaskan* was part of a five-ship support group attacked by Dornier 217s carrying HS 293 glider bombs in the early afternoon of 27 August. A new weapon, the HS 293 was a winged, radio-controlled missile with a 600-pound warhead which was capable of speeds up to 603 kilometres per hour. As the aircraft approached, the Canadian destroyer opened fire at 1303; soon the sky was filled with flak from the guns of the five warships. One of the ships, HMS *Egret*, was hit almost immediately and sank with heavy loss of life. Five aircraft then attacked *Athabaskan*, three releasing their glider bombs at the same time; one missile tore into the destroyer and out the other side before exploding — its fuse improperly set. But it did tremendous damage; five men were killed or died of their wounds, twelve were injured, and the ship was left down at the bow, on fire, and with a significant list. Escorted by the remaining ships in the group, *Athabaskan* limped back to port, arriving at Plymouth late on the 30th; the dead had already been buried at sea.

By the end of 1943, the RCN's transition from corvette navy — its chief task convoy escort — to something larger and more mature had begun. But what was that larger Royal Canadian Navy to be? At the height of the Allied submarine-killing offensive, the professional officers flirted with the idea that the RCN's chief ambition should be to build a second-to-none anti-submarine navy. That navy would use fast, manoeuvrable, and comfortable ships equipped with the best in radar, asdic, and anti-submarine weapons. But that would have taken a dedicated mid-war building and acquisition program because there was no practical way to re-fit the existing corvette fleet to become something it was not.

It was in this period of uncertainty that the RCN decided that its new River Class frigates would become the mainstay of the Canadian anti-U-boat offensive; sixty-one of these ships were built in Canada, and seven were acquired from the RN (in addition to three similarly sized Loch Class frigates also from the RN). Displacing some 1400 tonnes, the frigates carried two 4-inch guns as main armament and a variety of anti-aircraft weapons, as well as hedgehog and depth charges. The Loch Class ships mounted the new "squid," an ahead-throwing mortar that tossed three large, depth charge-size bombs automatically set to explode at a predetermined depth when they were linked to the newest asdic devices.

These better ships, with more advanced radars and asdic and more effective weapons, allowed the RCN to step up its war successfully against U-boats in 1944. Operating with these ships, but without the aid of baby flat-tops (which the RN steadfastly refused to give the RCN for anti-U-boat operations), the RCN performed well, especially in UK waters, in the summer and fall of 1944. Chummy Prentice's support group, Escort Group 11, formed in the spring of 1944, was the single most effective Allied anti-submarine group during the Normandy operations. At war's end, he and Commander Clarence King, of the RCNR, had participated in the destruction of four U-boats apiece.

But just as the RCN's overall performance at convoy escort suffered from the technological backwardness of its ships and equipment in 1942 and 1943, so too its performance at submarine-killing in 1944 and 1945 left something to be desired, also for reasons of equipment. The U-boats Dönitz sent to sea from late 1943 to the end of the war were not only better equipped, but they could dive much deeper. A new US-developed 3-centimetre radar was required to find submarines cruising at snorkel depth; the squid mortar linked to the Type 147B asdic was needed to kill them when they went deep. The RN mounted a crash program to equip its submarine-hunters with these new devices, but the RCN dragged its heels. Almost no RCN anti-submarine vessels had mounted the squid/147B asdic combination at war's end.

The reason the Royal Canadian Navy lagged behind in submarine-killing technology is that the "pusser" navy had greater things on its mind. Most RCN officers, and certainly those in the navy's upper echelons, thought of anti-submarine warfare as second class. They wanted the RCN to acquire fleet destroyers such as the Tribals, cruisers, light fleet carriers, and whatever else they thought their dream navy required. They thought of anti-submarine command as a dead end; true war and postwar advancement would come from service aboard the larger fleet ships. As Marc Milner has put it, "the period from late 1942 to the late summer of 1943 was the only time when the problems of the escort fleet dominated the RCN's agenda. That phase passed with the advancement of plans for the acquisition of major fleet units in the fall of 1943."[7] Thus the RCN's dreams of postwar RCN grandeur stood in the way of a better RCN wartime performance. What is truly ironic about those dreams is that the postwar RCN, under pressure from the government to define a realistic Cold War goal for itself, would choose to specialize in none other than anti-submarine warfare.

T he small Sicilian town of Nissoria sits astride a straight portion of the highway from the hilltop town of Agira to Leonforte, close to the centre of Sicily.
Most Sicilian towns perch, like eagles' nests, on high peaks, and are reachable
only by narrow roads that twist and climb over the mountains that dominate the
centre of the island. They are sited there because armies have fought over Sicily
since time immemorial; the Sicilians long ago learned the hard lesson that it is
easier to defend hilltops than valleys. But Nissoria is an exception; it is located in
a shallow valley about 6.5 kilometres west of Agira. On the morning of 24 July
1943 this otherwise unexceptional place was the initial objective of an attack
mounted by the Royal Canadian Regiment (RCR) of the 1st Canadian Infantry
Brigade, 1st Canadian Infantry Division. The ultimate goal for the day was not
Nissoria, but Agira, which overlooks an important road junction on the highway
from Catania, on the east coast of the island, to the Sicilian capital of Palermo, on
the north coast.

The assault plan, conceived by divisional commander Guy Granville Simonds,
was designed to use the massive firepower available to the Canadian division to
clear the way for the RCR attackers. Under cover of an air and artillery bombardment, the RCR's four rifle companies were to leapfrog astride the highway through
Nissoria and then make the long, hilly climb into Agira. Before the bombardment, the battalion commanding officer, Lieutenant-Colonel Ralph Crowe, took
his company commanders forward to reconnoitre the ground over which they
would advance. One of them later described the scene: "Ahead lay undulating
ground covered with olive orchards and grapevines while Nissoria looked white
and deceptively clean in the burning sun."[1]

The barrage and the airstrike began, and the ground ahead of the advance
was covered with smoke and shook with the shock of exploding bombs and shells.
Then the infantry started its advance. The RCR tried to follow the creeping barrage, but the inevitable delays that accompany any infantry advance slowed them
down and the barrage moved on, the men falling farther and farther behind. As

soon as the shelling passed over, the Germans clambered out of their slit trenches and bunkers, sited their mortars and machine guns, and waited for the Canadians to draw within range. At about 1630, they opened fire. The RCR regimental history tells what happened:

> Just as [the RCR] began emerging from the eastern edge of [Nissoria] heavy fire was brought down upon them. At the same time the rear companies were breaking from cover, provided from orchard lands west of the town. Some of the troops were actually eating apples as they moved forward, when suddenly a terrific mortar barrage fell upon them and a low ridge they must of necessity cross was swept by machine gun fire.[2]

D Company was chewed up and the survivors pinned down. The other three companies took cover in a gully, advanced, and found themselves behind the German ambushers, in sight of Agira and in a good position to cut off the forward elements of the German defence. But they did nothing. While they were in the gully, the battle raged, but the three RCR company commanders were separated from their battalion headquarters and could not decide what to do. They remained where they were until the following day and were then ordered to withdraw. A golden opportunity had been lost to come up behind the Germans, shorten the battle, and keep Canadian casualties low.

The campaign to capture Agira was supposed to be over in two days or less. It was not. The heavy casualties suffered in the initial attack by D Company were just the beginning; Agira was not taken for five more days and the cost to the division was high — 438 killed, wounded, missing, or taken prisoner; the Canadian war cemetery at Agira is the largest in Sicily. The fight for Agira revealed both the strengths and the weaknesses of the way the Canadian Army had learned to wage war; both would become clear in the summer and fall of 1943 as the difficult battle for what Churchill had called "the soft underbelly of Europe" ground on without any apparent resolution.

The Mediterranean Sea has been a theatre of war since the dawn of time. On its periphery, Egyptians, Greeks, Romans, Byzantines, Arabs, and Crusaders have struggled and died for centuries to control trade routes, access to ports, strategic islands, and land routes to the east and to Africa. Phoenicians, Philistines,

Carthaginians, and other sea peoples have tried to assert their dominance over its blue waters. The Axis powers were no less interested in this strategically important sea; *Mare Nostrum* — "our sea" — declared Italian dictator Benito Mussolini's fascists, as they and their German allies tried to turn the Mediterranean into an Axis lake. To break that dominance, to secure the Suez Canal, and to prevent a possible link-up between the German Afrika Korps and the German armies in the Caucasus Mountains, Britain and the United States had fought to expel the Axis from North Africa. The British victory at El Alamein in October 1942 and the British and American Torch landings in Morocco and Algeria the following month had been the beginning of the end of that campaign; the surrender of the Germans in Tunisia in May 1943 set the stage for the next phase of the struggle — Operation Husky, the invasion of Sicily.

The men of the 1st Canadian Infantry Division, accompanied by the 1st Canadian Army Tank Brigade, were not the first Canadians in the Mediterranean theatre. The RCAF's No. 417 Fighter Squadron had been transferred to Egypt in June 1942 and had mounted its first offensive mission in March 1943, one month before it officially joined the Desert Air Force. In June 1943 three RCAF Wellington squadrons from No. 6 Group of Bomber Command — Nos. 420, 424, and 425 — were detached from the United Kingdom and sent to form No. 331 Wing based at Kairouan in Tunisia, where they were to fly missions in support of the upcoming Sicily landings. Their first bombing raid on Sicily was mounted on 26 June against an airfield.

The RCN had also taken part in Mediterranean operations prior to the Sicily invasions. In the fall of 1942, seventeen corvettes had been sent to the United Kingdom to have the 271 radar installed and their anti-aircraft defences improved before they proceeded to the Mediterranean to help guard convoys from Britain and Gibraltar to North Africa. Their numbers were briefly augmented when the Canadian Mid-Ocean Escort Force groups were put on the UK–Gibraltar and UK–Gibraltar–North Africa run in the late winter and early spring of 1943.

In addition to the RCAF and RCN, some 350 officers and noncommissioned officers (NCOs) from a variety of Canadian Army units had been rotated through the British forces in North Africa at three-month intervals in order to gain battle experience. They had gone not as observers but as participants; while they were there, they were fitted into British Army formations to carry out whatever tasks were assigned them. One of these men was Guy Simonds, then a Brigadier, who had been attached to General Bernard Montgomery's Eighth Army headquarters for about two weeks in April 1943, and who had returned to the United Kingdom convinced that "the day of blitzkrieg was over" and that "carefully prepared infantry attacks were required" to assault well-defended German positions successfully.[3]

While the battles for North Africa raged back and forth over desert sands and coastal blacktop roads, and from wadi to oasis to seaport, the Canadian Army in the United Kingdom — the "dagger pointed at the heart of Germany" — trained and trained and trained some more. By the spring of 1943 it had assumed the basic shape it would retain for the rest of the war — a headquarters (then commanded by A.G.L. McNaughton), two army corps headquarters, five divisions (three infantry and two armoured), and two independent armoured brigades. In addition, the 1st Canadian Parachute Battalion was being made ready to join the 6th British Airborne Division in July. Altogether, it was a formidable force that was doing almost nothing to defeat Germany — at a time when Americans and Britons were fighting and dying in several war theatres around the globe. This fact could not be hidden from the Canadian people — and especially not from the Canadian press.

One of the reasons that Canadian troops were doing virtually nothing was McNaughton's well-known antipathy to breaking up the First Canadian Army. By the late winter of 1942/43, however, the pressure on Prime Minister Mackenzie King to send Canadian soldiers into battle had increased to the point where he was willing to disregard McNaughton's views. In March 1943 Ottawa notified London that Canada was now in favour of larger units of the Canadian Army being used in extended operations outside the United Kingdom, with the understanding that they would be returned to Britain in time for the opening of the second front. In late April the British responded by asking Canada for permission to use a Canadian infantry division and armoured brigade in "operations based on Tunisia." Canada agreed, and the 1st Canadian Infantry Division and the 1st Canadian Army Tank Brigade were chosen to take part in the forthcoming landing in Sicily. The 1st Division was to replace the 3rd British Infantry Division. The Canadians were to be attached to the 30th Corps of the British Eighth Army under Montgomery. The rest of the invading force consisted of the United States Seventh Army under US General George S. Patton. The overall ground commander was British General Sir Harold Alexander, while the overall commander of air, land, and naval forces was US General Dwight D. Eisenhower, who had been in command of the Torch landings.

The first Canadian division to be mobilized and dispatched to the United

Kingdom, the men of the 1st Canadian Infantry Division wore the "old red patch" on their shoulders, the same divisional insignia worn by the 1st Canadian Division in the First World War. The division included the three prewar Permanent Force regiments — the Royal Canadian Regiment (RCR), the Princess Patricia's Canadian Light Infantry (PPCLI), and the Royal 22e Régiment (the Van Doos), one in each of its infantry brigades — and six militia battalions. Under the command of Major-General H.L.N. Salmon, it was assigned a landing zone at the extreme left flank of the British invasion force, but Salmon and many of his staff were killed on 29 April as their Tunis-bound plane crashed after takeoff from the United Kingdom. Simonds was assigned to take Salmon's place.

Born in the United Kingdom in 1903, Simonds came to Canada as a tot with his family before the First World War and settled in Victoria. He entered the Royal Military College in 1921 and graduated in 1925. He then joined the Royal Canadian Horse Artillery and began a long and distinguished career in the Canadian Army which ended only upon his retirement in 1955. Simonds was one of the best of the small corps of professional officers who kept the Canadian Army alive in the interwar years. He thought systematically about the craft of war and published articles on armour-infantry tactics in 1938. He went overseas with the 1st Canadian Infantry Division in 1939 and was noticed early for his brains, his devotion to his task, and his no-nonsense approach to soldiering.

Simonds is a controversial figure in Canadian military history. He was respected by the British as a man who understood war and the requirements for winning battles, and was admired by Montgomery himself as the best of the up-and-coming Canadian officers. Non-Canadian military historians today generally believe him to have been the best field commander Canada produced in the Second World War. Yet he was never loved by those who served under him. Simonds tried to be a teacher as much as a leader; as commander of the 2nd Canadian Corps from early 1944 to the end of the war, he constantly sent memos to his officers advising them on subjects as diverse as German defensive tactics and the importance of properly integrating reinforcements (replacement personnel) into their battalions. As a devotee of Montgomery's set-piece battle, his battle plans were invariably long and complicated and based on major applications of firepower. He firmly believed in the maxim, born of bitter experience in the trenches of the First World War, that it was better to waste shells than the lives of men; he seemed not to pay heed to another maxim, from the nineteenth-century German commander von Moltke, that no battle plan survives first contact with the enemy.

Roughly triangular in shape, Sicily is about 290 kilometres from western to eastern tips and 180 kilometres at its widest point from north to south. The major geophysical feature on the island is the active volcano Mt Etna, just inland from the island's east coast, north of the city of Catania. South of Etna is the marshy Catania plain. The capital is Palermo, on the north coast. Sicily is separated from Italy by the 3-kilometre-wide Strait of Messina, at its northeastern tip. Most of the island's interior is rugged and mountainous, with hilltop villages connected by a handful of narrow, twisting roads running through defiles and up the sides of steep, rugged hills. The terrain is easily defended from heights of land that give defenders vistas stretching for tens of kilometres. A few well-placed heavy mortars or artillery pieces and a well-sited ambush employing as few as a company of infantry could hold up an advance for many hours, if not days.

Sicily was defended by a mixed force of German and Italian troops; there were 300,000 Italians and the German 15th Panzer division on the island as late as June 1943. The British tried to convince the Germans and Italians that their next objective after North Africa was the Balkans, not Sicily. They left a dead body dressed as a Royal Marine officer and carrying secret papers where it would wash ashore on the Spanish coast (he was forever after known as "the man who never was"). The ruse largely worked, except that the Italian garrison commander, General Alfredo Guzzoni, remained unconvinced and sought reinforcements. The Germans sent the newly recreated Hermann Göring division (the original division had been lost in Tunisia) to augment the 15th Panzer and shore up the island's defences. Guzzoni wanted to position the two German divisions in eastern Sicily, out of range of possible naval gunfire, where they could rush forward with their armour to counter-attack an Allied landing force and throw them back into the sea. He convinced the Germans to put the Göring division there, but the 15th Panzer was divided into three battle groups (kampfgruppen) located across the breadth of the island.

The Allied plan had come together only after a long and fierce debate among British and American commanders as to what objectives, roles, and portions of the island were to be assigned to what forces. Alexander shirked his duty as ground commander in not imposing a plan and the discipline of command on Montgomery and Patton. In the end, a plan evolved that was to have the British land on the island's southeast coast, south of Syracuse, on a front of some 60 kilometres, while the Americans were to land on a front only slightly smaller to the east of Ricata, on the south coast. The Allies were then to attack northward, cut Sicily in half, pivot eastward, and then destroy the enemy forces between them and the east coast. The Canadians were assigned a beach near the southernmost tip of Sicily, opposite the town and airfield of Pacino. D-Day was set for 10 July.

On 19 June the first transports carrying the Canadians from the United Kingdom directly to Sicily left Scotland; a second group of transports sailed five days later. Together, they were known as the Slow Assault Convoy. Another convoy, known as the Fast Assault Convoy, left the River Clyde on 28 June. Both proceeded to Gibraltar. The men did not know for certain where they were going, but the fact that they had traded their Canadian-built Ram tanks for the American Sherman medium tank, the standard battle tank used by both the British and the Americans in North Africa, must have given them a clue. They were also equipped with the Thompson .45 submachine gun, also the standard gun in that theatre, rather than the British Sten gun, used by Canadian and British troops in Northwest Europe. The voyage to Sicilian waters took many days and, after passing through the Strait of Gibraltar, enemy aircraft and submarines posed a serious threat. On 4 July three ships from the Slow Assault Convoy were torpedoed and sunk; fifty-eight Canadians were killed and more than 500 vehicles were lost, along with thirty artillery pieces and the radios intended for use by divisional headquarters.

In the predawn darkness of 10 July, American and British paratroopers assaulted the southern and southeastern coasts of Sicily. The mixed force of glider-borne troops and parachutists was badly scattered and there were heavy casualties. Then the naval support force opened up and the sounds of heavy gunfire and the flash of the long-range naval guns tore through the night. The Canadians' beach, code-named Bark West, was on the southwest side of the Pacino peninsula. The 1st Brigade was assigned to the right-flank beach — "roger" — and the 2nd Brigade to the left flank — "sugar." The landing on the left went well and the troops were quickly ashore with no opposition, but on the right there were delays because of the late arrival of the landing craft. Then, when the craft did nose towards shore, they grounded on a sand-bar about a hundred metres from the beach. Platoon commander Farley Mowat was there:

> This was the moment toward which all my years of army training had been building . . . Revolver in hand, Tommy gun slung over my shoulder, web

equipment bulging with grenades and ammo, tin hat pulled firmly down around my ears, I sprinted to the end of the ramp shouting "follow me, men!" . . . and leaped off into eight feet of water."[4]

All along the beachheads, the defenders offered little or no resistance; British, Canadians, and Americans were quickly ashore and they pushed inland rapidly. The airfield at Pacino was easily taken. Then the business of unloading the supplies and equipment began, as the battalion and company commanders huddled at brigade Orders Groups to look at maps and aerial photographs and to plan the next move. As the sun climbed higher, the flies and mosquitoes were everywhere, the vehicles produced thick clouds of dust and grit, and the heat increased by the minute. Since most of the vehicles had been lost at sea, the men would have to walk. Makeshift mule teams were organized, the animals "requisitioned" or hired from the locals, to carry the heavier equipment. After a night near the beach, the 1st and 2nd Brigades started out, the 1st on the right moving overland through the hills to the village of Giarratana, the 2nd on the left marching by road towards Modica and Ragusa, where they were to effect a junction with the US 45th Division. That first day set the pattern for most of those that followed: the men walked up steep roads or made their way over rocky hillsides under a broiling sun in unbearable heat, with water rationed and clouds of mosquitoes and flies to torment them every time they stopped for rest. As the division moved inland, it was accompanied by the Three Rivers Regiment of the 1st Canadian Army Tank Brigade; the rest of the brigade remained behind with the armoured reserve of the British Eighth Army. (The designation of this unit was soon to be changed to 1st Canadian Armoured Brigade, a pattern that was followed for all similar formations.)

To the left of the Canadians, the Americans had a much harder time of it. The Hermann Göring division struck hard the day after the landings and drove towards the beaches occupied by the US 1st Division. Had the Germans succeeded, they would have exposed the left flank of the US 45th Division, to the left of the Canadians, but the Americans put up a tenacious defence, aided by naval gunfire, and drove the panzers back. The Canadians encountered virtually no opposition for the first five days, and took the headquarters of Italian General Achilles d'Havet in Modica on 12 July without a struggle. Simonds went there personally to accept d'Havet's surrender. Riding in a jeep, CBC war correspondent Peter Stursburg was just behind the troops as they advanced beyond Modica:

- Milan

Venice

Po

Bologna
Reno
Senio
GOTHIC LINE

Pisa
Arno
Rimini
SAN MARINO
Foglio
Metauro

Ancona

N

Civitavecchia

ROME

Orsogna

Pescara
Ortona

ADRIATIC SEA

Sacco
Liri
Sangro

GUSTAV LINE

Anzio
HITLER
LINE
Castel di
Sangro
Cassino
Biferno

Campobasso

TYRRHENIAN SEA

Gaeta

Volturno

Naples

Foggia

Bari

Salerno

Potenza

Taranto

ITALY

Cassano
Spezzano

Catanzaro

IONIAN SEA

Palermo
San
Stefano
Messina

SICILY
Leonforte
Agira
Regalbuto

Reggio di Calabria

Enna
Mt Etna

Piazza
Amerina
Adrano
Catania

Gela

Syracuse

Pachino

MEDITERRANEAN SEA

0   100 miles
0   100 km

"We passed columns of Italian prisoners, who had fallen into our hands with the capture of General d'Havet's headquarters at Modica. There were thousands of them, and they were only too willing to cheer and raise their fingers in the V sign for the photographers."[5] This seemed to be the attitude of the great majority of Italian troops in Sicily: they were happy to resign from the war. It was a different story with a handful of crack Italian troops and, of course, with the Wehrmacht.

Despite the apparent ease with which the Canadians were advancing towards the centre of Sicily in the first days after the landings, important decisions had been made at higher levels which would soon translate into much heavier going. On 12 July Montgomery approached Alexander with a new plan for the capture of the island. The British would proceed north along the narrow coastal plain east of Mt Etna directly to Messina, in order to cut off the German and Italian escape route to the mainland. The Americans would protect the British left flank. This meant that the US 45th Division would change its axis of attack from northeast to northwest and that the main north–south highway in that sector would be given to the Canadians for their use in their advance towards Leonforte. To the consternation of the Americans, Alexander complied. Thus the Canadians were fated to run into major concentrations of German troops offering stiff resistance, while the US 45th Division, close on the Canadian left, had an easy time of it. In the words of US military historian Carlo D'Este:

> So ludicrous was the situation that once the orders were issued transfer-ring the disputed boundary and Route 124 to Montgomery, the Canadians encountered stiff resistance while the 45th Division stood helplessly by, unable to come to their aid even though their artillery was within one mile of the highway.[6]

The Canadians ran into their first firefight at Grammichele, about 65 kilo-metres northwest of Pacino as the crow flies, on 15 July. It was a short fight — the Canadians suffered only twenty-five casualties — and the village was taken by noon. Then it was on up the climbing, twisting road to Caltagirone and beyond that to Piazza Armerina, which the division reached on the 17th. The firefight at Grammichele set a pattern for most of the skirmishing that took place in the following days. Not strong enough in men or heavy weapons to block perma-nently the Canadian advance, the Germans used the terrain to set up ambushes manned by rearguards who were told to withdraw as soon as their positions ap-peared to become untenable or as soon as ordered. Most of the time the Germans would put up stiff resistance for several hours, then use the cover of darkness to withdraw to their next defensive position, usually at the next village, a few kilometres up the road.

With the almost total collapse of the Italian forces on the island, the Germans rushed the 29th Panzergrenadier division to Sicily, but soon concluded that they could not hold the island. Their strategy, therefore, was to delay the Allied advance at every opportunity, defend a main line of resistance roughly from Mt Etna northwest to the coast, and aim for the orderly evacuation of as much equipment and as many men as possible to the mainland via the Messina Strait. On the Allied right, the British advance north to Messina was stalled by fierce German resistance at the Primosole bridge spanning the Simeto River; the road to Catania and beyond ran over that bridge.

On 17 July, as the Canadians were moving up the highway beyond Piazza Armerina towards Valguarnera, General A.G.L. McNaughton, who had arrived in Algiers on 10 July with the intention of visiting the Canadian troops in Sicily, was told by Montgomery that "no visitors will be allowed on the island" as long as the fighting continued. McNaughton appealed to Alexander, who backed Montgomery; McNaughton returned to the United Kindom without seeing the Canadians and lodged a stiff complaint to General Sir Alan Brooke, Chief of the Imperial General Staff. Montgomery never liked visitors on the battlefield, no matter who they were, and was the operational commander of the Canadians in Sicily, but McNaughton was the General Officer Commanding-in-Chief of the army to which 1st Canadian Infantry Division belonged. Montgomery later claimed that Simonds had not wanted to deal with McNaughton in the midst of handling his first battlefield command, and that is entirely possible. Given McNaughton's temperament and his already demonstrated lack of understanding of how to run a modern battle, Montgomery may well have done the right thing militarily. But his action created friction between Canadian Army Headquarters and the British, and probably helped to bring about McNaughton's ultimate downfall.

As the Canadians moved towards Valguarnera, the division was still short of artillery and transport, but the battalions seemed to make good their shortages through innovation. The Hastings and Prince Edward Regiment, for example, infiltrated its rifle companies across country after dark, thereby outflanking the main German defences that faced west on Highway 117. An even better example of using darkness and terrain to mask movement came a few days later as the lead elements of the division approached Assoro and Leonforte. Simonds decided to advance at night: the 2nd Brigade would head for the town of Leonforte, on the highway; the 1st Brigade for the heights of Assoro, one of the highest peaks in the area, located about 3 kilometres southeast of Leonforte. The Germans were strongly entrenched in the region.

As the Hastings and Prince Edward Regiment formed up to attack, their Commanding Officer was killed by German shellfire. His replacement, Major the Lord Tweedsmuir, son of the prewar Governor General, decided on a bold night march and a steep climb up a height known as Castle Hill, which dominated the German positions. All night the men struggled upward over a steep rocky slope, weighted down by packs, rifles, and ammunition, and with the ever present necessity to keep absolutely quiet; before dawn they reached the peak, surprised the small German observation party camped there, and took control of the position. All the next day and night they called artillery fire down on the German defences. With the Hasty Ps already in their rear, those positions were no longer viable, and the Canadians soon took both Assoro and Leonforte with minimal casualties.

The Canadians had done well thus far. They had used brains and initiative to find the weak spots in the German defences, and they had adopted what military theorists call an "indirect approach" to outflank the Germans or to make German forward positions untenable. The Germans were impressed. Their initial assessment of the Canadians was "very mobile at night, surprise break-ins, clever infiltrations at night with small groups between our strong points."[7] The Germans undoubtedly admired those tactics because they were so like the ones they themselves employed. Emphasizing manoeuvre over firepower (artillery, tanks, tactical air support) as a way to achieve victory on the battlefield, the Germans habitually encouraged officers, NCOs, and men to think for themselves in battle, to find the point of least resistance in the enemy defences, and to exploit those weaknesses to outflank, to infiltrate, to flow through and around enemy strongpoints. The Germans respected firepower, but combined it with manoeuvre in a flexible manner to ensure that firepower did not dictate the shape of the attack. The Germans always eschewed rigid attacks, systems for centralized control of infantry movement, and pre-set fire plans to which the infantry was supposed to adhere. It was the infantry that determined what would happen in a German attack, not the artillery.

On 22 July Montgomery visited Simonds, to impress upon him that the British difficulties in moving north through the Catania plain and along the coast east of Mt Etna made a further change of plans necessary. Henceforth Montgomery would emphasize his left flank — where the Canadians were — in an effort to penetrate the German defences in the centre of the island, and then swing to the east, driving for the coast north of Catania and Etna. Simonds was directed to turn east, secure Agira, and continue to the Simeto River.

Simonds began to prepare the attack on Agira. By now most of his lost artillery had been replaced. He knew he was facing formidable German defences somewhere around Agira and he also knew that the Canadian division's role in the Sicily campaign was much more important than it had been previously. He decided to abandon the tactics of movement and flexibility that had worked so well up to this point and to lay on a fully fledged set-piece attack with air support, armour, and an intricate fire plan. Everything was to be centrally controlled and to depend on precision timing.

The forward elements of the 1st Canadian Division attacked towards Agira from the west on the afternoon of 24 July while the British 231st (Malta) Infantry Brigade, under Simonds's command for this operation, attacked from the south. Nissoria was easily taken, but, as we have seen, the RCR, which led the attack, suffered heavy losses in one company. The other three companies unwittingly infiltrated behind the German forward defences, but did nothing to take advantage of their good luck. That night, the Hastings and Prince Edward Regiment tried to follow the RCR assault up the road from Nissoria, but were also beaten back with heavy losses. The 48th Highlanders had no better luck the following day. The positions that dominated Nissoria were not taken until the 26th, when the PPCLI (of the 2nd Brigade) attacked under cover of a heavy barrage. The ridge beyond Nissoria taken, the Canadians moved towards Agira, captured a second German position on the 27th, and managed to take the town itself on the 28th.

Three days before Agira was secured, Italian dictator Benito Mussolini was overthrown by Marshal Pietro Badoglio, who formed a new ministry. Badoglio told the world that Mussolini's demise did not presage Italian withdrawal from the war, but Hitler did not trust him. Hitler could ill afford an Italian collapse followed by the hurried advance of the Allied armies to the Italian-Austrian border; massive German reinforcements were rushed into Italy virtually to occupy the country. Henceforth, it would not matter whether Italy surrendered or not; the Allies would still have to fight and die for every metre of the country.

In the fight for Agira, Simonds's division had consisted of his two Canadian brigades and the Malta Brigade; the 3rd Canadian Infantry Brigade had been attached directly to the British 30th Corps to aid in the clearing of the valley of the

Dittaino River, some 15 kilometres to the south of the Canadian division. It reverted to Simonds's command in early August, but not before capturing an important bridgehead at Catenanuova on 30 July from the 923rd German Fortress battalion. Thus Simonds continued his drive towards Regalbuto, about 8 kilometres east of Agira, with a mixed division. The village was strongly held by the Hermann Göring division, and the Malta Brigade was beaten back in the initial attack on 31 July. Then it was the turn of the RCR. They managed to get as far as a small bridge to the southeast of the town before being stopped by German fire. Throughout the day the RCR men clung to their positions in the heat, baked by the sun, and exposed to German machine-gun fire from two directions. The battalion was in an "unenviable situation," according to its regimental historian.[8] Simonds knew it would be useless to continue with a frontal assault and he pulled the RCR back after dark. But the Germans withdrew also, as they had so many times, and the town was occupied on 3 August.

With 3rd Brigade as the spearhead, the Canadians pushed on towards Adrano, crossing the Simeto River on 6 August. That was about as far as the division was going to go; on 7 August they were pulled out of action to prepare for the next round of fighting, the assault on southern Italy. On the other fronts, the Americans under Patton had swung wide to the western part of the island, taking Palermo on 22 July, then headed towards Messina along the north coast. Montgomery's troops finally entered Catania on 5 August and also began to push towards Messina. The Germans and those Italians who fought alongside them conducted a skilful defence and withdrawal, and pulled both men and equipment back towards Messina, where an elaborate shuttle operation brought them quickly over the strait to the Italian mainland. As the Allies advanced and the Germans withdrew, the front narrowed. Montgomery decided to pull the Canadians out of the line for a well-deserved rest.

As fighting formations, the previously untried 1st Canadian Infantry Division and the 1st Canadian Armoured Brigade had done well in their first test. The infantry battalions had shown skill and determination under difficult conditions of heat, mountainous terrain, dust, and the continued need to march, rather than be trucked, to the next objective. The Canadian infantry worked well with the artillery and the airforce. There were the usual mistakes, foul-ups, and failures of communication, made more difficult by the woeful inadequacy of the basic Mark 18 radio in hilly country (though it was not much better on flat ground). There were also weaknesses in leadership that did not show up in training but which emerged starkly under fire — Simonds always dealt ruthlessly with such situations. But the greatest single problem that the fighting in Sicily pointed to was not so much a failing as an inherent part of the thinking of many Canadian commanders, from Simonds on down: the idea that massive firepower, phased assaults, and centralized control were the keys to victory in battle. Too often, in the months ahead, this way of war produced as much failure as success.

The Allies entered Messina on 16 and 17 August; the Germans got away. Not a single able-bodied German soldier was left behind, aside from those who had been captured, and masses of armour, artillery, and transport vehicles were brought over to Italy as well. Given that the Allies' combined strength was roughly eight times that of the Germans, the campaign had taken far too long, had been too costly in casualties, and had not achieved its ultimate objective of destroying the German forces there. Sicily had been taken — at a cost of approximately 29,000 Allied casualties, 2310 of whom were Canadian (562 dead, 1664 wounded, 84 taken prisoner in the 1st Division) — but that event in itself would have little impact on the outcome of the war. Across the Straits of Messina, Italy, and a formidable German defensive force, awaited.

✹ X Ortona

O n Christmas Day, 1943, war artist Charles Comfort was still sleeping in the pre-dawn dark in Ortona when incoming German 88-millimetre rounds shattered his reverie. The shells seemed to be falling behind his position, raising his recurring fears of stray or short rounds.

> As I rose, all hell broke loose from our own guns, including the 7.2s whose thundery voice might well "wake the dead." The dawn was dark as the grave and chilly and the mud sucked powerfully at my rubber boots as I wandered over in the direction of "E" mess. Above the man-made thunder I heard myself humming the old traditional carol "God rest you merry, gentlemen, let nothing you dismay." "Let nothing you dismay" seemed to have a special significance this morning."[1]

The words of the old carol would have seemed more than a little ironic to the men of the 2nd Canadian Infantry Brigade and the 12th Canadian Armoured Regiment (Three Rivers Tanks) battling for every metre of the small Italian coastal town of Ortona. The fight for the town had started at nightfall on 20 December, when the Loyal Edmonton Regiment, supported by the Seaforth Highlanders of Canada, moved into the western outskirts of Ortona. The German paratroopers who defended the town were determined to make the Canadians pay for each building and for every block. "For some unknown reason, the Germans are staging a miniature Stalingrad in hapless Ortona," wrote one war correspondent,[2] a reality that the men in the town knew well. House by house, Ortona was eventually cleared of its defenders as the year 1943 and the first phase of the Canadian campaign in Italy dragged to its bloody conclusion. It is difficult, if not impossible, to find the name Ortona in most of the histories of the war in Italy written by non-Canadians. For them it seems to have been but a skirmish, compared with the dramatic near-disasters at Salerno and Anzio or the great Allied drive up the Liri Valley to open the *via ad Romam* — the road to Rome. But Canadians should long remember what happened at Ortona: that desperate fight in the ruins of that small Italian town showed beyond all doubt that the Canadian Army in Italy had truly come of age.

Although Sicily and Italy are separated only by the 3-kilometre-wide Strait of Messina, it had long been a point of contention between the British and the Americans whether the conquest of Sicily would immediately and logically lead to an attack on the Italian mainland itself. The overall view of the US military, and certainly of General George C. Marshall, US Army Chief of Staff, was that the Allies must invade Northwest Europe as soon as possible and smash their way directly towards Germany. The British, and in particular Winston Churchill, insisted that the Allies nibble around the edges, supposedly to bleed the Germans dry, while the Combined Bomber Offensive and the Soviet Red Army finished Hitler off.

In terms of overall war aims, Churchill's strategy made no sense, and the Americans knew it. The only way to ensure victory was to crush Nazism at its source and inflict a total defeat on Germany. That was not going to be done by slugging up the Italian peninsula, or worse, as some suggested, through the Balkans. Churchill always fancied himself a grand strategist; the Australians and New Zealanders whose lives were thrown away at Gallipoli, in Turkey, in 1915 might have argued otherwise. Churchill had conjured Gallipoli up as a grand flanking manoeuvre to achieve victory over Germany and Austria, not unlike his Second World War vision of a campaign in Italy.

In pressing for the Allies to move on to Italy, Churchill was probably motivated by two considerations. First, he undoubtedly believed casualties there would be less than they would be in a prolonged drive through France and the Low Countries to Germany. That was important because the British were desperately short of manpower throughout the war. It was also a factor in the thinking of Mackenzie King who, although having nothing to say about grand Allied strategy, certainly thought a campaign in Italy would cost fewer Canadian lives than one in France. The second factor behind Churchill's reasoning was probably his desire to restore the British imperial position in the Mediterranean after the war. That structure, built to ensure oil supplies from the Middle East and the safety of the Suez Canal link to the Far East and India, had virtually collapsed in 1940.

In the end, a compromise of sorts was arranged; the invasion of Italy would go ahead, but so, too, would the invasion of Northwest Europe in 1944. The latter would have first call on men and on equipment. Two Allied armies would conduct the campaign in Italy, the newly structured US Fifth Army, under General Mark

C. Clark, which would fight on the west slopes of the Apennines Mountains; and the British Eighth Army, first under Montgomery, then under Oliver Leese (after "Monty" returned to the United Kingdom to begin preparing for the D-Day landings), which would fight on the east slopes. The Canadians would continue to fight with the British. What exactly these two great armies were supposed to achieve in terms of the overall Allied strategy, other than to keep pressure on the Germans or to draw German strength from other fronts, was only vaguely spelled out. The Allies were in secret contact with the Badoglio government, trying to convince it to surrender, but although such a surrender would remove the large Italian army from the field, the Italians were never the main threat. The Germans were, and they had no intention of allowing their defence of Italy to be affected in any way by an Italian surrender. As US military historian Carlo D'Este has put it, "What was lacking . . . throughout the Italian campaign was a statement of Allied grand strategy. If the political goals were vague, the aims of the forthcoming military operations were even less clear."[3]

Italy is a defender's dream and an attacker's nightmare. Since the Apennine range runs down the centre of much of the peninsula, the water-courses from the mountains to the Mediterranean on the west and to the Adriatic on the east virtually all flow across Italy. Thus, for anyone advancing up the coasts, there was, in a very real sense, always "one more river to cross." The land between these rivers was rugged, and the few coastal roads were narrow and twisty — and easily covered by shellfire or cut by the blowing of numerous bridges or culverts. Mule trains were as necessary for military transport in the mountains of Italy as they had been in Sicily. There was precious little open ground anywhere suitable for tank warfare, nullifying the Allies' overwhelming numerical advantage in armoured fighting vehicles. The many small villages, usually built of stone with walled courtyards and narrow streets, were easy to defend. Summers were hot and dry, and winters cold and rainy, especially in the mountains.

The German defence was coordinated by one of the best defensively minded German officers, Field Marshal Albert Kesselring. His overall strategy was to withdraw virtually all his troops from Calabria, the southernmost province of Italy, allow the Allies to advance rapidly north through most of southern Italy up to the Sangro River, and then mount an aggressive defence along a series of fortified lines anchored in the mountains. In the opening stages of the fight, this strategy would put the main body of his troops outside the range of Allied tactical air power based in Sicily. At his disposal was the German Tenth army and other veteran units, including most of the troops who had escaped from Sicily. The most important of the major defensive positions, comprising several defence lines strung across the peninsula about 120 kilometres south-east of Rome, was collectively known as the Gustav Line.

The Allies had no real clues as to Kesselring's strategy; Sir Harold Alexander, who commanded the 15th Army Group, decided on an initial two-pronged landing. The British Eighth Army was to proceed directly across the Strait of Messina on 3 September (Operation Baytown), to draw the Germans south, it was hoped; then the US Fifth Army (consisting of one British and one US corp) was to land at the Bay of Salerno six days later (Operation Avalanche). Montgomery hated the plan. He later claimed in his memoirs that he had been ordered to take his army into Italy with no clear military objective. It was his view that the Avalanche landing should have gone first and that, if it had then proven successful, his army should have added its strength to it. Then the Germans in southern Italy would have had to retreat north or risk being cut off.

Canada had no say in these strategic decisions, either at the top political level of Roosevelt, Churchill, and Stalin, or at the Combined Chiefs of Staff in Washington, where US and British military planners oversaw the war against the Axis. As far as the Americans were concerned, the Canadian Army was part of larger British formations and there was no need to consult the Canadians about how their troops were to be used. The British agreed, since to agree meant that their traditional position of imperial superiority over Canada could be maintained. Canadian commanders in the field always had the option to refuse assignments of various sorts, but the people of Canada generally saw their war effort as part of a great Allied venture led by the British, the Americans, and the Soviet Union. The overwhelming majority of Canadians backed the war and wanted to see Canadian soldiers fighting it. The Canadian government had little leverage to try to influence the making of grand strategy, even had Mackenzie King been so inclined. But he was not.

In the pre-dawn darkness of 3 September 1943, the 13th British Corps under the command of Lieutenant-General Miles Dempsey, led by the 5th British and the 1st Canadian Infantry Divisions, slipped across the Strait of Messina under cover of a massive artillery bombardment of the mostly deserted coast. The Canadian 3rd Brigade headed for Reggio di Calabria, the capital of Calabria, just on the coast, and took it without opposition; the 1st Brigade moved straight into the mountains, pushing over the high Aspromonte range towards the small town of Locri, on the other side of the "toe" of Italy. The weak Italian opposition caused few delays; the Germans were nowhere to be found. The countryside was almost idyllic and mostly untouched by war, as Charles Comfort noted: "The grape harvest was going on everywhere. The principal native traffic of the road was concerned with the harvest and with wine. The grapes were contained in large tubs, carried on low wagons. As we passed, bunches were thrown at us, sweet and lush."[4] Within one week, the Canadians had reached Catanzaro, about 120 kilometres from Regio as the crow flies.

The Salerno landings were another matter. Kesselring was well aware that the Bay of Salerno was the northernmost suitable landing place available to the Allies that was within fighter cover of Sicily; the Germans were ready with the 16th Panzer division, 15,000 men strong with more than one hundred tanks and an experienced core of officers and NCOs. The announcement on the night of 8 September that Italy was surrendering to the Allies gave Kesselring ample warning of the invasion. Allied troops going ashore the morning of 9 September knew about the surrender and expected a walkover; they were bitterly surprised. It took more than five days of heavy fighting and some 13,000 Allied casualties before the Fifth Army broke out of the beachhead and headed for Naples, which they entered on 1 October.

While the Fifth Army struggled at Salerno, Simonds was ordered to take his division inland to seize the important road-junction town of Potenza, about 90 kilometres east of Salerno. Simonds assigned the task to the 3rd Brigade, to be led by a scratch unit known as "Boforce" commanded by Lieutenant-Colonel M.P. Bogert, Commanding Officer of the West Nova Scotia Regiment. Boforce consisted of the West Novas, the Calgary Tanks, and other units; it was to rush the defences of Potenza and seize key positions before the rest of the brigade could follow. On 19 September Bogert's troops approached Potenza after a sixty-hour dash; Bogert feared that the many new apartment blocks in Potenza might be well defended and he waited for nightfall before ordering his troops in. Three West Nova companies moved in, ran into about one hundred German paratroopers, and were soon engaged in a furious firefight. Simonds sent the Royal 22e (the Van Doos) to outflank the German positions as tanks moved into the town; the

Germans decided to pull out. The rest of the brigade moved in quickly to prepare for an expected counter-attack that did not materialize.

By the end of September, the Fifth and Eighth Armies held a line across Italy that ran northeast from just north of Naples on the Mediterranean to the Adriatic. The British 5th Corps had come up from the south to seize the Foggia Plain and the strategic airfields located there, but the formidable defences of the Gustav Line lay between the Allies and Rome. It was becoming more obvious by the day that Kesselring had no plans to abandon Rome, as the Allies had thought he might do once they had broken out of the Salerno beachhead.

It must remain a matter of conjecture why Allied commanders chose to ignore the age-old maxim of military operations — concentration of effort — to position each of their armies on a different slope of the Apennines on a line across Italy. Perhaps they underestimated the task facing them in breaking through the German mountain positions in the now deteriorating weather. It would have been far better for them to have deployed token forces east of the Apennines and concentrated the bulk of their divisions west of the mountains.

The heat and dust of the summer were long gone by the beginning of October. Cold nights, rainy weather, and mud plagued the Canadians as they struggled westward from the Foggia Plain and upward into the mountains along narrow roads and mountain paths. Their immediate objective was the Fortore River, where the Germans were strongly dug in on the north bank. One company of the Van Doos tried to force its way across the river on the night of 5/6 October, but was driven back by German shellfire from the 15th Panzer Grenadier regiment. Two days later the West Novas and the Carleton and York Regiment captured Gambatesa, on the important Highway 17 that led west to Campobasso. That victory precipitated a general German withdrawal from the north bank of the Fortore. The race to Campobasso was now on in earnest.

The task assigned to the Canadian Division by Miles Dempsey, the corps commander, was to take the left flank of the 13th British Corps front and to drive towards Campobasso; meanwhile, the 78th British Division would fight its way north on the right or coastal flank. From height to height, and town to town, the advance was slow and deliberate. At every opportunity the Germans held fast as long as they could, and usually long enough to force the Canadians to redeploy from line-of-march into attack formation, thus causing more delays. Each hilltop seemed to hold another fortified position; every valley road was cut by a blown bridge. Mines were strewn everywhere. The rainy weather and the bad roads made a mess of logistics; the division had to move slowly in order not to outrun its supplies.

On 14 October the Royal Canadian Regiment finally entered Campobasso, high in the mountains. A small city of some 17,000 people, the town was destined to be a leave and administrative centre. The troops quickly dubbed it Maple Leaf City, as thousands were given short leaves to sample the local culture. Comfort and his fellow war artists put on an exhibition of their paintings and sketches, which was a huge success. For the average infantryman, however, war art was not first on the priority list. As Major-General Chris Vokes later put it in his memoirs: "The personal view of a private soldier in war is 'I'm here today and gone tomorrow . . . ' So, the mentality of a soldier in the field is that he wants to get drunk and he wants to get laid, because these are pleasant things he may perhaps never experience again."[5] The Canadians did their best to get their fill of those simple pleasures in Campobasso.

Because German shells continued to fall sporadically on Campobasso, Simonds was forced to push further north to the Biferno River, which flows about 9 kilometres to the north and west of Campobasso. The RCR crossed on 23 October; the Hastings and Prince Edward Regiment followed two days later. Farley Mowat was there: "On a rain-dark night we slipped and slithered down to a roaring river swollen by the endless downpours and spanned by a decrepit power dam over which the waters foamed so fiercely that the Germans must have assumed the dam was impassable and so had failed to defend or even mine it."[6] The 1st and 2nd Brigades stayed in position about 15 kilometres north of the Biferno throughout November. They engaged in vigorous patrolling to determine the location and strength of the enemy and, if possible, to drive him further back. But Montgomery had had second thoughts about assaulting the Gustav Line defences on his left flank and had started to prepare for a new thrust along the coast. To cover his intentions, the 3rd Canadian Infantry Brigade advanced beyond the divisional area towards the upper Sangro, reached it, and then mounted a series of limited attacks to try to convince the Germans that the entire division was operating in that vicinity. They remained there until they were ordered to rejoin the division after it moved to the coast.

As Montgomery laid plans to pierce the Gustav Line along the Adriatic, the officers and men of the 5th Canadian Armoured Division began to arrive in Naples. The move to add a second Canadian division to the Allied contingent in the

Mediterranean had been initiated by J.L. Ralston, Minister of National Defence, and Ken Stuart, Chief of the General Staff. They managed to convince Mackenzie King that doing so would allow Canada to form a corps in Italy, give more officers and men battle and command experience, and, by keeping the troops there, avoid the inevitable high casualties that a Northwest Europe landing would entail. McNaughton was given little choice but to agree, even though transferring a second division and a corps headquarters to Italy made it less likely that these Canadians would be returned to the United Kingdom in time for a cross-channel assault.

With McNaughton cowed into submission, Ottawa approached London with the offer of an armoured division and a corps headquarters. The British were just then in the process of pulling 30th Corps headquarters and their famous 7th Armoured Division (the Desert Rats) back to the United Kingdom to prepare for the invasion of Europe, but they hoped to replace it with an infantry division. Ottawa nevertheless persisted (King still believing that units sent to Italy would suffer fewer casualties) and, over Montgomery's objections, London eventually agreed. Since switching two armoured divisions would severely tax Allied shipping capacity, an agreement was worked out. The Canadians would leave their equipment in Britain, to be taken over by the returning British formations, and would, in turn, take over the British equipment on their arrival in Italy. That the British equipment was worn, in need of repair, and often obsolete, while the Canadian equipment was new and up-to-date, seems not to have occurred to Ottawa. It would be many months before the 5th Canadian Armoured Division was ready for battle, especially since Lieutenant-General H.D.G. Crerar, the designated commander of the 1st Canadian Corps, diverted part of the new equipment that did arrive in Italy for the 5th Armoured to his own corps units.

The arrival of the new formation signalled changes in the Canadian command structure. Simonds was transferred to command of the newly arriving 5th Canadian Armoured Division, Vokes was promoted to lead the 1st Canadian Infantry Division, and Crerar was earmarked as General Officer Commanding the 1st Canadian Corps, scheduled to be activated in January. It would be the first Canadian corps in the field since the end of the First World War, even though it would be roughly half the size of its illustrious predecessor.

On 29 November the 1st Canadian Infantry Division began to pull out of the Campobasso area and to head for the coast. It was to occupy positions being vacated by the British 78th Division, which had managed to push across the lower Sangro in heavy fighting and with many casualties. The Canadians were to take over the hard-won British positions and, accompanied by the 1st Canadian Armoured Brigade, assault across the Moro River and capture the small coastal town of Ortona, about 3 kilometres further on. By 4 December the Canadians found themselves in their new positions on a ridge overlooking the south bank of the Moro.

Dating back to the ancient Trojans, Ortona was dominated by a cathedral, two massive defensive towers, and a fortress standing on a promontory alongside the small harbour. The streets were narrow and the buildings made of stone or brick, with many common walls. There were three large open squares in Ortona, the centremost and largest being the Piazza Municipale. The Germans laid out their defences to make killing grounds of these piazzas, by demolishing buildings and blocking streets to force vehicle and foot traffic through them. Every metre of those squares was covered by heavy concentrations of automatic weapons, mortars, and even flame-throwers.

Ortona could not be approached along the sea front or from the west; there were two roads into the town, one from the south, the other from the southeast paralleling the coast. To reach Ortona, the Canadians would have to cross the Moro, work their way up the bluffs on the other side of the river, then cross a deep but narrow gully that paralleled the river about 3 kilometres to the west, before they gained the Orsogna–Ortona highway that ran at right angles to the coast. They would then have to wheel to the right, and advance northeast up that highway into Ortona. The German paratroopers defending Ortona and its vicinity would contest every step of the way.

Why was Ortona attacked at all? By itself it was not a vital crossroads that the Canadians had to capture in order to push further up the coast; the area's important road junction was located 3 kilometres to the southwest. Once that junction was in Canadian possession, the town could have been masked off and the German defenders isolated and bypassed. That possibility does not appear to have occurred to anyone in command. The prevailing mindset of the day was that Ortona was in the way and had to be taken. At least one Canadian military historian believes that the battle of Ortona took place because both sides had been trapped by their own publicity-mongers. Brereton Greenhous has written: "The struggle for Ortona . . . assumed a public relations importance out of all proportion to its military significance."[7] That view fits with Kesselring's Christmas Day message to his Tenth army commander: "We do not want to defend Ortona decisively, but the English have made it as important as Rome . . . you can do nothing when things develop in this manner."[8] It is important to note that when the Allies won the Battle of Normandy eight months later and raced towards the Low Countries and Germany, they bypassed Dunkirk, which was not liberated until the very end of the war.

Vokes planned the attack on Ortona in three stages: first, cross the Moro; second, cross the gully to get onto the Orsogna–Ortona highway; third, advance into Ortona and capture it. In the waning daylight hours of 5 December, the three battalions of the 1st Brigade led the attempt to force the Moro crossing. On the coast road the Hastings and Prince Edward Regiment crossed the river near its mouth and set up a defensive bridgehead just atop the bluffs on the west bank of the river. This was intended as a diversion; when the regiment ran into stiff opposition, it withdrew back across the river. What was intended as the main attack was launched about 1.5 kilometres to the south of the Hastings and Prince Edward bridgehead. There, the Seaforth Highlanders moved across the Moro and worked their way up a narrow, twisting road towards the hamlet of San Leonardo, perched near the edge of the bluffs. Three kilometres further south the PPCLI forded the river and stormed the hamlet of Villa Roatti, taking the Germans by surprise.

As dawn broke, the PPCLI was counter-attacked by both tanks and infantry. They held on with the help of British armour from the 44th Royal Tank Regiment (which managed to move a number of Shermans across the river and up its steep and muddy sides), but on the night of 7/8 December they handed their positions over to troops of the 8th Indian Division and pulled back over the river. The Seaforths also faced formidable opposition, but, unlike the PPCLI, had no armour support and had to be withdrawn on the evening of 6 December.

On 6 December the Hasty Ps were sent back across the Moro River. Farley Mowat wrote about that attack years later:

> What followed was the kind of night men dream about in after years, waking in a cold sweat to a surge of gratitude that it is but a dream. It was a delirium of sustained violence. Small pockets of Germans that had been cut off throughout our bridgehead fired their automatic weapons in

hysterical dismay at every shadow. The grind of enemy tanks and self-propelled guns working their way along the crest was multiplied by echoes until it sounded like an entire Panzer army.[9]

To top it all off, it began to rain, and a bitter wind chilled the men through and through.

With the Hasty Ps holding the only Canadian bridgehead across the Moro, Vokes now hatched a new plan; the 1st Brigade would attack with two battalions, the 48th Highlanders moving directly across the river east of San Leonardo and the RCR breaking out of the bridgehead held by the Hasty Ps and attacking southwest towards San Leonardo. The attack began on the afternoon of 8 December; the 48th Highlanders achieved their crossing, but the RCR ran into a strong German counter-attack. The regimental history describes the ordeal:

> Throughout the night of December 8th–9th the RCR maintained its position on the feature which came to be known regimentally as "Slaughterhouse Hill." The fighting was most confused, the enemy appearing on several sides of the perimeter as well as within it. The sound of armoured vehicles moving gave the impression that a counter-attack would come in at dawn, and the incessant shellfire from both sides turned the night into pandemonium.[10]

The RCR beat off the counter-attack, but not without heavy casualties. In the meantime, the engineers used the cover of darkness to build a bridge across the river and, by the morning of 9 December, tanks and anti-tank guns were crossing over to the west side to reinforce the bridgehead. By nightfall on the 9th, the RCR and the 48th Highlanders had linked up; San Leonardo was in Canadian hands.

The next objective was Casa Berardi, a cluster of walled farm buildings on the west side of the gully, about 3 kilometres cross-country from San Leonardo. The task of securing this vital position was given to the Van Doos; on 14 December C Company, courageously led by Captain Paul Triquet and supported by the Sherman tanks of C Squadron of the Ontario Tank Regiment, battled their way across the gully, through German paratroopers and armour, to the stout walls of the main house. Though down to a handful of men and just six tanks, the small force stormed the house, captured it, and held it until after dark, when reinforcements arrived. Triquet was awarded the Victoria Cross for his courage, the first Canadian VC in the Mediterranean theatre.

Now, on the Orsogna–Ortona road, the 3rd Brigade was ordered to take the vital crossroads southwest of Ortona. Under cover of a massive artillery bombardment that began at 0800 on 18 December, the 48th Highlanders and the Three Rivers Tanks began the advance, which was then continued by the RCR. But Canadian shells began falling on the advancing troops and the barrage was lifted; once again the Germans had time to emerge from their bunkers and slit trenches, site their weapons, and open fire on the Canadian infantry. In the words of the RCR regimental history, "the slaughter was terrible." The regiment halted short of the crossroads, unable to continue. The next morning, the advance resumed with closely coordinated tank and artillery fire, and the crossroads were taken.

The battle for Ortona itself began the following day, when the Loyal Edmonton Regiment of the 2nd Brigade, already well below strength, advanced towards the town from the newly captured crossroads. By nightfall they and the Seaforths, who covered their right flank, were into the western edge of the town. The German paratroopers who held Ortona were determined to keep it. Their machine guns were sited for interlocking fire and they had dug tanks into the rubble, with turrets exposed, as mini-fortresses. Houses were fortified with everything imaginable, chicken wire was attached over windows and other openings to keep out grenades. Virtually every tempting object lying in the street, from full wine bottles to Bibles, was boobytrapped.

The Canadians advanced house by house in small actions involving platoons, sections, even half-sections. As two or three men gave cover with a Bren gun, the others eased up to a front door, kicked it in, lobbed grenades inside, then rushed in, Tommy guns blazing, as soon as the grenades had gone off. The Loyal Eddies found a new use for their new 6-pounder anti-tank guns: "We used the anti-tanks in a unique way. The shells could not penetrate the granite walls, sometimes 4 ft thick. So we just put them through the windows [and fired] and they (i.e., the shells) bounced around inside much like they would in an enemy tank doing horrible damage."[11]

Another technique perfected by the Canadian infantry was "mouse-holing." The streets were a death trap, so the Canadians moved under cover from house to house by blasting through the walls. Using high explosives, they would blow a hole from one house to another on the top floor, then clear the neighbouring building from top down. Although the Three Rivers Tanks gave valuable support, the battle for Ortona was primarily an infantry fight. Germans and Canadians were too close together for the Canadians to use artillery, and many streets were too strewn with rubble and mines for armour. Besides, the new German anti-tank weapon known as the *panzerfaust* was coming into use — the best infantry anti-tank weapon in the war — making the streets exceedingly dangerous for armour.

As the Canadians inched painfully forward towards the Piazza Municipale, preparations were completed to give the men Christmas dinner as close to the lines as possible. A sumptuous meal was prepared and tables were set, usually in church courtyards. As the battle roared around them, the men at the fighting front were brought back a few at a time, fed, given Christmas sweets and cigarettes, then returned to action. The Seaforths held their dinner in a parish church near the Piazza Vittoria. Norman Pope of the Canadian Army Historical Section witnessed the spectacle and later described it to Charles Comfort:

> Over the crash and din of the surrounding battle came the skirl of bagpipes and the raised voices of men singing Christmas carols. Through a smoky haze [Pope] saw men seated at tables covered with white napery. Three hundred yards away the enemy had active machine-gun posts, mortar bombs and shells were creating a hellish dissonance, as cool young subalterns (in true Christmas tradition) served Canadian turkey with dressing and vegetables.[12]

The Germans prepared a deadly Boxing Day for Lieutenant E.B. Allen and his platoon of twenty-three Loyal Eddies by mining a building near the Piazza Tommaso. When Allen and his men entered the building, the Germans blew it up. Canadian pioneers rushed forward to dig the men out, but were met by grenades and rifle fire. Only five men were rescued from Allen's platoon, one after being pinned in the rubble for seventy-two hours.

Two days before Christmas Vokes had sent the 1st Brigade to cut off the German escape and supply routes to the west of the town. At first the Hasty Ps and the 48th Highlanders made it through to the high ground west of Ortona, but had then been cut off; on Christmas night a party of the Saskatoon Light Infantry reached them with supplies and ammunition, and the next day tanks from the Ontario Regiment broke through. The German position in Ortona was now untenable; they had suffered heavy casualties and all their escape routes were about to be cut off. On the 27th the survivors began to pull out of Ortona; they were gone by the 28th, their unburied dead rotting in the streets.

The fight for the Moro River crossing and the capture of Ortona had cost the 1st Canadian Infantry Division 2339 officers and men killed and wounded, and another 1617 men taken out of the line because of illness, many afflicted with battle exhaustion. Since hitting the beaches at Pacino, Sicily, in July, the division had earned a reputation for doggedness and determination. Officers and men had overcome high-calibre German troops mounting skilled and innovative defences. The campaign in Italy thus far was more like the battles of attrition fought in the First World War than the blitzkrieg-style warfare that some had expected. By the end of 1943 it was clear that Canadian officers and men could fight the set-piece battle as well as any army. What was not so clear was whether they could excel at a war of swiftness and manoeuvrability. They would find that out a few short months later in Italy's Liri Valley.

As 1943 drew to a close, the Axis was on the defensive everywhere. In the Pacific, the Japanese navy had suffered a stunning blow in June 1942 at the Battle of Midway. This defeat had been followed by the American invasion of Guadalcanal, the start of the United States Navy's island-hopping campaign in the central Pacific, and the American-Australian thrust to recapture New Guinea. Mired in China and the jungles of Southeast Asia, the Japanese were being pushed back, with heavy losses on virtually all fronts. American submarines were taking a huge toll of Japanese merchant shipping, and American shipyards were turning out new fleet and escort carriers, fast battleships, and modern cruisers and destroyers by the score.

On the eastern front, the battle of Stalingrad had ended in early 1943 with a crushing German defeat. The German summer offensive of July 1943 had been stopped almost as soon as it began in the massive tank battle of Kursk, a dramatic Soviet victory. Over the course of the year the Soviets deployed thousands of new tanks and attack bombers, scores of new infantry divisions, and hundreds of additional artillery brigades. It seemed only a matter of time before the Soviets drew up to the German borders.

In southern Europe and the Mediterranean, the Axis had been expelled from North Africa and Sicily, and Italy had surrendered. Rome remained out of reach, behind the defences of the Gustav Line, as British and Americans fought over how many further resources should be devoted to the bloody war there. Everyone, Hitler included, knew that 1944 would bring the cross-channel invasion and the opening of the second front.

With two divisions and a corps in Italy, and virtually no chance of returning them to the United Kingdom before D-Day, it was obvious at the end of 1943 that the First Canadian Army would fight the war in Northwest Europe as a part-Canadian, part-British, part-Polish formation (though under Canadian command) and not as an all-Canadian unit. It was also clear by December 1943 that the army would not go into action commanded by A.G.L. McNaughton. The British had lobbied hard for McNaughton's removal ever since the Spartan debacle in March 1943 and had been helped behind the scene by Crerar, who saw himself as McNaughton's successor. McNaughton's political views about the unity of the Canadian Army, and his clash with Montgomery over his plans to visit Sicily, had not helped his position. But the foremost reason why the Canadian government was prepared to sack him was the mounting evidence that he was not competent to command a field army.

Mackenzie King liked McNaughton, knew he was popular with the troops, and did not want to fire him, in part because McNaughton opposed conscription. But Sir Alan Brooke and others had convinced Ralston that McNaughton had to go, and King had little choice but to accept Ralston's advice. McNaughton was sacked in December 1943 — the government claimed he had resigned because of ill health — and replaced by Crerar, who would command the First Canadian Army for the duration. Crerar was eventually succeeded at the 1st Canadian Corps by E.L.M. "Tommy" Burns. Vokes stayed in command of 1st Canadian Infantry Division, and Bert Hoffmeister, a Vancouver militia officer originally with the Seaforth Highlanders, took command of 5th Canadian Armoured Division in March 1944. Simonds was brought back to the United Kingdom to become commander of the 2nd Canadian Corps. That corps would be the premier Canadian component of the First Canadian Army (the other corps was to be the British 1st under Lieutenant-General J.T. Crocker) until the 1st Canadian Corps was brought back from Italy to rejoin First Canadian Army in early 1945.

On New Year's Eve, 1943, the 48th Highlanders captured the hamlets of San Tommaso and San Nicola, a little more than 3 kilometres west of Ortona. An assault on Point 59, a small hill on the coast about 3 kilometres northwest of Ortona, was less successful, and more than fifty Canadians were killed, wounded, or captured. Point 59 was finally secured by the Carleton and York Regiment on 4 January, and the Canadian front on the Adriatic then fell quiet. There was no point in trying to go any further on this coast when the road to Rome, on the Mediterranean side of Italy, was still blocked by the fierce resistance of Kesselring's troops. The Allies now paused to rethink their priorities and their strategy; the hiatus was more than welcomed by the tired, dishevelled, and understrength Canadians, who badly needed a rest.

On 24 May 1944 Lieutenant Edward J. Perkins and his small band of reconnaissance troops struggled across the Melfa River in mid-afternoon to blaze
a trail for the lead elements of the 5th Canadian Armoured Division. The river
banks were steep, but Perkins and his men had coaxed their three small General
Stuart (or "Honey") reconnaissance tanks up the other side and captured a small
house occupied by eight German paratroopers. Perkins then placed his tanks in a
hull-down position and organized his men for the inevitable German counter-
attack. He expected the infantry of A Company of the Westminster Regiment to
follow in short order. Until they did, the Sherman tanks of A Squadron of Lord
Strathcona's Horse would provide covering fire from the other side of the river.

The Melfa River flows from the north to intersect the Liri River some 20
kilometres due west of the Italian town of Cassino. The Liri River is one of the
few south of Rome which flows in a general east–west direction. The river valley
has long been used as an invasion route to Rome; the Germans, in full knowledge
of the history and geography of the region, had strongly fortified the eastern end
of the valley. If the Allies could reduce or bypass those defences, they would penetrate the Gustav Line and have a chance to turn the flank of Kesselring's Tenth
army.

The battle for the Liri Valley had raged for many months; the latest phase
had started on 11 May with a massive barrage from one thousand guns which
shook the valley to its foundations. British, Indian, Canadian, and French troops
then broke through the Gustav Line and through the more lightly defended Hitler Line, about 12 kilometres further west. On 23 May the 5th Canadian Armoured
Division made for the Melfa River, in the first attack of the entire division fighting
together since its arrival in Italy. Perkins's small force was the lead element of
that attack.

Under fire, and alone in their small perimeter for several hours, Perkins's men
were joined at about 1700 by infantry from the Westminster Regiment. The infantry had taken several casualties, but as soon as they arrived on the west bank of

the Melfa, they pushed out on the left flank to expand the bridgehead. At dusk, three German Panther tanks and about one hundred infantry started to advance towards the Canadian position. Perkins's men and the men of the Westminster Regiment fired everything they had at the approaching enemy, including PIATs (projector, infantry, anti-tank), even though the range was too great for the PIATs to have any effect. Perkins himself was slightly wounded when he was hit by fragments from a high-explosive shell as he leaped into his tank. There was little to stop the Germans from pushing the Canadians into the river, but the daylight was almost gone and the Germans were thrown off balance by the ferocity of the Canadian fire. They decided to play it safe and failed to press their attack home. The Canadians held their positions and remained in control of the bridgehead until they were joined by stronger forces the following day. The Canadian armour then roared across the Melfa as the Allies drove for Rome.

After the capture of Ortona and the high ground to the west, the Eighth Army's offensive on the Adriatic coast closed down for the winter. The Allies had hoped to take Rome by the end of 1943, but a skilled and tenacious enemy still held the Gustav Line from the Adriatic to the Mediterranean. There was no use in trying to push further north when the winter mud, rain, cold, and snow in the high passes made the going even more difficult than it had been before. A new strategy seemed necessary; the Allies decided to outflank the Gustav Line defences with a landing at Anzio (Operation Shingle), about 50 kilometres due south of Rome and well past the Gustav Line defences. The landing was due to take place 22 January 1944.

While British and Americans (and the Canadians of the First Special Service Force) made preparations for the Anzio landings, the 5th Canadian Armoured Division's 11th Canadian Infantry Brigade saw its first action at the Arieli River, north of Ortona, on 17 January 1944. At that time the cutting edge of British and Canadian armoured divisions consisted of one infantry and one armoured brigade (in this case, the 5th Armoured Brigade). In December Guy Simonds, now in command of the 5th Armoured Division, asked that the 11th Brigade be brought into action as soon as possible to get a taste of the enemy. Since the 5th Armoured Division was not yet fully concentrated, the 11th Brigade was temporarily attached to the 1st Canadian Infantry Division and ordered to mount limited attacks across the Arieli to divert German attention from the Anzio and Cassino areas. On 17 January the Cape Breton Highlanders and the Perth Regiment mounted their first real action against the Germans. Incredibly, they attacked successively, instead of together. With each accompanied by a squadron of tanks, they "went in across open ground in daylight against well-prepared river defences manned by experienced veterans of the German 1st Parachute Division. The combination of a disjointed plan, inexperienced units and strong defences produced a dismal failure."[1]

The problems that underlay the brigade's failure at the Arieli would plague the 5th Armoured for many months. Equipment shortages hampered training, command assignments were changed constantly (for example, the division had three commanders in less than five months), and the units had had precious little practical experience in tank-infantry cooperation, which is the essence of an armoured division. Despite these difficulties, the full division was put into the front lines in the Orsogna sector, replacing the 4th Indian Division, at the beginning of February — just eighty-five days after its arrival in Italy. At virtually the same time (31 January/1 February), the 1st Canadian Corps was activated and relieved the 5th British Corps in the coastal area. By 9 February, Corps Commander H.D.G. Crerar had both Canadian divisions under command.

Some of the problems plaguing the 5th Armoured Division were tackled directly over the next few months, when the division was withdrawn from the Ortona front for intensive training in mobile warfare and especially in tank-infantry cooperation. The 1st Division remained in the Ortona area until late April, but its battalions were rotated to rear areas for similar training. All this was in preparation for the Liri Valley offensive that was made necessary by the near-disaster at Anzio.

From the end of the Ortona fighting to the opening of the Liri Valley offensive, the Canadians took no part in any major operations, yet the war of attrition in the mountains and on the coast continued to take a dreary toll of casualties. By the start of the Liri Valley offensive, 9934 Canadians had become casualties in the Italian campaign, 2119 of them fatal. Many were battle exhaustion casualties, which had started to mount even during the summer fighting in Sicily.

Because the Canadian Army had had no truly sustained contact with the enemy until the Sicily campaign, battle exhaustion had posed no significant problem. Since then, the nature of the war in Italy and the daily dangers faced by the men had caused battle exhaustion casualties to mount at a rapid pace. There is a wealth of evidence that all soldiers face battle exhaustion. Once known as shell-shock or battle fatigue, battle exhaustion generally results from a soldier's being too long in a combat zone with too little apparent prospect of survival. It is a phenomenon far more evident in long campaigns, even of relatively low intensity, than in short ones, including ones as horrific as the Dieppe landing.

Any soldier in a line unit, of any rank, can be stricken with battle exhaustion. Men too long under fire, watching comrades being killed in the most horrible fashion, getting more and more fatigued from lack of sleep and constant move-ment, living in mud and dirt with little or no news from home, would eventually crack. Even the bravest had their limits: no one was exempt, and battalion com-manders were afflicted no less than riflemen. (Battle exhaustion afflicted the bomber crews as well, and for much the same reason. In the first years of the war, aircrew who refused to fly were labelled as LMF — lacking moral fibre — and removed from active service. They were treated harshly for the balance of their service, and were sometimes sent to work in the coal mines.)

The Canadian Army in the Second World War tried to mitigate battle ex-haustion in two basic ways: prevention and, where possible, quick cure. Preven-tion was best served by trying to keep troop morale up with hot food whenever possible, regular mail, mobile baths, and fresh changes of clothes. Most of these amenities were not available at the front during periods of intense action, so units were rotated out of the line and placed in reserve as often as the combat situation would allow. In addition, men would take turns being LOB — left out of battle — to ensure that some men in a platoon or company were always fresh. When in reserve, the British-run NAAFI — the Navy, Army, Air Force Institute, a civil-ian-run organization — provided canteens, movies, and sometimes live entertain-ment, while the army supplied beer and hearty meals. The more often a soldier could rest, clean up, eat a few good hot meals, and generally recover from the constant pressures of front-line existence, the less chance he would be quickly afflicted with battle exhaustion. High-quality leadership on the part of company and battalion commanders also mitigated the problem.

No matter how well rested or fed a soldier was, virtually any man was bound to crack in a prolonged campaign. In the Italian theatre, men marched for days on end over bad roads, crossed rivers without apparent end, slept in the open in cold rainy winters and hot dusty summers, endured flies and disease, and witnessed the poverty and misery of the population. Combined with the tenacious and deadly defence of the German enemy, these conditions inevitably produced battle exhaustion in large numbers. Thus treatment was as important as prevention.

Canadian army psychiatry was in its infancy at the beginning of the war, but knowledge about battle exhaustion eventually expanded and, with it, sensitivity to the problem. The key breakthrough was to recognize that anyone could be afflicted and that those who did succumb were not "slackers" or cowards, but men who had reached their limit. Also important was the realization that much battle exhaustion was temporary — a good sleep and a few calm days with food and rest usually restored a man's sense of balance and allowed him to return to his unit. In other cases, reassignment to other, noncombat duties was called for. In very rare cases, complete discharge was necessary. The experiences gained in Italy taught the Canadian Army's medical staff a great deal about battle exhaustion, but it still took some convincing to win over old-line army officers who thought of battle exhaustion as cowardice. Simonds is a case in point. After weeks of hard fighting in Normandy, he concluded that infantry battalion commanding officers had to be replaced every four months because of the constant strain they were under and the consequent danger of mental breakdown. He also realized that adverse fighting conditions — poor weather, bad food, static warfare — were major factors producing battle exhaustion. At the same time, however, he cautioned army medical officers not to take too lenient a view of battle exhaustion. In a late August 1944 memo to his divisional commanders he warned: "It requires the close attention of commanders to see that malingering is not only discouraged, but made a disgraceful offence and disciplinary action taken to counter it."

❦

By January 1944 US General Mark Clark's Fifth Army had reached the Gustav Line at the entrance to the Liri Valley, but every step of the way had been costly. On the night of 20 January, for example, the US 36th Division tried to force a crossing of the Rapido River; by the time dawn broke, 143 had been killed, 663 had been wounded, and 875 were missing (about 500 of those had been taken prisoner). It was "one of the bloodiest failures of the war,"[2] but it was only one of many in the fighting along the Rapido and near the town of Cassino at the entrance to the Liri Valley.

This tough going prompted Generals Alexander and Eisenhower to hatch Operation Shingle, the landing at Anzio, which was intended to outflank the

Gustav Line defences. The VI Corps with 50,000 troops was to land at the small port of Anzio on 22 January, outflank the Gustav Line, and drive towards Rome. That did not happen. The Allies met stiff and determined resistance from the approximately 14,000 German troops already in the Anzio area and from another 20,000 or so German reserves near Rome, which Kesselring immediately ordered to Anzio. The Allies had expected that the Germans would weaken the Gustav Line by moving troops to the Anzio front; instead, the Allies were now forced to consider stripping troops from the main US Fifth and British Eighth Armies to shore up their position at Anzio.

There was a small Canadian contingent at Anzio — the Canadian participants of the First Special Service Force, a mixed American-Canadian commando unit under the command of US Lieutenant-Colonel Robert T. Frederick, which was later immortalized in films as "the Devil's Brigade." The force had been activated in Helena, Montana, in July 1942 and had received intensive training in amphibious, parachute, and ski commando tactics. Originally conceived to attack power plants and other strategic installations behind enemy lines in northern Europe (Project Plough), the force had its introduction to operations in the Aleutian campaign in August 1943. It saw no combat, however, since no enemy forces were encountered.

The First Special Service Force was then shifted to the Italian front, where it distinguished itself with a spectacular climb up the steep Monte La Difensa to surprise the German defenders and gain control of a key point in Kesselring's Winter Line. In that and subsequent battles, it suffered heavy casualties and was used less and less for commando-style operations and increasingly as a highly skilled and aggressive infantry unit. It was assigned a key sector of the front line on the Anzio perimeter and played an important role in the eventual breakout from Anzio and the pursuit to Rome.

The failure to break out of the Anzio perimeter only worsened the Allied position south of Rome. With the equivalent of more than three divisions bottled up and taking a daily pounding from artillery and aircraft, it was soon apparent that unless Anzio was abandoned altogether — which would have been an unmitigated disaster on a par with the Gallipoli disaster of the First World War — the Fifth Army was going to have to come to the rescue of the troops in the beachhead. It could only do that, of course, by breaking through the Gustav Line — a formidable task.

It was Lieutenant-General Sir John Harding, a skilled staff officer newly arrived from the United Kingdon with extensive combat experience, who conceived Operation Diadem. Harding had been sent to Sir Harold Alexander's headquarters by Sir Alan Brooke, who believed that Alexander's loose control of his army group and his shortcomings as a strategist were prolonging the drive to Rome. Harding produced a plan for a joint Fifth Army/Eighth Army attack through the Liri Valley which was dubbed Diadem. It called for the Eighth Army to transfer the great bulk of its fighting power secretly over the Apennines and to mount a massive armoured assault westward, from the area east of the Gari River. At the same time, the Fifth Army would be shifted southward to the left flank of the attack; the French Expeditionary Corps would form the right flank of the Fifth Army. Thus, the Eighth Army would make the main thrust — a fact that the American Mark Clark brooded over. Sir Oliver Leese, GOC-in-C of the Eighth Army, would have three corps under command — 13th British, 2nd Polish, and 1st Canadian.

The attack began an hour before midnight on 11 May with a massive artillery barrage. One Canadian officer described it this way:

> In those few miles between the hills, a thousand guns suddenly let go as one, and then they kept on firing. We'd never seen or heard or imagined anything quite like this. You could see the flashes of nearby guns and you could hear the thunder of dozens and hundreds more on every side and you could only imagine what sort of Hell was falling on the German lines. It damn near deafened you.[3]

The 1st Canadian Corps was in reserve for the initial assault across the Gari River, but the 1st Canadian Armoured Brigade (the independent armoured brigade) assisted the 8th Indian Division, which had been assigned to effect a crossing, hold a bridgehead, and erect bridging in the Sant'Angelo sector for the armour and vehicles to follow. The Indian infantry, assisted by the Canadian armour, made slow going at first, but by the late afternoon of 13 May they had penetrated through the initial Gustav Line defences to establish a number of bridgeheads across the Gari. Then the tanks and troops of the British 78th Division moved across and began to advance towards the Hitler Line. On the left flank the skilled mountain troops of the French Expeditionary Corps made a wide sweeping advance through rugged terrain south of the Liri; had Leese been prepared to take advantage of the French breakthrough, the Canadian armour might have been used to form a northern pincer to entrap the Germans manning the Hitler Line. But he did not. Never prone to react quickly or with boldness, the plodding Leese let the opportunity slip by; the classic set-piece battle would continue as planned.

The Indian breakthrough of the Gustav Line and the rapid French advance south of the Liri rendered the line untenable. Those Germans not killed, wounded, or captured withdrew to the weaker defences of the Hitler Line, some 13 kilometres west of the Gari. To assault that secondary defence position, Leese called upon Lieutenant-General E.L.M. Burns and the troops of the 1st Canadian Corps. In typical fashion, Burns prepared for a set-piece attack with heavy artillery support: he hoped that the 1st Division infantry would take the lead and break through the Hitler Line, and that the 5th Armoured (under the command of Hoffmeister) would exploit the infantry breakthrough and advance as quickly as possible up the Liri Valley. The 3rd Brigade was positioned on the right, the 1st Brigade on the left, with the Pignataro–Cassino road as the start-line.

The attack began in the early morning hours of 17 May, part of an Allied offensive designed to close up the Hitler Line along its length. Although the Germans resisted the Canadian advance through the day, they melted away at nightfall and both Canadian brigades failed to make contact the following day as they advanced to the vicinity of the Hitler Line. It was a different story when the Canadians finally reached the line itself on the 19th; the Ontario Regiment lost thirteen tanks destroyed and many others damaged supporting an attack on the line by the British 78th Division, while the Royal 22e suffered heavy casualties in an ill-conceived direct assault on the line's barbed wire. There would be no penetration of the line and no breakthrough advance by the Canadian armour that day. The attack had run out of steam.

Burns decided to lay on another set-piece attack to punch through the Hitler Line at a point about 2 kilometres southwest of the hamlet of Aquino. To Leese's disgust, he took the better part of three days to lay out the attack. It would begin with a bombardment over a front of some 2000 metres, followed by an advance by two brigades from 1st Division: 2nd Brigade on the right, 3rd Brigade on the left. The 5th Armoured would then advance towards the Melfa River, cross it, and proceed westward on Highway 6 towards Rome.

The renewed attack began in the morning haze of 23 May. On the right the 2nd Brigade struggled forward under heavy fire to its first objective, and went no further. The PPCLI was especially hard hit:

Against the advancing Patricias the enemy garrison in Aquino . . . intervened in disastrous fashion. From the right flank the . . . report lines were raked continuously . . . "B" Company, following in its mopping-up role, pushed ahead through the woods; the trees, the standing crops, the dust, smoke, and mist reduced visibility to a few yards. Capt. A.M. Campbell and his men eventually reached the enemy wire, where they were brought to a halt by machine-guns firing from cupolas at point blank range.[4]

The attack on the right flank was an abject failure.

Things went much better on the left, where there was no German flanking fire; the infantry battalions moved quickly through the German defences and over the Pontecorvo–Aquino road. Vokes decided to reinforce success and threw his divisional reserve into the battle behind the 3rd Brigade. The advance started late in the afternoon in a heavy rain and caught the Germans in the open, preparing to counter-attack. The Canadian reserves killed many Germans and widened the breach. To their left the Princess Louise, a reconnaissance regiment, and the 1st Brigade cleared the town of Pontecorvo.

The next morning, 24 May, Hoffmeister sent his tanks through the gap made by the infantry and towards the Melfa River. Three infantry/tank battlegroups of the 5th Armoured Brigade forced a crossing by nightfall and held the bridgehead while the 11th Infantry Brigade began to pass through the next morning (25 May). By midday the division was across the Melfa on a two-battalion front. But then problems arose. The rear area of the division was a confused and tangled mass of vehicles and men from different corps; supplies, ammunition, and bridging equipment could not be brought up quickly, and the infantry of the 11th Brigade were forced to curtail their advance towards the Liri. They did not cross that river until 26 May, and it was a full day again until they were able to occupy the town of Ceprano, near Highway 6 on the way to Rome.

The Canadians did not spearhead the drive to Rome; that honour was given to other Allied units in whom Leese had more confidence. The 1st Canadian Corps returned to reserve. Leese, who had failed to organize his own battle properly in the narrow Liri Valley and who was as ponderous as always in battle management, believed that Burns and the Canadians had not done a good job. In his view, the Canadian units had been too slow and Burns had been too deliberate. In the weeks following the Liri Valley campaign, Leese sought to have Burns fired and the Canadian Corps broken up. That action was as much the result of his imperious attitude towards colonials as it was a reflection of any Canadian shortcomings. In fact, the 1st Canadian Corps had performed well given the constraints under which it operated — the 5th Canadian Armoured Division's lack of battle experience and the tendency of Canadian commanders to depend on massive firepower, rather than bold manoeuvre, to win battles. Ironically, Leese suffered from the latter handicap as much as or even more than most Canadian commanders.

The Allies entered Rome on 4 June, the Canadians of the First Special Service Force among them. But while Clark's Fifth Army seized Rome, he allowed the bulk of the German Tenth army to slip away to the north. It was a major error, and it gave Kesselring ample troops and weapons to man strong defensive positions, such as the Gothic Line, which ran from north of Pisa on the west coast of Italy to south of Rimini on the east coast (sometimes referred to as the Pisa–Rimini Line). Thus the Allies would continue to slog north through difficult terrain fighting a well-armed and resourceful enemy determined to make them pay for every metre of advance. To make matters worse for the Allied campaign in Italy, seven veteran divisions were withdrawn from Alexander's command to be made ready for Anvil, the proposed invasion of southern France to be carried out in August. The weakening of the forces committed to Italy, and the arrival on 6 June of the long-expected news that the Allies had landed on the coast of France (Overlord), made it clear that the Italian campaign was to be a secondary front from now on, a sideshow to the decisive battles that would bring the Allies to the very borders of Germany.

Sideshow or not, Churchill and Alexander were determined to push ahead with the conquest of Italy. An assault on the Gothic Line would be necessary. The 1st Canadian Corps would have a two-month hiatus before that happened, time enough for the 5th Canadian Armoured Division to continue tank-infantry training and to be reorganized to take into account lessons learned by British and Canadians in the Italian campaign thus far. The 1st Canadian Armoured Brigade had no such luxury as it accompanied British forces in their drive to Florence. The most important of those lessons was that the armoured divisions were too poor in infantry to be effective in a country that did not lend itself to mobile warfare. It was therefore decided to add a second infantry brigade (the 12th) to the armoured division, formed from reconnaissance, motorized, and anti-aircraft regiments converted to infantry. The reason was simple: shortages of trained infantry were already becoming apparent only weeks after the Normandy landing. The Canadian Army staff, using figures supplied by the British and based on the war in the North African desert, had greatly underestimated infantry casualties and overestimated how many other troops it would need when allocating manpower resources. This would become a serious problem by the fall and would precipitate a general manpower crisis in the Canadian Army.

On 25 August 1944 Operation Olive — Leese's attempt to smash the Gothic Line on the Adriatic coast — began. Of the two Allied armies in Italy, Leese's Eighth Army had been the least affected by the transfer of troops to France for Anvil, and he had persuaded Alexander to allow him to move his forces back over the Apennines to attack the Gothic Line at its right anchor. For three weeks the transfer was carried out with great care and secrecy. Kesselring was taken by surprise. Leese's offensive began with three corps up front — 2nd Polish on the right, 1st Canadian in the centre, and 5th British on the left. At first Kesselring believed the attack was a feint designed to pin his troops down as the Allies pushed through southern France; he was convinced that this was a major offensive only when his intelligence captured a communication from Leese which outlined the plans for the operation. But by then it was too late for him to reinforce the northern front. Although the Poles and the Canadians ran into the usual tenacious defence put up by the German troops in the line, the Germans had neither the troops nor the heavy weapons to hold for long.

In command of the Canadian troops, Burns planned a four-stage assault that would take them from the Metauro River, about 16 kilometres east of and parallel to the Gothic Line defences, to Rimini. It took the Canadians four days to clear the ground between the Metauro and the Foglia Rivers, but when they closed up to the Gothic Line on 30 August, Hoffmeister quickly realized that the Germans were not present in great strength. On his own initiative, he committed his 5th Armoured Division to attempt a breakout and to turn the northern flank of the German defences. By the afternoon of 30 August, Hoffmeister's armour was through the line and onto the high ground beyond it. In the words of US military historian Carlo D'Este:

> The timing and boldness of the Canadian attack left the Germans in considerable disarray and helpless to prevent an exploitation, provided it was

carried out before they regrouped. In fact, if a drive had been mounted . . . Eighth Army might have outflanked the Gothic Line entirely and unleashed its armour onto the plains of the Po Valley.[5]

But a drive was not mounted: Burns had no reserve to exploit Hoffmeister's breakthrough, and Leese, never trusting the Canadians to accomplish much, had nothing behind Burns to throw into the fight. He had left the 1st British Armoured Division some 160 kilometres to the rear, out of the battle entirely. The same 5th Canadian Armoured Division that had struggled at the Melfa River just three months before had scored one of the finest Canadian victories of the war and had handed Leese an opportunity to end the war in Italy, but Leese was unprepared to take advantage of it. In this one battle, Leese showed that he was mediocre at best as an army commander, but he liked to blame others — usually Burns — for his shortcomings. As William McAndrew has observed of his performance in this battle:

> The Canadians were placed on the best ground for movement but lacked reserves to exploit . . . Leese had [given away] his capability to influence the battle directly. Had he retained control [of his armoured reserve] Leese could have had it in hand to exploit where and when the decisive breakthrough occurred: on the Canadian Corps' front.[6]

The Germans recovered. The British and Canadians (minus the Poles, who had been "pinched out" on the right) fought their way towards Rimini as the hot, dry weather broke and the rains of late summer began to turn the ground into a muddy morass. The infantry of the 1st Division had a particularly difficult time dislodging the Germans from the small village of San Martino as German shellfire from the San Fortunato Ridge beyond made life hell for the Canadians. That ridge was the key to the German defences in the sector. On the night of 19/20 September, it was the objective of an all-out assault by 3rd Brigade, with the Hasty Ps from 1st Brigade under command. The attack began at 0400. By first light two Hasty P companies, supported by tanks, were in position to attack the crest of the ridge. Many of the tanks were hit by anti-tank fire; the German paratroopers on the crest poured machine-gun, mortar, and rifle fire down the slopes at the approaching Canadians. The Hasty Ps were too close to the Germans to call on artillery support, so had to withdraw before shell explosions began to blanket the crest. Then they tried again: "Up through mangled vineyards and orchards the platoons clawed their ways to reach their objectives under the lee of the last slope. Here, engaged in bitter hand-to-hand fighting they dug in to hold the ground."[7]

But the battle was not yet over. The other battalions of 3rd Brigade had not done so well and the Hasty Ps were in danger of being out-flanked and cut off. They were forced to withdraw once again to allow the artillery to have its way. Through the remainder of the day and into the night, the shells rained down on the hill, the Germans, and on the men of 14 platoon of C Company of the Hasty Ps, who had failed to get the word to withdraw. The intense shellfire and a renewed assault finally carried the day; by the next morning the ridge was firmly in Canadian hands.

The fighting on the Adriatic front did not end with the capture of the San Fortunato Ridge. The Eighth Army offensive, and the Canadians with it, ground on across seven more rivers before it reached the Ronco River and went into reserve at the end of October. Even then the interlude was relatively brief. The Canadians were back in action and driving towards the Senio River in early December. They reached it on 21 December — the farthest north they would go in Italy.

On 5 November Burns was relieved of command of the 1st Canadian Corps and replaced by newly promoted Lieutenant-General Charles Foulkes. Foulkes had commanded the 2nd Canadian Infantry Division in Normandy and had been Acting Officer Commander of the 2nd Canadian Corps during the Battle of the Scheldt Estuary (see chapter 14). A dour intellectual, Burns had not made friends with his two divisional commanders and his senior staff officers, and he was intensely disliked by Leese. Although he had certainly not been among the best of the Allied corps commanders in Italy, he had performed tolerably well considering the initial inexperience of his armoured division. The communications foul-ups at the Melfa were at least as much Leese's fault as they were his, and Leese was surely the more culpable of the two in the failure to exploit Hoffmeister's Gothic Line breakthrough at the end of August. But no matter. A corps commander who did not have the respect of his divisional commanders could not function well. That was especially important because, in the words of Sir Brian Horrocks, GOC of the 30th British Corps in the last year of the war, "a Corps is the highest formation in the British Army which fights the day to day tactical battles."[8] That applied equally well to the Canadian Army. At the same time that Burns was relieved,

Vokes was sent to Holland to assume command of the 4th Canadian Armoured Division. Harry Foster, who had been in command of the 4th since late August, was sent to Italy to take over the 1st Division.

When the troops of the 1st Canadian Infantry Division and the 1st Canadian Armoured Brigade had left the United Kingdom in June 1943, it had been assumed that they would rejoin their countrymen in time for the invasion of the continent. Instead, they had been joined by the 5th Canadian Armoured Division and a corps headquarters, and had continued in the battle for Italy long after it was obvious that the war in Europe would be decided elsewhere. In February 1945 the Combined Chiefs of Staff, meeting in Malta, decided to move more troops out of Italy to reinforce those about to fight the final battles for Germany. The 1st Canadian Corps was to be among those troops. Beginning that month, slowly, and with as much secrecy as possible, the Canadians pulled out of the front lines, withdrew to the coast, and boarded transports for southern France. They began to form up in northern Europe in late February and early March, too late for the Battle of the Rhineland, but just in time for the final push into Occupied Holland.

In all, some 92,757 Canadians served in the Italian theatre of operations, including those in the First Special Service Force. They left behind them 5764 of their comrades either killed in action or who died of other causes while on active service. A further 19,486 Canadians had been wounded in the campaign, and 1004 taken prisoner. The Canadians in Italy poked a bit of fun at themselves as Overlord was launched on 6 June and the battle for Normandy began; they called themselves the "D-Day Dodgers." But their role in the liberation of Italy stands among the finest achievements of Canadian arms anywhere.

It was pitch dark when Charles Martin and the other men of the Queen's Own Rifles of Canada began one of the most momentous days in history aboard the pitching transport SS *Monowai*. The men knew that when daylight finally came on 6 June 1944, they would be among the first wave of Canadian infantry to hit the Normandy beaches in front of the little resort town of Bernières-sur-Mer. It may have occurred to some of those men that behind them stood the combined armies of three nations with millions of fighting men, thousands of armoured vehicles and warplanes, and an invasion armada such that the world had never seen. Some may even have taken comfort in that thought. Most knew in their guts that when they ran across the sand, each man would be utterly alone with his fears, his courage, and his determination to survive.

Just before 0600, with a faint hint of the approaching dawn on the eastern horizon, the men began the tricky climb down the loading nets into the assault landing craft (LCAs) that pitched below them. The men were heavily laden with extra ammunition, a full pack, extra grenades, shells for the 2-inch mortars, spare barrels for the light machine guns, and the other accoutrements of war. It was not easy to climb down the nets and time their leaps to the deck of the bucking landing craft, which were tied loosely alongside the transport with their motors running. It took time, but if the men were hurried, some would miss their jump and sink like cannon-balls into the cold depths.

The assault boats were finally loaded. As they cast off, they began their long voyage to the breakers about 8 kilometres away. At 0715, as they moved towards a still-darkened shore, the sky was lit around them by the gun flashes of hundreds of ships and landing craft. Each ship was supposed to be firing at a pre-selected target; the great weight of explosives was intended to ensure that D-Day would not be another Dieppe. The craft moved closer and closer to the maelstrom of fire and explosion that had been a peaceful beach not long before. Then, at 0720, they learned that their landing had been put back by half an hour: some of the specialized assault vehicles, such as the Duplex-Drive (DD) tanks, were having trouble in the rough sea. These waterproofed Sherman tanks had special canvas shielding and propellers hooked up to their engines which allowed them to float. They were designed to be disembarked off-shore and to "swim" to the beaches. The lateness of the DD tanks meant that the Queen's Own would land in the full light of dawn; the absence of the tanks meant there would be no close-in covering fire.

Martin peered through the mist and light drizzle and caught sight of Bernières-sur-Mer. Untouched by the barrage, it seemed postcard perfect in the dim morning light. He later remembered: "There wasn't much talk . . . as we came closer, it was the strange silence that gripped us."[1] The landing craft spread out as they neared the beaches. A nervous German gunner opened fire when the boats were still too far out, wounding one of the men. Martin, in charge of the platoon in the LCA, ordered the Royal Navy lieutenant in command of the boat to move ashore as fast as possible. At about 0805 the prow grated on the sand and the ramp at the front of the boat dropped. Mortar and machine-gun fire opened up all along the beach front. "Move! Fast!" Martin shouted. "Don't stop for anything. Go! Go! Go!" They all raced down the ramp, fanned out, and headed for the sea wall as fast as they could.[2] The invasion of Occupied Europe — Operation Overlord — had begun.

Martin's platoon was one small part of the 8th Canadian Infantry Brigade, 3rd Canadian Infantry Division. That division had been selected to play a key role in the largest invasion in history. Across a front of some 100 kilometres along the south shore of the Bay of the Seine, elements of eight Allied divisions (three of them airborne) — three British, one Canadian, and four American — stormed ashore or landed by glider and parachute to begin what the Germans later called "the longest day." Both sides had been preparing for Overlord for at least three years; they knew that the outcome of the invasion would have a major impact on the course of the war. Both sides were prepared to commit all the resources at their command to ensure victory.

Canadians were proud when they learned that their countrymen were part of the first wave of Allied soldiers to hit the beaches, and they anxiously watched the unfolding drama of the long battle of Normandy that followed D-Day. What many of them did not fully realize, however, was that Martin's platoon and the other soldiers of the 3rd Canadian Infantry Division were not the first group of Canadians to be directly involved in the battle for Normandy. Even the paratroopers of the 1st Canadian Parachute Battalion, who had landed not long after midnight on 6 June to the northeast of Caen as part of the 6th British Airborne Division, were not the first. That honour went to the men of the Royal Canadian Air Force and the Royal Canadian Navy, both of which played an important part in the pre-invasion preparations.

Allied invasion planners were well aware that the Germans had begun 1944 with some thirty-eight divisions in France and the Low Countries. These divisions, in various states of readiness, differed both in fighting quality and in intended role. For example, there was a major difference between a low-grade infantry division assigned to defend a particular stretch of coastline, or one that contained many eastern Europeans and Russians impressed into the Wehrmacht, and a crack division such as the 12th SS Panzer (Hitlerjugend), a well-equipped, motivated, first-line division. The Allies were also aware that more German divisions were being shifted to France and the Low Countries as the date of a likely invasion drew closer.

The key to victory in battle, as Confederate General Nathan Bedford Forrest once said, is to "get there first with the most men." That was what the Allies intended to do when the invasion began. The problem was that the Germans had many more divisions in France and the Low Countries than the Allies could ever hope to land on the beaches or send ashore shortly after the landings took place. The Allies did two things to solve that problem. First, they succeeded in convincing the Germans through a variety of subterfuges that they would land in the Pas de Calais area. The Germans placed their Fifteenth army there and held much of their armour in reserve near Calais long after the D-Day landings, which they initially thought might be a diversion. Second, British air ministry adviser Solly Zuckerman devised the transportation plan designed to make the actual landing zones as inaccessible as possible by road or rail to the rest of France. This was to be done by destroying railway marshalling yards, rolling stock, bridges, and tunnels, and by levelling major transportation centres. The heavy bombers of the US Eighth Air Force and Bomber Command were to be used, as well as the light and medium bombers and the fighter-bombers of the Allied Expeditionary Air Force. The object was to stop the Germans from reinforcing their troops in the landing zone, giving the Allies time to push enough men and weapons ashore to overwhelm the Germans on the beaches and in the lodgement areas immediately behind the beaches.

General Dwight D. Eisenhower, who had been designated Supreme Allied Commander in Europe and who therefore was in overall charge of the invasion and the subsequent fighting, asked for and received control of the heavy-bomber forces as part of the invasion preparation. That was vital, since the commanders of the US Eighth Air Force and the RAF's Bomber Command were reluctant to pull their bombers off their strategic bombing campaigns to bomb railway track. They were still convinced that they could win the war through bombing alone. Eisenhower assumed control of the heavy-bomber forces through his deputy for air, RAF Air Chief Marshal Sir Arthur Tedder, on 27 March 1944. In fact, however, the transportation-plan bombings had started well before that. On the night of 6/7 March 1944, 267 Halifaxes from Nos. 4 and 6 Groups, guided by Mosquitoes from No. 8 Group, attacked the marshalling yards at Trappes, near Paris. These attacks gave Sir Arthur Harris a chance to use the many Halifax IIs and Vs in his squadrons which had been proven increasingly unable to survive deep penetration raids into Germany. The raid of 6/7 March was a test mounted in response to a directive by Sir Charles Portal, Chief of the Air Staff; it demonstrated the tremendous damage that the heavy bombers could do to the rail network. The raid was followed by a second experimental attack the very next night against the key rail centre at Le Mans. This time bombers from No. 3 Group also participated. No aircraft were lost and the target suffered heavy damage.

Harris was surprised by the accuracy his crews were able to achieve on these precision night raids against difficult targets. But time after time throughout March, April, and May the post-raid reconnaissance photos showed that the "heavies" had achieved good concentrations and inflicted punishing damage. Of course, there were casualties among French and Belgian civilians, as Eisenhower and Churchill knew there would be. On the night of 9/10 April, for example, Bomber Command severely damaged the railyards at Lille, but at a cost of 456 French civilian casualties. The next night, 428 Belgians were killed and 300 injured when the bombers attacked rail targets near Ghent, Brussels, and locations in Belgium. Even though the civilian casualties were lower than had been forecast, Churchill and the Free French Minister of the Interior, General Koenig, agonized over these deaths. Eisenhower knew, however, that there was simply no choice but to carry on with the bombings if the Allied troops were to have a chance to make a successful lodgement and hold their ground.

Bomber Command did not restrict itself to attacks on the French and Belgian transportation networks in the months preceding the invasion. Area raids were mounted against Berlin (24/25 March), Nuremberg (30/31 March), Essen (26/27 April), Friedrichshafen (27/28 April), and other German cities. The great bulk of the missions flown, however, were against rail and other transportation targets. The German night-fighter defences were less effective in countering the bombers on these raids, primarily because the missions into France and Belgium were far shorter in duration and the night-fighters had long ago concentrated in Germany itself. Casualties fell dramatically during this period; the No. 6 Group loss rate fell to 2.8 percent in March, 2.1 percent in April, and 1.8 percent in May. These figures include the much heavier losses suffered in raids into Germany itself, even the disastrous Nuremberg attack of 30/31 March. Night after night the bombers flew out to attack marshalling yards or rail centres, to return with no losses at all.

Bomber Command took these "easy" missions into consideration when it ended the thirty-mission tour of duty and substituted a point system instead, with crew members collecting so many points per mission and needing so many to complete a tour of duty (the number changed as the war progressed). The points were allocated on the basis of perceived difficulty of the target attacked. And yet, although loss rates were small compared with those of the Battle of Berlin, there were still losses. During the months in which Bomber Command attacked transportation targets, its crews flew 24,600 sorties and dropped some 78,000 tonnes of bombs; 523 aircraft were lost, thirty-six from No. 6 Group.

At the beginning of June, the heavy bombers switched targets from rail and transportation centres to coastal batteries and other purely military targets near the French coast. In order to hide the fact that the Normandy beaches had been selected as the landing ground, more sorties were flown to other locations, particularly the Pas de Calais area. On the night of 4/5 June, for example, Bomber Command attacked three coastal batteries near Calais and one located between the designated US landing beaches of Utah and Omaha.

On the night of 5/6 June, as the Allied flotilla drew near to the landing beaches, Bomber Command set out to destroy ten strategically located coastal batteries using some 6000 tonnes of bombs. Virtually every serviceable bomber that could be mustered took off into the darkening sky and headed for the French coast. One of the men flying that night was Flying Officer Murray Peden, a Canadian piloting an RAF Flying Fortress with No. 214 Squadron. Peden's mission was to patrol the coast north and east of Dieppe, dropping Window and jamming the German radar. Towards dawn, mission completed, Peden headed the bomber back to England.

Suddenly we saw a sight that brought a lump into my throat. A tremendous aerial armada was passing us in extended formation a mile or two on our left side — not bombers, but C-47s: an airborne army. They were going in. We were coming out. For a long minute I watched them sailing silently onward to their date with destiny.[3]

The heavy bombers did not bear the total burden of disrupting the French and Belgian transportation network. On 13 November 1943 the Allied Expeditionary Air Force was born. Its dual mission was to attack transportation targets, airfields, and coastal defences in France prior to the invasion, and to provide tactical air support for the Allied armies in France after it had occurred. The American contribution to the AEAF was the Ninth United States Air Force; the British contribution was the Second Tactical Air Force, which included the light and medium bombers of No. 2 Group of Bomber Command and the fighters and fighter-bombers of Nos. 83 and 84 Groups. Fifteen of the twenty-nine squadrons in No. 83 Group were RCAF flying Spitfire IXs and XIs, Mustang Is, and Typhoon IBs, one of the deadliest Allied fighter-bombers of the war. When the Second Tactical Air Force was formed, the RAF's Fighter Command (which lost many squadrons to the new force) was renamed Air Defence of Great Britain (the name was later changed back to Fighter Command). ADGB retained three RCAF fighter squadrons.

The primary mission of No. 83 Group was to provide air support for the Second British Army. This was ironic, since the First Canadian Army was to receive its air cover and support from No. 84 Group, which had no Canadian squadrons. To provide air support meant to gain and maintain air superiority over the battlefield (the prime task of pure fighters such as the Spitfire IXs), to prevent the flow of enemy men and supplies to the front, to attack designated ground targets, and to strike other targets as needed at the request of the fighting units on the ground. The ground attack missions were flown primarily by the Typhoon squadrons, armed with cannon, bombs, and/or 3-inch-high explosive or armour-piercing rockets. As the German day-fighter force all but disappeared from the skies over western Europe, the Spitfires were also increasingly used as fighter-bombers.

When the AEAF was first formed, Allied airmen believed that the Luftwaffe would pose a serious threat not only to the invasion, but to subsequent battles to liberate France and the Low Countries and to subdue Germany. In fact, Normandy was, in part, selected as the landing site because it was within easy fighter range of Britain. When the great day arrived, however, the Luftwaffe barely made a showing and, in the long battle for Normandy that followed, it was hardly a factor. The Allies enjoyed almost total air superiority in Normandy, making it difficult for the Germans to bring up large numbers of troops, armour, or other essential war equipment in daylight. The battle for the skies over western Europe had been won by the Allies, especially by the Americans, in early 1944, when long-range Mustang fighters began to accompany the US heavy bombers on raids deep into Germany. The original Mustang was US-designed, and was built and equipped with a US Allison engine. It was simply adequate as a fighter, although it performed well in the ground attack mode. When it was mated to the British Merlin engine, however, it became the best propeller fighter of the war. When the Luftwaffe's fighters rose to meet the US bombers in early 1944, they were slaughtered by the Mustangs; when the bombers returned home to the United Kingdom, the Mustangs roamed free to attack German airfields. This wholesale destruction of German aircraft, combined with heavy bomber attacks on German aircraft plants and fuel-production facilities and a less than intelligent Luftwaffe deployment of its fighter resources, gave the Allies virtually complete control of the air by the time of D-Day.

Like everyone else in the Allied tactical airforces, the Canadians had to learn the science of ground support from scratch. Attacking preassigned targets — especially supply depots or artillery parks — behind the lines was easy enough; hitting enemy troops or tanks while a battle was actually in progress was another matter. The RAF had been working on the technique of tactical ground attack since the war in North Africa, when the famed Desert Air Force had proven itself against the Afrika Korps. The problem of using aircraft in support of ground troops was two-fold: it required identifying enemy targets and attacking them in a timely fashion; it also involved hitting these targets. Neither was especially easy. For example, if a company of Canadian infantry were ambushed by German troops in a strongpoint near a road junction, then those endangered Canadians could not afford to wait until their request for an air strike on the strongpoint was passed up from company to battalion to brigade to air liaison officer to wing, then back down to squadron to flight leader, who then took off with his flight, searched the ground for some sort of marker (panels, flares, or coloured smoke), and attacked what he hoped was the correct target (which he tried to pick out while flying over the ground at, say, 250 kilometres per hour). If the flight leader did arrive at the right place in time to save someone, he had the additional problem of hitting the target.

The eventual solution, first worked on by the RAF in the desert but not perfected for some time after the Normandy landings, was the "cab rank" system in which one-third of a squadron was in the air loitering near the battle zone, one-third was preparing to take off at a moment's notice, and one-third was returning to be refuelled and rearmed. The aircraft near the battle zone could then be called quickly in support of ground troops by a forward air controller — an airforce officer assigned to battalion headquarters and equipped with a radio that could transmit directly to the flight leader. The aircraft so summoned would then attack, using cannon or rockets, both of which proved to be far more accurate than bombs for hitting targets such as tanks, self-propelled guns, or strongpoints. This system worked well, but it was not much in evidence on the Canadian front even by the winter of 1944/45.

In the months leading up to the Normandy landings, the fighters and fighter-bombers of No. 83 Group attacked German airfields, coastal defence installations, radar sites, and road and rail targets, especially bridges and rolling stock. Specially equipped Spitfires and Mosquitoes flew thousands of aerial reconnaissance missions, taking photographs of beach areas, inland defences, tank parks, and the like. The fighters also flew escort missions for the medium and heavy bombers that were taking part in the transportation-plan raids. Many squadrons moved to advance airfields along the British coast to be closer to the future battle zone. Still others prepared for quick transfer to France to begin operating from makeshift fighter strips as soon as a bridgehead was secured.

The RCAF's No. 401 Fighter Squadron, which had been the first RCAF fighter squadron to arrive in the United Kingdom in 1940, was now flying the highly manoeuvrable and fast Spitfire IX. Moved to Tangmere airfield for forward operations, the pilots spent the weeks before D-Day flying intercept and search-and-destroy missions against enemy aircraft, and attacking ground targets, something the Spitfire was not especially designed to do. The last two weeks of April 1944 were typical, as recorded in the squadron record book:

April 19 F/L (flight lieutenant) Scotty Murray could not release his bomb nor [bomb] rack out over the sea . . . and after much effort was forced to abandon his a/c (aircraft) over Beachy Head.
April 24 P/O (pilot officer) T.W. Dowbiggin spotted an ME-110 which he attacked, and it burst into flames and crashed and exploded on the ground . . .

April 27 The Squadron was airborne at 1215 to dive bomb a railway bridge. F/O (flying officer) W.E. Cummings did not recover from the dive after releasing his bomb, and was last seen diving past the vertical, apparently out of control.

April 30 F/O G.D. Billing nearly flew straight into the target . . . after dropping his bomb all attempts to pull out proved futile. Just when he had given up hope of recovery, he wound on full right rudder and the a/c came out in a tight diving turn only a hundred-odd feet from the ground.[4]

Such were the hazards of dive-bombing in a high-speed fighter.

The men and ships of the Royal Canadian Navy were also destined to play an important role in the Normandy landings and were an integral part of the pre-invasion preparations. The RCN's duties included offensive night sweeps in the English Channel carried out by the four Tribal Class destroyers, minesweeping, escort work, the transport of men and equipment from the United Kingdom to the beaches, and helping the RN maintain standing anti-U-boat patrols in strategic areas near the entrances to the channel. When the invasion began, the Canadian Tribals added their gunfire to the other Allied ships that were supporting the men going ashore. In all, some 10,000 Canadian sailors aboard 110 Canadian warships took part in the invasion, 4 percent of the total naval strength involved. Although this total was not high, it must be remembered that RCN ships were still carrying about half the convoy escort burden in the North Atlantic. By the spring of 1944 the RCN was also putting its own support groups to sea in the fight to sink U-boats.

In January 1944 the four Canadian Tribals were reassigned from Scapa Flow to Plymouth to become part of the RN's 10th Destroyer Flotilla, operating under the Commander-in-Chief, Plymouth. The Canadian Tribals thus joined their British counterparts in preparing for regular offensive night sweeps of the English Channel from Ostend, Belgium, to the Bay of Biscay. The operations were carried out at night to avoid the Luftwaffe and its new glider bombs; they were directed at hunting and sinking German destroyers, disrupting channel convoys, hunting U-boats passing through the Bay of Biscay, and acting as screens for British minelaying operations.

The Canadian and British Tribals fought in four ship divisions. Thus, the four Canadian Tribals often sailed with RN ships. They first sortied in January 1944, but did not meet any German naval units until the night of 25–26 April, when *Haida*, *Huron*, *Athabaskan*, and the RN Tribal *Ashanti*, combined with the RN cruiser *Black Prince*, ran into three German destroyers. As the cruiser laid back to fire starshells, battle was joined. One German destroyer was sunk, the others escaped. *Ashanti* and *Huron* suffered minor damage from a collision that occurred as the ships returned to Plymouth.

Three nights later, *Athabaskan* and *Haida* and two motor torpedo boats sortied in support of an RN minelaying flotilla. The two destroyers took up station off the French coast in a spot where they would be able to intercept any German destroyers or E-boats (torpedo boats) coming from the east. At about 0200 on the morning of 29 April, Plymouth alerted them to two enemy vessels steaming westward at about 20 knots. The two Canadian destroyers altered course to the southwest and went to full speed to intercept. At 0412 two German destroyers were sighted; within moments starshells illuminated the seascape. The Germans were about 7300 metres away. They fired two torpedo spreads, before turning back sharply to the east; the two Tribals opened up with their main armament and chased after the fleeing destroyers, altering course to avoid the torpedoes. The Germans returned the shellfire, shrapnel peppering *Athabaskan*'s decks. Suddenly Captain John H. Stubbs received word that his ship's radar had detected two objects travelling off his port quarter at high speed. E-boats! Then, thirty seconds later, a terrific explosion ripped apart the starboard stern quarter. Whether the explosion was caused by an E-boat torpedo or a torpedo fired by one of the German destroyers was never clear. It did not matter, anyway. What did matter was that the explosion caused tremendous casualties and much damage; *Athabaskan* lost headway and began to founder almost immediately. The "abandon ship" order was given and, moments later, *Athabaskan* disappeared beneath the waves, stern first. Stubbs and 128 crew were killed; *Haida* returned to rescue forty-two survivors, but had to abandon the search just before daybreak because she was less than 10 kilometres from shore and well within range of German guns and aircraft. Nevertheless, *Haida*'s captain, Harry DeWolf, left the ship's motor launch behind; it was able to pick up six more men and make its way back to Plymouth, though it was dogged by engine trouble and German minesweepers and fighter aircraft. The destroyer sweeps went on until September, but no more Canadian Tribals were lost in the channel.

While the channel battles reached their climax in late April, a fleet of nineteen

Canadian corvettes to be used for convoy escort and other anti-submarine duties gathered in UK ports. On 28 April the first such operations began when Canadian corvettes *Woodstock* and *Regina* began to escort small convoys to and from ports on the Thames Estuary. On the last day of April, nine Canadian destroyers and eleven corvettes arrived at Moelfre Bay in North Wales and set to work to establish a 90,000-square-kilometre submarine exclusion zone covering the western entrance to the channel.

The role played by the Royal Canadian Navy in the landings themselves is often overlooked, but that role was by no means a minor one. The RCN's contribution included not only the pre-invasion channel sweeps by the Canadian Tribals and the anti-U-boat patrol duties of the corvettes, but also the vital work performed by the RCN's minesweepers, including the 31st Minesweeping Flotilla, in helping to clear mines from the waters off the beaches. The Canadian infantry landing ships (LSIs) *Prince Henry* and *Prince David* ferried men from the United Kingdom to the Normandy coast, while five flotillas of RCN landing craft of various sorts brought infantry, tanks, trucks, self-propelled artillery, and other equipment directly to the beaches.

❧

The C-47s (Dakotas) that passed Murray Peden's B-17 as he and his crew returned to the United Kingdom in the early morning hours of 6 June carried elements of three airborne divisions — the US 82nd and 101st and the British 6th — destined to be the first of the Allied invaders to land on French soil. The two US airborne divisions were to land to the south and west of the beach designated "Utah," which was on the southeast corner of the Cotentin Peninsula. They were supposed to secure the key inland routes that led to the beaches so as to stop the Germans from reinforcing their coastal defence troops as the US infantry stormed ashore. The British 6th Airborne, which included the 1st Canadian Parachute Battalion, was to be air dropped or glider landed to the east of the Orne River, south of the easternmost British beach ("Sword"), so as to secure the river crossings and stop German troops and armour from mounting a flanking attack against Sword Beach.

The great bulk of the Canadian troops were to assault "Juno" Beach, which stretched from St Aubin-sur-Mer on the east to half-way between La Rivière and Courseulles-sur-Mer on the west. The 3rd Canadian Infantry Division under

Major-General R.L. Keller was picked for the task. This was not surprising, since the 1st Division was heavily engaged in Italy and the 2nd was still considered shaky owing to the tremendous losses it had suffered at Dieppe. Keller selected the 7th and 8th Brigades to make the initial assault, with the 9th in reserve. The 7th was assigned to hit "Mike" Beach on the division's right, and was to be supported by the 6th Canadian Armoured Regiment (1st Hussars). The 8th would take "Nan" Beach on the left, with the village of Bernières-sur-Mer right in the middle of the landing ground; it was to be accompanied by the 10th Canadian Armoured Regiment (Fort Garry Horse). To the right of Juno Beach lay "Gold" Beach, to be assaulted by the 50th British Infantry Division. To its left was Sword Beach, the objective of the 3rd British Infantry Division. The three beaches were to be under the command of the 1st British Corps, then attached to the British Second Army; once a successful lodgement had taken place, the Canadians were to revert to the command of the 2nd Canadian Corps. Montgomery did not intend to bring Crerar and his First Canadian Army Headquarters to Normandy for some time yet.

Much controversy would erupt in the years after the war about what Field Marshal Montgomery had planned for D-Day and the days following. He himself claimed that he had always intended to fight a defensive battle on the British-Canadian front; draw the bulk of the German troops and especially armour to his front; and then loose the Americans on his left (they also landed at "Omaha" Beach, which lay to the west of Gold Beach) to break through the German defences and make a wide sweep towards both the Brittany ports and the River Seine and Paris beyond. The historical record shows otherwise. Montgomery clearly intended to seize Caen on the first day and then drive rapidly beyond it to take the high ground to the south (Verrières and Bourguébus Ridges). Caen was the chief administrative centre of Normandy, the main rail, road, and canal junction in the area of the beaches, and the key to any further inland advance on the left flank. The quicker this could be done the better, since the land south of Caen was ideal for airfields to be used by the forwardmost units of the tactical airforces. The role given to the Canadians after they had secured their bridgehead was to drive eastward, and to capture the important ports of Le Havre and Rouen. This latter operation was dubbed Axehead.

The British and Canadians were assigned the easternmost beaches, and the United States the two on the west, because of the locality where those armies had been based in the United Kingdom (the Americans in the south and west, the Canadians and British in the southeast), and because it was thought that the

American troops might be resupplied by ships arriving directly from the United States. That created a major strategic imbroglio for the Allies in the coming weeks. The Americans were by far the strongest of the three Allies in both men and equipment. They therefore had the best chance of fighting a successful battle to break out of the bridgehead. But inland from them was the *bocage* country — hundreds of square kilometres of small fields and pastures bordered by earthen embankments with thick hedgerows growing on the top. Each field afforded the Germans excellent defensive positions and, when they did push inland, the Americans had literally to fight a small battle for each one. It was slow and it was very costly. Inland from the British and Canadians, in contrast, lay mostly open rolling country, excellent for tank warfare. But the Canadian Army was small, and both armies suffered from severe manpower shortages. Montgomery could not afford to risk heavy casualties in a breakout battle, so he chose to be much more cautious than an American commander might have been facing the same terrain.

The German defenders had stepped up their preparations for D-Day since the beginning of the year, when Field Marshal Erwin Rommel had been designated Inspector of Fortifications for the western front (he was also in command of Army Group B). Field Marshal Gerd von Rundstedt was in overall charge of German forces in France. The two men disagreed on how best to meet an Allied invasion, and their disagreement was reflected in the way the Germans deployed their troops. Rommel wanted to stop the Allies on the beaches with powerful armoured thrusts from panzer units located only a short distance away. Von Rundstedt took the more traditional German approach to defence; he wanted to keep the German armour farther back, to be used in a powerful counter-attack once the Allies got ashore. Most of the German commanders (but not Rommel) also fell for the Allied ruse that Calais was to be the invasion point, not Normandy. Thus the Fifteenth army (with its panzer divisions) was to be held in reserve near Calais until Hitler himself agreed to release it, or its tanks, to be used elsewhere. This left a number of static infantry divisions manning the coastal defences, with a handful of armoured divisions stationed from 10 to 20 kilometres south of the beaches. On the Sword-Juno-Gold front, the Germans placed the 716th Infantry division; the armoured backbone was initially to be provided by the 21st Panzer division.

As dawn broke along the beach, the British, Canadian, and American infantry climbed down into their landing craft and waited. Ashore, the paratroopers of the

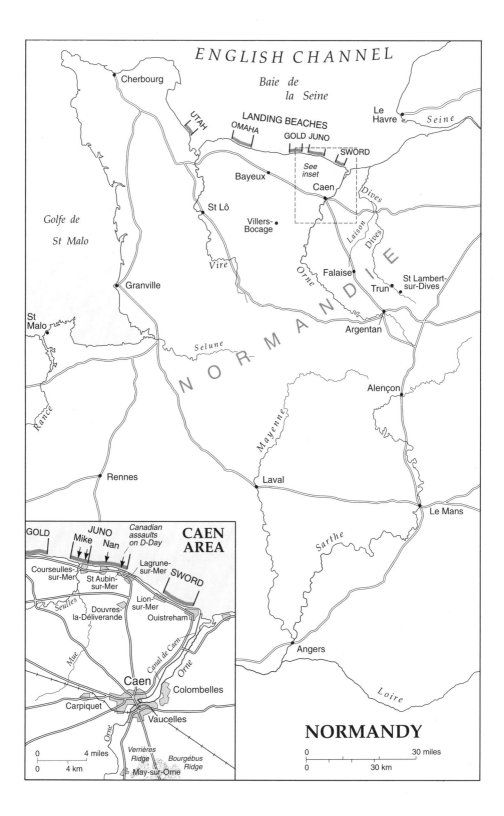

ENGLISH CHANNEL

Baie de
la Seine

Cherbourg

Le
Havre

Seine

UTAH

LANDING BEACHES

OMAHA

GOLD JUNO

SWORD

See
inset

Bayeux

Caen

Dives

St Lô

Golfe de

St Malo

Villers-
Bocage

Laison

Dives

N
O
R
M
A
N
D
I
E

Vire

Orne

Falaise

St Lambert-
sur-Dives

Granville

Trun

St
Malo

Selune

Argentan

Rance

Alençon

Mayenne

Rennes

Laval

Le Mans

Sarthe

GOLD

JUNO

Mike

Nan

*Canadian
assaults
on D-Day*

CAEN
AREA

Courseulles-
sur-Mer

St Aubin-
sur-Mer

Lagrune-
sur-Mer

SWORD

Seulles

Lion-
sur-Mer

Mue

Douvres-
la-Déliverande

Canal de Caen

Orne

Ouistreham

Angers

Loire

Caen

Colombelles

Carpiquet

Orne

Vaucelles

0   4 miles

0   4 km

*Verrières
Ridge*

*Bourgébus
Ridge*

May-sur-Orne

NORMANDY

0   30 miles

0   30 km

207

6th British Airborne had seized the bridge across the Orne River south of Ouistreham in the early hours of D-Day and had been beating back German counter-attacks ever since. The American paratroopers had an even more difficult time of it. Widely scattered in their drops, they suffered heavy casualties and were delayed by the need to reorganize and consolidate before moving to their objectives; they achieved most of them solely due to German confusion.

At approximately 0715, the heavy guns aboard the cruisers and battleships opened up on the beach defences. The fire plans had been carefully prepared. The largest calibre naval guns were used to bombard the massive concrete gun emplacements along and behind the beaches; the lesser guns of the destroyers were aimed directly at the smaller bunkers and gun emplacements along the beach fronts. Rocket-equipped landing craft and self-propelled artillery (105-millimetre "Priests") on other landing craft drenched the beaches with fire, designed not so much to destroy defences as to force the defenders to keep their heads down as the landing craft headed in to shore.

On the British and Canadian beaches, the infantry were to be supported by a variety of specially designed armoured fighting vehicles, such as flail-tanks to clear paths through minefields, fascine-carrying tanks to fill in gulleys and anti-tank ditches, and the Duplex-Drive (DD) tanks. The Americans, for the most part, eschewed these "funnies," as they were called by the British and Canadian troops, though they did use a small number of DD tanks. They had faith that their infantry could successfully assault the beaches without direct support from armour. By then, however, there was plenty of evidence from numerous assault landings carried out by US Marines in the South Pacific that unprotected infantry could be subject to heavy casualties in a well-opposed landing. They ignored the evidence; on Omaha Beach their troops would pay a high price for this shortsightedness.

On Gold, Juno, and Sword Beaches it was planned to have the DD tanks come ashore before the infantry to give them cover fire. On most of the beaches, the rough sea upset that scheme. Several DD tanks sank like stones, taking crew members with them; others were brought directly to the beaches in their tank landing craft (LCTs). In some sectors the tanks went ashore ahead of the infantry as planned, but in most cases they arrived well after the infantry.

The pre-invasion bombings and the bombardment had had only a limited effect on the beach fortifications; some of the Canadian assault battalions ran into heavy defensive fire immediately after they reached the beaches. It was largely a matter of luck whether a man lived or died in the rush across the sand and in the attacks on the sea wall and its integrated bunkers. On the 7th Brigade's Mike Beach, C Company of the Canadian Scottish landed on the right flank, on a stretch of relatively open sand, to find that its objective had already been destroyed by naval gunfire. They pushed inland with few casualties. A few hundred metres to their left, the two assault companies of the Royal Winnipeg Rifles came under heavy fire even before touching down; B Company suffered a great many casualties as it attacked four German strongpoints without any covering fire. Only one officer and twenty-five men managed to get off the beach unscathed. On the leftmost sector of the beach, the Regina Rifles A Company had been assigned to clear a strongpoint in the northwest corner of the village of Courseulles-sur-Mer. They received a nasty surprise as they neared their objective:

> The bombardment had not cracked the huge casemate . . . [the] fortress had reinforced concrete walls four feet thick and housed an 88-millimetre gun as well as machine-guns. In addition there were concrete trenches outside the fort liberally sprinkled with small arms posts. It was grim going but eventually they executed a left flanking attack and with the support of tanks succeeded in breaking through the defences.[5]

On the 8th Brigade's Nan Beach, the Queen's Own A Company was put ashore in front of a new German defensive position not indicated on the map. They took heavy casualties from mortars and machine guns. On the left of the beach, the farthest left platoon of the North Shore Regiment had practically a walkover and "went into the village in nothing flat," but the platoon to its right ran into intense small-arms fire and sought refuge behind the sea wall. Lieutenant G.V. Moran knew that he and his men could not stay there: "In order to get the men moving . . . I stood in the open and shouted at the top of my voice and, making vigorous motions with my arms, urged the sections around the wall forward."[6] A German sniper easily spotted Moran and aimed for the centre of his back. If shot there, Moran would have been killed, but the instant the German pulled the trigger, Moran began to turn around and was hit in the left arm instead. By midday, the assaulting companies were past the initial line of beach defences and into the towns or fields beyond, as the reserve companies came ashore. Later in the day the 9th Brigade Headquarters landed, as did Keller and his divisional headquarters. Despite the popular belief that the Canadians were the only troops to reach and hold their D-Day objectives on D-Day itself, none of the Allied soldiers on any of the beaches actually did so, despite the disorganized German resistance and the almost complete absence on the battlefield of German armour.

At Utah Beach the Americans had come ashore in the wrong spot, but had established a good lodgement on easily defended ground. They were lucky. Their compatriots at Omaha Beach became trapped among the dunes when the infantry could not fight its way past the German defenders to exit the beach. With virtually no armour, and no specialized armoured vehicles for help, they were pinned down below the bluffs that overlooked the beach for several hours as the outcome of the landing remained in doubt. Casualties were very heavy. For a time, General Omar Bradley, commander of the US First Army, considered evacuation, although to have done so would have left a gaping hole in the Allied landing zones. By mid-afternoon, a series of courageous rushes combined with excellent demolition work under fire allowed them to begin to outflank the German defenders and get out of the killing zone.

At Gold Beach, the 50th British Infantry Division pushed about 6 kilometres inland and linked with the Canadians on Juno Beach. The Canadians had run into some of the stiffest resistance of any of the Commonwealth troops, but still managed to reach the farthest point inland. However, they failed to establish a contiguous front with the 3rd British Infantry Division on their left, a fact that the Germans were well aware of and tried to exploit with an attack by the 21st Panzer division late in the afternoon. The Germans were stopped by British troops, who managed to destroy thirteen of the forty tanks taking part. That gave the rest of the attacking German tanks second thoughts about continuing; even though there was little else between the Germans and the sea at that point, they withdrew without pressing the attack home.

The forwardmost company of the Queen's Own Rifles advanced as far as the small hamlet of Anisy before setting up their defences for the night. It was only then, when the mad rush to get off the beach and to push inland as far as possible, had expended itself, that Martin and his comrades had time to think about the awful reality of war:

> It was on this evening that a moment came when some reality sank in about all the things that had happened during the day. It hurt. We had reached only the edges of Bernières-sur-Mer when we learned that half of our original company — those I had joined up with in June of 1940 — had been killed or

wounded. And we'd taken still more casualties as we'd gone on to Anguerny. The tears came. I went behind a wall. So many had been lost.[7]

That was true for the other battalions as well. Although the casualties were not nearly as high as the most pessimistic of the predictions (the worst had forecast 1980 casualties), they were high enough; more than 600 men were wounded, and 335 killed.

The Canadians finally met the German armour the morning after D-Day, when spearheads of the 12th SS Panzer counter-attacked the North Novas and the 27th Canadian Armoured Regiment at Authie. That town lay just to the north of the Caen–Bayeux road, the initial overall Canadian objective for D-Day itself. If Authie had been taken and held as planned, the Canadians would have been in a good position to advance on Carpiquet, just to the west of Caen, as the first part of a manoeuvre to outflank Caen and encircle it. Caen was the key to virtually everything around it and, as long as the Germans held it, the British and Canadian forces would move neither eastwards nor to the south. The Germans were determined to defend Caen at all costs, and Authie was as good a place as any to drive back the Canadian spearheads. They quickly moved two more armoured divisions into the Caen sector, in addition to 21st Panzer that had been there before D-Day. The 12th SS marched all night and was the first of the two to arrive. It deployed before dawn on 7 June; the other, Panzer Lehr, followed in short order. A heavy division of almost 20,000 men, the 12th SS was known as the Hitlerjugend since most of its recruits were young and fanatical Nazis from the Hitler Youth organization. Although not yet battle tested, they had been thoroughly trained and were led by veteran officers and NCOs, most of whom had served prolonged periods on the eastern front.

The 12th SS attack was coordinated by the commander of the 25th SS Panzer Grenadier regiment, SS Obersturmbannführer Kurt Meyer — a battle-hardened and committed Nazi. Meyer stationed himself in the Abbaye d'Ardenne, an abandoned Gothic ruin in the fields to the northwest of Caen. From atop one of the towers, he could see almost all the way to the beaches and track the progress of the oncoming Canadian armour:

Did I see right? An enemy tank pushed through the orchards of St. Contest. Suddenly it stops. The commander opens the hatch and scours the countryside before him. Is the fellow blind? Has he not noticed that he stands barely 200 yards from the grenadiers of my 2nd Battalion, and that the barrels of their anti-tank guns are pointed at him?[8]

Meyer suddenly realized that the Canadians were heading to Authie and that their eastern flank was totally unprotected. That was where he would strike.

As the Canadians rolled towards the Caen–Bayeux road, Carpiquet ahead of them, the Germans attacked. There was a short, sharp tank battle before the Germans swept past the lead Canadian tanks and into Authie. Then they overran Authie. The North Novas there, and those between Authie and Buron, just to the north of it, were badly shot up. With support from the Canadian armour, they tried to hold in Buron, but were driven back. They were forced to retreat to a point about 5 kilometres northwest of Caen, where they held and dug in; they suffered 245 killed, wounded, or missing in one day.

Meyer's 25th SS Panzer Grenadiers hit the Canadians the next day. This time it was the Royal Winnipeg Rifles in Putot-en-Bessin, about 8 kilometres west of Authie and on the south side of the Caen–Bayeux road. The three forward companies of the Winnipegs were encircled by Meyer's tanks and infantry; they took heavy casualties before they managed to withdraw. The 7th Brigade Commander, Harry Foster, then ordered a counter-attack by the Canadian Scottish, which went in at nightfall and drove the SS back. Putot was recovered and held. Then the SS came at the Regina Rifles at Norrey-en-Bessin. A desperate night-long tank/infantry battle swirled around the Reginas' battalion headquarters before the Germans were driven back with heavy casualties, leaving several destroyed tanks, including Mark V Panthers, in the smoking ruins of the town.

As the survivors of the Royal Winnipeg Rifles withdrew from Putot-en-Bessin, they were forced to leave a number of men behind, some of whom were wounded. The SS took them to the Abbaye d'Ardenne. After being punched and beaten, eighteen were systematically murdered in a little courtyard of the abbey (two more were shot some ten days later). Their bodies were hastily buried there and not discovered for some time after. Meyer, who took command of the 12th SS Panzer division on 14 June, was charged with war crimes after the war, tried by a military court, found guilty, and sentenced to death. His sentence was then commuted to life in prison, which he was supposed to serve in Canada. He was brought to Dorchester Penitentiary in New Brunswick, but sent back to Germany in September 1954. He was subsequently released.

The Canadians battled the 12th SS again on 11 June, when the 6th Canadian Armoured Regiment (1st Hussars) and the Queen's Own attempted to advance from Norrey-en-Bessin through Le Mesnil-Patry towards Cheux, thereby beginning to outflank Carpiquet to the west. As they approached Le Mesnil, the Germans poured heavy mortar and machine-gun fire down on the infantry who were riding aboard the Shermans. Then they opened up with 88-millimetre anti-tank guns. The tanks slewed and swerved to avoid being hit. The infantry jumped off and headed for cover as the Shermans drove on to try to deal with the German fire. Some penetrated into the town. "We were just sitting ducks with that kind of exposure," Martin would later write, "and we could move just as fast on foot."[9] In the town, the 1st Hussars were slaughtered by German tanks and anti-tank guns. Only two of the Shermans that had entered the town survived; fifty-nine men were killed and twenty-one wounded. The Queen's Own lost fifty-five killed and forty-four wounded. The attack was a total failure. The men were learning the hard way just how vulnerable the Shermans were to German anti-tank fire. The men nicknamed them Ronsons (as in Ronson Lighters) because they "brewed up" (caught fire) so easily when hit by an 88-millimetre armour-piercing shell.

Le Mesnil-Patry should have taught the Canadians something else: that piecemeal attacks with perhaps a single infantry battalion backed by an armoured regiment were not enough to penetrate the well-laid-out German defensive screen. Time after time in the Normandy fighting, the British and the Canadians mounted attacks with too few men and too few armoured vehicles, depending on artillery support to smooth the way. Time after time such attacks failed, with heavy casualties. The Germans quickly learned this pattern, and noticed as well that even when British and Canadian assaults were initially successful, the advancing troops almost always failed to follow through; instead, they stopped to consolidate, to rest, and to bring up the all-important artillery. That fatal pause usually gave the Germans the chance to do what they did so well — to counter-attack to regain lost ground.

After the failure at Le Mesnil-Patry, the 3rd Canadian Infantry Division was effectively withdrawn for the better part of the next three weeks while the British and the Americans bore the brunt of the fighting. The failure to take Caen produced a long and deadly stalemate as the Germans strengthened their defences in an effort to hold the Allies to a relatively small and shallow bridgehead. Although the US forces were able to drive westward across the Cotentin peninsula, then north to Cherbourg to take that port, the Allies could not advance to the south. Thus, a deadly war of attrition followed the quick success of Overlord itself.

In the six days between the D-Day landings and the nightfall of 11 June, 1017 Canadian soldiers were killed in action and 1814 were wounded on or near the Normandy beaches. As bad as they were, however, the mounting casualties were only a sombre sign of the terrible price that would have to be paid before the battle for Normandy was won.

XIII The Ordeal of Normandy

The fifth anniversary of Britain's declaration of war against Germany, 3 September 1944, was to be a solemn one for the men of the 2nd Canadian Infantry Division; a little over two years after assaulting Dieppe, the division had returned to the place of its greatest single-day loss of the war. Two days earlier the division's lead elements had entered Dieppe from the south after a long and almost uneventful drive from Rouen, the cathedral city on the north bank of the Seine. They had encountered no Germans; the port town had been taken without a shot being fired.

On the morning of 3 September the survivors of the Dieppe attack and others from the division attended religious services at the Canadian war cemetery on the southern outskirts of the town. The people of Dieppe had built and maintained the cemetery during the many long months of German occupation since the Canadian raid. In that cemetery lay more than 700 of the Canadians killed on 23 August 1942, as well as other Allied servicemen killed in the raid or shot down in the vicinity of Dieppe in the months that followed.

In the afternoon, the citizens of Dieppe officially welcomed their liberators as the entire division paraded through the main part of the town, led by the massed pipe bands of its Highland regiments. At the head of the parade were the armoured cars of the 8th Reconnaissance Regiment, followed in order by its three infantry brigades. Army commander Harry Crerar took the salute; standing beside him was divisional commander Charles Foulkes and the mayor of Dieppe. Ross Ellis, battle-adjutant of the Calgary Highlanders, was there. At the end of the day he wrote to his wife, Marjorie: "This is quite a day in history, 5 years of war . . . Today also brought back memories of another Sunday 5 years ago and I find that I can remember several points quite clearly . . . Day by day doesn't count anymore because so often there is no distinction between days."[1] For Ellis, as for so many other Canadian soldiers, one day of war was pretty much like another.

The road to Dieppe had been long and bloody for the 2nd Canadian Infantry Division. It had landed in France at the beginning of July and had gone into action on 18 July in Operation Atlantic — the final stage of the capture of Caen. Within a week of its first day in battle, one of its battalions — the Black Watch (Royal Highland Regiment) of Canada of the 5th Canadian Infantry Brigade — had walked up Verrières Ridge and, after a matter of hours, had suffered the worst single-day defeat inflicted on a Canadian battalion since the start of the Normandy campaign. By the time the battle for Normandy ended, the 2nd Division had changed almost beyond recognition from what it had been when it first landed in France. But then, so had the other two Canadian divisions of the 2nd Canadian Corps and the many other units that fell under corps command. From D-Day until the crossing of the Seine in late August, 18,444 Canadians had become casualties in Normandy, and 5021 of them were dead. The story of the Battle of Normandy is often ignored when the history of the successful D-Day landings is related, but Normandy was one of the bloodiest campaigns of attrition in the history of modern war.

Although the focus of most Canadians was fixed firmly on the battle for Normandy in the weeks after D-Day, the RCAF and the RCN continued to make important contributions to the Normandy campaign in particular and to the Allied war effort in general. The heavy bombers of No. 6 Group, in conjunction with the rest of Bomber Command, kept up their attacks against communications targets in France and the Low Countries. On one of these raids, against Cambrai on 12 June, a Lancaster bomber of No. 419 Squadron was attacked by a night-fighter and set ablaze. Pilot Officer Andrew Mynarski of Winnipeg was about to leap to safety when he caught sight of the tail gunner who was trapped and struggling to free himself. Mynarski made his way to the rear of the burning bomber and tried desperately to free the man. As he did so, his own clothes caught fire. Finally concluding that he could not save the gunner, Mynarski struggled to an escape hatch, saluted the trapped man, and reluctantly bailed out. It was too late; he made it to the ground, but died of his burns shortly after. Miraculously, the gunner survived the crash and lived to tell Mynarski's story; as a result, Mynarski was posthumously awarded a Victoria Cross.

The bombing attacks on communications targets continued until mid-August, as did occasional area attacks on German cities such as Stuttgart (24/25 July) or Hamburg (28/29 July), but two more types of targets were added to Bomber

Command's list in the weeks after D-Day: launching sites for the V-1 "buzz-bomb" and German synthetic-oil production and storage facilities. The Germans began launching the V-1s against London shortly after D-Day. Air-breathing, pilotless flying-bombs, the V-1s were powered by a ramjet engine. They were fast, but not so fast that they could not be destroyed by the fastest British fighters, or by very accurate anti-aircraft fire. Nonetheless, the most effective method of dealing with them was to bomb their launching sites. This campaign was initiated on the night of 16/17 June, when all of Bomber Command's groups, except No. 3, were dispatched to destroy four V-1 launching sites in the Pas de Calais area.

Attacks on German oil-production facilities were part of a combined Allied effort to starve Germany of its all-important oil supplies. For the balance of 1944, synthetic-oil factories, crude-oil refining facilities, oil storage dumps, and the like were repeatedly bombed by the "heavies" of Bomber Command and the Eighth US Army Air Force. The campaign was a singular success. German oil supplies fell off dramatically as the bombing campaign took hold. The results of the "oil plan," as it was called, proved conclusively that the heavy bombers, properly used, were making a major contribution to Allied victory.

It is important here to point out that the detractors of the heavy-bombing campaign, then and now, claim that heavy bombing did little or nothing to hinder German industrial production. They often point to German aircraft production figures — which rose dramatically after mid-1943 — as evidence that, despite Allied bombing, German determination, organization, and productive energy prevailed. This is sheer nonsense. When aircraft factories were repeatedly attacked, production fell. When the Allied bombers turned their attention to other targets — such as oil — aircraft production recovered. It should be no surprise that the Germans were able to increase aircraft production after mid-1943 because their aircraft production facilities had been so badly organized to begin with. But when all those new German fighters emerged from the factories in mid-to-late 1944, there was no aviation gas for them because of the sustained Allied air offensive against German oil targets. Surely, that is what really counted.

On the sea, the RCN continued to screen the channel approaches to the landing zones and to carry out offensive sweeps against German naval and merchant targets. *Haida* participated in the destruction of a U-boat west of the channel on 24 June, while other Canadian destroyers and corvettes sank four more U-boats in the Bay of Biscay and the channel before the end of August. *Ottawa* and *Kootenay* took part in three of those four sinkings.

While Canadian destroyers and corvettes hunted U-boats in the channel vicinity, Canadian destroyers and motor torpedo boats patrolled the channel waters aggressively, sometimes encountering German naval vessels. On 9 June *Haida* and *Huron* sank two German destroyers, effectively breaking the back of the German destroyer force in the channel area. Canadian ships also took part in Operation Kinetic, launched on 31 July, intended to break up German coastal supply links and tighten the sea blockade of Germany west of the Kiel Canal. In early August the RCN's first escort carrier, *Nabob* (a RN carrier crewed by the RCN, but with RN pilots), accompanied by Tribals HMCS *Algonquin* and HMCS *Sioux*, sortied from Scapa Flow to launch air attacks against German shipping on the Norwegian coast. All this naval activity in English or northern European waters did not come cheaply. On 8 August the corvette *Regina* was sunk off Trevose Head while it was trying to salvage a torpedoed freighter; *Alberni* went down on 21 August off the Isle of Wight.

On land, the battle of Normandy had degenerated into a costly stalemate after the initial success of the D-Day landings and the establishment of a contiguous Allied lodgement in the days immediately afterward. The failure of a thrust to the southwest of Caen by the British 7th Armoured Division on 12 June had left the front lines about 6 kilometres to the north of Caen, except on the eastern side of the Orne and the Caen Canal where the British 51st (Highland) Division had taken over the ground won by the 6th British Airborne Division on D-Day. On that flank the front looped to the south, almost touching the industrial suburb of Colombelles, immediately east of Caen.

The 7th Armoured Division's failure on 12 June was all too typical of the way the fighting was going for the Allies; in an advance west of Caen, the British thought they had discovered a hole in the German defences and they rushed the 7th Armoured into it. That famed and battle-hardened division headed rapidly towards the strategic hilltop town of Villers-Bocage, about 16 kilometres southwest of Caen. But instead of pushing through as far and as fast as possible, the column stopped and rested at Villers-Bocage, watched by SS Captain Michael Wittman, leader of a group of five Tiger tanks. Singlehandedly, Wittman attacked, badly shot up armoured cars, trucks, and tanks, and prompted the division to begin a withdrawal. In five short minutes, one German tank crew had turned aside the entire 7th Armoured Division.

Because of Allied air superiority, the Germans had great difficulty moving reinforcements up by day, but they could and did move them by night, as Wittman's Tiger tanks had. In the weeks following the invasion, three more panzer divisions were moved to the Caen front, in addition to the two sent there just after D-Day and the one in place when the landings took place. The armour stiffened German resistance; the ponderous tactics of the Allies and the piecemeal insertion of their units to battle left the front virtually unchanged. The Germans could not hope to throw the Allies into the channel, but they just might be able to make Normandy into a costly battle of attrition and bottle the Allies up in the bridgehead.

There were four basic reasons why the German defences in Normandy were able to hold out as long as they did. First, it is much more difficult to attack successfully than it is to defend stubbornly. The Allies were not in Normandy just to hold on; they were there to attack and to keep on attacking until the Germans were destroyed or driven from the battlefield. The Germans could "win" just by holding out. Second, much of the German equipment was better than that of the Allies. Although the bulk of the German tanks in Normandy were the older Mark IVs, a match for the Sherman medium tank, the Sherman was no match for the newer and much heavier armoured and better gunned Panthers and Tigers. The Sherman was also easily destroyed by the 88-millimetre anti-tank gun. The British had engineered a solution to the Sherman's inability to kill the new German tanks. Called the Firefly, it combined the effective British high-velocity 17-pounder anti-tank gun with the Sherman in a modified turret. There were never enough Fireflies. British and Canadian armoured regiments eventually managed to deploy two per tank troop, but the Americans were late to receive them and never got enough to make a major difference on the battlefield. Third, German small-unit tactics, and the training in those tactics given to their ranks, their NCOs, and their junior officers, were superb and better than the small-unit tactics and training of the Allies. Finally, though lacking air cover, the Germans took full advantage of the stone-walled villages, narrow roads, thick hedgerows, tall wheat, and other terrain features when they laid out their defences.

In response to the German build-up, Montgomery altered his original intentions at the end of June. He decided to fight an essentially defensive battle on the Caen front in such a way as to convince the Germans that his object was to break out near Caen and strike for Paris. This, he believed, would lead them to place the bulk of their armour opposite him, giving the Americans a chance to break out. The trouble with that strategy was that the Americans had first to fight their way through the *bocage*, a difficult and costly operation.

Virtually all the units of the 3rd Canadian Infantry Division spent the last half of June in reserve. That hiatus ended on 4 July, when Keller's troops opened an attack on the town of Carpiquet and the airport that lay to the south of the town. The offensive was to be the first stage of a major British effort to take Caen — Operation Charnwood. The 8th Brigade, with the Royal Winnipeg Rifles under command, had already suffered heavy casualties on D-Day (as had the Winnipegs), but was given the assignment anyway. It was supported by the 10th Canadian Armoured Regiment (Fort Garry Horse) and the "funnies" or AVRE (Assault Vehicles, Royal Engineers) of the 79th British Armoured Division.

With support from the artillery, RAF Typhoons, and the guns of the Battleship HMS *Rodney*, the Canadians swept in from the west to meet the formidable firepower of the well-dug-in SS defenders. As so often happened, the massive barrages left the bulk of the defenders still alive and the core of the defence unshaken. From low concrete bunkers surrounding the control buildings and hangars, the SS made the airfield into a killing zone, with interlocking fields of machine-gun fire backed by mortars and artillery. Major J.E. Anderson of the North Shore Regiment, which sustained more casualties on that day than on any other of the war, later reflected on the nature of the battle: "I am sure that at some time during the attack every man felt he could not go on. Men were being killed or wounded on all sides and the advance seemed pointless as well as hopeless."[2] The Canadians took the town, but could not secure the southern part of the airfield, even after a second attempt mounted by two battalions. The attack was only a partial success, bought at very high cost. There were too few tanks and too little direct fire support. Again, a hesitant effort had produced disappointing results. Charlie Martin and the Queen's Own were there:

> It was terrible. We had to dig in along the runway and in part of an old hanger building. The enemy were watching every move from a slightly higher level. At best it's difficult crossing open ground, but the terrain surrounding an airport is about as level as can be found anywhere.[3]

Keller's two superior officers, army commander Miles Dempsey and corps commander Sir John Crocker, blamed him for failing to control the battle and for not recognizing when to throw additional resources into it. They thought him unfit for divisional command. Canadian military historian John English, who has done

one of the most sophisticated analyses of the Canadian Army's performance in the Normandy campaign, essentially agreed with them when he wrote: "The decision to send the [reinforcements] over two kilometers of open ground without any intimate direct fire support was questionable. The decision to hurl them in again with the minimum tank support they should have had in the first place could also be categorized as too little, too late."[4]

For the next five days, the 8th Brigade remained in its exposed salient in Carpiquet and the northern portion of the airfield until the Germans were driven out of Caen by the Charnwood attack. That offensive began with a massive bombing of the northern fringe of Caen in the early morning hours of 8 July. Then the entire 1st British Corps, assisted by the 3rd Canadian Division, moved into the city. The 9th Canadian Infantry Brigade captured Buron and Authie, to the northwest of Caen, the 7th Brigade captured the small hamlets of Cussy and Ardenne, while the 8th completed its capture of Carpiquet as the Germans pulled back.

Caen, or what was left of it after the heavy bombing and fighting, was secured by the night of 9 July; 1194 Canadians had become casualties in taking the city, 334 of them fatal. But the suburbs of Colombelles, east of Caen, and Vaucelles, across the Caen Canal to the south of it, remained in German hands, as did the key Verrières and Bourguébus Ridges that lay about 6 kilometres to the south of Vaucelles. Those were to be Montgomery's next objectives. The Orne had to be crossed on the western side of Vaucelles, and Colombelles had to be secured; that would leave the Germans outflanked and force their withdrawal further south. Once that happened, the Canadians and British could continue their push towards Falaise, southwest of Caen, preferably along Route Nationale 158, which ran straight as an arrow from Caen to Falaise. In the meantime, General Omar Bradley, commander of the US First Army to the west, would continue to prepare for the breakout offensive.

The country to the south of Caen was ideal for defence. From the stone-walled Norman villages atop Bourguébus and Verrières Ridges, the Germans could see many kilometres to the north; it would be virtually impossible to surprise them in daylight, yet mounting a well-coordinated night attack is one of the most difficult things to do in war. The old villages provided excellent protection for German troops and armour; the tall grain and the many clumps of woods could hide troops and even armour when properly camouflaged. Demolished, the towns provided excellent cover, as in the case of the hamlet of Tilly-la-Campagne, situated near the Caen–Falaise highway. There the Germans built bunkers in the basements of the houses, then blew up the houses atop the bunkers. The rubble gave excellent protection to the defenders. Backed by German armour, they threw back repeated British and Canadian attacks in July and August, exacting a heavy toll.

On 11 July Guy Simonds's 2nd Canadian Corps took over operational command of the 3rd Canadian Infantry Division from the British. It also assumed control of the 2nd Canadian Infantry Division, which had started to arrive in France from the United Kingdom on 6 July, as well as the independent 2nd Canadian Armoured Brigade. The 4th Canadian Armoured Division was to be held in the United Kingdom until near the end of the month, primarily because there was simply no room for it in the increasingly crowded Allied bridgehead. Although Crerar and much of the staff of the First Canadian Army Headquarters had arrived in France before the end of June, Crerar was not due to activate his command until the end of July. At that point the 1st British Corps was to pass under his control, along with the 2nd Canadian Corps. Still later, on 5 August, the 1st Polish Armoured Division would also be placed under Simonds's (and Crerar's) command. First Canadian Army's eventual configuration until early 1945 would thus basically consist of two corps, one British and one Canadian, with the Canadian being made up of three Canadian divisions and one Polish. From time to time additional corps and divisions were also placed temporarily under Crerar's command for specific missions: 104th US Division in the Battle of the Scheldt in October 1944, for example, and 30th British Corps in the initial stages of the Battle of the Rhineland in February 1945.

Simonds's first battle as GOC 2nd Corps was Operation Atlantic, the Canadian end of a joint Canadian-British effort (Operation Goodwood/Atlantic) to secure Vaucelles and Colombelles, to draw the Germans to the eastern end of the Allied lodgement and away from the Americans, and, if possible, to punch an armoured fist through the German defences which the infantry could then exploit. The British part of the operation was known as Goodwood and was aimed at securing the high ground to the east and south of Caen, particularly Bourguébus Ridge. Simonds planned Atlantic as a two-pronged assault. First, Keller's 3rd Division would lead, cross the Orne in the vicinity of Colombelles, and then move south to secure the country to the west of Route Nationale 158. It would stay in contact with the British 8th Corps, attacking to its left. Second, Foulkes's 2nd Division would follow with an attack southeastward from Caen, across the Orne into the western outskirts of Vaucelles, to secure the territory between the Orne and Route Nationale 158.

The attack began early on 18 July. On the left the British ran into the 1st SS Panzer division (Leibstandarte Adolf Hitler), with its Panther tanks and anti-tank guns deployed well forward. The British 11th Armoured Division lost 126 tanks in short order and was forced to halt its attack well short of its objective. The 7th Armoured Division tried without success to capture Verrières and Bourguébus Ridges and got set to resume the attempt the next day. To the British right, the 3rd Canadian Division's troops, aided by artillery and following a massive bombing attack against the German positions, pushed across the river into Colombelles and to the south and east of the steel works there. Despite great disorder in the attack, the Queen's Own was able to capture Giberville, while the rest of the 8th Brigade worked its way south. By nightfall 3rd Division's troops were in Cormelles, just to the east of the main highway, and had secured the eastern part of Vaucelles.

On the Canadian right, engineers trying to bridge the Orne came under heavy mortar fire and were unable to complete their task on the 18th. On the 19th, the 5th Brigade's Black Watch made a successful assault crossing of the river, which was followed up by further advances to St André-sur-Orne on the right and to the northern edge of Verrières Ridge on the left. The following day Simonds sent the 6th Brigade, with the Essex Scottish under command, into the centre to take Verrières Ridge. Backed by artillery and air support, their assault began at 1500. It went well at first, but then a torrential rain swept the battlefield, putting to an end the work of the Typhoons and making it difficult for the artillery observers to see the battle develop. The Germans took advantage of the rain to launch a heavy counter-attack; their tank fire and machine guns quickly killed and wounded scores of Canadian infantrymen and destroyed the few Canadian tanks that had ventured forward. In danger of being encircled and losing men by the minute, the Canadian troops in the centre broke; they threw away their weapons and ran back, chased by the advancing Germans. Two companies of the Fusiliers Mont-Royal were cut off and virtually wiped out. The German attacks resumed at dawn, and the Canadians lost more men before a counter-attack by the Black Watch helped to stabilize the situation. The Essex Scottish lost more than 300 men killed and wounded in the fighting. Atlantic was a failure; the 2nd Division suffered 1149 casualties, and Simonds blamed Foulkes. He concluded that Foulkes was not competent to run a division, and was determined to fire him if he could. In the end he could not; Foulkes, protected by Crerar, would end the war as a Corps Commander.

The failure of Operation Goodwood/Atlantic put great pressure on Montgomery to try again, especially since Bradley was finally ready to launch his major effort to break out (Operation Cobra). This time the main thrust would be made on Montgomery's right; Simonds's Canadians, with the British Guards Armoured and 7th Armoured Divisions under command, would mount Operation Spring at dawn on 25 July with heavy artillery support and tactical air power. The goal was to use the two Canadian infantry divisions to create a gap in the German defences on Verrières Ridge, then to send the two armoured divisions through the hole to exploit as far south as possible, and certainly as far as the high ground around Bretteville-sur-Laize and Cintheaux. Although Simonds was to claim after the war that Spring was intended only as a "holding action" to draw German armour to his front while the Americans broke out to his right, there is no indication of that in the pre-attack orders circulated to his divisional commanders.

Spring was to be fought in four phases; the first and most important was to begin at 0330 on the morning of 25 July and be completed by 0530 with the first light of dawn. Within that two hours, troops of the two Canadian infantry divisions were to secure May-sur-Orne, at the bottom of the western slope of Verrières Ridge, Verrières village, on the crest of the ridge, and Tilly-la-Campagne, about 1.5 kilometres east of Verrières village, across the N158. Once secured, the ground between these villages would give the armoured divisions a good assembly area from which to launch their attacks southward. The 7th Armoured would lead, the Guards Armoured would follow, then both they and the 3rd Canadian Infantry Division would leapfrog towards Falaise. The initial night attacks would be aided by artificial moonlight — searchlights played against the clouds.

In the pre-dawn darkness of 25 July, the North Nova Scotia Highlanders moved off as planned on the 3rd Division front, supported by tanks of the Fort Garry Horse. One company went straight at Tilly from the start-line, two others moved around to outflank it from the south and east. At 0545 they reported that they had reached their objective and had taken it. But dawn broke to reveal that they had only half of Tilly in their possession, that the Germans had the other half, and that the Germans were moving back in strength, supported by armour, to launch a counter-attack. Most of the Canadian tanks were destroyed; the North Novas in and around Tilly were cut off. After nightfall, the remnant made it back to the start-lines.

In the centre, the Royal Hamilton Light Infantry stormed up the gentle forward slope of Verrières Ridge and took Verrières village. They held it despite intense

Some of the underwater obstacles carrying deadly charges that Canadian troops faced on the Normandy beachhead, France, 10 June 1944.
PHOTOGRAPHER F.L. DUBERVILL. PA 131541

The first Nazi prisoners captured by Canadians are guarded by military police and soldiers with fixed bayonets. Normandy beachhead, France, 10 June 1944. PHOTOGRAPHER F.L. DUBERVILL. PA 136290

Canadian troops before going inland on D-Day, Normandy, France, 6 June 1944.
PHOTOGRAPHER F.L. DUBERVILL. PA 132652

General H.D.G. Crerar (RIGHT) and Lieutenant-Colonel J.C. Spragge, Commanding Officer of the Queen's Own Rifles of Canada, drive through Bretteville-le-Rabet, France, 23 June 1944.
PHOTOGRAPHER F.L. DUBERVILL.
PA 115543

German prisoners, members of the SS, captured by Canadian troops in Normandy, France, 17 June 1944.
PHOTOGRAPHER F.L. DUBERVILL.
PA 163919

Four Ack-Ack gunners near the front line, with one Junkers 88 to their credit, France, 17 June 1944. PHOTOGRAPHER F.L. DUBERVILL.
PA 132652

Members of the Royal Canadian Artillery with a 17-pounder anti-tank gun in Normandy, France, 22 June 1944.
PHOTOGRAPHER KEN BELL.
PA 169273

French rescue workers remove bodies from destroyed buildings following an air raid, Caen, France, 18 July 1944.

PHOTOGRAPHER KEN BELL. PA 138268

Members of the Royal Canadian Artillery firing a 5.5-inch Howitzer near Voucelles, France, 23 July 1944.

PHOTOGRAPHER KEN BELL. PA 168703

Bombing on the Caen–Falaise road, Normandy, France, August 1944. PA 154826

Avro Lancaster in flight.
PA 145613

Vickers Wellington aircraft in flight.
PA 144537

Major David Currie of the South Alberta Regiment (LEFT) directs the successful three-day defence of St Lambert-sur-Dives, France, 19 August 1944. As commander of a mixed force of tanks, infantry, and artillery, he was awarded the VC for his part in this action.
PHOTOGRAPHER D.I. GRANT. PA 111565

Consolidated Liberator GR VI aircraft 372 Q of No. 11 (BR) Squadron, RCAF, 2 January 1945. PA 100815

Officers of the 6th Canadian Infantry Brigade watch the warm-up of Hawker Typhoon aircraft of No. 121 Squadron, RAF, Antwerp, Belgium, 22 September 1944. PHOTOGRAPHER KEN BELL. PA 177798

Consolidated Canso A flying-boat of the RCAF built by Canadian Vickers Ltd in Montreal, 1944. C 32420

Ferrying Bren guns across the Afwalnings Canal, the Netherlands, 7 April 1945. PHOTOGRAPHER DANIEL GURAVICH. PA 167198

Dutch children watch Canadian vehicles cross a home-made bridge in Balkbrug, the Netherlands, 11 April 1945. PHOTOGRAPHER DANIEL GURAVICH. PA 134486

Sherman tanks of the 4th Canadian Armoured Division near a German position at the Dortmund-Ems Canal, Germany, 8 April 1945. PHOTOGRAPHER A.M. STIRTON. PA 113696

Sherman tank of the Sherbrooke Fusiliers entering Xanten, Germany.
PHOTOGRAPHER KEN BELL. PA 114965

General Kurt Meyer, handcuffed to Major Arthur Russel, during his exercise period, Aurich, Germany, 12 November 1945.
PHOTOGRAPHER B.J. GLOSTEN. PA 132443

Generals of the First Canadian Army: LEFT TO RIGHT, seated, H.S. Maczek, G. Simonds, H.D.G. Crerar, C. Foulkes, B.M. Hoffmeister; standing, R.H. Keefler, A.B. Matthews, H.W. Foster, R.W. Moncel, S.B. Rowlins, 20 May 1945. PA 137473

Canadian and British prisoners in Hong Kong waiting to be liberated by a landing party from HMCS *Prince Robert*, 30 August 1945. Photographer Jack Hawes. PA 115875

German fire, but the Royal Regiment of Canada, due to use the village as a starting-point for an attack on Rocquancourt, about 3 kilometres further south, could move almost no further. The capture of Verrières village was the only success, partial as it was, that Spring was to produce.

One of the blackest days of Canadian arms occurred on the morning of 25 July, on the far right flank of Operation Spring. In that sector the attack of 5th Brigade went wrong from the beginning. The start-line was not secured on time. The forwardmost companies of the Calgary Highlanders reached the vicinity of May-sur-Orne after a confused and somewhat disorganized night approach, but were quickly driven out by German armour and self-propelled guns. As the Germans counter-attacked, the Highlanders were first driven back to a locality known as "the factory" (actually a set of mine buildings), about halfway between their original start-line and May-sur-Orne. Later they were again driven back, this time to the vicinity of their start-line.

According to the plans laid down by Simonds, the Highlanders should have completed the capture of May-sur-Orne by first light. This would have secured the right flank of the Black Watch as it moved southwest up the slope of Verrières Ridge towards its objective, Fontenay-le-Marmion. The Black Watch advance should have started at 0530 after May-sur-Orne was supposed to have been secured. But the Black Watch were delayed by having to fight their way to their own start-line; in that fighting, the Commanding Officer (CO) and the senior company commander were killed. The delay meant that a new artillery plan needed to be laid on. At 0930 acting battalion CO Major F.P. Griffin, not knowing for certain where the Calgary Highlanders were, advanced up the slope. He and his men were caught in a maelstrom of tank, anti-tank, mortar, machine-gun, and sniper fire. It came from behind, from air and mine shafts that the Germans had hidden in as the Canadians passed, from ahead, from sniper and machine-gun positions, and from tanks disguised as hay stacks. It also came from the flanks: from the high ground west of the Orne and from May-sur-Orne, and from Germans dug in on the northern crest of the ridge. Griffin and a handful of survivors reached the crest of the ridge, where he, and most of them, were killed. On that one morning, the Black Watch lost 123 men killed in action or who died of their wounds, 101 wounded, and eighty-three taken prisoner, of whom twenty-one were wounded.

In Simonds's mind, the overall plan for Spring had been sound, but subordinate units — 2nd Division, 5th Brigade, and the attacking infantry battalions — had dropped the ball. It was "errors of judgment in minor tactics" that had produced the debacle, he subsequently declared; he was more ready than ever to fire Foulkes. Canadian military historian John English agrees with Simonds's assessment.[5] But Simonds's analysis was as much self-seeking rationalization as it was cool judgment on events. To succeed, Simonds's concept would have required virtually split-second timing, by troops and commanders who were still very green, in an uncoordinated series of night attacks across a front of some 8 to 10 kilometres over largely unknown and unreconnoitred ground. It was too much to ask, too much to expect, even of brave men. Simonds's intelligence also underestimated the German strength on the ridge as badly as he overestimated the abilities of his subordinate units.

Although Spring was a failure, it did serve one valuable purpose; it continued to persuade the Germans that the main Allied push would come on Montgomery's front at the very moment when Bradley's US First Army was launching Cobra. In the words of US military historian Russel Weigley: "Through the critical first hours of Cobra the Canadians [with Operation Spring] reinforced Field Marshal von Kluge's fatal conviction that the Anglo-Americans remained principally interested in rolling across the Falaise plain, and that it was the American attack farther west that was diversionary."[6] Weigley points out that on 25 July von Kluge went to the Canadian front, not the American, to direct the German defence.

Bradley's Operation Cobra had been twice stalled owing to bad weather; it went ahead on the morning of 25 July, opening with the standard massive heavy-bomber attack that killed many front-line US troops. At first the offensive stumbled, but then the US VII Corps commander, J. Lawton "Lightning Joe" Collins, realized that his troops had slogged their way right through the main German line of resistance and had broken into open country. He drove his corps forward like a man possessed; his division commanders were ordered to keep moving no matter what, to bypass and isolate German strongpoints if necessary, and to push ahead at all costs. It was the right move; in the next few days the VII Corps spearheaded the American First Army's drive to the south and opened the door for General George S. Patton's Third Army, just activated, to swing westward into Brittany, as the original Overlord plan had called for. At that point Brittany was of no immediate value to the Allies; Bradley should have hustled Patton's army eastward towards the Seine at top speed. He did not. Although Montgomery, to his credit, quickly saw the opportunity opened up to trap the Germans, Bradley and Eisenhower were slow to modify the original intent to meet the new circumstances.

The Germans on the Caen front were in danger of encirclement and should have withdrawn south of the Seine, but instead Hitler ordered a counter-attack

(Operation Luttich) westward towards Mortain in an attempt to cut off the south-ward thrusting US spearheads. Before Luttich could be launched, however, Montgomery ordered his army commanders to keep pressure on the Germans with a series of local attacks; in response, Dempsey sent his 8th and 30th Corps southward on 30 July, while Crerar called for a renewed effort to take Tilly-la-Campagne. The Calgary Highlanders tried unsuccessfully to capture it on 1 August, while units of the newly arrived 4th Canadian Armoured Division, under Major-General George Kitching, tried again on 2 and 5 August, also without success.

On 6 August the Germans launched Operation Luttich, using virtually every German armoured unit north of the Seine. It was a disaster. Warned of the impend-ing attack by Ultra, the Americans fought it to a stop. The Germans had gambled all and had lost; the failed attack had brought the great bulk of their armour into a threatened encirclement. If the Americans to the south and the Canadians and Brit-ish to the north could join up and close the gap to the east, near the key road junc-tion at Falaise, the German army would be finished in France. On 8 August Bradley decided to order Patton to send his XV Corps north to Alençon, then to Argentan to meet the Canadians, whom Montgomery was sending southeastward. Instead of try-ing a "long" envelopment, to encircle the Germans along the line of the Seine, the Allies (Patton dissenting) decided on a "short" envelopment in the Falaise area.

❧

On 23 July Crerar's First Canadian Army had assumed operational command of Simonds's 2nd Canadian Corps and Crocker's 1st British Corps. His relationship with Crocker got off to a bad start when Crocker questioned the utility of an opera-tion Crerar ordered him to carry out; the matter was settled within a day or so, but it appears to have confirmed Montgomery in his view that Crerar and his Canadian Army were simply not as competent at war as were the British. He observed: "Harry Crerar has started off his career as an Army Commander by thoroughly upsetting everyone . . . I fear he thinks he is a great soldier and he was determined to show it the very moment he took over command at 1200 hrs on 23 July. He made his first mis-take at 1205 hrs; and his second after lunch."[7]

Notwithstanding these views, Montgomery had no choice but to give the Ca-nadians the most important task of the campaign thus far: the link-up with the Americans at Falaise to trap the Germans. Crerar's 2nd Canadian Corps was on the far left of Montgomery's flank and was clearly in the best position to attack towards Falaise; to realign the front south of Caen, and to switch whole divisions from one part of the front to another, would have involved a lengthy delay. Time was of the essence. On 4 August Montgomery ordered Crerar to launch a heavy attack towards Falaise so as to trap the German armour retreating from the front of the British Second Army. Simonds was given the job, and planning began for Operation Totalize, the most ambitious Canadian attack of the war to that point.

Simonds is generally acknowledged to have been one of the most innovative and imaginative Canadian army commanders of all time. He certainly demonstrated both qualities in planning Totalize. The attack was to be preceded by a massive heavy-bomber assault on five fortified villages that stood in the way of the advancing troops. Then, in the pre-dawn hours of 8 August, the British 51st (Highland) Division on the left, accompanied by the 33rd Armoured Brigade, and the 2nd Canadian Infantry Division on the right, accompanied by the 2nd Canadian Armoured Brigade, were to advance down both sides of the Caen–Falaise road. They would be kept going in the right direction, despite the dark, by light beams, radio beacons, and tracer fired parallel to their advance. They would be aided by artificial moonlight. There would be no massive artillery barrage preceding the attack, so as to preserve surprise. The infantry would be carried in armoured personnel carriers (APCs) — Priest self-propelled guns with the guns removed and reinforced by steel plate welded on at key places. The APC was Simonds's own invention; the new vehicles, prepared in Canadian army repair shops, were dubbed "kangaroos." When the initial phase of the assault was completed, there was to be an eight-hour hiatus; then the attack was to resume with the 4th Canadian Armoured Division on the right and the 1st Polish Armoured Division on the left. Ahead lay the German infantry, considerably weakened by the westward movement of the panzers, but with enough armour, anti-tank weapons, and SS infantry to make things very difficult.

The attack began as planned the night of 7/8 August, with the infantry jumping off at 2330. There was some confusion, owing to the massive amounts of dust thrown up by the columns of APCs and tanks and the resistance of the Germans in some localities, but for the most part the great weight of men and tanks succeeded in smashing through the main German defences that had held firm for many weeks. Then, as planned, the great mass of men and vehicles halted to regroup and to bring up the field artillery. During the hiatus between Totalize I and II, Kurt Meyer brought forward two battle groups of his 12th SS Panzer division, as well as a number of assault guns and Tiger tanks, and positioned them across the Canadian front.

Nothing illustrates better the continuing weakness in Canadian (and British) tactical thinking than a contrast between the Canadian Simonds during Totalize I and the American Collins in the first phase of Cobra. When Collins realized that his troops had broken through, he spurred them ahead to give the Germans no chance to regroup. Simonds, too, broke through — at least through the front-line positions — but did not alter the plan and cancel the halt. That was because he believed, wrongly, that the 1st SS Panzer division was manning the second German defence line. Having twice had his nose bloodied by the SS, he did not relish a third pummelling. Thus he insisted on the halt in order to bring two fresh armoured divisions forward to spearhead the second phase of the attack. Simonds also erred in his choice of the two divisions; both were inexperienced and it would have been a near miracle if they had known instinctively how to attack successfully against a tenacious German defence. In the event, they did not. Had Crerar been a knowledgeable army commander with a feel for the battlefield, he might have ordered Simonds to press on rapidly, or to use two other divisions for the second phase of his attack, but he was not. Thus, all would proceed as planned.

The second phase of Totalize, a daylight attack designed to punch through the second German line of defence, was much less successful than the first phase had been. Essentially a repeat of the first phase, it got off to a very bad start when the preparatory bombing by the Eighth US Air Force also hit the 3rd Canadian and 1st Polish Divisions, killing and wounding a great many men. Among the wounded was 3rd Canadian Division's commander, R.L. Keller. Making matters worse, the few tanks but many 88-millimetre anti-tank guns that Meyer had positioned in front of the Canadians rushed back and forth across the front of the attack and destroyed large numbers of advancing tanks. Instead of flowing around the German resistance points and pushing on, the Canadian and Polish armoured divisions wasted time and momentum by trying to deal with every strongpoint. Their advances ground to a halt before nightfall. Although the two divisions tried to get forward the next day, they could make no further progress.

Casualties mounted all day; the 4th Canadian Armoured Brigade was especially hard hit. Its 28th Armoured Regiment (the British Columbia Regiment), led by Lieutenant-Colonel D.G. Worthington, with two companies of infantry from the Algonquin Regiment — the combined unit was known as Worthington Force — was supposed to swing right from the main line of advance and capture Point 195, about two kilometres west of the Caen–Falaise highway. They got lost, went left, and stopped atop a hill they mistakenly believed to be their objective. In fact, they were isolated and surrounded; over the course of a long hot day the Germans exacted a heavy toll of the trapped force. Hundreds of men were killed or wounded, including Worthington — killed by a mortar shell — and forty-seven tanks were destroyed. After nightfall, the survivors made their way back to the Polish lines. Totalize was over. The combined assaults had moved the Canadian lines about 12 kilometres to the south, but they were nowhere near Falaise or even the high ground to its north.

Simonds was not pleased by the performance of Kitching's division or of the Poles. In his memoirs, Kitching chalked up his division's failure to high casualties among senior officers, poor radio communications, and general inexperience in a very green division: "I do not think these factors were appreciated sufficiently by General Simonds whose vision was focussed on the horizon and whose thoughts were often a day or two ahead of us," he later wrote.[8] He did not know it, but he was a marked man in Simonds's eyes. Keller was also through as a divisional commander. He had wanted Simonds to relieve him days before on medical grounds; now his wounds from the American bombing made that a foregone conclusion. He was relieved on 8 August, to be replaced ten days later by Major-General D.C. "Dan" Spry, who was brought from Italy to command the 3rd Division until late March 1945.

The situation on the morning of 10 August was completely fluid; the bulk of the German armour was still in the Mortain area, as the Germans tried to decide whether to withdraw. The American XV Corps had reached Le Mans and was swinging north towards Argentan. The Americans may well have been able to drive most of the way to the Canadian sector — they had more men and armour, and had seen less grinding combat — but Montgomery overestimated Crerar's ability to push south with great speed and underestimated the American ability to drive northward. Monty ought to have sent an additional armoured division or two from the Second British Army to bolster the Canadian thrust, but he did not. He insisted, instead, that the Canadians meet the Americans at the pre-established boundary between the 12th Army Group (American) and the 21st Army Group (British and Canadian) just south of Argentan. Since Montgomery, in overall command of both army groups, made no move to shift that boundary to the north, the Americans had no choice but to pull up and wait for Crerar to meet them. In any case, the American drive into Argentan stalled when Leclerc's 2nd French Armoured Division — attached to the XV Corps — disobeyed orders to drive directly into the town and took a more circuitous route instead. By the time they approached Argentan, the Germans had greatly strengthened their troops there.

On 11 August, Montgomery ordered Crerar to capture Falaise as quickly as possible. If that key road junction were in Allied hands, it would be difficult for the Germans to withdraw their armour to the east. On that very day German commander Field Marshal Gunther von Kluge decided to risk Hitler's wrath and do just that. Once again, Crerar handed the job to Simonds; once again Simonds designed a large set-piece attack much along the lines of Totalize. This time the offensive was code-named Tractable, but unlike Totalize, it would be launched in daylight, its attacking elements and its flanks hidden from the enemy by smoke laid down by artillery. Before Simonds could actually launch the attack, Montgomery changed his mind and gave the job of capturing Falaise to the Second British Army (he would later change this yet again). Montgomery also directed Crerar to take the high ground north and east of Falaise, then drive southeast to Trun, a key road junction about 18 kilometres east of Falaise. The left flank of the attack was to be made by Kitching's 4th Armoured, and the right by the 3rd Infantry, with the 2nd Armoured Brigade under command. H Hour was set for 14 August; the Germans learned of the attack the day before when a Canadian officer lost his way and drove into enemy lines. He was killed and his driver taken prisoner; in the jeep was a copy of Simonds's orders.

Tractable began on time with a short preliminary bombardment by medium bombers flying low over the battlefield. Then smoke shells fired by the artillery began to hide the men and the armour. The Germans could not see much because of the smoke and the dust thrown up by the vehicles, but, warned of the attack, they had sited their artillery and anti-tank guns on the expected line of approach. They fired furiously into the smoke and dust, hitting many tanks and causing many casualties, including Brigadier Leslie Booth, commander of the 4th Armoured Brigade, who was killed. Many of the Canadian tanks bunched up at the few crossing-points over the Laison River, which ran across the line of advance, though the infantry got forward as planned. Much territory was captured, but the attackers ended the day short of the objective, a hill immediately to the north of Falaise known as Point 159. Despite their paucity in both men and armour, the German resistance was still too fierce for the Canadians to overcome easily. Little progress was made the next day; it was not until 16 August that Point 159 was taken. That same day troops of the 2nd Canadian Division finally entered Falaise.

That did not close the gap. It was still about 18 kilometres wide and the Germans were pouring through it to the east. Simonds ordered the Poles and Kitching's division to attack southeast to Trun, to cut the Germans off; the next day orders were changed again and the Poles were directed to Chambois, about 6 kilometres east of Trun, to meet the Americans, who were about to attack to the north. As the Germans desperately tried to keep the gap open, the Canadians and the Poles struggled just as desperately to close it. The Canadians reached Trun early on the 18th, but the Poles, under heavy attack, could not reach Chambois until the next day. That same day first contact was made with advancing US troops from the south.

As thousands of Germans streamed eastward through the narrowing pocket, others attacked the Poles and Canadians from the west in order to keep the escape route open. Now Allied fighter-bombers began to exact a fearful toll of men, equipment, and horses (much of the German equipment was still horse drawn). Even battle-hardened veterans would find the carnage incredible. On the 19th, in the midst of the intense ground fighting and the air attacks, a unit of the 4th Canadian Armoured Division under Major D.V. Currie fought its way into St Lambert-sur-Dives and held for the next three days as the Germans tried to break out. In those three days, they captured about 2000 Germans and killed many others. Not far to the east, but cut off totally from the Canadians, the Poles held Chambois and Point 262, a strategic hill that commanded what was left of the German escape route. They were attacked violently and continuously by German forces on the 20th, but managed to hold while destroying much German equipment and taking many prisoners; on 21 August they were so low on ammunition that they had to be resupplied by air drop.

Late on the afternoon of 21 August, the Canadians finally struggled through to the Poles on Point 262 and in Chambois. The Falaise gap was closed and the battle for Normandy was effectively over. The Germans lost about 300,000 men in total; the Canadians alone took more than 13,000 prisoners in the closing phases of the Falaise battle. Many thousands more Germans were slaughtered by Allied fighter-bombers as they pushed towards the ever narrowing gap; their heaviest casualties came in the last three days of the fight. The fate of two of the SS's once-powerful divisions was typical. Meyer's 12th SS had been a division of more than 20,000 men, with 150 tanks on D-Day; by 25 August it had been reduced to fewer than 300 men, ten tanks, and no artillery. The 1st SS Panzer was left with no tanks, no artillery, and only a handful of men.

Despite the heavy losses, many thousands of Germans did manage to escape as the Poles and Canadians struggled to close the gap in the week from the beginning of Tractable (14 August) until the gap was closed on the 21st. Among those who got away were a large number of divisional, corps, and army staff officers who would later form the basis on which destroyed and new German army units would be rebuilt. Precious days had been lost as the bedraggled German defenders had succeeded time after time in delaying the advances of the numerically powerful Canadian and Polish armour, backed by an overwhelming preponderance of artillery and air support. The 4th Canadian Armoured Brigade — the armoured component of Kitching's division — was especially to blame for having been ponderous and indecisive in its operations. Kitching would later explain that failure in terms of Booth's death in the first hours of Tractable, and his division's inexperience in battle.

Simonds was not happy about the performance of his two leading armoured divisions in Tractable or in the closing of the gap. He had no authority to remove the Polish commander, Major-General S. Maczek, but Kitching was another matter. Simonds relieved him on 21 August, and replaced him with Harry Foster, who was still in Italy. Within a matter of days, then, two out of the three Canadian divisional commanders in France were gone. It was one measure of how difficult an ordeal the Battle of Normandy had been.

In the end, the failure to close the gap more quickly and score a truly decisive victory in the west must be shared around. Bradley and Eisenhower must take part of the blame for allowing large numbers of American troops to advance into Brittany after the Cobra breakout as though nothing had changed. Montgomery gave the Canadians too large a job to do without adequately backing them up. (He would do that again in the opening phase of the Battle of the Scheldt Estuary.) Leclerc's 2nd French Armoured Division's failure to move quickly into Argentan when ordered gave the Germans a chance to block the American move north. Simonds's failure to exploit the initial success of Totalize gave Kurt Meyer a chance to reorganize his defences and thwart the second phase of Totalize, thereby delaying the closure even further. The tactical shortcomings of the rookie 4th Canadian and 1st Polish Armoured Divisions gave the Germans further chances to escape.

With the Falaise gap closed, Montgomery directed Crerar's troops to advance from the Trun-Chambois area to Elboeuf, where they were to cross the River Seine near Rouen. The Second British Army was to advance to the right of the Canadians. Units of the 2nd and 3rd Canadian Divisions began to move on 20 August, even before the gap was fully closed. They made good progress, only occasionally meeting German rearguards or being attacked from the air at night. What remained of the German army in Normandy made quick tracks to the Seine, where other German rearguards, including a handful of SS panzer troops, fought as long as possible to hold up the Allied advance until their comrades could get across the river. The Germans took a heavy toll of units of the 2nd Canadian Infantry Division advancing through the Forêt de la Londe, just south of the Seine, in the last days of August. The tragedy was that the division should not have fought in the forest in the first place. By the time that Foulkes issued the orders to clear it, the other two Canadian divisions had bypassed it and were crossing the river at Elboeuf.

By 30 August the 2nd Canadian Corps was across the Seine and pushing towards the channel coast. The 2nd Division was directed to Dieppe, the other troops to the important channel ports of Boulogne and Calais, around which large numbers of V-1 sites were to be found. For a time it was feared that the Germans would put up a ferocious struggle for Dieppe, but they did not. Early on the morning of 1 September, the lead elements of the 2nd Canadian Infantry Division crossed the height of land to the south of the port and cautiously began the long descent to the town itself. As the citizens cheered the Canadians on, the division's long journey back to Dieppe finally ended.

XIV The Scheldt

At 0130 on 22 September 1944, Sergeant Clarence Kenneth Crockett and nine men of C Company, the Calgary Highlanders, of the 5th Canadian Infantry Brigade, left their forward positions on the south bank of the Albert Canal near Antwerp and crept stealthily towards the damaged lock gate that awaited them in the drizzly gloom. A veteran of many battles, Crockett had been selected by his company commander to lead a small patrol over the lock gate and seize a bridgehead on the north bank of the canal. All the men of his platoon had volunteered to go, but Crockett could take only nine with him. He chose two Bren gunners and seven others armed with Sten guns. Each man carried two or three bandoliers of ammunition over his shoulders. One took a PIAT (Projector, Infantry, Anti-Tank), another a 2-inch mortar, and a third carried a small Mark 38 radio set. For better footing, they doffed their combat boots and put on sneakers. The lock gate was damaged half way across and they would have to make the last part of the crossing on a water pipe 15 centimetres in diameter with just a bent catwalk rail to hold on to.

In the fall of 1944 the canal ran through open farm country about 3 kilometres north of the Antwerp suburb of Wommelgem. It was about 30 metres wide and connected the port of Antwerp to Liège, about 130 kilometres to the east. The north side of the canal was lined by fields, brush, and patches of woods and was regularly patrolled by its German defenders. If the Germans were going to be rooted out of the northern suburbs of Antwerp, the Canadians would have to take and hold a bridgehead over the canal from which to begin the clearing operations. The Black Watch, also of the 5th Brigade, had attempted to cross the canal at roughly the same spot the night before, but had been discovered and beaten back.

Crockett inched his way over the south part of the lock gate, walking carefully on an undamaged catwalk until he reached a small island in the middle of the canal. When he saw it was all clear, he returned to the south bank to beckon his men forward. They moved silently over the catwalk, then waited on the island while Crockett made his way carefully over the water pipe to the north side of the canal. The night was damp and the pipe was slippery; Crockett slung his Sten gun on his back so that he could better grasp the partly demolished hand rail. When he reached the north side of the canal, he found a barbed-wire barrier blocking his way. He returned to the island to bring the rest of the patrol forward with him. In complete silence they crept along until they reached the north bank; then Crockett and Corporal R.A. Harold, crouched behind him, carefully inched the barbed-wire barrier out of the way.

Suddenly a flare popped and a voice called out in German. The men on the pipe froze in position as machine guns opened up in the dark. One man was hit immediately; the others rushed on to the north side of the canal, automatic weapons blazing away at the machine-gun flashes. Crockett cut down one German soldier with his Sten, then poured several clips into a machine-gun position, silencing it. He and one of his men then destroyed two more German machine guns with the PIAT. The mortar man quickly went into action, killing yet another German gun crew.

As Crockett's men battled for their lives on the north bank of the canal, the rest of his company began to pour over the lock gate from the south bank. Then A and D Companies followed. The Germans brought up reinforcements, and German mortar fire began to blanket the Canadian perimeter. For the next several hours the fight raged back and forth, first one side holding the upper hand, then the other. It was not until early afternoon, as the drizzle stopped and the sun began to push through the clouds, that the Highlanders were able to secure the area. Then a unit of engineers came up to construct a bridge across the canal. By nightfall, most of the 5th Brigade were across and the job of clearing the entire area began in earnest. The Highlanders paid a heavy price for this first permanent Canadian foothold across the canal — fifteen killed and thirty-four wounded; Crockett was awarded the Distinguished Conduct Medal for his incredible act of bravery. For the Calgary Highlanders and the 5th Brigade, the Battle of the Scheldt Estuary had commenced in memorable fashion.

The struggle of the First Canadian Army to clear the banks of the Scheldt Estuary dominated Canadian war news in September and October 1944. Even as that battle raged, however, other Canadian soldiers, airmen, and sailors were fighting the forces of the Axis over thousands of kilometres of land, sea, and sky and on

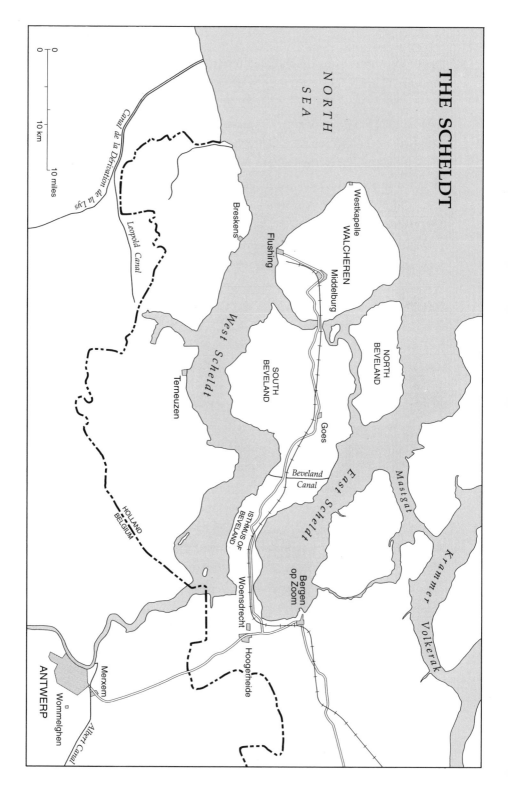

THE SCHELDT

NORTH SEA

Westkapelle

WALCHEREN

Flushing

Middelburg

NORTH BEVELAND

SOUTH BEVELAND

Goes

Beveland Canal

East Scheldt

Mastgat

ISTHMUS OF BEVELAND

Bergen op Zoom

Kramer Volkerak

Breskens

West Scheldt

Terneuzen

Leopold Canal

Canal de la Dérivation de la Lys

HOLLAND
BELGIUM

Woensdrecht

Hoogerheide

Merxem

ANTWERP

Wommelghem

Albert Canal

0
0
10 km
10 miles

237

almost every war front. In the Mediterranean theatre, for example, the 1st Canadian Corps in Italy spent the first two weeks of September deeply engaged in the struggle to break the Pisa–Rimini line. At the same time, Canadians of the RAF and the RCAF in Bomber Command increasingly took advantage of the weakness of the German day-fighter forces (and the strength of the Allied day-fighter escorts) to fly daylight raids into Germany itself. Such missions included an area attack against Emden on 6 September and raids against synthetic-oil installations at Dortmund and other locations in Germany on 12 September and against the key communications centre of Osnabrück on the 13th. On the night of 15/16 September the bombers returned to Kiel for the only night raid of the month. No. 6 Group lost only six aircraft in all of September; the crews of three bombers were saved after ditching in the North Sea. Most of its twenty-three missions that month were against tactical targets or synthetic oil plants.

As the bombers took to the air day after day, so too did the fighters and fighter-bombers of No. 83 Group, flying thousands of sorties in support of the Allied armies drawing nearer to the borders of Germany. The experiences of the RCAF's No. 126 Wing were typical. Having begun to fly from forward airstrips near the invasion beaches only twenty-four hours after the D-Day landings, the wing moved east behind the advancing Allies. Groundcrews and aircrews lived a Gypsy life of almost constant movement in tents, trailers, and other temporary shelters, as army engineers prepared new airstrips close to the fighting fronts. By the beginning of September, the wing was operating out of an airfield designated B4, its seventh airfield since transferring to France. Located near Amiens, it allowed the fighters and fighter-bombers to give close support to the Second British Army as it closed up to the Albert Canal east of Antwerp. Just as the wing began to settle in to B4 on 5 September, it received orders to move again, this time to airfield B56, at Evère, just north of Brussels. Even this stay was brief. On 20 September the wing transferred to B68, near Le Culot. Monty Berger, the wing's intelligence officer, described the field:

> The barracks were badly damaged . . . [the] new quarters were damp, unheated and overcrowded. The lack of indoor plumbing and flush toilets . . . was also keenly felt. Pilots drove sixteen kilometres to a nearby town just to bathe . . . respiratory afflictions increased, and morale was affected.[1]

Morale was especially affected by the daily grind of flying operations, especially missions against ground targets. Attacking a ground target was one of the most dangerous tasks a pilot could attempt. Ground fire from the enemy, friendly fire, pilot error, bad weather, and mechanical malfunction all took their toll. When a Spitfire or Typhoon was diving on a target at close to 450 kilometres per hour, anything could go wrong, and in a split second, the aircraft could plunge out of control. There was little room for error, almost no time for recovery or bail out. Even when there was no battle, men died. On 22 September, for example, Spitfires from No. 401 Squadron were returning from an uneventful sweep near Arnhem when two of them collided. Lieutenant-Commander A.C. Wallace went into an inverted spin and was killed as his plane ploughed into the ground. The other pilot made a forced landing and was unhurt, though badly shaken up.

The RCN's war had changed since the days of the wolfpack attacks in the mid-ocean, but its primary mission was still the escort of convoys and the hunt for U-boats. The German submarines now rarely attacked in packs. Equipped with the snorkel device that allowed the boat to stay under water indefinitely, the U-boats now tended to hunt singly, often in coastal waters. The mass slaughter of merchant vessels that had occurred in the early years of the war was not repeated, but merchant ships were still torpedoed and men still died in the cold North Atlantic waters. The story of convoy ONS 251 was typical.

Sailing for North America at the beginning of September, ONS 251 was escorted by the RCN's Escort Group C 4. At 2215 on the night of 2 September, the moon was shining on a flat sea north-northwest of Ireland when the Norwegian cargo ship *Fjordheim* was torpedoed on the starboard side. The officer of the watch in the RCN frigate *Montreal* saw "what looked like a giant roman candle sputtering in the convoy" and raced to the scene to begin the search for the assailant. But no submarine was found, despite an extensive sweep by *Montreal* and other ships of the convoy escort. Other RCN vessels had better luck that month; in the first half of September, *St John* and *Swansea* sank U-247 off Land's End, while *Dunver* and *Hespeler* destroyed U-484 in the Atlantic off the New Hebrides.

As the First Canadian Army moved up the channel coast in the first two weeks of September, a growing shortage of infantry reinforcements stymied efforts to keep the front-line rifle companies up to war-establishment strength. The problem was not an overall shortage of reinforcements in the army as a whole; just too few trained infantrymen available. A projected shortfall of some 20,000 men was expected to occur by the spring of 1945. How and why had this happened?

The key reason was that the Canadian Army had too few infantry and too many of everything else. When new recruits entered the army, most had been taken up by the artillery, the engineers, the pay corps, the military police, and so on. What's more, the army had tended since the beginning of the war to pick what it considered the best men — intelligent, ambitious, well-educated — for everything but the infantry. A second important reason was that the army had used British combat loss projections based on the fighting in the North African desert to forecast how many casualties (the army called this "wastage") it would need to replace once the fighting in Italy and Northwest Europe began in earnest. Those figures were far too low. The intense ground combat in Italy and Normandy produced far more infantry casualties than had been expected — 75 percent of the total — and fewer casualties in most other branches of the army. As one example, the weakness of the German airforce left many thousands of Canadian soldiers in anti-aircraft units doing very little in the way of combat in the summer and fall of 1944, while their counterparts in the infantry could barely carry out their assigned tasks.

After the war, the former commander of the 1st Canadian Corps, E.L.M. Burns, produced a study of manpower in the Canadian Army which told the tale succinctly. By the fall of 1944, Burns found, the Canadian Army had expanded to almost half a million men and women, with a quarter million serving in Northwest Europe, Italy, or the United Kingdom. About 100,000 of these people worked at jobs in supply depots, hospitals, offices, communications centres, and in other non-combat situations, or were waiting for assignment in reinforcement units. Some 158,000 served in the field formations — the five divisions and two independent armoured brigades of the First Canadian Army. But few people in a Canadian division actually fought; most did something else. What all this boiled down to was that the actual front-line fighting strength of an infantry division consisted of the riflemen, Bren gunners, mortarmen, and anti-tank gunners in the four rifle companies and the one support company of each infantry battalion — about 5400 men in a division of more than 17,000.

One solution to the shortage of infantry was to remuster men from noninfantry units into the infantry. There was great potential in remustering, but it was a slow process to retrain men for the infantry. In the meantime, the army worried, its infantry battalions would fall far below strength and be rendered ineffective before any appreciable number of reinforcements could be trained. Thus the army's top commanders put pressure on the government, through J.L. Ralston, Minister of National Defence, to send overseas those trained infantrymen serving in Canada who had been conscripted under the National Resources Mobilization Act (NRMA) of 1940. Often referred to disparagingly as "zombies," these men had been conscripted for home defence and, under the laws of Canada, could not be sent to an active theatre of war overseas. Many NRMA men volunteered for active (overseas) service during the war, but by the fall of 1944 a hard core had emerged in Canada who appeared dead set against going active. Eventually, after a serious crisis in the Canadian cabinet, which led to Ralston's ouster and the appointment of A.G.L. McNaughton to replace him, 16,000 of these men were ordered sent to the fighting fronts. About 2400 actually reached front-line units before the war ended; in virtually all cases, they were welcomed by the veterans and integrated without difficulty into the line rifle companies.

🍁

On 4 September 1944 the 11th British Armoured Division of the 30th British Corps entered the port of Antwerp. Located on the Scheldt Estuary, the massive port (second largest in Northwest Europe) was protected from the rising and falling of the North Sea tide by two sets of massive locks. The Germans had neglected to destroy those locks until almost the last minute before they pulled out of the dock area; when they did try, they were prevented from doing so by the Belgian White Brigade, a royalist resistance movement. Thus the port of Antwerp — with its almost 50 kilometres of quays, its hydraulic and electric fixed and floating cranes, its grain elevators, its hundreds of kilometres of railway track, and its capacity to handle well in excess of 10,000 tonnes of cargo per day — was taken virtually intact.

That was vitally important because, by the late summer of 1944, the Allied armies were facing a severe supply problem. Most of the food, ammunition, gasoline, and other necessities of war were still being unloaded over the original Normandy invasion beaches and trucked forward hundreds of kilometres. The Allies possessed no major ports near the front lines. The US armies, on the Allied right flank and farther from the coast than the British and Canadians, were especially hard pressed; shell rationing was imposed on American artillery regiments by late August. The problem was growing so severe that Eisenhower declared he would not permit an offensive into Germany until it was resolved.

The capture of Antwerp promised relief from the supply problem, but not until both banks of the Scheldt Estuary were taken from the Germans. When the British rolled into Antwerp at the start of September, they could have done that easily. The Germans were still in retreat and in disarray. All that was needed was for the commander of the Second British Army, Sir Miles Dempsey, to have ordered his units forward some 30 kilometres up the right bank of the Scheldt to seize the narrow neck of land where the South Beveland peninsula connects to the mainland; in so doing, he could have isolated any German defenders on South Beveland or the island of Walcheren. But he did not; Montgomery wanted Dempsey's troops for bigger and better things.

In the days and weeks that followed, the Germans, under express orders from Hitler to hold the Scheldt, reinforced their men and planted thousands of mines in the waterway. Needless to say, these mines could not be swept, and ships could not pass to Antwerp, as long as German guns dominated the waterway. The reinvigorated German presence in the Scheldt area was only one sign of a general stiffening of German resistance all across the Allied front. In what the Germans referred to as the "miracle in the west," new divisions and battle groups were scraped together, rearmed with new weapons, and dispatched to the front. By mid-September they were able to match the Allies almost man for man, although they were still vastly outnumbered in artillery, tanks, and, of course, in aircraft. That they could do this was a testament not only to their remarkable recuperative powers, but also to the Allied failure at Falaise and the Seine crossing to destroy the bulk of the German divisional and corps headquarters and staff.

The main reason why Montgomery did not make a full-scale effort earlier to take the banks of the Scheldt was that he was preoccupied with Operation Market Garden. Put together with Eisenhower's blessing, Market Garden was to consist of a combined airborne/ground assault to drive a narrow salient deep into German lines and seize the river and canal crossings leading into Germany. The ultimate objectives of the attack were the rail and road bridges across the Neder (Lower) Rhine at Arnhem, in Holland. Both Montgomery and Eisenhower believed that a victory at Arnhem would allow the Allies immediate entry to the Ruhr and bring a quick victory. If that happened, access to a major port might not be so crucial.

Market Garden was a wild gamble. The plan was intricate and required split-second timing and masterful coordination. Literally every part of it had to succeed, in sequence, if it was all to work; such happy circumstances are exceedingly rare in war. Launched with a massive drop of British and American paratroopers on 17 September, too many things went wrong. When Market Garden was called off on 26 September, the Allied salient reached just beyond the Nijmegen bridge; the bridges at Arnhem — or what was left of them — were still firmly in German hands. More than 6000 Allied prisoners, mostly British, were taken by the Germans; nearly half of them were wounded paratroopers who had been left behind because they could not be evacuated. The 1st British Airborne Division, given the task of taking Arnhem, was decimated.

❦

Market Garden was to be a British and American operation, and it did not call upon Crerar's First Canadian Army. For the Canadians, the war was to be less dramatic. Their initial job after crossing the Seine was to seize the channel coast and take its small river-mouth ports. The 3rd Infantry Division headed for the Boulogne/Calais/Cap Gris Nez area, the 2nd Infantry Division for Dunkirk and Ostend, and the 4th Armoured Division for Bruges and the Leopold Canal, south of the Scheldt.

Hitler had ordered his commanders to hold these ports at all costs, and the garrison commanders did their best to oblige. Extensive fortifications were prepared; artillery, mortars, and machine guns were sited; patrols were pushed out to find and harass the Canadians. To make matters worse, it seemed to rain constantly throughout the first weeks of September. Large stretches of the coastal plain lie below sea level near Dunkirk and Ostend, as do parts of the landward side of Calais. With the rains, this ground was sodden and muddy. Wherever they could, the Germans blew open canal locks and dykes to flood low-lying polders and to force the Canadians, men and vehicles, to stick to the roads — there they were easy targets for German shells or mortars.

The Canadians might have had an easier time had they concentrated on one port at a time and used sufficient power to overcome whatever opposition there was, but they did not. Crerar decided to mask Dunkirk, but to capture Boulogne and Calais, and then to concentrate on the Scheldt. Boulogne contained a

10,000-man garrison behind strong fortifications, backed by plenty of artillery. Much of the defence faced seaward, however, while the troops were not first class and morale was low. The initial Canadian ground assault on 17 September was preceded by a massive bombardment from the air with 690 Bomber Command aircraft taking part; the impact of this bombing was questionable. When the ground attack began, the Canadians were immediately met by strong defensive fire. It took five days, and thousands of shells and aerial sorties by fighter-bombers, before the outer defences could be overcome. Boulogne finally fell on 22 September; the Canadians took some 9500 German prisoners, but the harbour facilities had been systematically destroyed and were not usable until mid-October.

Calais and Cap Gris Nez came next. On 25 September the usual bombing and heavy artillery barrage signalled the start of a Canadian infantry and armoured offensive. On the evening of 28 September the German garrison commander met Canadian divisional commander Dan Spry to ask that Calais be declared on open city. Spry refused, but allowed twenty-four hours for the evacuation of the town's civilians. The following day the guns momentarily fell silent around Calais, but the fighting continued at Cap Gris Nez to the west as the 9th Canadian Infantry Brigade assaulted and captured the massive guns that the Germans had been using to bombard Dover and other points along the English coast since the summer of 1940. At noon on 30 September, the cease-fire at Calais ended and the Canadians resumed the assault, but the Germans had lost their taste for the fight. Resistance ceased the next day, and more than 7000 Germans were taken prisoner.

The Canadians took too long to take the two port areas. In the case of Boulogne, particularly, a large German garrison was attacked by a relatively small Canadian force, and the result had been a hard slog which took five days of ground combat to complete. The delays do not absolve Montgomery of the ultimate responsibility he must bear for caring much more about the Ruhr than he did about the Scheldt, but the delays are surely one important reason behind Crerar's inability to concentrate his forces more rapidly than he did for the start of the Scheldt operation. At one point in late September, his 2nd Corps was spread over some 320 kilometres of French and Belgian coast.

The taking of Dieppe, Boulogne, and Calais did very little to ease the Allied supply problem. The ports were too small (and in the case of Boulogne too damaged) to make any difference. Antwerp was still the prize, but a prize unusable until the seaward approaches to it were cleared. Throughout the first weeks of September, Montgomery had remained preoccupied with Market Garden, but on 15 September, two days before Market Garden was to begin, he had ordered Crerar to hurry on to the Scheldt Estuary.

Although British troops were trucked into the Dunkirk area in mid-September to relieve the 2nd Canadian Infantry Division (which was sent to Antwerp to begin the initial stage of the attack on the Scheldt), not much else was going to get done unless the Canadians either received substantial reinforcements, or were relieved of (or completed) the task of taking the channel ports, or both. Put simply, Montgomery underestimated both German strength and the need to take the Scheldt quickly. But then, he and Eisenhower were banking on Market Garden to shorten the war. In addition, Montgomery was placing burdens on Crerar's army that no small army could possibly carry. As if to emphasize his total disregard for the realistic when it came to the Canadians, he also ordered Crerar on 27 September to protect the left flank of the Second British Army (Crerar was to do this with his 1st British Corps), which was about to begin an offensive towards the Ruhr from the Nijmegen salient. Thus, when the 2nd Canadian Infantry Division began to clear the area north of the Albert Canal on 22 September — led by the Calgary Highlanders and the rest of the 5th Brigade when Crockett won his Distinguished Conduct Medal — that activity was really only preliminary to a major attack that still lay in the future. In effect, the 2nd Canadian Division was trying to establish the base from which an offensive aimed at capturing South Beveland might later be launched.

The very day that Montgomery ordered Crerar to cover Dempsey's left flank (27 September), Crerar took ill and flew to the United Kingdom to be admitted to hospital. The burden for planning and commanding the Scheldt battle now fell on Simonds, who became acting army commander in Crerar's absence (Foulkes took over temporarily from Simonds at 2nd Canadian Corps Headquarters). Simonds decided that the Scheldt offensive should be conducted in three stages. First, the area between the south bank of the Scheldt, the Leopold Canal, and the Canal de Dérivation de la Lys — called the Breskens pocket — would be cleared. This would be done primarily by the 3rd Canadian Infantry Division, aided by elements of the 52nd British (Lowland) Division and the 4th Canadian Armoured Division. Then, the neck of South Beveland would be cut and the rest of South Beveland taken, primarily by the 2nd Canadian Infantry Division. Finally, the island of Walcheren, which dominated the entrance to the estuary, would be assaulted from South Beveland over the Walcheren causeway and by seaborne landings by British troops at Westkapelle and Flushing. The last part of the plan depended on flooding Walcheren — most of which lay below sea level — to deny the German garrison movement and confine it to the small areas of the island that lay above sea level. It was a controversial proposal, but eventually it was approved by Eisenhower and Churchill. The Walcheren dykes were destroyed from the air beginning on 3 October, when 243 heavy bombers dropped more than 1200 tonnes of high explosive on the dykes. Other attacks followed on subsequent days; by the third week of October, most of the island lay under water.

In the last week of September, the 2nd Canadian Infantry Division pushed the Germans back on the north side of the Albert Canal, cleared the area between it and the Turnhout Canal, and forced a crossing over the Turnhout Canal as well. Then, on 2 October, it began the long-awaited push towards the point where the isthmus of South Beveland joins the mainland. The 4th Brigade struck north from Antwerp, while the 6th Brigade attacked westward from the Turnhout Canal. Their objective was to push the Germans back from Antwerp and to clear the ground for a 5th Brigade attack towards Hoogerheide and Woensdrecht, two small towns barely 3 kilometres apart which dominated the road and rail links from the mainland through South Beveland to Walcheren.

W. Denis Whitaker, then commanding officer of the Royal Hamilton Light Infantry, 4th Canadian Infantry Brigade, later described the opening moments of the attack:

> At H-Hour, a deafening barrage went up and C Company began its advance. To our horror, we observed that one of our own field guns was firing short, right into the path of my advancing men. I had a terrible decision to make — and it had to be made instantly. If I aborted the operation at this point many lives would be lost, more than if I risked some of the troops being hit by fragments from our own shellfire. I had little choice but to carry on.[2]

Whitaker's terrible gamble paid off; the opening stages of the attack were successful and the two brigades spent the next few days advancing steadily to the northwest, the 6th Brigade protecting the flank of the 4th Brigade.

On 6 October the offensive to crush German resistance in the Breskens pocket began. The attack started with a flame-throwing assault by 27 Wasps — Bren carriers equipped with flame-throwers — on the north bank of the Leopold Canal, followed by an assault crossing of the canal by two battalions of the 7th Canadian Infantry Brigade. The flame-throwers momentarily stunned the German defenders, but they quickly recovered and counter-attacked. The two Canadian battalions managed to hold on to their bridgeheads, but could not link them up, even with the assistance of a third battalion that crossed soon after. The German troops in the Breskens area were very good and were determined to follow Hitler's orders to the last man.

To the east, in the battle for South Beveland, the Calgary Highlanders began to lead the 5th Brigade advance towards Hoogerheide and Woensdrecht on 7 October. By nightfall they had pushed into Hoogerheide against stiffening German resistance. The following day they and the other battalions of the 5th Brigade — the Black Watch and the Maisonneuves — began to advance cautiously towards Woensdrecht, just a few kilometres to the west. But the Germans were ready to push back with Kampfgruppe Chill, a force of some 2000 men, many of them paratroopers, backed by tanks, self-propelled artillery (SPs), and assault guns. Battle was joined in the afternoon when the Germans slammed into the Canadian positions; it raged all night and into the next day. The Black Watch intelligence officer observed: "The [German] troops we are now meeting are the cream of the crop . . . fine physical specimens, keen to fight and with excellent morale."[3] At one point an entire Highlander company went missing for several hours; cut off and with its radios malfunctioning, battalion headquarters had no idea of its status. After dark a 68-tonne German "Ferdinand" SP packing an 88-millimetre gun penetrated to the very centre of the Black Watch positions before it was destroyed.

The 5th Brigade held; the German attack was spent by dawn on 10 October. Now preparations began for the seizure of Woensdrecht and the final push to the East Scheldt, just beyond it, to cut off the supply lines and line of retreat for the German defenders on South Beveland. In the meantime, in the Breskens area, the 9th Canadian Infantry Brigade climbed into amphibious "Buffalo" vehicles at Terneuzen just after midnight on 9 October and began a 7-kilometre journey westward to land behind the German lines just after 0200. As dawn broke, the surprised German defenders reorganized themselves and began counter-attacking. Nonetheless, the 9th Brigade was soon reinforced by the 8th Brigade, and the Germans began to give ground.

In the Breskens pocket, the fighting seemed unending, the men had little respite, the water was everywhere, and death came quickly and sometimes unexpectedly. Donald Pearce was serving with the North Nova Scotia Highlanders of the 9th Brigade on 10 October, leading a small convoy of Bren carriers of the anti-tank platoon to B Company:

> Tense ride down an open one mile stretch of country road, every moment expecting a big explosion to occur underneath us . . . We have to make a sharp turn up a little lane that heads to Baker Company, so I stop just beyond the intersection to ask for covering fire before turning into the exposed laneway. The second carrier pulls up just a few yards back of ours and with a noise like the bursting of a ship's boiler simply blows up — men, equipment everything . . . My gun crew and I were appalled . . . I was sick all day.[4]

As the 8th and 9th Brigades pushed westward, the 10th Infantry Brigade of the 4th Canadian Armoured Division joined the battle, pushing west along the north side of the Leopold Canal. On 14 October the three brigades linked up; five days later they joined the lead elements of the 52nd (Lowland) Division, which had pushed across the Leopold Canal from the south, using the bridgehead originally established by the 7th Brigade. By now the original Breskens pocket had been reduced by about half, but the Germans fought on, their guns at Breskens still dominating the water passage between Breskens and Flushing, on Walcheren. The town of Breskens fell on 22 October, but the Germans still refused to quit. The Canadians pushed on to the west, bypassing a large flooded area north of the Bruges-Sluis Canal, and closed in on the remnant of the German defenders, near Zeebrugge. Charlie Martin and the men of the Queen's Own were given the dubious honour of assaulting the last German stronghold. As usual, the attack was preceded by an artillery bombardment:

> We were on both sides of the road, spaced, running fast and making ourselves as difficult targets as possible. The moment we hit the gate our artillery stopped — perfect timing . . . now we had to cover open ground to get close enough to drop in our grenades or smoke bombs . . . so we're all running at top speed . . . the miracle we prayed for happened. Out from all the slits in the strong point came the white flags. They had surrendered. The battle for Breskens was won.[5]

As the 10th Brigade neared its intended junction with the 8th and 9th Brigades southeast of Breskens on 13 October, the fight for Woensdrecht was beginning to

reach a bloody climax some 40 kilometres to the northeast. At 0645 that morning, C Company of the Black Watch passed through positions of the Royal Regiment of Canada some 3 kilometres west of Woensdrecht, to begin an advance
towards the railway embankment carrying the main line from Bergen-op-Zoom to
Walcheren. The plan was to shoot two companies onto the position with the aid
of tank, mortar, and artillery fire; the aim of the advance was to cut the rail line
leading to South Beveland.

The attack ran into difficulty almost from the start. C Company began to
take heavy casualties from small-arms fire not long after leaving its jumping-off
point. B Company, assigned to pass through C Company, was heavily mortared at
its start-line. Under cover of smoke, these two companies were eventually able to
advance to the embankment, but were then pinned down, taking more casualties.
Both company commanders were wounded. Later, under cover of artillery fire and
air strikes, and accompanied by Wasp flame-throwers, the other two Black Watch
rifle companies tried to complete the battalion's assigned task. But the artillery
spotters found it difficult to pinpoint targets in the almost featureless landscape,
while the fighter-bombers could not attack the far side of the curving railway
embankment without gravely endangering the Canadian troops. By nightfall, the
offensive was called off. It was a complete failure; fifty-six Black Watch were killed
or died of their wounds, sixty-two were wounded, twenty-seven were taken prisoner. It was the second, and second worse, disaster to befall the regiment since the
start of the campaign. Most of the Black Watch dead lay exposed and unburied
along the railway embankment until 24 October, when the Calgary Highlanders
finally took and held this small piece of contested and bloody ground.

The Black Watch attack was a disaster for many reasons, including the failure
of the infantry to use their artillery cover properly. But some of the blame must
also be laid at higher levels. Put simply, the advance was another case of too few
men asked to do too difficult a job against a well-dug-in enemy especially skilled
at defence. Even though Simonds had only about half of his army to work with,
and certainly no reinforcements from Montgomery, his plan had called for two
widely separated campaigns at the same time, one in the Breskens area and one at
the eastern end of South Beveland. Had he masked the Breskens pocket with, say,
the 3rd Canadian Infantry Division and assigned the 4th Canadian Armoured Division to the South Beveland attack in a two-divisional operation, the fight for
Woensdrecht might have been completed much quicker and with fewer casualties.

Ultimately, the fault lay at Montgomery's door. He had given the First Canadian Army too much to do and it could not accomplish everything he was asking of it. With the failure of Market Garden, it became obvious that the Allies would need to mount a coordinated offensive into Germany and that they would need the Antwerp port facilities as quickly as possible. But Montgomery continued to have his eye on the Ruhr. As October dragged on, Eisenhower put increasing pressure on Montgomery to make the Scheldt battle his first priority. Eventually, on 16 October, Monty was forced to give in. He closed his Ruhr offensive down, ordered Dempsey's army to cover the Canadians' right flank and help them take Bergen-op-Zoom, and gave Simonds two additional divisions, one British and one American, to work with. As C.P. Stacey noted: "As soon as the new orders took effect, the situation north of Antwerp was transformed."[6] Montgomery was not ordinarily a man to concede that he ever made a mistake, but he did admit to making one when it came to the Scheldt battle. In his memoirs he wrote: "Here I must admit a bad mistake on my part — I underestimated the difficulties of opening up the approaches to Antwerp so that we could get the free use of that port. I reckoned that the Canadian Army could do it *while* we were going for the Ruhr. I was wrong."[7]

On the morning of 16 October, the Royal Hamilton Light Infantry finally took Woensdrecht; in the days that followed the 5th Brigade cut the road and rail links between the mainland and Walcheren, while the rest of the 2nd Division turned westward along the South Beveland peninsula. Led by the 4th Brigade, the advance began 23 October as the division's other two brigades completed the task of securing the area north of Woensdrecht. They were aided by units of the 4th Canadian Armoured Division, which joined the fight the following day. Then they, too, headed westward.

Despite heavy traffic, German shelling, and German demolition of the bridges over the Beveland Canal, the division made steady progress. On 26 October the 52nd (Lowland) Division crossed the Scheldt from Terneuzen and began landing on the southeast coast of South Beveland. Then it, too, began to advance towards the western end of the peninsula. On the 29th it linked with the Canadians. By the 31st, all resistance had ceased on South Beveland; the island of Walcheren lay ahead.

Simonds's plan called for a three-pronged attack on Walcheren. On 1 November the British 4th Special Service Brigade was to land near Westkapelle, on the western tip of Walcheren, while the British No. 4 Commando, accompanied by a brigade of the 52nd (Lowland) Division, were to storm Flushing from Breskens. The land attack from South Beveland over the long and narrow Walcheren Causeway was to get underway as soon as possible. The 5th Canadian Infantry Brigade was given the task.

The western end of the causeway was well fortified by the Germans; their mortars and artillery were sited on every metre. The salt marshes on both sides of the causeway did not have enough water to float assault boats, but were too muddy to support men and vehicles. The only way to get across to Walcheren was to get there by crossing the almost totally exposed causeway. The Black Watch were the first to try. At about 1040 on 31 October they sent three companies forward; German shells rained down, forcing the men to hit the ground. Some were lucky enough to be near brick-lined slit trenches that the Germans had built for their own use. Most lay exposed, with little prospect for movement. They remained on the causeway until dark, then pulled back.

The Calgary Highlanders went next. After a heavy barrage on the German positions atop the dykes to the north and south of the western end of the causeway, the Highlanders moved out just after midnight. German mortar, machine gun, and shellfire blanketed the causeway. Some men got as far as a large tank trap on the south slope of the causeway, about two-thirds of the way across; others took refuge in slit trenches and shell holes. Company Commander Francis "Nobby" Clarke set up his headquarters in a large crater that the Germans had blasted out of the middle of the causeway, and quickly concluded that he could not hold. By 0300 the Highlanders had pulled back, taking some Black Watch wounded with them. Three hours later, the Highlanders moved back onto the causeway under cover of a new and more extensive fire plan. This time they made it all the way across and began to fan out on the eastern end of Walcheren. By midday it began to look as if they might succeed, but the Germans counter-attacked with flame-throwers, threatening to cut off at least one Highlander company. Late in the day, the Highlanders pulled back, their rifle companies reduced to about twenty men each.

That same day, to the west, the landing at Flushing was a complete success. Although the troops coming ashore at Westkapelle met stiff resistance at first, they were able to fan out to the north and south before the day ended. It was clear that the German hold on Walcheren was loosening fast, but the 5th Brigade was still under orders to assault over the causeway. Thus the Maisonneuves sent two companies onto the causeway after midnight on the night of 1/2 November. They never came closer than 200 metres from Walcheren and had to be rescued by the Scottish troops of the 52nd (Lowland) Division.

Foulkes, still in temporary command of the 2nd Canadian Corps, insisted on another go across the causeway and turned to Major-General Hakewell-Smith, GOC of the 52nd (Lowland) Division. Hakewell-Smith refused to make a direct assault and ordered his men to find another way. This they did when scouts discovered a place where troops could, in fact, walk across the mud flats. They outflanked the Germans at the end of the causeway, hastening the surrender of the last defenders on Walcheren on 8 November. It then took almost three weeks to clear the mines from the Scheldt. The first cargoes did not arrive until 28 November; symbolically, a Canadian merchantman led that first convoy.

As the Battle of the Scheldt Estuary ended, the men of the First Canadian Army retired eastward to the vicinity of Nijmegen. Taking over from the US 82nd Airborne Division, which had captured the town and its dominant highway bridge during Market Garden, the men encamped in the forests to the southeast of Nijmegen (against the German border), in the town itself, and in nearby towns and villages to the west. Much of the land near Nijmegen was dotted with the wreckage of American gliders, relics of Market Garden. For the next few months, the war would largely be fought elsewhere on the western front; the Canadians were only too happy to be left out. As they dug their slit trenches, sited their mortars and machine guns, and watched the falling snow cover the war-scarred countryside, they awaited the sixth Christmas of the war.

✿ XV Victory

In late August 1945, the slave labour prisoners at Camp B of the Nippon Kokan shipyards in Kawasaki, Japan, had known for at least a week that Japan had announced its surrender. The Canadians among them had been prisoners since that bleak December day in 1941 when the Commonwealth forces on Hong Kong Island had surrendered to Japan. They had survived the unspeakable horrors of the post-surrender atrocities that the Japanese had meted out. They had lived through almost four years of captivity in Hong Kong and Japan in conditions of filth, starvation, brutality, and constant physical exhaustion. They had endured months of air raids from US carrier-borne aircraft and the massive fire raids of the great silver American B-29 bombers. Now they waited to be rescued and to go home.

One of the men was William Allister. An army signaller, Allister had been born in Montreal and had grown up in Manitoba. In the fall of 1941 he had been attending a signals course in Nova Scotia, with little prospect of going overseas for at least a year, when the chance arose to volunteer for a secret mission to an unknown destination. He grabbed it and, within weeks, was aboard the SS *Awatea* bound for Hong Kong. Allister became a prisoner of war on Christmas Day, 1941; it had been the beginning of his life as a slave to the Japanese Empire — an ordeal that changed him forever.

The news of the Japanese surrender brought the promise of release, but days went by with no sign of the Americans. Most of the thousands of American, British, Canadian, and other Allied prisoners in Japan were in desperate straits; even a few days' early release could mean the difference between life and death. Then fighter planes began to appear in the sky, circling, searching for POW camps. Usually they were too far away to signal. Each day the aircraft seemed to come nearer, but not near enough. The men grew frustrated: "We felt like castaways on a desert island trying to signal ships," Allister later remembered.[1]

Then one day, about 21 August, it happened. A fighter plane circled closer and spotted the camp. The pilot flew straight at the jubilant men, then swooped low, coming in just over the telephone wires. As he flew past he dipped his wing in salute. It was a moment Allister would remember all his life:

> I was shrieking, waving, laughing, howling insane gibberish, freaking, weeping uncontrollably — the tears spurting up like an irrepressible orgasmic release. My dam had burst at last and out it all came, as though all the anguish of the planet had found me, and out of my bowels all the murders, tortures, all the Jews burning in Belsen, all the hellish years, had gathered in a million voices bursting all bounds.[2]

Allister and his comrades-in-arms were among the first Canadian soldiers taken prisoner in the Second World War; they were the last to be liberated.

As 1944 ended, one of the coldest winters on record gripped northern Europe. Along the western front from Holland to southern France stood seven Allied armies — one Canadian, one British, four American, and one French — close to ninety divisions. Opposing them were the supposedly defeated remnants of the Wehrmacht, which had suddenly come to life to put up a skilled and tenacious defence against the British at Arnhem, the Canadians at the Scheldt, and the Americans and French advancing towards the Saar.

In the other theatres of war, Allied victory had become certain, though months of hard fighting and heavy casualties obviously remained. In Italy, the American and British forces had broken through the Gothic Line, but stalled south of Bologna as winter closed in among the high passes of the Apennines and along the Adriatic coastal plain. On the eastern front, three Soviet army groups with fifteen armies stood poised for the last great Soviet offensive of the war. By then the Soviets had regained all of the Soviet Union and most of Poland, stood on the borders of East Prussia, and were preparing to take Warsaw. In the southwest Pacific, the United States had regained most of the Philippines and prepared to invade Luzon, the principal island and site of Manila, the Philippine capital. In the central Pacific, US Marines prepared to invade Iwo Jima, close enough to Japan to be used as an air base for long-range fighters to attack Japan directly.

As the Allied commanders on the western front bickered about what to do next, the Canadian Army gathered in and around Nijmegen. The Canadian mission was simple — to hold the Nijmegen salient and the small piece of

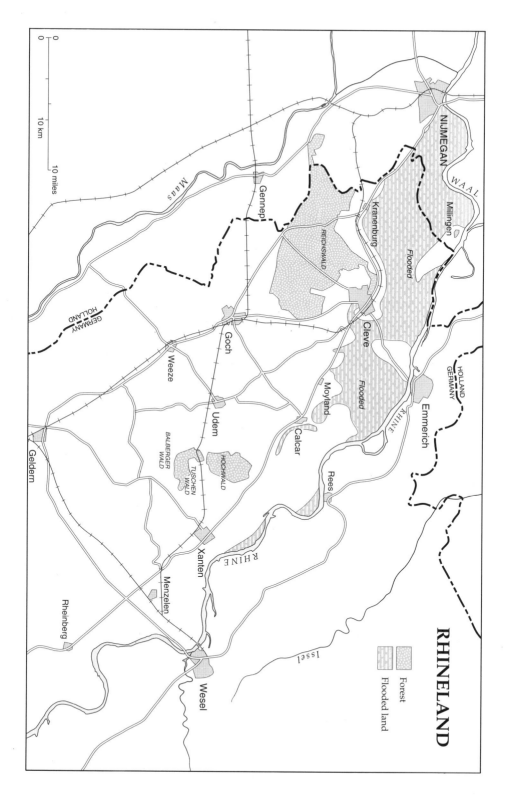

RHINELAND

Forest
Flooded land

Allied-held territory north of the Maas, across the Nijmegen bridge, known as "the island." Montgomery was planning a major offensive to start in early January aimed at clearing the Germans from the Rhineland as a first step to crossing the Rhine. He planned to use the Nijmegen salient as the jumping-off point for the initial attack.

The three months that the Canadians spent in the vicinity of Nijmegen was the longest period of time after D-Day in which the Canadians in Northwest Europe mounted no major operations. That does not mean there was no action. North of the Maas the Germans did their best to push the Canadians out of "the island." The flood-gates of the Neder (Lower) Rhine were opened, and the flood waters rose in the polderland between that river and the Maas. The Canadians north of the Maas were confined to an ever smaller slice of dry land, and were under constant German harassment.

Southeast of Nijmegen, near the towns of Berg-en-Daal and Groesbeek, the Canadian and German positions faced each other along the Dutch-German border. The German positions were the outposts of the much vaunted Siegfried Line, with its concrete fortifications, pillboxes, dragons' teeth, and other obstacles, that lay just a few kilometres out of sight in the forest to the east. Both sides patrolled aggressively to probe positions, take prisoners, and gather intelligence. Artillery barrages regularly made life difficult, if not deadly. The men dug deep slit trenches, covered them with whatever was handy — often portions of the gliders that still dotted the landscape — and tried to keep warm. On Christmas Day and New Year's Eve they serenaded one another with both music and mortar fire before returning to the grim business of survival in a hostile environment.

As much as they may have grumbled about the snow and the cold and the need for constant vigilance, especially at night, the Canadians had nothing to complain about compared with their American allies further south in the Ardennes Forest. There, on 16 December, the Germans loosed two panzer armies through General Courtney Hodges's US First Army. The Germans called the attack Autumn Fog; the Americans dubbed it The Battle of the Bulge. New armour from German tank factories had been channelled to reinvigorated units smashed in the Normandy fighting or to new units recently formed. Gasoline, in ever shorter supply in the Reich, had been hoarded for months to fuel the attack. It was all part of Hitler's last great gamble; if his troops could cut deep into Allied territory and retake Brussels and Antwerp, the Allied cause in the west would suffer a serious setback. Then Hitler could turn the bulk of his troops eastward to meet the

Russians. The German plan called for the Fifth and Sixth Panzer armies to drive west and north, and then to form the anvil for Army Group H, which would attack westward across the Maas to encircle and then destroy the 21st Army Group. Allied air superiority was neutralized by the bad weather; for days Hitler's tanks moved underneath a cover of thick clouds.

Stunned, the Americans managed to rush the 101st Airborne Division to the key Belgian road-junction town of Bastogne; there they were besieged but refused to surrender. Other American troops fought tenaciously at St Vith, another important crossroads, until they were forced to pull back. The Germans drove to within 30 kilometres of Namur on the Meuse River, but could get no farther. Their lines of supply and communication were hopelessly snarled. Even if they had reached the Meuse, however, they would have encountered a stiffened defence organized by Montgomery, who had been asked by Eisenhower to take the US Ninth Army under command for the duration of the emergency because Bradley's 12th US Army Group Headquarters was on the other side of the bulge from it. Monty placed US and British troops at strategic locations to hold the shoulder of the Bulge, and alerted Crerar's Canadians for a possible attack on the Nijmegen salient by the German First Parachute Army.

That attack never came. The US Army suffered thousands of casualties — dead, wounded, and missing — but fought back stubbornly after the initial panic. Patton's Third Army, which had been poised to launch an attack against the Saar, swung north in one of the most difficult manoeuvres called for in war, and broke through to Bastogne just after Christmas. Then, when the weather cleared, Allied fighter-bombers took a frightful toll of German troops and tanks. Hitler had gambled his last significant reserve and had lost. The Germans would still put up a determined defence of their borders, but the panzers that would have added so much punch to that defence lay wrecked on the roads and among the trees of the Ardennes Forest.

As the Allied armies had driven to the very borders of Germany in the late fall of 1944, Bomber Command's assault on Germany had intensified. Harris's bombers had been tied in to the Normandy operations since the spring; when Normandy was finally won, he regained control over his aircraft. For a time in late summer the RAF and RCAF "heavies" had concentrated on V-1 sites, but for the most part these aircraft were ineffective against such targets, which were better attacked by medium bombers and fighter-bombers. Harris's heavies also attacked oil and other strategic targets in a somewhat grudging and belated acknowledgement that the systematic destruction of German energy sources was having a major impact on the war. For the most part, however, Harris returned to his favourite tactic — area attacks against German cities.

By now the bomber war had swung in favour of the RAF; as the Allies advanced towards Germany, Oboe stations had been set up on the continent, thereby improving the crews' ability to pinpoint their positions. The aircraft also carried improved H2S, which allowed them to locate their targets with much greater accuracy at night or when bombing through clouds in daylight. The acute German shortage of aviation gasoline played havoc with the Luftwaffe's efforts to field an effective night-fighter force. The German propeller day-fighter force had long since been driven from the skies. The new ME 262 jets, much faster than Spitfires or Mustangs, were almost invincible when they attacked bombers in daylight, but large numbers of these jets were either destroyed on the ground or shot down when landing or taking off. A few were even destroyed in air-to-air combat.

Through the fall and into the winter, the bomber force attacked city after city, wreaking havoc at little cost. In fact, of the more than 300,000 tonnes of bombs dropped in area raids on Germany throughout the war, the greatest part by far was used after 1 July 1944. In just one week in October, for example, the RCAF's No. 6 Group took part in four area bombing attacks against Duisburg (twice), Wilhelmshaven, and Stuttgart. A total of 677 aircraft sortied in these raids; only eight failed to return. The pace of the attacks picked up in November and December, with No. 6 Group routinely dispatching 150 or more bombers to a single target each night for the loss of just one or two aircraft.

The previous summer the Air Ministry had examined, then shelved, Operation Thunderclap — a series of "overwhelming raids" designed to destroy German morale and to end the war.[3] Now, after the Battle of the Bulge, and with Germany apparently teetering on the brink of collapse, Churchill urged the revival of the plan. The target selected for the first Thunderclap attack was Dresden, a rail and communications centre in eastern Germany which lay in the path of the Red Army and which was jammed with refugees fleeing from the east. Dresden was the largest German city still intact, and one that contained important war plants. To those who accepted both the logic and the necessity of area bombing, there was no reason why Dresden should be spared when other German cities had not been.

As Carter and Dunmore concluded in their history of No. 6 Group: "At this stage of the conflict, the Allies were in no mood to show mercy to the perpetrators of such horrors as Auschwitz, Belsen, and Dachau. The pressure had to be maintained . . . The Allies had already suffered far too many casualties in the invasion of Europe. The bloodletting had to be brought to a halt as rapidly as possible."[4]

On the night of 13/14 February 1945, Bomber Command sent close to 800 Lancasters and nine Mosquitoes to Dresden. They started bombing at 2215; within forty-five minutes the heart of the city was engulfed in a firestorm. The blaze could be seen by approaching bombers at least 200 kilometres away. Bomber Command later estimated that 85 percent of the built-up area of Dresden was destroyed. As many as 150,000 people were killed; since the city was filled with refugees, an accurate death count was not possible. Many No. 6 Group squadrons were still flying Halifaxes of various types, so only sixty-seven RCAF Lancasters took part in the raid; none was lost.

In one of the greatest acts of hypocrisy of the entire war, Churchill now sought to distance himself from the Dresden bombing in particular and the area bombing campaign in general. It was time to re-examine the policy, he wrote in late March 1945, when the Allied armies were already deep into Germany and victory was both certain and only weeks away. His reversal was shameless and had no impact on the course of the war, but it helped to create a postwar climate of disapproval both of Harris and of the area bombing campaign. This condemnation was manifested in a number of ways, from failure to honour Harris as the other Allied military leaders had been to refusal to issue a special medal to Bomber Command aircrew. Echoes of this hypocrisy reverberate to this day, as the drums against the area bombing campaign continue to be beaten by people who experienced nothing of the horror of the Second World War and who ignore the context within which the bombing campaign took place.

The bombing continued until late April, even as the Russians closed in on Berlin. As city after city was occupied by the Allies, target after target was removed from the Bomber Command list. By the end of the fighting, thousands of square kilometres of Germany's most important cities lay ruined, hundreds of thousands of city dwellers had been killed, and many more people had been injured or rendered homeless. The debate about the strategic effectiveness of the bomber war will continue for a long time, but there was one indisputable result of that bombing campaign: when the German people dug themselves out of the ruins of their cities, they knew beyond doubt that they had suffered a terrible and costly defeat and had paid a heavy price for the war they had begun and waged. As the *Globe and Mail* put it in March 1945:

> The real victory of Allied air power [was] a thing of the mind — a lesson so
> terrible as never to be forgotten . . . The German People will not need the
> presence of Allied armies to persuade them that they lost this war. The
> storm which is engulfing them from the air . . . is convincing them that
> they have suffered the most terrible defeat ever inflicted on a people in all
> history.[5]

That was as good a guarantee as any that Germany would not repeat the mistake a third time in the twentieth century.

In the early hours of 16 April 1945 the RCN Bangor Class minesweeper *Esquimalt* departed Halifax on a routine anti-submarine sweep on the approaches to Halifax harbour. The ship was to meet up with HMCS *Sarnia* just before noon. It was calm and clear.

Esquimalt was not using its radar, which was, in any case, obsolete. The ship's asdic beam swept the waters close ahead, but *Esquimalt* was neither zigzagging nor streaming its CAT gear. At 0635, near the Sambro light ship, an acoustic torpedo tore into the minesweeper. It had been fired by U-190, which had been lying at ambush ready to attack ships coming into or leaving Halifax harbour. *Esquimalt* went down in less than four minutes, with no chance to issue a distress call. The survivors clung to four carley-floats in the bone-chilling water for some seven hours before they were spotted by *Sarnia*. Many died of exposure; the final death toll was forty-four. *Esquimalt* was the last RCN vessel to be lost in the war; its sinking was all too typical of the last phases of the Allied campaign against the U-boats.

From the late summer of 1944 until the end of the war, Dönitz sent his U-boats into the shallow waters of the English Channel and the approaches to the major east-coast ports of North America such as Halifax. His reasoning was simple: Allied anti-submarine capability had developed to the point where a renewal of the wolfpack tactics of 1940–43 was unthinkable; thus, his submarines would have to hunt alone. Sending lone submarines to search the vast areas of the mid-ocean for convoys was a waste of precious resources — it was too easy for a lone boat to miss a convoy. But the experiences of his submariners in the Gulf of St

Lawrence in 1942 had demonstrated two things: tricky currents and thermal layers made it easy for U-boats to hide in coastal waters; and it was also easy for them to find targets at particular choke-points, especially approaches to harbours.

The Canadians had had a difficult enough time hunting U-boats in their own coastal waters in 1942; they and their Allies had an even tougher time in late 1944 and 1945 because the U-boats were much better equipped than they had been two years earlier. The newest snorkel heads carried the latest in radar-detection equipment, while the submarines had the still dangerous Gnat acoustic torpedo. It is therefore understandable, though ironic, that of the fifteen RCN ships sunk by submarines during the war, three were destroyed in Canadian coastal waters in the last six months of the conflict: *Shawinigan* in the Cabot Strait on 25 November 1944; *Clayoquot* near Halifax on 24 December 1944; and *Esquimalt*.

The new tactics and equipment enabled the U-boats to approach close to the east-coast ports of both Canada and the United States as they had done in 1942. Even the much vaunted United States Navy's hunter-killer groups had a difficult time finding and sinking the inshore invaders. Because of the overwhelming presence of Allied air cover and ocean-going escorts, however, there was nothing like the slaughter that had taken place more than two years before. Snorkelling U-boats still had to stay submerged to avoid detection from the air. This restricted their speed and their ability to get into attack position. When they placed themselves on known routes into and out of major ports, they could sink merchantmen in relatively large numbers, as U-1232 had done in early January 1945 when it had destroyed three ships near Halifax in only a matter of hours. But the days of wide-open roving of the convoy lanes, on the surface or submerged, were over. Even the best-equipped U-boats could not sink ships they could not detect or reach.

In the final months of the war, Dönitz dreamed about a great new submarine offensive using the new, faster, longer-range submersibles still on the drawing boards or being built in German shipyards. Reports appeared in some North American newspapers that the Germans would use these U-boats to launch V-2 rockets at east-coast cities. But dreams of submarine-launched missiles were still dreams (or nightmares), and the advanced U-boats Dönitz needed to renew his mid-ocean campaign against Allied shipping were destroyed, still in their dry-docks, by Allied bombers.

The RCN lost twenty-four ships and 1800 sailors to all causes in the Second World War; more than a thousand other Canadians were killed at sea aboard

Canadian-registry merchant ships. But four of every five U-boat crew members who left European ports on war patrol never returned, and the RCN could take some satisfaction from that; it and the RCAF had sunk, or participated in the sinking of, fifty-two Axis submarines in the course of the war. More to the point, its vessels had escorted millions of tonnes of vital Allied shipping from North America to the United Kingdom and back. Without that shipping, Allied victory in Europe would have been impossible. That was quite an achievement for a navy that had all but disappeared in the early 1930s.

In the pre-dawn darkness of 8 February 1945, the rifle companies of the Calgary Highlanders took up their forward positions in the dense but leafless woods on the road to the German border town of Wyler. They and the Régiment de Maisonneuve had been chosen to lead the 2nd Canadian Infantry Division in the great attack about to begin. That attack, code-named Veritable, was to be the first stage in Montgomery's campaign to clear the Rhineland. Its object was to secure the ground between the Dutch-German border and the Hochwald, a forest reserve that guarded the approaches to the crossroads town of Xanten. Xanten was the key to the Rhine crossings at Wesel. After the Hochwald had been reached, the attacking forces were to halt for regrouping and redeployment. The artillery would be brought forward in classic set-piece fashion. Then stage two of the offensive — code-named Blockbuster — would begin.

To the south, along the Roer River, the US Ninth Army under the command of Lieutenant-General W.H. Simpson had been placed under Montgomery's command for this operation; it was to attack northward (Operation Grenade) to meet the British and Canadian forces opposite Wesel. Montgomery had put the entire 30th Corps and several other British divisions under command of the First Canadian Army to ensure that Crerar had the strength he needed to break through the German frontier defences. For a time, Crerar's headquarters would control thirteen divisions, of which only three were Canadian, while the total manpower strength of the forces under his command would reach almost half a million. Montgomery believed that the Germans would never suspect that his major offensive would begin on the Canadian front, and he was right.

The attack began at 0500 on 8 February with a huge artillery barrage. The field, medium, heavy, and super-heavy guns of seven British and Canadian divisions and five Army Groups Royal Artillery were joined by the deadly projectiles of the 1st Canadian Rocket Battery and virtually every anti-aircraft gun, tank gun, medium machine gun, and 4.2-inch mortar along the front. The initial barrage lasted for 160 minutes, then ceased abruptly for ten minutes as spotters and listeners pinpointed answering German artillery. Those guns were then targeted when the firing resumed. Five hours after the initial barrage, a moving barrage led the first waves of British and Canadian troops towards their assigned objectives. One Calgary Highlander was awed by the spectacle: "I never saw anything like that in my life," William Powell would remember. "The ground just rocked . . . that was the first time I saw those multiple rockets fired. There was a farm and a grove of trees near Wyler . . . that place just disintegrated, all in one smack."[6] Behind the front, heavy bombers attacked and virtually destroyed the road-junction towns of Cleve, Goch, and Emmerich. The fighter-bombers and medium bombers of the RAF's Second Tactical Air Force and the US Ninth Air Force provided close air support whenever the weather permitted.

Canadian divisions played a small but vital role in Veritable. On the northern or left flank the 3rd Division, aptly nicknamed the Water Rats because of the polder fighting they had done during the Scheldt campaign, advanced in amphibious vehicles across flooded fields to take possession of the area between the Waal and the Nijmegen–Cleve–Calcar road, which was one of the main axes of attack. The task of the 2nd Division (especially the 5th Brigade) was to secure the left flank of the 15th (Scottish) Division by taking the fortified towns of Wyler and Den Heuvel. The Calgary Highlanders and the Maisonneuve did that in one day, though the Highlanders suffered heavy casualties when one of their assault companies ran into a well-prepared killing zone sown with mines and covered by German mortars and machine guns. Only quick thinking by battalion Commanding Officer Lieutenant-Colonel Ross Ellis saved the situation; he crawled forward under fire to do his own reconnaissance, and then ordered a new fire plan to send his reserve company on to its objective and to the rescue of the men who were pinned down.

The 2nd Division got into the fight once again, several days later, when it was called upon to clear a thick forest reserve known as the Moyland wood about 8 kilometres southeast of Cleve, but for the most part this first stage of the offensive was borne by the British troops of 30th Corps who slogged their way forward over muddy and congested roads, through bombed-out or shelled-out villages, and, worst of all, through the thick wood of the Reichswald.

Like many of the forests which dotted the Rhineland, the Reichswald was actually a forest reserve. Hiking and bicycle paths ran through it, along with a number of narrow dirt roads. In the forest itself, thick stands of both evergreen and deciduous trees made movement difficult, as did the snow, mud, wet leaves, and pine needles on the forest floor. The Germans had planted mines and booby-traps everywhere and had constructed low bunkers to protect their machine-gun and sniper emplacements. Using the paths and narrow roads in the forest was suicide; pushing through the thick brush was almost impossible. Tree bursts from 88-millimetre guns sent deadly shards of wood and shell fragments crashing on the advancing infantry. It was slow going against a determined enemy, but by nightfall of the first day the Siegfried Line (which ran through the western part of the forest) had been breached and the defending German 84th Division smashed.

At first the Veritable offensive went well. Within forty-eight hours 30th Corps had captured "virtually all its objectives for Phase One of 'Veritable.'"[7] But no battle ever runs smoothly, and major problems began to beset Montgomery's armies on the third day of the attack. The northward thrust of Simpson's Ninth Army from the Roer River had to be postponed when the Germans blew up the Roer dams, flooding the river and inundating the land over which the attack was to be launched. For the most part the German defenders who faced the British and Canadians were not as skilled at war as the well-trained Wehrmacht and SS troops who had fought in Normandy, but the Germans were now defending the soil of their own country and they battled with great determination.

On the northern flank of the attack, the rising flood-waters made the area between Cleve and the Rhine into a shallow lake; movement was all but impossible. Donald Pearce of the North Nova Scotia Highlanders was one of the Canadians who fought there. He kept a diary of his time on that sodden battlefield:

February 15
Took up new positions on the flooded dykes and farms bordering the Rhine opposite Emmerich. Our duties purely defensive — maintaining constant contact with neighbouring companies and, at night, patrolling the dykes, most of which were submerged . . . we managed our night patrols in row boats, splashing from one flooded farm to another, docking at windows, or at high points along the dykes . . . this was one of the ugliest assignments we have ever been handed — cold, wet, cut off from the rest of the brigade by acres of standing water.[8]

In the centre of the front an early thaw turned the dirt roads into morasses, forcing the British armour to use only the few paved roads in the region. To add to their troubles, the destruction of Cleve and Goch by bombing made movement through those towns very difficult. Whereas the British and Canadians had made good progress on the first two days, it took six more days to move an additional 15 kilometres. Veritable was running out of steam well short of its initial objective, the Hochwald.

On the night of 19/20 February, the Royal Hamilton Light Infantry and the Essex Scottish of the 4th Brigade were hit hard in their positions on the Goch–Calcar road by a German battle group scrounged from elements of the 116 Panzer division. It took almost twenty-four hours of continuous fighting before the German counter-attack was thwarted, and the cost was very high. The brigade, and the Queen's Own Cameron Highlanders from the 6th Brigade, suffered some 400 casualties in that time period. The Essex Scottish alone lost 204 killed, wounded and missing.

On 23 February the US Ninth Army finally launched its long-delayed attack, code-named Grenade. But the Germans continued to maintain a strong presence west of the Rhine, especially in the Hochwald and the area to the east and south of Xanten. Crerar's army would have to move much farther to the southeast to effect a junction with Simpson's forces than was originally planned. That advance, code-named Blockbuster, was set to start on 26 February. This time the 2nd Canadian Corps would play the major role, and the 30th British Corps would guard the right flank of the Canadians.

The Canadian attack plan was simple in conception. The 2nd and 3rd Canadian Infantry Divisions were to take possession of the Hochwald and the smaller Tuschenwald and Balbergerwald that lay to the south of it, and which were separated from it by a cleared area about 2 kilometres wide. The rail line from Goch to Wesel ran through that gap. Once in possession of the forest north and south of the gap, the 4th Canadian Armoured Division was to sweep through the gap, south of Xanten, and then towards Wesel. Then the two infantry divisions would follow, with the 2nd directed to take Xanten itself. The British 43rd Division would cover the Canadian left flank between the Rhine and the Calcar–Xanten road.

The Hochwald is on a plateau that slopes up from west to east. Like the Reichswald, it is thickly forested and was easily defended. In front of the Hochwald was the Schleiffen Position, a belt of strong defences backed up by nine German infantry divisions. It stretched from Rees, on the south bank of the Rhine, to Geldern. The line would have to be assaulted by infantry in a dawn attack because the land to the west of the forest was gently rolling and mostly open farm country; infantry or armour trying to cross that area by daylight would be cut down by machine gun, mortar, and anti-tank fire from the woods. Just prior to the main attack, a diversionary assault would be launched at a height of land to the west of the forest and south of Calcar. Simonds hoped this attack would draw the main German strength to the north.

Blockbuster began on schedule and, for a time, the diversion worked, but German resistance soon stiffened; the fighting on the edges of the Hochwald and in the forest itself was especially vicious and costly. Crack German paratroopers defended the gap, and other German soldiers the forest itself. Although troops of the 2nd and 3rd Divisions pushed through the Schlieffen Position on the first morning of the attack (26 February) to reach the edge of the Hochwald, the forest itself was not cleared for another six days.

To the south, the US Ninth Army continued its attack to the north, threatening the German defenders west of the river with encirclement. On 3 March troops of 30th Corps effected a junction with the Americans south of Udem. Henceforth, the Germans began to concentrate on getting over the Rhine with as many men and as much equipment as possible. As the German paratroopers prepared to defend Xanten to the last man, their comrades in arms started to pull back to the highway and rail bridges at Wesel and to the east bank of the river.

On 7 March came the electrifying news that the US First Army had captured a railway bridge across the Rhine at Remagen, between Bonn and Coblenz, and was pushing straight across the river. The next day the 5th Brigade of the 2nd Canadian Infantry Division began the battle for Xanten, while other troops from the division moved past it to the Alter Rhine, an oxbow lake some three kilometres south of the Rhine River.

By 9 March the battle for the Rhineland was almost over. Three British divisions — the 3rd, the Guards Armoured, and the 53rd — were sweeping towards Wesel from Geldern in the west, while the Americans closed in from the south. As his troops neared the river, Simonds gave some thought to seizing one or both of the bridges there, despite being warned not to do so by Montgomery. But at 0700 on the morning of 10 March, with the bulk of their surviving forces withdrawn to the east bank of the Rhine, the Germans blew the bridges. By 2200 hours that night all resistance west of the river ceased; now, only the Rhine stood between the Canadians and Germany itself.

Though the Americans in the Remagen bridgehead were driving as many troops and as much equipment across the Rhine as they could, Montgomery characteristically made extensive and careful preparations for a massive assault crossing of the great river in his sector. That operation, code-named Plunder, began at 2100 on 23 March. The crossing took place on a wide front between Wesel and Rees. Though the Canadians had played such a key role in clearing the ground for the crossing, Montgomery reserved the bulk of the operation for the British Second Army — only the 9th Canadian Infantry Brigade took part on the extreme left of the bridgehead. The 3rd Canadian Infantry Division crossed the Rhine five days later over a pontoon bridge at Rees, and the 2nd Division followed soon after.

The crossing of the Rhine by Montgomery's 21st Army Group was one of the last acts of the war. Victory was now finally in sight. On the eastern front the Soviet armies, two million strong with more than 40,000 artillery pieces, 6000 tanks, and some 500 ground assault aircraft, stood on the Oder River 65 kilometres from Berlin. In the west, four American armies were across the Rhine; two were driving east into Austria and Czechoslovakia, and two others began to encircle the Ruhr. On the northern flank Dempsey's Second British Army prepared to assault northeast towards Bremen, Hamburg, and Kiel — Montgomery was especially anxious to beat the Russians to Denmark. Canada's Cinderella army was to be denied the chance to help cut out the heart of the Nazi enemy. Instead, Crerar's forces — united at last with the arrival from Italy of the 1st Corps — were given the less glamorous but no less important task of liberating Holland.

Simonds's 2nd Canadian Corps was initially directed north and east from its Rhine bridgehead to push the Germans out of eastern Holland, secure the Dutch coast along the north sea, and move into northern Germany on the left flank of the British Second Army. Foulkes's 1st Canadian Corps, which had formally come under Crerar's command on 15 March, was to clear the "island" north of the Waal, capture Arnhem, then drive to the Ijsselmeer (once known as the Zuider Zee). Following those operations, it was to swing westward to clear northwestern Holland, including the major cities of Amsterdam, Rotterdam, The Hague, and Utrecht.

The 2nd Corps drive began on 1 April, with the 2nd Division moving up the central axis of advance to Groningen; the 3rd Division, to the left of the 2nd Division, directed towards Leeuwarden; and the 4th Canadian and 1st Polish Armoured Divisions, on the corps' right flank, advancing northeast towards the Dutch-German border. In the words of one Canadian Army report, the objective was to drive the Germans "into the [POW] cage, into the grave, or into the North Sea." The corps swept north, delayed primarily by blown bridges, flooded polders, and mined roads. A German SP (self-propelled artillery) might occasionally lob some shells towards the advancing Canadians, before scuttling away or being destroyed. In some of the more important road-junction towns, scattered units of the German army or SS tried to delay the advance, but they could not. Brigadiers would assign a battalion to clear them out, while the rest of the brigade would sweep around the centre of resistance and continue on the move. The Canadians made little effort to protect their divisional flanks, but the Germans were hardly in a position to threaten those flanks. On the night of 7/8 April, French paratroopers were dropped forward of the advancing corp to seize bridges and other important positions and to help clear the way for the Canadians. The Canadian spearheads met up with the paratroopers three days later.

Within two weeks of beginning the advance, the 3rd and 2nd Divisions were in reach of the North Sea. Then, on 13 April, the battle for Groningen was joined. A one-time port city dating back to the thirteenth century, Groningen was home to some 100,000 people and was capital of Groningen province. It was defended by a mixed force of German troops, including naval personnel, members of the Dutch Nazi party (NSB), and Dutch SS. This last group was made up of Dutchmen who had joined the SS after Holland had been occupied by the Germans. Many had fought on the eastern front. Knowing they would be killed either in battle or at the hands of their compatriots once Holland was liberated, they mounted a fanatical resistance. The fight was long and bloody, and much of the historic town centre was destroyed. The Canadians were handicapped by Simonds's order not to use artillery unless absolutely necessary so as to preserve civilian lives. On 16 April, however, the German garrison commander surrendered and resistance died out. Thereafter, the 2nd and 3rd Divisions were trucked rapidly over the Dutch-German border to begin operations aimed at clearing the area between the Kusten Canal and the North Sea, taking the important port of Wilhelmshaven.

The 1st Canadian Corps went into action on 2 April, with the 5th Canadian Armoured and the British 49th (West Riding) Divisions under Foulkes's command (the 1st Canadian Infantry Division began operations under Simonds, then switched back to Foulkes). There was some hope that the Germans might withdraw from western Holland, because they were now in great danger of being entirely cut off from Germany, but they did not. Accordingly, Foulkes launched his forces at Arnhem from across the Ijssel River. The Germans fought for each house in the already battered town; by 14 April, however, Arnhem — or, what was left of it — was in Canadian hands. As one visiting Canadian officer later wrote: "This city is one of the most saddening sights I have seen in this war, for though the destruction is very far from total every building is smashed in some degree . . . the greater part of it . . . entirely empty of civilians, and the doors of many houses . . . standing open."9

On 11 April the 1st Canadian Infantry Division joined the battle by attacking westward across the Ijssel towards Apeldoorn. Then Foulkes sent the 5th Canadian Armoured Division northward towards the Ijsselmeer; it reached Harderwijk, on the edge of the Ijsselmeer, on 18 April. Foulkes's corps now stood on a north-south line from the Ijsselmeer to the Neder Rhine, poised for a major assault westward towards Utrecht.

The Germans had about 120,000 troops in western Holland, still a formidable opposition for Foulkes's two division corps. Those Germans were isolated and could have no further impact on the outcome of the war, so there was a good argument to be made to leave them in place. The most important problem facing the Allies in this sector, however, was not a military one; the civilian population of western Holland was slowly starving to death. It was far more important to get food supplies to them than it was to defeat the Germans there. An agreement was worked out under Eisenhower's threat to deal harshly with the Nazi occupation authorities and the puppet Dutch government of Arthur Seyss-Inquart if they did not agree to allow food supplies to be sent into their administrative area. The Canadian offensive would be halted and, in turn, the Germans would allow food convoys in to feed the civilian population and would take no further repressive measures against them. On 22 April Montgomery ordered Crerar to cease operations in western Holland; six days later a full truce went into effect. On 29 April Allied aircraft began dropping tonnes of food supplies into the beleaguered area, and truck convoys rolled in shortly after.

On 25 April Soviet and American troops met at Torgau on the Elbe; Germany had been cut in half. In the north, the Second British Army penetrated to the centre of Bremen, while Crerar's forces prepared to attack Wilhelmshaven. In southern Germany, US forces had swept through to the Czech border. In Berlin, the Soviet army was taking the German capital block by block in some of the bitterest and bloodiest fighting of the war. In Italy, German troops prepared to surrender. SS Chief Heinrich Himmler betrayed Hitler by offering to surrender the German armies on the western front, an offer that was refused. Hitler prepared for his marriage and his suicide.

By 4 May Simonds's corps was within 15 kilometres of Wilhelmshaven and preparing to enter the city. Just after noon, Crerar received a telephone call from 21st Army Group Headquarters with the news that the Germans were meeting with Montgomery to discuss the surrender of all their forces on the 21st Army Group front. Crerar called Simonds and told him to hold his troops until further word came. That evening the news broke that the Germans on the northern front would definitely surrender the next day. On the evening of 5 May, German Generals Blaskowitz and Straube formally surrendered the troops under their command to Foulkes and to Simonds, respectively. The formal surrender of Germany was received by Eisenhower at his headquarters at Rheims on 7 May, and 8 May was declared VE-Day. For the Canadians in Europe, the war was over. In the days between the launching of Veritable and the end of the war, they had lost 5515 officers and men killed, wounded, and missing. The fighting had continued almost to the last; Canadian units were still taking significant casualties right up to the truce.

The war did not end on 8 May 1945. In the Pacific theatre the Japanese fought on; their army exacted a terrible toll of US Marines on Okinawa, while their kamikaze pilots accounted for many good ships and good sailors. Canada had played little part in the Pacific war, but it was prepared to field naval, air, and ground forces that would participate in the looming invasion of Japan. That invasion never took place; Japan surrendered after losing two entire cities — Hiroshima and Nagasaki — to atomic bombs. Those bombs killed tens of thousands of Japanese, but spared tens of thousands of Allied soldiers' lives, including those of the many Canadians who would have been killed in the final battle for Japan.

In the end, they went home — to wives, husbands, lovers, children (some they had never seen), and families. Most rebuilt their lives; all participated in some way in Canada's postwar economic growth and in its maturity and development as a modern nation. Although many chose to join veterans' organizations, and some continued to participate in the militia, most wanted nothing more than to put the war behind them. Over the years, however, the memories often flooded back — of men trapped in the engine room of a sinking destroyer, of bombers exploding like fireworks in the night skies, of close friends lying with bodies shattered in sodden polderland or in the dusty wheat fields of Normandy. Just as war begins and ends inside each individual human being, so, too, does the process of healing. Victory is a concept celebrated by nations, but to warriors from time immemorial to now it really means only one thing: a chance to go home, a promise of a normal existence, and a good possibility of surviving the next twenty-four hours. As a beleaguered Europe celebrated its liberation from Nazi tyranny, the Canadians turned to home and to peace.

Afterword

There were only four Allied nations that fielded a force of at least five divisions in Western Europe in the fight to destroy Nazi barbarism — the United States, Britain, France, and Canada. That was a distinction Canada earned at a high price — 12,579 officers and men killed in action in the Canadian Army, and 35,373 wounded, missing, or taken prisoner. Those losses must be added to the casualty totals for the RCAF, the RCN, and those Canadians serving in other, mostly British, formations. The total for the nation was 42,042 dead and 54,414 wounded out of about 1.1 million who served. For a nation of just over 11 million people, it was a marvellous achievement. For a country that began the war six years earlier with fewer than 10,000 soldiers, sailors, and airmen, it was a miracle.

The Canadian war was as sweeping as it was varied. Canada's fleet of escort vessels, from the lowly corvettes to the thoroughbred Tribal Class destroyers, patrolled from the warm waters of the Caribbean to the freezing ocean on the run to northern Russia. Canadian airmen flew transport and supply missions over the jungles of Burma and bombing missions in the dark night air over Germany. Canadian soldiers fought and died from Hong Kong to northern Germany. Canadian dead can be found at Commonwealth War Graves Commission cemeteries from the Japanese home islands to the islands of the United Kingdom.

The Canadian war did not begin well. In the time-honoured way of virtually all Canadian governments past and present, those who governed Canada between 1919 and 1939 thought not of war but of political advantage. As in the First World War, Canada's soldiers, sailors, and airmen went to war undertrained, poorly equipped, and, for the most part, badly led. They had no choice but to learn on the job. They did learn, but the initial price — Hong Kong, Dieppe, Verrières Ridge, the disastrous convoy battles of late 1942, the heavy losses suffered by No. 6 Group in the first eight months of 1943 — was very high.

It is sometimes observed that Canada was fortunate in its total casualties in the Second World War compared with those in the First World War. In the first war, there were 60,661 fatal casualties, or 9.28 percent of all those who served. In the second war, only 3.86 percent of the total who served were killed or died on active service. But the figure is misleading. Although aircrew casualties were much higher than anticipated in the Second World War, especially among bomber crews, nothing destroys lives quicker and in larger numbers than sustained ground combat. In the First World War, the Canadians fought in virtually every major battle on the western front from April 1915 on — three years and seven months. In the Second World War, sustained Canadian ground action did not begin until July 1943 and, even then, the bulk of the Canadian ground forces were not committed to action until the summer of 1944. Thus they went in harm's way for a much shorter time. The simple fact is that in several major battles in which Canadians participated during the Second World War, casualty rates were the equal of, and sometimes even higher than, some of the more famous battles of the First World War. Normandy was as ferocious and as costly a campaign as any Great War battle on the western front.

There will always be controversy about the quality of the military leaders during the 1939–45 war. It ought not to be surprising that the quality of that leadership was at best uneven, on the ground, at sea, and in the air, for at least the first half of the war. Then, however, Canada's military leaders either learned how to make modern war or were forced out of their leadership positions. As that happened — as the brutal but inexorable battlefield process of the "survival of the fittest" took hold — the quality of Canada's military leadership increased dramatically. And, when Canada's forces began to receive the very best in equipment, Canadian performance on the ground, at sea, and in the air improved as well. By the end of the war it was second to none.

War is a terrible evil. Among the many species that share this good Earth, homo sapiens is the only one that wilfully organizes wars for abstract purposes or for purposeless conquest. War has been part of human history and human civilization from time immemorial and, barring some fundamental change in human nature, it will form part of human activity far into the future. But although war in the abstract is both terrible and evil, human beings have, from time to time, rightly chosen to fight wars rather than allow themselves to be enslaved. That is as it should be. All human beings are destined to die, but slavery is the deserved destiny of no one. As long as evil men and women plot to enslave and murder other men and women, and use the force of arms to achieve their tyrannical goals, there will be a need to take up arms to preserve the basic human right to be free. The Talmud declares: "He who saves one life saves the whole world." Between 1939 and 1945, Canada's soldiers, sailors, and airmen willingly went into harm's way to fight the Axis, until it was shattered. In doing so, they helped save the world many times over.

Organizational Structures of the Canadian Armed Forces and Officer Ranks

Canadian Army Organization

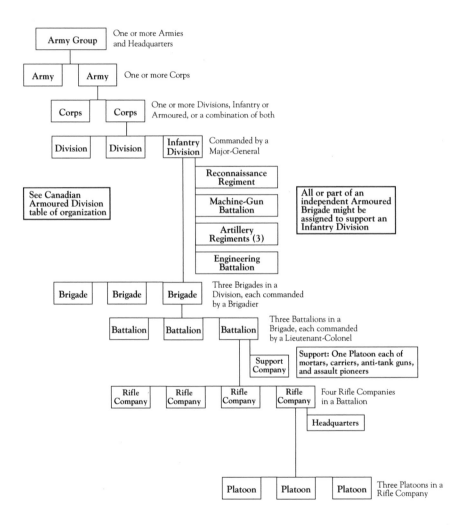

Army Group — One or more Armies and Headquarters

Army | Army — One or more Corps

Corps | Corps — One or more Divisions, Infantry or Armoured, or a combination of both

Division | Division | **Infantry Division** — Commanded by a Major-General

Reconnaissance Regiment

Machine-Gun Battalion

Artillery Regiments (3)

Engineering Battalion

See Canadian Armoured Division table of organization

All or part of an independent Armoured Brigade might be assigned to support an Infantry Division

Brigade | **Brigade** | **Brigade** — Three Brigades in a Division, each commanded by a Brigadier

Battalion | **Battalion** | **Battalion** — Three Battalions in a Brigade, each commanded by a Lieutenant-Colonel

Support Company — **Support: One Platoon each of mortars, carriers, anti-tank guns, and assault pioneers**

Rifle Company | Rifle Company | Rifle Company | Rifle Company — Four Rifle Companies in a Battalion

Headquarters

Platoon | Platoon | Platoon — Three Platoons in a Rifle Company

Canadian Armoured Division

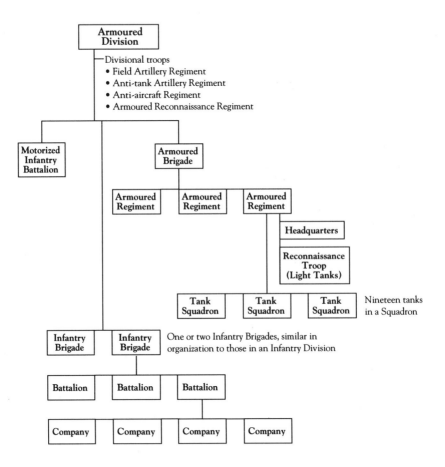

- Armoured Division
  - Divisional troops
    - Field Artillery Regiment
    - Anti-tank Artillery Regiment
    - Anti-aircraft Regiment
    - Armoured Reconnaissance Regiment
  - Motorized Infantry Battalion
  - Armoured Brigade
    - Armoured Regiment
    - Armoured Regiment
    - Armoured Regiment
      - Headquarters
      - Reconnaissance Troop (Light Tanks)
      - Tank Squadron
      - Tank Squadron
      - Tank Squadron — Nineteen tanks in a Squadron
  - Infantry Brigade
  - Infantry Brigade — One or two Infantry Brigades, similar in organization to those in an Infantry Division
    - Battalion
    - Battalion
    - Battalion
      - Company
      - Company
      - Company
      - Company

Royal Canadian Air Force
Organizational Chart of No. 6 Group

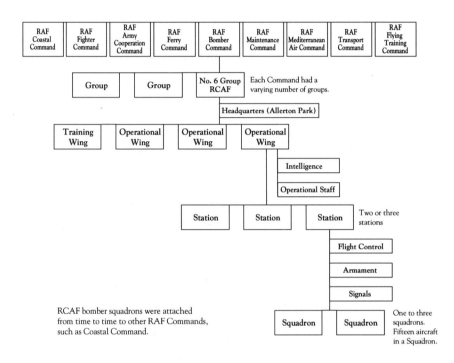

| RAF Coastal Command | RAF Fighter Command | RAF Army Cooperation Command | RAF Ferry Command | RAF Bomber Command | RAF Maintenance Command | RAF Mediterranean Air Command | RAF Transport Command | RAF Flying Training Command |

Group | Group | No. 6 Group RCAF | Each Command had a varying number of groups.

Headquarters (Allerton Park)

Training Wing | Operational Wing | Operational Wing | Operational Wing

Intelligence

Operational Staff

Station | Station | Station | Two or three stations

Flight Control

Armament

Signals

RCAF bomber squadrons were attached from time to time to other RAF Commands, such as Coastal Command.

Squadron | Squadron | One to three squadrons. Fifteen aircraft in a Squadron.

Allied Expeditionary Air Forces

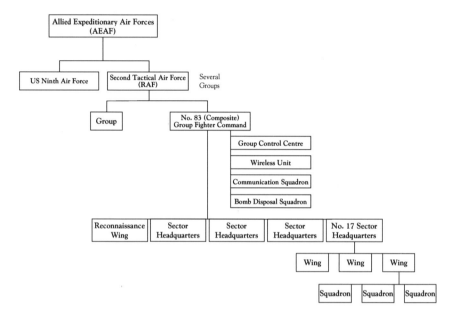

Royal Canadian Navy

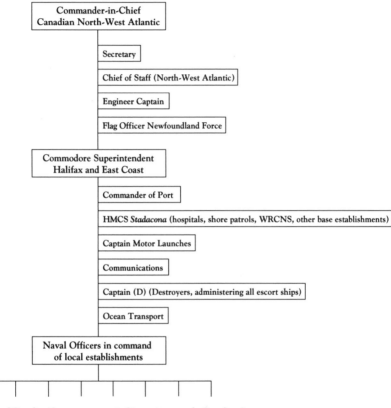

The Royal Canadian Navy was not organized into units as was the Canadian Army.
This table of organization shows the command organization of the Canadian
North-West Atlantic, an independent Canadian theatre as of 30 April 1943. As
such, the Commander-in-Chief answered directly to the Combined Chiefs of Staff.

Officer Ranks

RCN	ARMY	RCAF
Admiral	General	Air Chief Marshal
Vice-Admiral	Lieutenant-General	Air Marshal
Rear-Admiral	Major-General	Air Vice-Marshal
Commodore	Brigadier	Air Commodore
Captain	Colonel	Group Captain
Commander	Lieutenant-Colonel	Wing Commander
Lieutenant-Commander	Major	Squadron Leader
Lieutenant	Captain	Flight Lieutenant
Sub-Lieutenant	Lieutenant	Flying Officer
Midshipman	2nd Lieutenant	Pilot Officer
	Warrant Officer I	Warrant Officer I
Chief Petty Officer	Warrant Officer II	Warrant Officer II
Petty Officer	Staff Sergeant	Flight Sergeant
Leading Seaman	Sergeant	Sergeant
Able Seaman	Corporal	Corporal
Ordinary Seaman	Lance Corporal	Leading Aircraftman
	Private	Aircraftman First Class
		Aircraftman Second Class

✹ Notes

INTRODUCTION

1. John A. English, *The Canadian Army and the Normandy Campaign* (New York: Praeger 1991), 47

2. Stephen Harris, *Canadian Brass* (Toronto: University of Toronto Press 1988), 210–11

3. David Zimmerman, *The Great Naval Battle of Ottawa* (Toronto: University of Toronto Press 1989), 10

4. Ibid., 11

5. W.A.B. Douglas, *The Creation of a National Air Force: The Official History of the Royal Canadian Air Force*, vol. 2 (Toronto: University of Toronto Press 1986), 341

I   RUDE AWAKENING

1. Farley Mowat, *The Regiment* (Toronto: McClelland & Stewart 1973), 30–31

2. Quoted in J.L. Granatstein, *The Generals: The Canadian Army's Senior Commanders in the Second World War* (Toronto: Stoddart 1993), 21

3. Marc Milner, "The Battle of the Atlantic" in John Gooch, ed., *Decisive Campaigns of the Second World War* (London: Frank Cass 1990), 45

4. Marc Milner, *The U-Boat Hunters: The Royal Canadian Navy and the Offensive against Germany's Submarines* (Toronto: University of Toronto Press 1994), 51

5. W.A.B. Douglas, *The Creation of a National Air Force* (Toronto: University of Toronto Press 1986), 343

6. Mowat, *The Regiment*, 31

7. Dave McIntosh, ed., *High Blue Battle: The War Diary of No. 1 (401) Fighter Squadron, RCAF* (Toronto: Stoddart 1990), 38

II   THE RCN ENTERS THE BATTLE OF THE ATLANTIC

1. Marc Milner, "The Battle of the Atlantic," in John Gooch, ed., *Decisive Campaigns of*

the *Second World War* (London: Frank Cass 1990), 45–66

2. James B. Lamb, *The Corvette Navy: True Stories from Canada's Atlantic War* (Toronto: Signet 1977), 21

3. Marc Milner, *North Atlantic Run: The Royal Canadian Navy and the Battle for the Convoys* (Toronto: University of Toronto Press 1985), 41–42

4. Lamb, *The Corvette Navy*, 22–23

5. Hal Lawrence, *A Bloody War: One Man's Memories of the Canadian Navy, 1939–1945* (Toronto: Macmillan 1979), 52

III   CANADA AGAINST JAPAN

1. C.M. Maltby, "Operations in Hong Kong from 8th to 25th December, 1941," January 1948 (the Maltby Report), Public Record Office, UK

2. Oliver Lindsay, *The Lasting Honour: The Fall of Hong Kong, 1941* (London: Hamish Hamilton 1978), 96

IV   THE AGONY OF DIEPPE

1. W. Denis Whitaker and Shelagh Whitaker, *Dieppe: Tragedy to Triumph* (Toronto: McGraw-Hill Ryerson 1993), 252

2. Ibid., 253.

3. Quoted in John English, *The Canadian Army and the Normandy Campaign* (New York: Praeger 1991), 107

4. Nigel Hamilton, *Monty: The Making of a General, 1887–1942* (Toronto: Fleet Books 1982), 546–47

5. This is the conclusion of Brian Loring Villa in *Unauthorized Action: Mountbatten and the Dieppe Raid* (Toronto: Oxford University Press 1990).

6. Dave McIntosh, ed., *High Blue Battle: The War Diary of No. 1(401) Fighter Squadron, RCAF* (Toronto: Stoddart 1990), 104

7. John Mellor, *Forgotten Heroes: The Canadians at Dieppe* (Toronto: Methuen 1975), 74

8. C.P. Stacey, *Six Years of War: The Army in Canada, Britain and the Pacific* (Ottawa: Queen's Printer 1966), 332

9. Quoted in J.L. Granatstein, *The Generals: The Canadian Army's Senior Commanders in the Second World War* (Toronto: Stoddart 1993), 72

10. Whitaker and Whitaker, *Dieppe*, 290

V   THE DEADLY SKIES

1. Max Hastings, *Bomber Command* (London: Pan Books 1981), 178

2. W.A.B. Douglas and Brereton Greenhous, *Out of the Shadows: Canada in the Second World War* (Toronto: Oxford 1977), quoting Jerrold Morris, *Canadian Artists and Airmen* (Toronto 1975), 89

3. Quoted in Brian Nolan, *Hero: The Buzz Beurling Story* (Toronto: Lester & Orpen Dennys 1981), 84

4. Dave McIntosh, ed., *High Blue Battle: The War Diary of No. 1 (401) Fighter Squadron, RCAF* (Toronto: Stoddart 1990), 99

5. Jerrold Morris, quoted in Heather Robertson, *A Terrible Beauty: The Art of Canada at War* (Toronto: Lorimer 1977), 158

6. These conclusions can be found in Brereton Greenhous et al., *The Crucible of War, 1939–1945: The Official History of the Royal Canadian Air Force*, vol. 3 (Toronto: University of Toronto Press 1994), 864–67

7. Williamson Murray, *Luftwaffe* (Baltimore: Nautical & Aviation Publishing 1985), 283–84

VI   THE RCN ON TRIAL

1. James B. Lamb, *The Corvette Navy: True Stories from Canada's Atlantic War* (Toronto: Signet 1977), 92

2. Alan Easton, *50 North* (Toronto: Ryerson 1963), 99

3. Ibid., 139

4. Roger Sarty and Jurgen Rohwer, "Intelligence and the Air Forces in the Battle of the Atlantic 1943–1945," *International Commission of Military History*, Helsinki, 1991

VII   BOMBING GERMANY

1. Brereton Greenhous et al., *The Crucible of War, 1939–1945* (Toronto: University of Toronto Press 1994), 764

2. Walter Thompson, *Lancaster to Berlin* (Toronto: Totem 1987), 67

3. Quoted in L. Nuttal, "Canadianization and the No. 6 Bomber Group, RCAF" (PhD dissertation, University of Calgary, 1990), 265

4. Quoted in Spencer Dunmore and William Carter, *Reap the Whirlwind: The Untold Story of 6 Group* (Toronto: McClelland & Stewart 1991), 129

5. Quoted in John Terraine, *The Right of the Line: The Royal Air Force in the European War* (London: Hodder and Stoughton 1985), 548

6. Quoted in Max Hastings, *Bomber Command* (London: Pan Books 1981), 147

7. Martin Middlebrook, *The Peenemünde Raid* (London: Allen Lane 1982), 125

8. Quoted in Hastings, *Bomber Command*, 306

9. J. Douglas Harvey, *Boys, Bombs and Brussel Sprouts* (Toronto: McClelland & Stewart 1981), 96

10. Gordon W. Webb, "Nuremberg — A Night to Remember," *Airforce*, March 1982, 12

11. Ibid., 13

VIII VICTORY AT SEA

1. Alan Easton, *50 North: An Atlantic Battleground* (Toronto: Ryerson 1963), 192

2. Dan van der Vat, *The Atlantic Campaign* (New York: Harper & Row 1988), 315

3. Tony German, *The Sea Is at Our Gates* (Toronto: McClelland & Stewart 1990), 136

4. Peter Cremer, *U-Boat Commander* (Annapolis: Naval Institute Press 1984), 147

5. Ibid., 1

6. Marc Milner, *North Atlantic Run: The Royal Canadian Navy and the Battle for the Convoys* (Toronto: University of Toronto Press 1985), 263

7. Marc Milner, *The U-Boat Hunters: The Royal Canadian Navy and the Offensive against Germany's Submarines* (Toronto: University of Toronto Press 1994), 259

IX SICILY

1. Quoted in W.J. McAndrew, "Fire or Movement? Canadian Tactical Doctrine, Sicily — 1943," *Military Affairs*, July 1987, 143

2. Strome Galloway, *A Regiment at War: The Story of the Royal Canadian Regiment, 1939–1945* (Privately printed 1979), 81

3. Dominick Graham, *The Price of Command: A Biography of General Guy Simonds* (Toronto: Stoddart 1993), 68

4. Farley Mowat, *And No Birds Sang* (Toronto: Seal Books 1980), 52

5. Peter Stursburg, *The Sound of War* (Toronto: University of Toronto Press 1993), 100

6. Carlo D'Este, *World War II in the Mediterranean* (Chapel Hill: University of North Carolina Press 1990), 63

7. Quoted in McAndrew, "Fire or Movement?" This excellent article explains much about Simonds and Canadian tactical doctrine generally. My observations here are based upon it.

8. Galloway, *A Regiment at War*, 85

X ORTONA

1. Charles Comfort, *Artist at War* (Toronto: Ryerson 1956), 104–5

2. Quoted in G.W.L. Nicholson, *The Canadians in Italy* (Ottawa: Queen's Printer 1957), 328

3. Carlo D'Este, *World War II in the Mediterranean* (Chapel Hill: University of North Carolina Press 1990), 79

4. Comfort, *Artist at War*, 21

5. C. Vokes, *Vokes: My Story* (Ottawa: Gallery Books 1985), 123

6. Farley Mowat, *And No Birds Sang* (Toronto: Seal Books 1990), 154

7. Brereton Greenhous, "Would it not have been better to bypass Ortona completely . . . ? A Canadian Christmas, 1943," *Canadian Defence Quarterly*, April 1989, 55

8. Quoted Ibid.

9. Mowat, *And No Birds Sang*, 175

10. Strome Galloway, *A Regiment at War: The Story of the Royal Canadian Regiment, 1939–1945* (Privately printed 1979), 109

11. Quoted in Shaun R.G. Brown, "'The Rock of Accomplishment': The Loyal Edmonton Regiment at Ortona," *Canadian Military History* 2, 2 (1994): 16

12. Comfort, *Artist at War*, 109

XI VIA AD ROMAM

1. William McAndrew, "Fifth Canadian Armoured Division: Introduction to Battle," *Canadian Military History* 2, 2 (1994): 45

2. Carlo D'Este, *World War II in the Mediterranean* (Chapel Hill: University of North Carolina Press 1990), 126

3. Quoted in Carlo D'Este, *Fatal Decision: Anzio and the Battle for Rome* (New York: HarperCollins 1991), 347

4. G.R. Stevens, *Princess Patricia's Canadian Light Infantry: 1919–1957*, vol. 3 (Griesbach, Alberta: PPCLI, nd), 159

5. D'Este, *World War II in the Mediterranean*, 185

6. William J. McAndrew, "Eighth Army at the Gothic Line: The Dog-Fight," *Journal of the Royal United Service Institute*, June 1986, 62

7. Farley Mowat, *The Regiment* (Toronto: McClelland & Stewart 1973), 227

8. Brian Horrocks, *Corps Commander* (London: Magnum Books 1977), xiii

XII JUNO BEACH

1. Charles Cromwell Martin (with Roy Whitsed), *Battle Diary: From D-Day and Normandy to the Zuider Zee and VE* (Toronto: Dundurn 1994), 1–6

2. Ibid.

3. Murray Peden, *A Thousand Shall Fall* (Stittsville, Ontario: Canada's Wings Books 1979), 383

4. Quoted in Dave McIntosh, ed., *High Blue Battle: The War Diary of No. 1 (401) Fighter Squadron, RCAF* (Toronto: Stoddart 1990), 145

5. The quotation is from the regimental war diary, cited in Reg Roy, *1944: The Canadians in Normandy* (Toronto: Macmillan 1984), 13.

6. Quoted in Terry Copp and Robert Vogel, *Maple Leaf Route: Caen* (Alma, Ontario: Maple Leaf Route Books 1983), 42

7. Martin, *Battle Diary*, 14

8. Craig W.H. Luther, *Blood and Honor: The 12th SS Panzer Division* (San José: R.J. Benner Publishing 1987), 133

9. Martin, *Battle Diary*, 10

XIII THE ORDEAL OF NORMANDY

1. Quoted in D.J. Bercuson, *Battalion of Heroes: The Calgary Highlanders in World War II* (Calgary: The Calgary Highlanders Regimental Funds Foundation 1994), 124

2. Quoted in Terry Copp and Robert Vogel, *Maple Leaf Route: Caen* (Alma, Ontario: Maple Leaf Route Books 1983), 98

3. Charles Cromwell Martin, *Battle Diary: From D-Day to Normandy to the Zuider Zee and VE* (Toronto: Dundurn 1994), 37

4. John A. English, *The Canadian Army and the Normandy Campaign* (New York: Praeger 1991), 217

5. Ibid., 249

6. Russell F. Weigley, *Eisenhower's Lieutenants*, vol. 1 (Bloomington: Indiana University Press 1981), 241

7. Quoted in J.L. Granatstein, *The Generals: The Canadian Army's Senior Commanders in the Second World War* (Toronto: Stoddart 1993), 111

8. George Kitching, *Mud and Green Fields* (Langley, British Columbia: Battleline Books 1985), 219

XIV   THE SCHELDT

1. Monty Berger and Brian Jeffrey Street, *Invasions without Tears* (Toronto: Random House 1994), 93

2. W. Denis Whitaker and Shelagh Whitaker, *Tug of War* (Toronto: Stoddart 1984), 154

3. Quoted in D.J. Bercuson, *Battalion of Heroes: The Calgary Highlanders in World War II* (Calgary: The Calgary Highlanders Regimental Funds Foundation 1994), 169–70

4. Donald Pearce, *Journal of a War* (Toronto: Macmillan 1965), 76

5. Charles Cromwell Martin, *Battle Diary: From D-Day and Normandy to the Zuider Zee and VE* (Toronto: Dundurn 1994), 97

6. C.P. Stacey, *The Victory Campaign* (Ottawa: The Queen's Printer 1960), 390

7. B.L. Montgomery, *The Memoirs of Field Marshal Montgomery* (London: Collins 1958), 297 (emphasis in the original)

XV   VICTORY

1. William Allister, *Where Life and Death Hold Hands* (Toronto: Stoddart 1989), 218

2. Ibid., 219

3. Spencer Dunmore and William Carter, *Reap the Whirlwind: The Untold Story of 6 Group* (Toronto: McClelland & Stewart 1991), 344

4. Ibid., 346

5. Toronto *Globe and Mail*, 23 March 1945

6. Quoted in D.J. Bercuson, *Battalion of Heroes: The Calgary Highlanders in World War II* (Calgary: The Calgary Highlanders Regimental Funds Foundation 1994), 202

7. C.P. Stacey, *The Victory Campaign* (Ottawa: The Queen's Printer 1960), 474

8. Donald Pearce, *Journal of a War* (Toronto: Macmillan 1965), 140

9. C.P. Stacey, *The Canadian Army, 1939–1945: An Official Historical Summary* (Ottawa: King's Printer 1948), 265

ARMY

C.P. Stacey's *Six Years of War: The Army in Canada, Britain and the Pacific* (Ottawa 1966) is an excellent overview of the army's activities from 1939 to 1945, while W.A.B. Douglas and Brereton Greenhous's *Out of the Shadows: Canada in the Second World War* (Toronto 1977) is a more lively attempt to consider Canada's war effort. The performance of the army has been scrutinized in several works. Most notably, John English's *The Canadian Army and the Normandy Campaign* (New York 1991) argues that the army was insufficiently prepared for the Normandy onslaught, and that it paid dearly in the initial battles. English places the blame for the failure at the feet of the high command, but traces the responsibility to the inadequacies of prewar training and, ultimately, to the difficulties of maintaining a war-ready army in peacetime Canada. The making of that professional army is examined by Stephen Harris in *Canadian Brass* (Toronto 1988), while J.L. Granatstein's *The Generals* (Toronto 1993) considers the personal and professional strengths and weaknesses of Canada's senior army commanders of the Second World War. While Guy Simonds, the most controversial Canadian general of the war, is devoted a chapter in *The Generals*, he is the subject of *The Price of Command* (Toronto 1993), a flattering biography by Dominick Graham. An adequate biography of A.G.L. McNaughton is John Swettenham's *McNaughton* (Toronto 1969), volume 2 dealing with the Second World War.

In addition to English's examination of the Normandy bloodbath, a less critical, but good narrative of the Canadian Army's exploits in this campaign is Reginald Roy's *1944: The Canadians in Normandy* (Toronto 1984). C.P. Stacey's *The Victory Campaign* (Ottawa 1960) examines the army's role in the Allies' march from the beaches of Normandy in June 1944 through to Berlin in 1945. The Canadians were part of a larger Allied force, however, and subject to the overall command of British and American generals. They were often at odds during the war, and it has been argued that their squabbles led to military errors. Martin Blumenson, *The Battle of the Generals: The Untold Story of the Falaise Pocket — The Campaign That*

Should Have Won World War II (New York 1993), makes this argument. Max Hastings's *Overlord* (New York 1984) examines the operation from a broad perspective, and the best study to date of the poor communicaton between Montgomery and Eisenhower is Carlo D'Este's *Decision in Normandy* (London 1983). Terry Copp and Robert Vogel's *Maple Leaf Route* (Alma, Ont. 1983) describes the Canadian Army's trek through Northwest Europe, and Denis and Shelagh Whitaker's *Tug of War* (Toronto 1984) examines the army at the Scheldt. It should be read after J.L. Moulton's *Battle for Antwerp* (New York 1978).

D'Este's *Fatal Decision: Anzio and the Battle for Rome* (New York 1991) is essential reading for anyone interested in the Italian campaign, as is Samuel W. Mitcham Jr. and Friedrich von Stauffenberg's *The Battle of Sicily* (New York 1991). William J. McAndrew's "Eighth Army at the Gothic Line: The Dog Fight" in the *Journal of the Royal United Services Institute* (June 1986), and "Fire or Movement? Canadian Tactical Doctrine, Sicily—1943" in *Military Affairs* (July 1987), examine critically the nuts and bolts of implementing plans in the Mediterranean theatre. G.W.L. Nicholson's *The Canadians in Italy* (Ottawa 1957) is a detailed, if sometimes dry, account of the First Canadian Division's landings in Sicily in the summer of 1943, and their ensuing struggle to conquer not only enemy soldiers but the imposing Italian terrain as well.

Controversy over the debacles at Hong Kong and Dieppe continues to raise tempers within the historical profession. Carl Vincent's *No Reason Why* (Stittsville, Ont. 1981) fails to consider adequately British strategy on Hong Kong, as pointed out by John Ferris's article "Savage Christmas" in D.J. Bercuson and S.F. Wise's edited volume *The Valour and the Horror Revisited* (Montreal 1994), but is a good starting point for the controversy over the stationing of ill-prepared Canadians at that garrison. Dieppe has been an endless churner of Canadian stomachs, mostly because of the accusations that British policy-makers threw the 2nd Canadian Division to the wolves early on that morning of 1942. Brian Loring Villa reinforces that position in *Unauthorized Action: Mountbatten and the Dieppe Raid* (Toronto 1990), as does John Mellor in *Forgotten Heroes* (Toronto 1975).

Conscription was also an explosive issue. The crisis that arose over the manpower shortage in 1944 was brought about by the heavy losses at Normandy. E.L.M. Burns analyses the army's use of manpower, concluding that it could have been more efficient, in *Manpower in the Canadian Army 1939–1945* (Toronto 1956). A corps commander in Italy, Burns has also left a memoir *General Mud* (Toronto 1970), joining George Kitching's *Mud and Green Fields* (Langley 1985) and Tony

Foster's *A Meeting of Generals* (Toronto 1986) as the best produced by or about Canadian senior officers.

A number of regimental histories exist, including Farley Mowat, *The Regiment* (Toronto 1955), and David J. Bercuson, *Battalion of Heroes: The Calgary Highlanders in World War II* (Calgary 1994). Terry Copp's *The Brigade* (Stoney Creek 1992) is an excellent account of the activities of the 5th Canadian Infantry Brigade from 1939 to 1945.

AIRFORCE

Readers interested in Canada's effort in the air during the Second World War will have to rely in part on studies of the larger Allied exploits. For instance, John Terraine's *The Right of the Line: The Royal Air Force in the European War* (London 1985) examines how Britain viewed and implemented its version of air power, which affected in turn how Canadian forces were used. Central to that vision of air power was the strategic bombing campaign, directed by Arthur "Bomber" Harris. Controversy still rages over the merits of the campaign to bring the war home to Germany, and the role of Harris. Much has been written on that subject, beginning with Harris himself in 1947 with *Bomber Offensive* (London), but the general reader will find Charles Messenger, *"Bomber" Harris and the Strategic Bomber Offensive, 1939–1945* (London 1984), a well-considered start. Max Hastings's *Bomber Command* (London 1981) and Martin Middlebrook and Chris Everitt's *The Bomber Command War Diaries* (London 1985) should be consulted, the latter as an essential reference to trace the actions of individual squadrons. For a look at the German airforce, readers should consult Williamson Murray's *Luftwaffe* (Baltimore 1985).

Canadian bomber squadrons were formed into an independent unit of the RAF, No. 6 Group. The story of that group is told well by Spencer Dunmore and William Carter in *Reap the Whirlwind: The Untold Story of 6 Group* (Toronto 1991) where, for the most part, they leave aside the larger issues of the bombing campaign. However, *Reap the Whirlwind* does discuss the effects of Canadianization: the policy of keeping Canadian airmen and formations distinctly Canadian. Murray Peden, a Canadian pilot who served with the RAF's No. 214 Squadron, offers some vivid accounts of the trials of airmen in his memoir, *A Thousand Shall Fall* (Stittsville, Ont. 1979). This is one of the best memoirs of Allied airmen in the Second World War. Fighter Command has received considerably less attention than Bomber Command, perhaps because of the controversy over the latter, but

Dave McIntosh has edited the war diaries of No. 1 (401), which took part in the Battle of Britain, in *High Blue Battle* (Toronto 1990). Biographies of senior Canadian airmen are noticeably absent, but Brian Nolan's *Hero: The Buzz Beurling Story* (Toronto 1981) gives some insight into the life of the Canadian ace.

The role of the RCAF in the Battle of the Atlantic, the Aleutian campaign, and other activities in the Western Hemisphere is covered in the second volume of the official history of the RCAF, W.A.B. Douglas's *The Creation of a National Air Force* (Toronto 1986). The recent publication of volume 3 of the official history is a valuable addition to the historiography of the RCAF: Brereton Greenhous, Stephen Harris, William Johnson, and William Rawling's *The Crucible of War, 1939–1945* (Toronto 1994) does a commendable job of covering air policy and operations of the RCAF in the Second World War. The authors raise again the question of the morality of the strategic bombing campaign, but fail to address adequately the reasons why American and British strategists opted to target Germany industry *and* morale.

NAVY

Two official histories of the RCN's war emerged in the early 1950s: Gilbert Tucker's *The Naval Service of Canada*, vol. 2 (Ottawa 1952), and Joseph Schull's *The Far Distant Ships* (Ottawa 1950). Tucker explored the administration of the navy as it grew between 1939 and 1945, and Schull wrote an uncritical, yet engaging, popular history of the achievements of the navy. A scholarly official history is still in the making.

More so than the Canadian Army and RCAF, much of the writing on the RCN has been in the form of memoir, with some excellent results. Alan Easton's *50 North* (Toronto 1963), James Lamb's *The Corvette Navy: True Stories from Canada's Atlantic War* (Toronto 1977), and Hal Lawrence's *A Bloody War: One Man's Memories of the Canadian Navy, 1939–1945* (Toronto 1979) are thoughtful accounts of the war from serving sailors. Lamb and Lawrence have produced further memoirs, and there are many others, but for readers who want an entertaining but not always pretty look at wartime anecdotes, the *Salty Dips* collection compiled by Mac Lynch (Ottawa 1983/85/88) is recommended. In his memoir *U-Boat Killer* (London 1956), Donald Macintyre offers a very unflattering polemic of the RCN's wartime shortcomings.

There are some useful articles on various aspects of the Second World War at sea in Jim Boutilier's *The RCN in Retrospect* (Vancouver 1982) and W.A.B. Douglas's

The RCN in Transition (Vancouver 1988). Tony German's *The Sea Is at Our Gates: The History of the Canadian Navy* (Toronto 1990) is a spirited popular history, containing six chapters on the Second World War.

German U-boats found their way into Canadian waters during the war, a story told in Michael Hadley's *U-Boats against Canada: German Submarines in Canadian Waters* (Montreal/Kingston 1985). Exploring the RCN's escort role in the Battle of the Atlantic — often a dull, frigid, and dreary experience — Marc Milner analyses the RCN's operational efficiency in two books: *North Atlantic Run* (Toronto 1985) covers the war to 1943, and *U-Boat Killers* (Toronto 1994) takes it to 1945. Milner's books are first class and should be read in conjunction with David Zimmerman's thoughtprovoking look at politics, science, and the war against submarines, *The Great Naval Battle of Ottawa* (Toronto 1989). Zimmerman and Milner describe a navy fighting for recognition at home as much as against U-boats in the Atlantic. The attempt by senior officers to establish a navy that would be viable after hostilities is examined in W.A.B. Douglas's article "Conflict and Innovation in the Royal Canadian Navy 1919–1945" in Gerald Jordan, ed., *Naval Warfare in the Twentieth Century* (New York 1977).

Index

landers
Canadian Infantry Brigade, 7th
  and D-Day, 205, 209, 212–213, 220
  in Normandy, 221
  and the Scheldt, 247, 248
  See also Canadian Scottish Regiment;
    Regina Rifles; Royal Winnipeg Rifles
Canadian Infantry Brigade, 8th
  and D-Day, 205, 209, 210–211, 220
  in Normandy, 220, 221, 223
  and the Scheldt, 247, 248
  See also North Shore Regiment; Queen's
    Own Rifles
Canadian Infantry Brigade, 9th
  and Battle of the Rhineland, 267
  and D-Day, 205, 209
  and English channel ports, 244
  in Normandy, 221
  and the Scheldt, 247–248
  See also North Nova Scotia Highlanders
Canadian Infantry Brigade, 10th, 248
Canadian Infantry Brigade, 11th, 181–182,
    188, 189. *See also* Cape Breton Highlanders; Perth Regiment
Canadian Infantry Brigade, 12th, 189–190
Canadian Infantry Division, 1st, 9, 19
  and France, 15, 28–29
  and Holland, 268–269
  initial mobilization of, 5, 16, 17, 18, 20–
    21
  in Italy, 164–179, 181–182, 187, 191–
    192, 193, 205
  leadership of, 65, 153, 163, 178
  in Mediterranean theatre, 149–163,
    164–179, 180–193, 205
  Princess Louise (reconnaissance regiment), 188
  Saskatoon Light Infantry, 176
  in Sicily, 149–150, 151, 152, 153, 155–
    156, 158–163
  Westminster Regiment, 180, 181
  See also Canadian Infantry Brigade, 1st;
    Canadian Infantry Brigade, 2nd;
    Canadian Infantry Brigade, 3rd
Canadian Infantry Division, 2nd, 5, 17, 19,
    29, 62

and Battle of the Rhineland, 262–264,
    265–267
and Dieppe, 67–75, 205, 215–216, 234
8th Reconnaissance Regiment, 215
and English Channel ports, 243
Fusiliers Mont-Royal (FMR), 29, 72–73,
    223
in Holland, 268
in Iceland, 29
leadership of, 65
in Normandy, 192, 215–216, 222, 224,
    225, 228, 231, 232, 234
Royal Regiment of Canada, 29, 69–70,
    72, 249
and the Scheldt, 235–236, 245, 246,
    247, 248–249, 250
South Saskatchewan Regiment, 71
See also Canadian Infantry Brigade, 4th;
    Canadian Infantry Brigade, 5th; Canadian Infantry Brigade, 6th
Canadian Infantry Division, 3rd, 29, 59, 62,
    263
  and Battle of Normandy, 220, 221, 222,
    223, 224, 229, 230, 231, 234
  and Battle of the Rhineland, 263, 264,
    265–267
  and D-Day, 194–195, 204–205
  and English Channel ports, 243–244
  and Holland, 263, 268
  leadership of, 65, 230
  and the Scheldt, 245, 247–248, 249, 263
  See also Canadian Armoured Regiment,
    6th; Canadian Armoured Regiment,
    10th; Canadian Armoured Regiment, 27th; Canadian Infantry Brigade, 7th; Canadian Infantry Brigade, 8th; Canadian Infantry Brigade, 9th
Canadian Infantry Division, 6th, 60
Canadianized war effort, 16, 119
Canadian Military Headquarters (CMHQ),
    20, 27
Canadian Northwest Atlantic Command,
    138
Canadian Parachute Battalion, 1st, 152,
    195–196, 204
Canadian Rocket Battery, 1st, 263
Canadian Scottish Regiment, 209
Canal de Dérivation de la Lys, 245

and volunteers, 17

See also Allied Expeditionary Air Force

Royal Canadian Army Service Corps (RCASC), 18, 28

Royal Canadian Electrical and Mechanical Engineers, 18

Royal Canadian Horse Artillery, 29

Royal Canadian Mounted Police, 5

Royal Canadian Naval Reserve (RCNR), 11, 25, 148

Royal Canadian Naval Volunteer Reserve (RCNVR), 11, 25

Royal Canadian Navy (RCN), 25, 147

  and Battle of the Atlantic, 21–26, 34–48, 101–105, 111, 130–149

  and Battle of Normandy, 216, 217–218

  and Battle of the St Lawrence, 94–101

  casualties/ships lost during war, 30, 261–262

  composition/size of at start of war, 17, 21, 25

  and convoy escort, 21, 23–24, 26, 30, 34–35, 36–48, 95–97, 99–100, 101–105, 107–111, 130–148, 151, 202, 204, 239

  and corvettes, 24–25, 26, 30, 39, 101–102, 140, 204

  and D-Day, 196, 202–204, 204

  and destroyers, 10–11, 12, 21, 24, 25, 26, 30–31, 102, 140, 146, 148

  during interwar period, 10–12, 13–14, 26

  and E-boats, 203

  and frigates, 140, 147

  initial involvement in war, 21–26

  and W.L. Mackenzie King, 15

  and Mediterranean theatre, 135–136, 151

  and minesweeping, 204

  and North Africa, 100

  and Pacific theatre, 59–60

  and Royal Canadian Air Force (RCAF), 46

  and Royal Navy (RN), 7, 11–12, 24, 30, 38–39

  and training, 26, 39, 135

  and U-boats/submarines, 23–24, 25–26, 30, 31, 39, 40, 102–105, 108–109, 130–131, 136, 137, 138, 140, 147–

148, 202, 217, 239, 260, 261, 262

  and United States Navy (USN), 47, 98

Royal Canadian Regiment (RCR), 16, 149–150, 153, 161, 162, 170, 174, 175

Royal Flying Corps, 6, 84

Royal Hamilton Light Infantry (RHLI), 61, 70, 72–73, 224–225, 246, 250, 265

Royal Highland Regiment. *See* Black Watch

Royal Marines, 72

Royal Military College (RMC), 9, 19–20

Royal Naval Air Service, 6

Royal Navy (RN)

  and Battle of the Atlantic, 35–36

  and Combined Operations, 66

  and convoy escort, 21, 23, 38, 44, 102, 137, 138, 140

  and D-Day, 202–204

  during interwar period, 11–12

  and First World War, 37, 84

  and Pacific theatre, 59

  and Royal Canadian Navy (RCN), 109

  and training, 39

  and U-boats/submarines, 30, 130–131, 142, 202

  See also Western Approaches Command

Royal Rifles of Canada, 51, 52, 53, 54, 55, 56

Royal Winnipeg Rifles, 209, 212, 220

Ruhr, 85, 86, 244, 250, 267

  Battle of the, 122–123, 126

Russia, 50. *See also* Red Army; Soviet Union

Rutherford, C.A., 109

Sackville, 102–103, 104–105, 130, 133

Saguenay, 10, 25, 30

St André-sur-Orne, 223

St Aubin, 67

St Aubin-sur-Mer, 1, 204

St Clair, 31

St Croix, 31, 34–35, 104, 107, 108, 109, 130, 131–132, 136, 145

St Eloi, 6

St Francis, 130

St John, 239

St John's, 36

St Julien, 6

St Lambert-sur-Dives, 232